Countertransference
in Couples
Therapy

Also by the Editors

Judith P. Siegel

Repairing Intimacy: An Object Relations Approach to Couples Therapy

Marion F. Solomon

Lean on Me: The Power of Positive Dependency in Intimate Relationships

Narcissism and Intimacy: Love and Marriage in an Age of Confusion

*The Borderline Patient: Emerging Concepts in Diagnosis, Etiology,
Psychodynamics and Treatment* (with J. Grotstein and J. Lang)

A Norton Professional Book

Countertransference *in* Couples Therapy

Edited by

Marion F. Solomon

and

Judith P. Siegel

W. W. Norton & Company • New York • London

Chapter 7, Transference and Countertransference in Clinical Interventions with Divorcing Families, by Judith S. Wallerstein, Ph.D., is reprinted from the *American Journal of Orthopsychiatry*, Vol. 60, copyright 1990 by the American Orthopsychiatric Association Inc. Reproduced by permission.

Parts of chapter 14, Countertransference in the Storying of a Child's Suicide, by Sharon McQuaide, Ph.D., previously appeared in *The Clinical Social Work Journal*, Vol. 23(4), 1995, under the title "Storying the Suicide of One's Child."

Composition by Bytheway Typesetting Services
Manufacturing by Haddon Craftsmen

Library of Congress Cataloging-in-Publication Data

Countertransference in couples therapy / edited by Marion F. Solomon
    and Judith P. Siegel.
        p.   cm.
    "A Norton professional book."
    Includes bibliographical references and index.
    ISBN 0-393-70244-8
    1. Marital psychotherapy.   2. Countertransference (Psychology)
    I. Solomon, Marion Fried.   II. Siegel, Judith P.
    RC488.5.C6796   1997
    616.89'156—dc21   97-9583   CIP

W. W. Norton & Company, Inc., 500 Fifth Avenue, New York, N.Y. 10110
http://www.wwnorton.com
W. W. Norton & Company Ltd., 10 Coptic Street, London WC1A 1PU

1 2 3 4 5 6 7 8 9 0

Dedicated to our husbands,
Matthew and Morris,
and our children,
Bonnie, Glenn, Mitchell, and Jenna

Acknowledgments

My DEEPEST appreciation goes to my colleagues represented in this volume whose contributions have greatly enriched this book. My discussions with Marion Solomon have expanded and clarified my own thinking, and added to the quality of my presentations. A special acknowledgement should be made to Drs. Justin Frank and Micheline K. Frank for their thoughtful comments and recommendations the first chapter. Susan Munro should also be thanked for an excellent editing job, and for her support and understanding when it was most needed. Beyond that I would like to thank Shelley, Wendy and Debbie for their interest, support, and editing suggestions, and my husband and children, without whose cooperation this book would have been impossible.

—Judith P. Siegel, Ph.D.

I THANK Judith Siegel for her stimulating presentation at AFTA. Her willingness to talk about her own countertransference responses was the impetus for this book. I thank my colleagues for the energy they put into their contributing chapters that so enrich this volume. And as always I appreciate Susan Munro for her help with this project.

I especially appreciate the support and encouragement of my children, Bonnie and Glenn and my husband, Matthew, who encourages me to take the time to write, and who has the patience and fortitude to function as a "holding environment" in times when I am temporarily preoccupied with my work.

A special acknowledgment to Dr. Rita Lynn, who shares my belief that therapists must have collegial partners with whom we can discuss all of our private thoughts and feelings as we immerse ourselves in the primitive emotional reactions of some couples.

—Marion F. Solomon, Ph.D.

Contents

Contributors

Ronald Alexander, Ph.D., is a psychotherapist in family practice in Santa Monica, California. He is the Chair of the Graduate Department of Psychology and Director of Clinical Training at Ryokan College in Los Angeles, and adjunct Instructor in the Departments of Psychology and Health Sciences at UCLA Extension.

Robert Carroll, M.D., is Assistant Clinical Professor of Psychiatry at UCLA and maintains a private practice of family psychiatry in Los Angeles.

Carol A. Francis, Psy.D., is a clinical psychologist practicing in the South Bay region of Los Angeles. In this area she has supervised at many family crisis clinics wherein violence and abuse in the family structure have been her primary focus.

Justin A. Frank, M.D., is a teaching analyst at the Washington Psychoanalytic Institute and a Clinical Professor of Psychiatry at George Washington University Medical Center. He is also on the faculty of the Object Relations Couples and Family Program at the Washington School of Psychiatry, and is Co-director of the Metropolitan Center for Object Relations Theory and Practice in New York.

Eda G. Goldstein, D.S.W., is Professor at the New York University Shirley M. Ehrenkranz School of Social Work and maintains a private practice. She is consulting editor of the *Clinical Social Work Journal, The Journal of Analytic Social Work*, and *Social Work*.

Kenneth Mann, Psy.D., is a psychologist in private practice in Westchester County, New York, and is a clinical psychologist in the Westchester school system. He is Associate Professor at College of New Rochelle and an adjunct Instructor at SUNY Purchase.

Bonnie S. Mark, Ph.D., is Project Coordinator of the Reiss-Davis Child Study Center in Los Angeles, and a supervisor at the Beverly Hills Maple Center. She maintains a private practice in Los Angeles.

Sharon McQuaide, Ph.D., is Assistant Professor at the Graduate School of Social Service of Fordham University. She maintains a private practice in Connecticut.

Joan Schain-West, Ph.D., is a clinical consulting faculty member at the California Institute for Clinical Social Work, and maintains a private practice in Los Angeles.

Sheila A. Sharpe, Ph.D., is on the faculty of the San Diego Psychoanalytic Society and Institute, and maintains a private practice in LaJolla, California.

Judith P. Siegel, Ph.D., is Associate Professor at the New York University Shirley M. Ehrenkranz School of Social Work. She is on the editorial board of the *Journal of Family Social Work* and maintains a private practice in Mamaroneck, New York.

Marion F. Solomon, LCSW, Ph.D., is director of clinical training at the Lifespan Learning Institute Continuing Education Seminars and is Coordinator of mental health training programs, Department of Humanities, Sciences and Social Sciences, UCLA Extension. She maintains a private practice in West Los Angeles.

Jeffrey L. Trop, M.D., is Assistant Clinical Professor of Psychiatry at the UCLA School of Medicine and is a training and supervising analyst and faculty member of the Institute of Contemporary Psychoanalysis in Los Angeles.

Nancy P. Van Der Heide, Psy.D., is in private practice in Brentwood, California and is an adjunct Professor of Clinical Psychology at Royokan College in Los Angeles.

Judith S. Wallerstein, Ph.D., is Senior Lecturer Emeritus at the University of California at Berkeley. She is also the founder of the Judith Wallerstein Center for the Family in Transition, and principal investigator for the California Children of Divorce project.

Joel Jay West, M.D., is Assistant Professor of Psychiatry at the UCLA Neuropsychiatric Institute. He is a member of the Los Angeles Psychoanalytic Society and Institute and maintains a private practice in Los Angeles.

Introduction

THE IDEA for this book first came out of an AFTA meeting workshop on countertransference. In a room of colleagues who wanted to debate whether or not the concept existed in any meaningful way, we (the co-editors) found ourselves cementing an alliance that had started years earlier around a shared interest in narcissistic vulnerability. We found that our theoretical differences added to our appreciation of the clinical material, and that our own work was remarkably similar. We were also both struggling to provide a place for honest reflection on real life issues and the ways in which the experiences of the therapist and couple connected.

We decided that the kind of book that was needed on the subject was one that covered the fullest range of experiences, with a level of honesty that we had not yet encountered in published form. We wanted to present real responses to real cases and introduce other therapists to the benefits of working on this basis. In order to accomplish this, we decided to invite certain colleagues to present and discuss their cases so that a full spectrum of clinical work based on countertransference could be considered.

The book begins with a section on theoretical issues. From Dr. Siegel there is an overview of the classical, totalist, and real aspects of counter-transference as developed in the analytic literature. Each is then applied to couples therapy and reconsidered through the concept of identification. From Dr. Solomon there is an inquiry into the relationship between coun-tertransference and empathy and into the mysterious psychological process of attunement. Dr. Sheila Sharpe gives a thoughtful presentation on the differing forms of countertransference reactions, which are related to the psychic structure and developmental conflicts of the marital partners. Adding to this approach is a contribution from Dr. Eda Goldstein on the specific countertransference challenges evoked by couples with borderline dynamics. Following this, Dr. Justin Frank presents an interesting discussion of oedipal countertransference, demonstrating how this theme permeates couples therapy in direct and indirect ways. Dr. Jeffrey Trop's discussion of countertransference as a normal intersubjective process balances the book's different theoretical positions and adds an important perspective to utilizing countertransference in clinical practice.

The second section of this book, Countertransference in Practice, covers a broad range of clinical situations and countertransference reactions. Dr. Judith Wallerstein presents her work practicing and supervising therapists who are working with divorced couples and notes the stressful reactions induced by this life crisis. Drs. Joel West and Joan Schain-West describe envy in the countertransference, a phenomenon that is often experienced but rarely discussed. Dr. Marion Solomon addresses a similarly ignored topic, erotic reactions and lust in the countertransference.

The intersecting values, beliefs, and life experiences of the couple and therapist are explored by Dr. Kenn Mann in his therapy with a gay couple on the verge of breakup. In a similar vein, Dr. Judith Siegel presents her work with couples whose problems around infertility and childbearing mirrored her own. Related to issues of children is a chapter contributed by Dr. Bonnie Mark on countertransference themes arising from therapy involving parenting. The therapist's countertransference in difficult life-and-death situations is addressed by Drs. Robert Carroll and Sharon McQuaide. Dr. Carroll presents his countertransference to a young couple who face one spouse's illness and death, while Dr. McQuaide writes about her work with a middle-aged couple recovering from the suicide of their son. The countertransference reactions stimulated by violence are addressed by two different authors: Dr. Carol Francis presents the range of totalistic and culturally induced responses evoked in a complicated case, while Drs. Ronald Alexander and Nancy Van Der Heide offer a treatment approach based on self psychology.

In keeping with the book's mission of helping therapists face issues that are all too frequently avoided, Dr. Marion Solomon discusses burnout and how it can be understood and corrected through attention to countertransference phenomena. The book concludes with a chapter on utilizing countertransference in supervision, prepared by Dr. Judith Siegel, which offers an example of how the therapist's reactions can be explored in ways that facilitate understanding.

We wish to thank our contributing authors for presentations that have excited and humbled us by their honesty and clarity. We see this book not as a set of independent chapters but as a gestalt that weaves through a vast range of ideas and experiences. It is our hope that readers become stimulated, validated, and challenged to develop their own style of practice that allows them to appreciate and draw upon the many facets of countertransference in couples therapy.

Countertransference
in Couples
Therapy

SECTION I

Countertransference in Theory

1

Applying Countertransference Theory to Couples Treatment

JUDITH P. SIEGEL

FOR YEARS, analytically informed couple therapists have struggled with ways of using the therapist's reactions as a valid and useful form of information about the couple and the treatment process. Knowledge of countertransference provides such a vehicle by allowing the therapist to tune into and make sense of his/her subjective states, which might otherwise be neglected or unconsciously acted out. The greatest challenge in utilizing countertransference in couples treatment is to apply the concept in a way that does not obscure or compromise meaning.

Defining countertransference in a single sentence that would adequately reflect its multiple meanings and the debate they provoke is an almost impossible task. While it is generally accepted that countertransference is composed of the therapist's personal or subjective reactions to the patient/client system, there is disagreement as to whether all reactions should be regarded as countertransference or only those that create a departure from the therapist's typical therapeutic style or frame. While there are some who view countertransference as the totality of the therapist's responses, others acknowledge only specific reactions, such as, for example, those to the client's transference. The meaning attached to this particular concept reveals the therapist's theoretical framework, as it underscores the differences among analysts espousing classical, totalist, and postmodern analytic approaches.

If the full range of the therapist's subjective experiences is respected as clinically relevant, the therapist must become attuned to multiple sources of stimuli and plausible interpretations. It is possible that some of the therapist's reactions stem from his/her own internalized family relationships and emotionally charged issues. Yet, it is also possible that some of what the therapist experiences has been stimulated by the couple and mirrors some aspect of the couple's relationship. At the same time, there are reactions that are more specific to the current situation of the couple, especially when the therapist is facing similar issues in his/her own life. When all reactions are considered as countertransference, the couples therapist must look honestly inward, outward to the dynamics of the couple as a system, and beyond, into the culturally determined beliefs and life events that influence both.

In order to work with countertransference the therapist must also shift his/her focus of attention so that personal reactions can be more readily accessed and processed. This adds to the complexity of focus in couples therapy, where the therapist's attention is already split between the two spouses and the systemic dynamics. However, the processing of countertransference is vitally important, since the format of couples therapy seems to evoke specific and intense kinds of reactions that do not necessarily occur in individual psychotherapy.

In order to conceptualize the different kinds of countertransference reactions potentially experienced in couples therapy, it seems useful to begin with an understanding of the concept. Rather than present an historical overview of countertransference, such as that provided by Epstein and Feiner (1979), Slakter (1987), or Tansey and Burke (1989), this chapter will examine the different meanings currently attached to the concept. These ideas will then be applied to couples therapy and expanded in order to achieve the broadest possible perspective.

CLASSICAL COUNTERTRANSFERENCE

In classical analysis, countertransference reactions include atypical affective or cognitive responses to the patient that may emerge as fantasies, preoccupation, dreams, a resurgence of memories that impairs the analyst's ability to concentrate on the task at hand, or unconscious defenses that prevent the analyst from maintaining the neutral stance that is critical for a successful analysis (Jacobs, 1983). Classical analysts regard countertransference as potentially dangerous, for it might be acted out by the analyst in such a way as to create a therapeutic breach or interfere with the patient's progress. The source of the analyst's reactions is believed to be either insufficiently analyzed and therefore unresolved neurotic conflicts, a consequent transference of past issues onto the patient, or an inappropriate reaction to the patient's transference (Reich, 1959; Slakter, 1987). Regardless of cause, countertransference in the classical sense is viewed as detrimental to the analysis.

The notion of countertransference as an obstacle to comprehension reflects Freud's position when he first proposed the notion of countertransference. It is this usage that leads to the observation that a patient can never get healthier than his/her analyst, as the analyst will unconsciously deflect or detour around his/her own unresolved conflicts. Sharpe referred to the analyst's "blind spots," which limit full comprehension or understanding (Slakter, 1987). As Rockland explains, the therapist may react in a defensive or "uncharacteristically opaque manner to material that is similar to the therapist's own conflicts" (1989, p. 118). This view of countertransference resonates with Schoenewolf's notion of characterological countertransference, in which the patient's resistance to the treatment reflects the therapist's personal limitations (Schoenewolf, 1993).

Because analysis of the transference is one of the most important tools available to the analyst, it is imperative that he/she be able to tolerate and interpret the ways in which patients relate to him/her as an aspect of their internalized representational world. If the analyst is threatened by the material that surfaces through the transference, he/she might react in ways that are either uncharacteristic or unanalytic. Of particular importance are oedipal strivings, which, if not adequately neutralized, are reactivated to the detriment of the patient's analysis. Themes of competition, approval, and envy are likely to emerge in the transference due to the analyst's perceived power and authority. The analyst must be prepared to utilize his/her own response in order to fully comprehend the patient's struggle.

The role of gender in this form of countertransference is worth considering. Racker (1953) speculated that the male analyst was predisposed to reexperience his oedipal relationship with his mother when working with a female patient, and so might unconsciously elicit from her affection or phallic adoration. Similarly, the male patient might revive the male analyst's feelings of envy and competition. It was also postulated that female analysts would avoid threatening their male patients' competency and independence and experience a need for approval from their female patients. Because of the unconscious nature of these reactions, analysts are advised to use self analysis, periodic reentry into analysis, or analytic supervision.

Another dimension of classical countertransference concerns the meaning of the patient to the analyst and irrational needs that may unconsciously be met in the analytic relationship. Little (1951) discussed the kind of countertransference that emerged when the patient became the analyst's love object. Analysts who are primarily informed by Freudian theory would discuss this in terms of oedipal strivings or infantile urges. Those who utilize an object relations perspective would describe how the therapist has formed a transference to the patient and has assigned him/her a role that reflects internalized self and object representations. Another example of this phenomenon is the analyst who assumes a rescuing posture in response to a patient perceived as victimized or helpless. While it is possible that the rescue impulse is a reaction formation against aggressive impulses, it is also possible that the analyst as a child had played a rescuing role with one or both of his/her parents, or that by rescuing the patient he/she identifies with an experience of being rescued that was yearned for but never realized in his/her own childhood. This form of countertransference is labeled by Chediak as the analyst's transference to the patient, best understood as the "reliving of early part object relationships as elicited by certain features in the patient" (1979, p. 117).

Miller has described parentified persons who "not only become mothers, confidants, comforters, advisors, supporters to their own mothers, but also take over the responsibility for their siblings and eventually develop a special sensitivity to unconscious signals manifesting the needs of others" (1981, p. 9). The selective factor in choosing psychotherapy as a career may be a need to relate more intimately to others, to understand oneself better, to repeat a pattern of caretaking that began in childhood, to resolve personal problems, or to meet needs for power, admiration, or love. Maeder (1989) has suggested that therapy is a relatively safe way of relating intimately with others. In their relatively powerful position, therapists are able to gratify many needs, including voyeurism, social connection, and dependency. Of particular importance are the narcissistic snares shared by too many therapists: the need to heal all, to know all, and to love or be loved by all (Reid, 1977). These again stem from the analyst's infantile motivations that have not been adequately neutralized. As Reich (1959) points out, the process of trial identification that is necessary to create empathy is a delicate one and may stimulate strivings that the analyst is not prepared to relinquish. For example, the analyst may be stimulated to feel hate toward a patient who hates him/her and may find him/herself maintaining this stance because unconscious needs are being met. In Reich's words, the analyst can become stuck in trial identifications because of the gratification and become unwilling or unable to relinquish them (Reich, 1959, p. 391).

CLASSICAL COUNTERTRANSFERENCE IN COUPLES THERAPY

Although the editors of this book do not agree with the classical position that countertransference necessarily interferes with the therapeutic process, the themes identified by the analysts who hold a classical viewpoint can be readily applied to couples therapy. It is quite likely that the couples therapist will avoid or fail to comprehend dynamics that resonate with his/her own unresolved internalized conflicts. The couples therapist is called upon to respond to a wide range of issues, including the ways which anger and sexuality are expressed. It would be difficult for a therapist who has not come to terms with his/her own discomfort in expressing or tolerating another person's anger to work effectively with a quarreling couple. In one scenario the therapist could choose to change the subject directly or through a trajectory reframe and move away from the underlying issue perpetuating the couple's conflict. In another scenario, the therapist could remain untherapeutically passive and vicariously experience the anger from a relatively safe position.

It is equally likely that the couple will meet irrational needs of the therapist, especially in the realms of caretaking and rescue. Many couples are on the verge of divorce when they decide to go for couples therapy. Their pain is intense and their need for help urgent, especially when there are young children involved. Other couples are beset by life pressures or tragedies that would stimulate rescue fantasies in any therapist who cares about the well-being of others. But for the therapist who attained power and recognition in his/her own family of origin by taking on a parentified, caretaking role, the desire for reenactment may be too strong. Likewise, the therapist who as a child was emotionally self-sufficient may be particularly responsive to spouses who feel unheard and disregarded, thus mending his/her own childhood pain.

Voyeurism is also potentially active in couples treatment. There is a broad range of ways in which couples can resolve shared living and relationship issues. It is possible that a therapist's curiosity may be activated by a known or not yet fully comprehended dissatisfaction in the way a specific issue is handled in his/her own intimate relationship. The therapist could inadvertently focus on this issue in the therapy, although more for the therapist's benefit than for the spouses'.

The very format of couples therapy also activates specific dynamics that can be best understood through the theory of classical analysis. For example, there is almost always a revival of oedipal themes, for in every conjoint session the therapist is either part of a twosome that excludes an outsider or an outsider who is excluded from the intimate dyad (Fisher, 1993). Appel (1966) is one of the few marital therapists who has published on this theme. He suggests that a male therapist may be especially threatened by an acting-out, seductive wife, as this creates "erotic, competitive, hostile and anxious oedipal reactions" (1966, p. 308). However, the theme of jealousy is just as likely to emerge when a female therapist is empathic and available to a male spouse. My work with one couple failed miserably when the husband, in response to an empathic inquiry, disclosed feelings that were unknown to his wife. Despite the fact that this was a conjoint session, co-led by an equally supportive male therapist, the wife's experience of being displaced by a more nurturing female aroused intense feelings that led to an abrupt, premature termination.

The sex of the therapist is also reflected in the kinds of alliances and perceived alliances that develop between the spouses and the therapist. Herman (1982) noticed that couples often believe there is an alliance between the therapist and the member or the couple of the same gender, leading the partner to feel disadvantaged. The ability of a therapist to bond with the spouse of the same gender may be influenced by a number of factors, but would surely include childhood family dynamics and gender-influenced belief systems.

In addition, the couple often appeals to the therapist to become both referee and judge, thus empowering the therapist but also relegating him/her to the role of parent of two quarreling siblings. Specific unresolved conflicts reflecting the therapist's own family and sibling relations may be revived under these circumstances. Too little has been written on the sibling position and sibling-related dynamics that might help couples therapists become alert to their management of this commonly encountered situation. Jacobs (1983) has noted that material disclosed by the patient about his/her marriage and family may activate the therapist's family myths and secrets; however, a direct encounter would stimulate more intense reactions than a story shared with the therapist. The format of couples therapy stimulates countertransference at a level of intensity that is well beyond that which might surface in the more protected setting of individual therapy.

Another format-related aspect of countertransference concerns reactions that can be stimulated by the direct observation of expressions of aggression and sexuality displayed by the couple. It is not uncommon for spouses to act ragefully or even violently toward each other in the therapist's presence. While a therapist who works with individuals may hear about episodes of marital violence, the couples therapist is often forced to witness and take responsibility for dynamics that can be frightening and repulsive. Child analysts have noted that countertransference reactions are more likely to arise when libidinal and aggressive drives are expressed as "direct actions rather than as wishes, fantasies or verbal musings" (Anthony, quoted in Schowalter, 1985, p. 40). Kohrman, Fineberg, Gelman, and Weiss (1971) similarly suggest that the quality of these contacts leads to greater regression or reactive defensive maneuvers on the part of the therapist.

Therapists who work with couples who are violent, sadistic, or in other ways antisocial may have intense reactions that can go beyond culturally induced disgust or disapproval. In some instances the nature of the couple's sadism or violence is so intense that the therapist may experience a kind of secondary traumatic stress reaction or compassion fatigue (Geller, 1992; Herman, 1992). In these situations the therapist may develop depression, anxiety, helplessness, or intrusive violent fantasies as a reaction to the trauma of working with this couple.

Direct exposure to the couple's interaction may also reveal unresolved issues, beliefs, or values that are consciously denied. For example, a couples therapist may find him-/herself reactive to or defended against homophobia. The same therapist who could listen to stories about a gay or lesbian sexual relationship may respond very differently to a gay or lesbian couple's demonstrations of affection or sexuality within the session.

TOTALIST COUNTERTRANSFERENCE

The totalist position on countertransference departs from the classical position in several ways, but most specifically by appreciating that the analyst's response to patients is not unhealthy, unhelpful, or entirely determined by personal psychopathology. Heimann (1950) viewed the totality of the analyst's reactions as useful to the analytic process and as carrying important information about the patient's unconscious. Without this knowledge, the analyst's understanding and interpretations would be incomplete. Anna Freud also described a process in which unintegrated self and object images or representations were externalized by a psychotic patient onto the analyst (Volkan, 1981). In this instance, the analyst's reaction was viewed as an identification with the patient's self or object world and as having been stimulated by the patient's interaction. Sandler (1987) speaks of this as acceptance of a role that the patient is forcing on him, although he stresses that a portion of the reaction stems from the intrapsychic susceptibilities of the analyst. Most analysts who use the totalist approach distinguish between those responses any therapist would have and those more reflective of unresolved or insufficiently neutralized instincts. Giovacchini (1985), for example, speaks about *homogeneous* countertransference reactions, which reflect basic human sensitivities and are relatively universal. In contrast, *idiosyncratic* responses are those that are unique to the particular character and background of each therapist and provide more information about the therapist than about the individual patient.

The totalist view of countertransference allows the therapist's reaction to be likened to projective identification, although the mechanism of introjective identification or counteridentification has been suggested as more accurate (Blum, 1987; Grotstein, 1981; Joseph, 1987). The therapist may be stimulated to form an identification with split-off aspects of the patient's self, an experience described by Racker as concordant countertransference

(Racker, 1953). Some analysts prefer to call this emotional reaction a form of empathic identification (Chediak, 1979), as the analyst is primed to temporarily identify with the patient in order to best understand him/her. The therapist's reactions mirror or replicate the patient's internal state, leading him/her to understand the patient's situation in a very personal way.

The therapist may also be induced to take a role from the patient's internalized object world, a reaction described by Racker as complementary countertransference. Once again the therapist is stimulated to assume a stance that allows a childhood relationship to be reenacted within the realm of therapy. For example, an analyst may become irritated or rejecting toward a passive-aggressive patient who devalues interpretations or never pays bills on time, repeating this patient's experience with a critical, withholding parent.

The therapist's ability to receive the stimulation is more accurately described as introjective identification. It is a process that allows for a sharing of experience, which facilitates the therapist's understanding of the patient's internalized object relations. Some analysts, such as Strupp (1977), suggest that this is the essence of psychotherapeutic change, as the patient's need is to relive and modify the historically meaningful patterns that emerge in the analytic work.

The importance of the use of self as both receiver and container for the patient's externalizations has been emphasized by Bollas (1983, 1987), who speaks about creating a readiness to accept and work with the "news from within." He proposes that what the patient needs to communicate may stem from preverbal experiences, which can only be acted out rather than verbalized. A similar position is taken by Renik (1993), who views the analyst's receptivity to countertransference as a vital aspect of the treatment. The act of internally processing a countertransference reaction, which requires self-awareness, and of generating meaningful hypotheses has been thoughtfully presented by Tansey and Burke (1989).

Most analysts agree that the projective identification aspect of countertransference is most intense in the treatment of borderline and psychotic patients (Searles, 1965; Volkan, 1981). Kernberg (1975, 1995) suggests that intense countertransference reactions indicate the presence of preoedipal structural pathology. The greater the psychopathology, the greater the corresponding countertransference.

TOTALIST COUNTERTRANSFERENCE CONCEPTS IN COUPLES THERAPY

Couples therapists are in an advantageous position: they are both participant and observer in the couple's dynamics. Typically the couple's primary source of conflict and marital disharmony reflects projective identifications in which unwanted aspects of self are externalized and then encountered as an aspect of the spouse. In the same way that the spouse is provoked to accept and respond in ways that bring to life a previously internalized conflict, the therapist is similarly stimulated to experience aspects of both partners' internalized object relations (Scharff, 1989; Siegel, 1992).

Conceptualizing countertransference as a dynamic similar to projective identification does not negate the possibility that the therapist may also be responding to classically defined impulses or yearnings that have been revived through the interaction with the couple. Slipp (1988) differentiates between subjective countertransference, which is due to unresolved neurotic issues, and objective countertransference, which is the response created from a family's projective identification. Scharff and Scharff (1987) have further divided the therapist's objective countertransference into those aspects pertaining to the repetition of internalized object relations and those specifically related to the holding functions of the therapist.

The therapist who is able to recognize his/her own reactions and question the ways in which they stem from or mirror the couple's relationship has several advantages. Countertransference becomes a tool that allows the therapist to experience important aspects of the spouses' inner worlds and of their relationship, for the issues externalized onto the therapist are those that invariably cause the couple the most conflict and tension. As the totalist analysts suggest, the nature and intensity of the therapist's response often reflect the stage of object relations development in the spouses (Sharpe, 1990; Siegel, 1995). For example, couples in which one or both of the partners have borderline structures are unusually reactive and chaotic (Goldstein, 1990). It would not be uncommon for the therapist working with such couples to feel overwhelmed and confused (Schwoeri & Schwoeri, 1981). Similarly, the couple's use of splitting and hunger for an "all good" object might be most clearly revealed to the therapist by countertransference feelings, including a fear of displeasing the couple or a wish to be rid of them altogether.

Countertransference reactions are also predictable in treatment of narcissistically vulnerable couples (Nelsen, 1995; Siegel, 1992; Solomon, 1985, 1989). Because narcissistic vulnerability stems from precarious esteem, the therapist is likely to experience feeling devalued or idealized by one or both spouses. The couple's struggle with envy might first be revealed to the therapist in his/her own intense feelings of envy toward the couple or feelings of inadequacy about some aspect of him-/herself. The therapist may also be pulled into a control struggle with one or both of the spouses, reflecting the couple's intrapsychic and interpersonal problems in this area.

Postmodern Countertransference

Recent developments in the theories of constructivism and intersubjectivity have led to recognition of the subjective reality of the therapist and its influence on the therapy process. Constructivism refers to the ways in which external events are processed and made sense of and postulates that "reality" is constructed. Experiences are filtered through specific lenses that provide meaning and are influenced by social elements (Fruggeri, 1992). The intersubjective perspective adds that because all reality is subjective, or influenced by personal belief systems, the therapist's version of therapeutic phenomenon cannot be accepted as necessarily accurate or complete. Countertransference thus moves beyond being perceived as the disruptive obstacle of the classical analysts or the assessment tool of the totalist analysts to a necessary clinical phenomenon that facilitates the recognition and negotiation of different subjective experiences. Langs (1978, 1979) has proposed that therapy is truly bipersonal, in that patient and therapist influence each other in a variety of ways. The therapist's countertransference is viewed as necessary to comprehend intrapsychic and interpersonal dynamics. As Renik (1993) suggests, there is a need for the patient not only to recreate a former relationship but also to have this felt and appreciated by the therapist. In this way, as Strupp (1977) and others have suggested, the human relationship becomes the curative factor.

Once this position is accepted, it is no longer possible to consider the therapist's perspective as truly objective. Because two persons are involved, there is a need to verify and make sense of the subjective reality of each. The question "Whose reality is it?" becomes the central issue in the creation of meaning and change (Treurniet, 1993). Because the intersubjective therapist respects the importance of verifying the patient's sense of reality about his/her inner experience (Brandchaft & Stolorow, 1990), the therapist must be willing to openly process and work with all aspects of countertransference reactions (Thomson, 1991).

In order to address the importance of the therapist's subjectivity, one must focus on the therapist's self in ways that are not completely defined in either classical or totalist approaches. The therapist's beliefs, values, current life situation, and practice environment must be recognized as factors that affect the patient's view of the therapist as well as the therapist's reaction to the patient.

The relevance of culture and personal belief systems has been acknowledged in the analytic literature but only recently given full consideration. Jacobs (1983) briefly mentions the importance of the analyst's values, especially in the countertransference reactions that develop toward the objects in the patient's world. Chediak (1979) also speaks about the analyst's reaction or counterreaction to the patient as a person, which includes his/her social, cultural, religious, and financial qualities. Schoenewolf (1993) identifies a similar phenomenon, calling it the therapist's cultural counterresistance, and notes that this kind of resistance is often the most pervasive and poorly understood. He proposes that the analyst's ideological, religious, political, racial, ethnic, sexual, and regional/national beliefs create biases that could hinder the therapeutic process by preventing genuine relating. As he points out, there is usually a power imbalance that accompanies these deeply held but silent assumptions. The analyst's culturally determined, stereotyped attitudes have been addressed by Thomas (1962), who points out that the therapist is not always conscious of the effect of a derogatory attitude, especially when the values are culturally sanctioned.

Feminist therapists have voiced similar concerns about gender-determined roles and the ways that personal beliefs affect therapy (Luepnitz, 1988; Walters, Carter, Papp, & Silverstein, 1988). For the most part, the therapist's own belief systems have been shaped by a patriarchal society in which women have frequently been degraded and yet given full responsibility for raising the children. The criteria that determine women's mental health are also based on a patriarchal belief system, leading to the pathologizing of certain female traits and the sanctioning of culturally determined male traits such as independence (Brown, 1992; Kaplan, 1983).

In addition to culturally determined values, the current life situation of the therapist has been considered a source of countertransference. The analyst's choice of profession, status, and financial situation were proposed by Racker (1953) to be relevant to the patient's transference to the analyst, and also the analyst's reaction to the patient. This theme has been discussed in greater depth by Heath (1991), who suggests that the analyst's vulnerability to depression could be exacerbated by personal factors such as prestige and money. For example, a therapist could easily compare himself to a wealthy patient and experience self-depreciation or envy. Lakovics (1983) speaks of personal events in the analyst's life that in conscious or unconscious ways influence the therapy. However, it is only in the past few years that analysts have begun to thoroughly examine the impact of a broad range of life events on the therapy (Gerson, 1996; Gold & Nemiah, 1993).

Situational factors pertaining to the therapist's work environment can also contribute to countertransference. Lakovics (1983) identified institutional countertransference as the therapist's reaction to transferences that were specific to clinic patients who had long relationships with a treatment institution. It was implied that the lack of personal connection, the repeated replacement of therapists, and the therapist's own view of clinic patients might create an impersonal and defeating way of relating. Heath (1991) expanded this notion by suggesting that many individuals are susceptible to accepting and acting out projective identifications created in their work environment, a concept similar to Racker's notion of indirect countertransference (1953). Heath questions the extent to which analysts might carry the "chaos, depressive anxieties and phantasies" present in their own psychiatric institutions and professional associations (1991, p. 140).

In an era of managed care and imposed brief treatment, it is likely that the practice milieu is of even greater importance today than ever before. It is quite possible that therapists who are concerned about managed care confidentiality conflicts or resentful about imposed brief treatment plans may feel less than enthusiastic to begin treatment with managed care clients. It is also possible that in a competitive therapy market therapists are more fearful of losing a full-paying patient through a premature termination and might avoid clinically sound confrontations or other interventions that might jeopardize the patient's commitment to stay in therapy.

POSTMODERN COUNTERTRANSFERENCE IN COUPLES THERAPY

The therapist's subjectivity is an area that has not been sufficiently addressed in couples treatment. Every facet of the therapist's life informs his/her response to the couple, either by creating the risk for overidentification, envy, avoidance or by stimulating defenses that alter perception and judgment. Scrupulous honesty is needed in order to process and take responsibility for reactions and departures from the typical treatment stance.

The therapist's values, beliefs, and expectations are carried into every therapy situation. This point has been made by feminist therapists, who thoughtfully outline the ways in which role expectations, power, and responsibility must be examined in every family (Goldner, 1985; Hare-Mustin, 1981). The ways in which gender bias surfaces in couples therapy have also been addressed by Kupers (1995), who stresses the need to analyze the unstated underlying assumptions about men and women. Kupers points out that the goal is not to be neutral, for this is not likely to be attained. However, the therapist who is aware of his/her own biases is able to act consciously and to avoid hindering the couples therapy by his/her own poorly understood issues.

The current reality of the therapist undoubtedly has a tremendous impact on work with the couple. This is especially so when their life situations are parallel, as, for example, when a therapist undergoing marital stress or divorce is working with a couple threatening to separate. For many therapists, the way issues have been resolved in their own intimate relationships may unconsciously become an ideal to be imposed upon the couple. It is just as likely that the therapist's relationship conflicts will become a source of discomfort, stimulating envy or shame. The nature of the themes examined in couples therapy increases the likelihood that the therapist will have strong reactions both to couples who are competently resolving issues he/she is not successfully negotiating and to those who are experiencing similar kinds of pain.

Despite the fact that most marriage therapists are, were, or seek to become involved in intimate relationships, the state of the therapist's own personal intimacy is rarely discussed as having an impact on the therapy (Flaherty, 1979). In the same way that the therapist's personal life may make him/her receptive or defensive to certain issues in the couple, unresolved countertransferences stimulated by the couple or client may be unconsciously acted out on the therapist's unsuspecting relationship partner. A therapist who has just concluded an exhausting session with a bitter, attacking couple may compare and reevaluate his/her own relationship partner.

UTILIZING COUNTERTRANSFERENCE IN INDIVIDUAL THERAPY

There are many ways that countertransference can be used in the therapy. As early as 1951 Little proposed that the analyst's reactions should be shared directly with the patient. This position is also shared by Searles (1965, 1987) and Tauber (1979), who were influenced by Winnicott's work with schizophrenics. Tauber argues for authenticity in the analytic work and believes that the classical position of silence protects the analyst, but "reduces the enrichment potential of the transactions" (1979, p. 68).

The majority of analysts seem uncomfortable disclosing countertransference directly to their patients. Many state that it violates the analytic frame of neutrality and imposes a burden on the patient. Blum likens countertransference disclosure to "exhibition" and suggests that the "patient is likely to be confused, seduced, or intimidated and hurt by the intrusion" (1987, p. 103). Reich (1959), one of the most vocal opponents of sharing countertransference, points out the difference between education and analysis and suggests that the former does not replace the latter. She stresses the importance of accurate interpretations that make discussion of countertransference unnecessary and countertherapeutic. For many therapists, the themes accessed through analysis of countertransference reactions can be introduced in a more general way and used to focus on dynamics that affect other interpersonal relationships as well. Other analysts choose to disclose their countertransference reactions only in specific situations (Tansey & Burke, 1989).

However, intersubjective analysts such as Trop (1994) and Stolorow, Atwood, and Brandchaft (1994) take a different position. They suggest that, because the reality of the therapist is not necessarily the only reality, it must be shared and worked with as part of the therapeutic process. The meaning that the therapist assigns to the patient's therapeutic activity is filtered through the therapist's own defenses, needs, and belief systems; consequently, it needs to be presented as part of the truth, but not necessarily the whole truth.

This concept has also been expressed by analysts who utilize constructivist concepts. Stern (1992) refers to the collaborative aspect of therapy and the learning that takes place by balancing the patient's observations with the analyst's. In order to accomplish this, the therapist's thoughts, feelings, and experiences must be directly shared. Hoffman (1992) describes the importance of sharing the analyst's subjective experience and the authenticity that is accomplished in this process.

UTILIZING COUNTERTRANSFERENCE IN COUPLES THERAPY

Not all couples therapists who use the concept of countertransference recognize its potential as a productive assessment and treatment tool. Weeks (1989), for example, holds the classical position that countertransference is an interference that is potentially dangerous to the therapy and should be worked through outside of the treatment. However, for many family therapists, work with countertransference is an essential aspect of the therapy. Skynner (1987) is well known for revealing feelings and fantasies directly to the family, in the belief that the information contained in his own response is vital to the family's way of relating. He shares his reactions not as facts but as hypotheses that can be accepted or rejected as being meaningless. The Scharffs (1987, 1992) also value the full set of reactions experienced by the therapist and argue that the information should be shared with the couple, even when his/her reactions stem from unresolved personal conflicts. Even in those instances, the aspects of the therapist and spouses that elicit a specific reaction could contain information useful to the couple's way of relating. For different reasons, Livingston (1995) also proposes that the therapist's reactions be fully processed with the couple. As a self psychologist practicing in "couplesland," he stresses the importance of a multisubjective attitude, which is an understanding created by negotiating the experiences of all three participants. The therapist who chooses to reveal his/her thoughts and reactions directly faces some risk and vulnerability, but also creates a working model of honesty, accountability, and self-scrutiny.

Other couples therapists have emphasized the value of the information that can be generated from countertransference, but argue that countertransference should be used to inform the therapist in a more silent way.

Slipp (1984), for example, bases interpretations on knowledge garnered through analyzing the countertransference without necessarily revealing his own subjective experience. The therapist can make sense of his/her own reaction and be more prepared to confront the same issue or dynamic when it next surfaces between the spouses. Even when the countertransference is not completely understood, it is often worthwhile to focus on the similar dynamic in the couple and pursue the subjective experience of each partner instead of allowing the incident to be glossed over.

The therapist who has experienced countertransference as projective identification is in an excellent position to understand the meaning of this role to the spouses and their relationship. Even if the therapist chooses to remain silent, the very act of containment, which involves accepting the projection without retaliation, provides the couple with a different experience. If the therapist is able to contain anxiety and explore the dynamic in a safe, accepting environment, the couple acquires a new way to increase understanding and to learn to tolerate and accept the difficult themes. The problems that have created and perpetuated relationship distress can be approached in a new way that allows the partners to feel supported in their mutual growth.

MULTIDETERMINISM

Waelder (1936) proposed that any behavior or fantasy could serve more than one psychic purpose at the same time. In the same way, countertransference reactions may stem from more than one source, leading to confusion about their meaning and utility in the treatment. Rather than view the multiple sources of countertransference as compromising the usefulness of the concept, it is the purpose of this book to create a framework that allows the therapist to think about his/her diverse reactions to the couple with depth and clarity.

One concept that can serve to bridge many arenas is *identification*. Identification in the analytic sense involves the belief system about self in relation to others that has been created in the representational world (Horner, 1984; Kernberg, 1975; Meissner, 1986; Volkan, 1976). The therapist, for example, possesses a belief system about relationships and about the helping process that has been developed through accumulated experiences that are both remembered and forgotten. The therapist's beliefs and values about relationships are created from his/her own identifications built upon internalized self and object representations. These representations were created in an interpersonal context and influenced by the therapist's early experiences in relation to his/her parents' relationship, as well as with each parent directly. Accordingly, there is an identification matrix within the representational world of the therapist that contains myriad affectively charged experiences and corresponding beliefs about relating that are easily stimulated by the couple's situation and magnified by the format of couples therapy.

In addition, the very nature of therapy invites the therapist to reach toward the client in an effort to understand and connect with his/her cognitive and emotional experiences. In this process the therapist is receptive to all levels of information and can easily be stimulated to take on aspects of the client through the process of trial identification. This process is the basis of empathy, as it allows the therapist to share the client's world in an experiential manner. It is also the basis of projective identification, which helps the therapist comprehend the couple's situation in an intense and immediate way.

The process of identification is also useful in understanding the therapist's reactions to specific aspects of the client's life. These reactions can also be considered trial identifications having more to do with the here and now than the past. Like Bandura's (1977) notion of social learning through observation, there is a process through which the therapist's self representations and knowledge are unmistakably altered. The therapist develops an understanding through vicarious identification and acquires a level of empathy that resonates from within.

Countertransference can thus be regarded as an interplay of activated representations, transitory and trial identifications. The classical, totalistic, and postmodern theories emphasize different aspects of what can be learned about the client, the therapist, and the therapy process. The classical countertransference themes reflect the therapist's internalized object relations and more permanent identification matrix, character, and defense patterns. The oedipal situation and experiences of other intimate triangles are particularly prone to reactivation because of the format of couples therapy sessions. Similarly, the culturally determined self representations, including beliefs about gender, are frequently activated in response to the characteristics and belief systems of the spouses and the couple as a system.

Totalist countertransference theory provides useful concepts to facilitate the understanding of projective identification between spouses and the therapist. In this aspect of the identification process, the therapist accepts stimulation that in some ways alters self representations. This process, a transitory or trial identification, allows the therapist to experience first-hand the relationship dynamics that stem from the spouses' internalized representational worlds.

The personal factors that often contribute to countertransference reactions also need to be appreciated as a vital aspect of the therapist's encounter with the couple. This seems especially important when therapist and couple share a situation or when the couple's predicament threatens the security of the therapist. Therapists who help couples through a catastrophe such as illness or the death of a loved one need to have some framework within which to process intense personal reactions that are not accurately reflected by analysis of classical or totalist themes. Here there appears to be a different form of trial identification—one which, in certain instances, can lead to more enduring changes within the internalized representational identity.

Each aspect of the identification that has been stimulated brings a unique piece of information about the therapeutic experience. When we understand the different threads that combine to produce the total countertransference experience, the therapist and the therapy are immeasurably enriched.

REFERENCES

Aaron, R. (1974). The analyst's emotional life during work. *Journal of the American Psychoanalytic Association, 22*, 160–169.

Anthony, E. J. (1964). Communicating therapeutically with the child. *Journal of the American Academy of Child Psychiatry, 3*, 106–125.

Appel, G. (1966). Some aspects of transference and countertransference in marital counselling. *Social Casework, 47*, 307–312.

Bandura, A. (1977). *Social learning theory*. Englewood Cliffs, NJ: Prentice-Hall.

Blum, H. (1987). Countertransference: Concepts and controversies. In E. Slakter (Ed.), *Countertransference*. Northvale, NJ: Jason Aronson.

Bollas, C. (1983). Expressive uses of countertransference. *Contemporary Psychoanalysis, 19*(1), 1–34.

Bollas, C. (1987). *The shadow of the object*. New York: Columbia University Press.

Brandchaft, B., & Stolorow, R. (1990). Varieties of therapeutic alliance. *Annual of Psychoanalysis, 18*, 99–114.

Brown, L. S. (1992). A feminist critique of the personality disorders. In L. S. Brown & M. Ballou (Eds.), *Personality and psychopathology: Feminist reappraisals* (pp. 206–228). New York: Guilford.

Chediak, C. (1979). Counter-reactions and countertransference. *Journal of Psycho-Analysis, 60*, 117–129.

Epstein, L., & Feiner, A. H. (Eds.). (1979). *Countertransference: The therapist's contribution to the therapeutic situation*. Northvale, NJ: Jason Aronson.

Felton, J. F. (1986). Sex makes a difference: How gender affects the therapeutic relationship. *Clinical Social Work Journal, 14*, 127–138.

Fisher, J. (1993). The impenetrable other: Ambivalence and the oedipal conflict in work with couples. In S. Ruszcznsky (Ed.), *Psychotherapy with couples: Theory and practice at the Tavistock Institute of Marital Studies*. London: Karnac Books.

Flaherty, J. A. (1979). Self-disclosure in therapy: Marriage of the therapist. *American Journal of Psychotherapy, 33*, 442–451.

Fruggeri, L. (1992). Therapeutic process as the social construction of change. In S. McNamee & K. J. Gergen (Eds.), *Therapy as social construction*. London: Sage.

Geller, J. (1992). *Breaking destructive patterns*. New York: Free Press.

Gerson, B. (1996). *The therapist as a person*. Hillsdale, NJ: Analytic Press.

Giovacchini, P. L. (1979). Countertransference with primitive mental states. In L. Epstein &

A. H. Feiner (Eds.), *Countertransference: The therapist's contribution to the therapeutic situation*. Northvale, NJ: Jason Aronson.

Giovacchini, P. L. (1985). Countertransference and the severely disturbed adolescent. *Adolescent Psychiatry, 12*, 449–467.

Gold, J. H. & Nemiah, J. C. (1993). *Beyond transference*. Washington, D.C.: American Psychiatric Press.

Goldner, V. (1985). Feminism and family therapy. *Family Process, 24*, 31–47.

Goldstein, E. (1990). *Borderline disorders: Clinical models and techniques*. New York: Guilford.

Grinberg, L. (1979). Countertransference and projective counteridentification. In L. Epstein & A. H. Feiner (Eds.), *Countertransference: The therapist's contribution to the therapeutic situation*. Northvale, NJ: Jason Aronson.

Grotstein, J. S. (1981). *Splitting and projective identification*. Northvale, NJ: Jason Aronson.

Hare-Mustin, R. T. (1981). A feminist approach to family therapy. In E. Howell & M. Bayes (Eds.), *Women and mental health*. New York: Basic.

Heath, S. (1991). *Dealing with the therapist's vulnerability to depression*. Northvale, NJ: Jason Aronson.

Heimann, P. (1950). On countertransference. *International Journal of Psycho Analysis, 31*, 81–84.

Herman, E. (1982). Marital couples in stress: Therapeutic strategy. In F. Liegerman (Ed.), *Clinical social workers as psychotherapists*. New York: Gardner.

Herman, J. (1992). *Trauma and recovery*. New York: Basic.

Hoffman, I. Z. (1992). Some practical implications of a social-constructivist view of the psychoanalytic situation. *Psychoanalytic Dialogues, 2*, 287–304.

Horner, A. J. (1984). *Object relations and the developing ego in psychotherapy*. Northvale, NJ: Aronson.

Jacobs, T. J. (1983). The analyst and the patient's object world: Notes on an aspect of countertransference. *Journal of the American Psychoanalytic Association, 31*, 619–642.

Jacobs, T. J. (1991). *The use of self: Countertransference and communication in the analytic situation*. Madison, CT: International Universities Press.

Joseph, B. (1987). Projective identification: Clinical aspects. In J. Sandler (ed.), *Projection, identification, and projective identification* (pp. 65–76). Madison, CT: International Universities Press.

Kaplan, M. (1983). A woman's view of *DSM-III*. *American Psychologist, 71*, 786–792.

Kernberg, O. (1965). Notes on countertransference. *Journal of the American Psychoanalytic Association, 13*, 38–56.

Kernberg, O. (1975). *Borderline conditions and pathological narcissism*. New York: Jason Aronson.

Kernberg, O. (1995). Interview in *Psychoanalytic Dialogues, 5*(2), 325–349.

Kohrman, R., Fineberg, H. H., Gelman, R., & Weiss, S. (1971). Problems of countertransference. *International Journal of Psychoanalysis, 52*, 487–497.

Kupers, T. A. (1995). Gender bias, countertransference and couples therapy. *Journal of Couples Therapy, 5*, 71–78.

Lakovics, M. (1983). Classification of countertransference for utilization in supervision. *American Journal of Psychotherapy, 37*(2), 245–257.

Langs, R. (1978). *The listening process*. New York: Jason Aronson.

Langs, R. (1979). The interactional dimension of countertransference. In L. Epstein & A. H. Feiner (Eds.), *Countertransference: The therapist's contribution to the therapeutic situations*. Northvale, NJ: Jason Aronson.

Little, M. (1951). Countertransference and the patient's response to it. *International Journal of Psychoanalysis, 32*, 32–40.

Livingston, M. S. (1995). A self psychologist in couplesland: Multisubjective approach to transference and countertransference-like phenomena in marital relationships. *Family Process, 34*, 427–439.

Luepnitz, D. A. (1988). *The family interpreted: Feminist theory in clinical practice*. New York: Basic.

Maeder, T. (Jan., 1989). Wounded healers. *The Atlantic Monthly*, 37–47.

Meissner, W. W. (1986). The earliest internalizations. In R. Lax & S. Bach (Eds.), *Self and object constancy* (pp. 29–72). New York: Guilford.

Miller, A. (1981). *Prisoners of childhood*. New York: Basic.

Mustin-Hare, R. (1981). A feminist approach to family therapy. In E. Howell & M. Bayes (Eds.), *Women and mental health*. New York: Basic.

Nelsen, J. (1995). Varieties of narcissistically vulnerable couples: Dynamics and practice implications. *Clinical Social Work Journal, 23*, 59–70.

Ogden, T. H. (1979). On projective identification. *Journal of Psychoanalysis, 60*, 357–373.

Racker, H. (1953). A contribution to the problem of counter-transference. *International Journal of Psychoanalysis, 34*, 313–324.

Raphling, D. L., & Chused, J. F. (1988). Transference across gender lines. *Journal of the American Psychoanalytic Association, 36*, 77–104.

Reich, A. (1959). Further remarks on counter-transference. *International Journal of Psychoanalysis, 41*, 389–394.

Reid, K. D. (1977). Nonrational dynamics of the client-worker interaction. *Social Casework, 58*, 600–608.

Renik, O. (1993). Countertransference enactment and the psychoanalytic process. In M. Horowitz, O., Kernberg, & E. Weinshel (Eds.), *Psychic structure and psychic change*. Madison, CT: International Universities Press.

Rockland, L. H. (1989). *Supportive therapy: A psychodynamic approach*. New York: Basic.

Ruderman, E. B. (1986). Gender related themes of women psychotherapists in their treatment of women patients: The creative and reparative use of countertransference as a mutual growth experience. *Clinical Social Work Journal, 14*, 103–126.

Sandler, J. (1976). Countertransference and role-responsiveness. *International Review of Psychoanalysis, 3*, 43–47.

Scharff, D., & Scharff, J. (1987). *Object relations family therapy*. Northvale, NJ: Jason Aronson.

Scharff, J. S. (1989). Object relations theory and its application to family therapy. In J. S. Scharff (ed.), *Foundations of object relations family therapy* (pp. 11–22). Northvale, NJ: Aronson.

Scharff, J. S. (1992). *Projective and introjective identification and the use of the therapist's self*. Northvale, NJ: Jason Aronson.

Schoenewolf, G. (1993). *Counterresistance: The therapist's interference with the therapeutic process*. Northvale, NJ: Jason Aronson.

Schowalter, J. E. (1985). Countertransference in work with children: Review of a neglected concept. *Journal of the American Academy of Child Psychiatry, 25*, 40–45.

Schwoeri, L., & Schwoeri, F. (1981). Family therapy of borderline patients: Diagnostic and treatment issues. *International Journal of Family Psychiatry, 2*, 237–250.

Searles, H. F. (1965). *Collected papers on schizophrenia and related subjects*. New York: International Universities Press.

Searles, H. F. (1987). Countertransference as a path to understanding and helping the patient. In E. Slakter (Ed.), *Countertransference*. Northvale, NJ: Jason Aronson.

Sharpe, S. (1990). The oppositional couple: A developmental object relations approach to diagnosis and treatment. In R. A. Nemiroff & C. A. Colarusso (Eds.), *New dimensions in adult development*. New York: Basic.

Siegel, J. (1992). *Repairing intimacy: An object relations approach to couples therapy*. Northvale, NJ: Jason Aronson.

Siegel, J. (1995). Countertransference as projective identification. *Journal of Couples Therapy, 5*(3), 61–69.

Skynner, A. C. R. (1987). *Explorations with families: Group analysis and family therapy*. New York: Routledge.

Slakter, E. (Ed.). (1987). *Countertransference*. Northvale, NJ: Jason Aronson.

Slipp, S. (1984). *Object relations: A dynamic bridge between individual and family treatment*. New York: Jason Aronson.

Solomon, M. (July, 1985). Treatment of narcissistic and borderline disorders in marital therapy: Suggestions toward an enhanced therapeutic approach. *Clinical Social Work*, 141–156.

Solomon, M. (1989). *Narcissism and intimacy: Love and marriage in an age of confusion.* New York: Norton.

Stern, D. B. (1992). Commentary on constuctivism in clinical psychoanalysis. *Psychoanalytic Dialogues, 2*, 331–363.

Stolorow, D., Atwood, G. E., & Brandchaft, B. (Eds.). (1994). *The intersubjective perspective.* Northvale, NJ: Jason Aronson.

Strupp, H. H. (1977). A reformulation of the dynamics of the therapist's contribution. In A. Gurman & A. M. Razin (Eds.), *Effective psychotherapy.* New York: Pergamon.

Tansey, M. J., & Burke, W. F. (1989). *Understanding countertransference: From projective identification to empathy.* Hillsdale, NJ: Analytic Press.

Tauber, E. S. (1954). Exploring the therapeutic use of countertransference data. *Psychiatry, 17*, 331–336.

Tauber, E. S. (1979). Countertransference re-examined. In L. Epstein & A. H. Feiner (Eds.), *Countertransference: The therapist's contribution to the therapeutic situation.* Northvale, NJ: Jason Aronson.

Thomas, A. (1962). Pseudo transference reactions due to cultural stereotyping. *American Journal of Orthopsychiatry, 32*, 894–900.

Thomson, P. (1991). Countertransference in an intersubjective perspective. In A. Goldberg (Ed.), *The evolution of self psychology.* Hillsdale, NJ: Analytic Press.

Treurniet, N. (1993). Support of the analytical process and structural change. In M. Horowitz, O. Kernberg, & E. Weinshel (Eds.), *Psychic structure and psychic change.* Madison, CT: International Universities Press.

Trop, J. (1984). Conjoint therapy: An intersubjective approach. In A. Goldberg (Ed.), *Progress in self psychology.* Hillsdale, NJ: Analytic Press.

Volkan, V. D. (1976). *Primitive internalized object relations.* New York: International Universities Press.

Volkan, V. D. (1981). Transference and countertransference: An examination from the point of view of internalized object relations. In S. Tuthman, C. Kaye, & M. Zimmerman (Eds.), *Object and self: A developmental approach.* New York: International Universities Press.

Waelder, R. (1936). The principle of multiple function: Observations on overdetermination. *Psychoanalytic Quarterly, 5*, 45–62.

Walters, M., Carter, B., Papp, P., & Silverstein, O. (1988). *The invisible web: Gender patterns in family relationships.* New York: Guilford.

Weeks, G. R. (1989). *Treating couples.* New York: Brunner/Mazel.

2

Countertransference and Empathy in Couples Therapy

MARION F. SOLOMON

EVEN MORE THAN individual treatment, marital therapy is influenced by countertransference reactions of the therapist. Skynner (1976) has noted that the emergence of these reactions while treating a couple or family can feel chaotic and overwhelming, possibly interfering with the therapeutic process. Alternatively, the therapist's emotional responses can be utilized as an effective tool of treatment when they provide a route to understanding the internal experience of the partners.

Couples usually seek help when they are at an impasse in resolving their problems. Often they feel close to hopeless. If the relationship is in the process of breaking down, partners are particularly vulnerable both as individuals and as a couple. Notwithstanding the best efforts of a therapist, it is not possible to work with a couple without becoming, in some ways, immersed in the dynamics of the relationship. In conjoint therapy, not only do the husband's and wife's boundaries open toward each other and the therapist, but the boundaries of the couple as a unit open toward the therapist as well. Indeed, this permeability of boundaries offers a means of promoting the relationship by allowing destructive aspects to emerge for examination under safe and protected circumstances. Clinical understanding alone is rarely helpful; it must be shared in a manner that conveys an empathic understanding of the way each partner's core issues and emotions impact on the other and the relationship.

EMPATHY

The term *empathy* is often used as a synonym for caring and sympathetic listening, but empathy is not limited to positive regard (Kohut, 1984). Empathic understanding of another can be used to humiliate or destroy that person, because empathy confers the ability to "read" underlying affects and utilize awareness of the other's experience.

The mental health field has long sought to understand the empathic process more completely because of its importance to treatment. Fliess (1942) referred to "trial identification" in which the therapist actively welcomes and openly receives transitory affective states in a manner similar to the way a theater audience eagerly awaits being stimulated and moved by the actors. Empathy, Fliess wrote, is the ability to put oneself in the other's place, to step into his or her shoes, in this way obtaining inside knowledge that is almost firsthand. As the therapist opens up and willingly takes in—as if on a trial basis—whatever is sent by a patient, the process of understanding deepens.

Questions arise concerning the difference between countertransference reactions based upon the therapist's pathological unconscious processes and those derived from "healthier" counteridentification with the patient's projective identifications. Answers to questions such as these make arbitrary distinctions where there should be none. Empathy requires the totality of the therapist's response; the whole person of the therapist is involved in the dynamic interaction that takes place in treatment. In fact, empathic attunement requires the therapist's willingness to allow free flow of the full range of feelings throughout the session. Very often, what we "pick up" depends upon our own internal experience and familiarity with precisely those aspects of the unconscious material that is being transmitted to us. The important difference is whether the therapist has an awareness of the internal forces that are being pulled into play. If highly charged emotions are emerging, and the therapist is unconscious of them, it is more likely that some damaging enactments will occur, precipitated either by the partners or by the therapist.

What makes the work of empathy difficult is to attune both to the emotions of the partners and to the responses within the self of the therapist. Empathy comes from a genuine sense of underlying commonality, of the shared experience of humanness; it is not the imposition of unwanted or unfamiliar ideas by one party on another. Nor is it a unilateral intrapsychic experience. On the contrary, empathy is an intersubjective phenomenon in which there is an inner experience of sharing and comprehending the momentary psychological state of the other (Schafer, 1959). In an empathic encounter, identification takes place not with the other person, per se, but with his or her experience (Basch, 1983). Two people describing the same encounter between them may describe totally different experiences. A therapist, listening to a couple, may hold different, perhaps conflicting feelings, attuning to each of the partners.

Because empathy is part of a mutual communication process, the therapist's subjective experience throughout the session is as important as understanding what is going on in the interaction between the partners. When the therapist observes the unfolding interaction — maintaining a receptive capacity to how he or she is used by each mate in the relational space between them — various needs, feelings, and defenses emerge and become available for examination and modification. In order to operate therapeutically within that relational space, the therapist must be able to maintain a stance of open-minded curiosity about what is occurring within the spouses as well as in him-/herself, listening for messages from within and making some determinations about their source. The internal experience of the therapist often reflects the emotional experience of the individual or partners in the interactional space of the relationship.

It is a matter of recognizing that one's own affective state replicates that of the other, permitting a form of temporary identification. Such vicarious attunement to the internal state of another occurs quite commonly between people. Mothers of newborns, for example, accurately harmonize with the needs of their babies (Winnicott, 1971). Infants and children have been reported to be "unerringly attuned" to the affective state of the mother (Stern, 1985). In the course of development, "the parent transforms the infant's affective reactions into signals, consciously through reasoned evaluation of the significance of the child's facial expressions, cries, body posture, and movements, and, more importantly, *unconsciously in reaction to the affective state that is produced in the parent by the child's affective expression*" (Basch, 1983, p. 108).

WHEN EMOTIONS CROSS BOUNDARIES

The same transfer of emotional reactions that characterizes the parent-child relationship is at work between marriage partners, as well as between analyst and patient, marital therapist and couples. With some couples, a therapist will experience this transfer of emotions in the form of boredom broken by periods of interest, or as unexpected anxiety and insecurity. These are the times to recognize that some indirect messages are probably passing into the therapist's unconscious from the unconscious of one or both partners. It may be an effort to share some of their unacknowledged sense of helplessness, or an expression of fear that the therapist will be threatened by the intensity of their closeted emotions. Perhaps the partners, out of a deathly fear of their own emotions, are daring the therapist to react.

I think about a couple with whom I became extremely sleepy each time we met. I actually had to force myself to keep my eyes open. This couple was referred by a close friend and colleague who asked me to please help her "dear friends," who were going through a marital crisis. "She is a wonderful, superbly confident and successful career woman, and he is a brilliant, creative artist with a dark side," my colleague had told me.

I looked forward to meeting them at the time of our first session. They indeed had an unusual story to tell about how, before they had met, both independently made names for themselves in the same industry, and then, upon first meeting, realized instantly that they must spend their lives together. Jan and Rollo believed that by pooling their talents and resources, they could conquer their world together. I was fascinated by their talent and joint charisma. By the third session, however, I found that I could stay awake only by exerting great effort.

Jan contended that everything was going great for them — until they married. Rollo had gotten drunk at the wedding and was rude to all the guests. Then, after four weeks of partying and lovemaking, Jan discovered that she was pregnant. Rollo wouldn't come near her upon hearing this unwelcome news and gave every possible excuse to avoid sex.

When relating their history and family backgrounds, each described a series of tragedies. Jan described being abducted, raped, and nearly murdered when she was 18. She survived "by chance" after being left for dead. Rollo described the death of his best friend in a swimming accident, the separation of his parents, the loss of the first woman he loved in an airplane crash as she was returning home to be with him, the cancer that killed his father, and his own bout with a serious illness. Both Jan and Rollo described their horrific ordeals with great calmness, as I continued to crave sleep.

Finally I remarked that I was experiencing something strange as I listened to their stories. It was as though something was telling me *not* to listen, to lock it out, to go to sleep. I wondered if they had tried to bury their emotions, to put to rest the painful feelings around all of these traumas. Once we began talking about this, a door to deeper communication opened, and we had access to Jan's terror and grief around the abduction and abuse. We then looked at Rollo's hidden feelings of being toxic, unable to touch anyone or anything without causing death, and of needing to disconnect from his wife and unborn daughter to protect them from the poisons he believed he emitted.

As these discoveries were made, my sleepiness evaporated. I was able to work with this couple and help them explore the emotions as each described the pain of their traumas. The three of us began the process of expelling the deadening virus that had infected their marriage. Although there were times of intense pain, the therapeutic alliance allowed us to go together into areas that had felt unbearable to each of them alone.

The therapist's reception of one or both partners' unwanted affectivity can become the basis for pathological collusions or a tool for empathic understanding. The process of understanding the transference through empathic attunement helps the therapist to recognize and respond appropriately to the unconscious needs and the defenses against unconscious anxiety that emerge. One of the keys to achieving such attunement to the affectivity between the partners is enhanced utilization of the countertransference. Throughout the session, the therapist must remain attuned to his or her own fluctuating emotional and physical reactions. Pondering questions such as, "Who am I to them? . . . Whom does she represent to me? . . . Are my reactions unique to this couple? . . . Do I feel differently in this particular session than I generally feel with this couple?" provides information that is vital to the treatment.

In sessions with a couple, responses to such questions help the therapist recognize the way the partners deal with such issues as intolerable emotional states, fragile self-cohesion, and permeable or impenetrable boundaries. Understanding these issues is crucial to intervening at the level at which spouses are interacting with each other and with the therapist. Sometimes it is necessary to share with the couple certain aspects of one's response. Other times it is enough to know that an unusual therapeutic reaction may signify identification with some part of the couple's experience. The goal is then to listen with an open mind for clues to what the partners are trying to convey at an unconscious level.

Hedges, in *Strategic Emotional Involvement* (1996), suggests that the most important component of treatment is therapists' willingness to risk extending themselves emotionally by entering unknown areas and resonating with their patients' unconscious affects. Emotional resonance is both a method of gathering information about the internal state of the partners and a way of communicating caring. For people who have buried feelings, primitive affects, intolerable anxiety, and nameless terrors, their intimate relationships may be filled with stories about why living with the other is causing them so much misery. The ability to attune evenly to both partners, to point out the commonalties, and to demonstrate acceptance of each partner's inner experience is the basis of successful treatment of couples.

Although an empathic, absolutely evenhanded response is an ideal condition of treatment, such a response is often difficult to achieve, particularly when complex issues arise that do not allow easy resolution. The need to take charge and make the situation manageable may pressure the therapist into focusing on problems that can be resolved, while putting aside those issues that stir up too many of the therapist's own unresolved memories and emotions. A therapist who keeps the dialogue at a rational, intellectual level may be colluding with one or both partners' avoidance and fear of uncovering core issues. By remaining neutral, the therapist stays above the fray, while the partners, who relate to each other primarily on the basis of primitive emotions, are left to deal with torrents of affect and have no safe route to their unconscious process.

EMPATHIC FAILURES

Sometimes there are factors that cause a therapist to align with one spouse at the expense of the other, to the detriment of the treatment. One partner's facade of grandiosity or narcissistic demands, for example, may drive the therapist into alignment with the other. This can increase the level of the acting-out partner's rage, even to the point of dropping out of treatment. If the unfavored spouse stays in the treatment for a time, there is a defensive reaction against narcissistic injury caused by the sessions. Feelings of shame or humiliation may emerge as one partner feels blame and the other feels guilt. The blamed partner may be labeled "resistant" or "disturbed." Every therapist at some point is likely to experience such a misalignment with a particular couple. We all have blind spots and unconscious countertransference reactions. It is when it occurs repeatedly that consultation is necessary. The unfortunate aspect of such lack of empathic attunement is that the therapist may never recognize the countertransference problem, attributing treatment failures to "difficult" patients or dysfunctional couples.

The dynamic process of transference and countertransference in conscious and unconscious dialogue between patient and therapist reflects the totality of the intersubjective encounter (Stolorow & Atwood, 1992). Table 2.1 outlines the many different aspects of countertransference that were described in Chapter 1. These factors influence how a therapist attunes, or fails to attune, to the transmission of emotions between the partners and within him-/herself.

CONCORDANT AND COMPLEMENTARY COUNTERTRANSFERENCE

As noted in Chapter 1, classical descriptions of the unconscious emotional reactions of the therapist view them as something to be overcome through supervision or analysis. In this older model of countertransference, the unconscious transference reactions that the therapist brings to treatment are seen as being caused by unresolved issues in the therapist's life. The concept of totalist countertransference does not abrogate prior understanding of the structure and types of countertransference reactions and recognizes the dangers inherent in countertransference reactions. At the same

TABLE 2.1
Totalist Countertransference

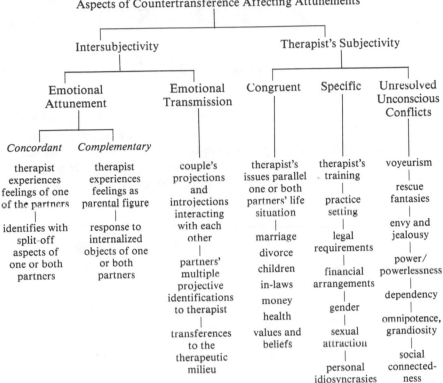

Aspects of Countertransference Affecting Attunements				
Intersubjectivity		**Therapist's Subjectivity**		
Emotional Attunement	Emotional Transmission	Congruent	Specific	Unresolved Unconscious Conflicts
Concordant *Complementary*				
therapist experiences feelings of one of the partners	therapist experiences feelings as parental figure	couple's projections and introjections interacting with each other	therapist's issues parallel one or both partners' life situation	therapist's training	voyeurism
identifies with split-off aspects of one or both partners	response to internalized objects of one or both partners	partners' multiple projective identifications to therapist	marriage divorce children in-laws money health	practice setting	rescue fantasies
				legal requirements	envy and jealousy
		transferences to the therapeutic milieu	values and beliefs	financial arrangements	power/ powerlessness
				gender	dependency
				sexual attraction	omnipotence, grandiosity
				personal idiosyncrasies	social connected-ness

time, this new view considers all the conscious and unconscious reactions of the therapist to be part of totalist countertransference and emphasizes the connection between those responses and the empathic response so essential to effective treatment.

Patients' vulnerabilities, idealizations, and projections—summarized in their expectations of the therapist—engender either "concordant" or "complementary" countertransference responses. According to Racker (1968), when a patient has disavowed untenable internal experiences, the therapist, through *concordant* countertransference, may experience what that person cannot consciously feel. For example, as a wife blandly describes enduring severe abuse by her husband, the therapist's anger at the husband emerges. Or, a therapist who experiences detachment, sleepiness, or boredom may be responding concordantly to the inner emotional deadness of a couple's relationship. When the therapist's affect closely tracks the patient's affect, concordant identification becomes the basis of the therapist's empathy.

Racker has suggested that in *complementary* countertransference, the therapist attunes to the patient's internalized parental object. The therapist then unconsciously identifies him-/herself as this object (Grayer & Sax, 1986). Thus, in complementary countertransference the therapist's emotional response is tracking the internalized objects of one or both partners. For example, the therapist may momentarily feel like, and begin to behave as, the parent of one of the mates. Such countertransference reactions are likely to occur with patients who developed primitive patterns of defense in response to recurring painful encounters very early in life. Learned behaviors, repeated in new situations, tend to elicit familiar responses, a repetitious pattern that may be recreated in the treatment setting. The danger is that the therapist may become angry, withholding, or seductive in a countertransference reaction to the patient's provocative behavior.

THE THERAPIST'S SUBJECTIVITY

In recent decades the concept of countertransference has been integrated with the concept of the therapist's subjectivity. No longer do we view the therapist as a dispassionate observer of intrapsychic conflicts or the neutral interpreter of interactive encounters between partners. We now understand that the therapist may experience feelings similar to those that stir patients and often with the same degree of passion. Love, hate, sexual arousal, envy, contempt, boredom, and a multitude of other feelings are part of an intersubjective experience. Both subjectivity and intersubjectivity become part of countertransference, but the latter enhances the ability for empathy, while the former may focus the treatment on issues important to the therapist—i.e., anxieties around sexual abuse or substance abuse may provide the lens through which all couples are seen.

Consider all the ways in which therapists may bring their personal issues into the therapy. All adults have made decisions about relationships: to marry or stay single, to remain married or get a divorce. The decisions a therapist has made about his or her own life are likely to affect reactions to those who are dealing with similar issues. The therapist who has decided to leave what feels like an intolerable marital situation may think in those terms when he or she sees a similarly unhappy situation in a patient's life. Although a therapist's personal history is not shared with patients, thoughts, affects, and attitudes are communicated in many nonverbal ways.

In trying to come to terms with what the therapist may bring into the session, many different issues may emerge: for example, there is the *self as a voyeur*—wanting information about a couple, feeling envious of, or titillated by, what emerges in sessions but not knowing what to do with it — or the *dependent self* — the desire to be loved and needed, even being seduced into believing in our own enhanced importance by individuals or couples with whom we are working, meeting narcissistic needs of omnipotence and grandiosity. These are the issues that can make or break a therapist's effectiveness. For therapists whose life situation revolves around their work ("I don't really need friends because I feel so connected to my patients"), there is an unconscious expectation that patients fill emotional needs of the therapist, most probably to the detriment of the therapy. The litigious tendencies of people who feel wronged may make empathy impossible. A therapist afraid of being sued may be overly cautious about trying innovative treatment and may not feel very empathic toward a patient who threatens to become an adversary.

Reality issues of therapists' and patients' lives can either enhance the therapist's empathic attunement or block the therapist's ability to hear one or both partners. Financial and sociocultural backgrounds, gender, sexual attraction, and the personal idiosyncrasies of both patient and therapist may cause distractions or distortions and a failure of empathy. Social and cultural issues are likely to influence values and beliefs. "She should not have to put up with the way he allows his parents to interfere with his life," I heard one therapist say in discussing a couple she was seeing. But the therapist had little understanding of the cultural factors in the husband's family that made what seemed pathological to the wife and the therapist quite natural and acceptable to the husband. The therapist felt empathically attuned to the wife and supported her position as the only reasonable one. The result was that the wife threatened divorce unless her husband distanced himself from his very close-knit family.

An essential part of the therapeutic communication with a couple is the exchange of ideas and ideals based upon personal histories and cultural socialization. Many issues, often out of conscious awareness, include the values and beliefs of the therapist, unexamined assumptions about health and pathology, good and evil, courage and failure, responsibilities and prohibitions, dependence and independence. These become part of the therapeutic dialogue and influence the course of treatment with a couple. The ideals and beliefs of the therapist, as well as the ability to tolerate ambiguity and "not knowing," determine the capacity to attune empathically to primitive, chaotic emotions that emerge in work with couples. Therapists with strong sociopolitical bents, feminist orientations, or pro-/anti-abortion stances are similarly faced with distortions in attunement and may fail to help partners deal with issues that are tearing the fabric of the relationship.

A "pro-life" therapist in a countertransference seminar described her dilemma: a couple with four children had suddenly found out that the wife was pregnant — after the husband had had a vasectomy — and were now disputing whether or not to have an abortion. The wife cried and said that God wanted them to have this baby. "I can't do it," the husband said over and over again about having a baby. "I'm just not in a place where I can take on another child."

"I didn't have the right to tell them what I felt," the therapist said. "But there was no way that I could be empathic with the husband!" We all experience certain moral and ethical dilemmas in our work, and our ability to attune to the emotions of the couple at these times is impaired.

EMPATHY AND PROJECTIVE IDENTIFICATION WITH PRIMITIVE MENTAL STATES

Many people who appear to function quite successfully in most aspects of their lives carry deep within their core borderline and narcissistic defenses against severe pathology or early trauma. In stressful situations, those with narcissistic defenses may become emotionally detached, encapsulating the self as protection against the slings and arrows of a partner's anger. The result is a feeling of emotional deadness or emptiness that is experienced by others around such people as boredom, lack of interest, or disconnection. Other means of protecting a vulnerable self, usually identified as borderline defenses, include splitting and projective identification. People employing these defenses may carry old injunctions against showing their true feelings because they believe there is something bad inside. They cut off the "bad-ness," but go through life feeling that a part of them is missing.

Individuals with such primitive defenses against being injured look for partners who have what is missing in their lives. So often couples find and marry each other because their unconscious defenses "fit" together. In later chapters we will see how boundaries are traversed through projective identi-fication and the therapist's projective counteridentification (Grotstein, 1981), which in marital therapy provides a freely moving pattern of interac-tions between the partners and between the couple and the therapist.

One of the main challenges in dealing with primitive defenses is that such people may engage in behaviors that discount, anger, or deaden those present, even as the extreme behaviors demand total involvement and em-pathic responses. No matter how hard a therapist tries to preclude it, the transference process with such couples invariably engenders countertrans-ference reactions — love or hate or some mixture of intense feelings.

Challenging behavior is often a highly active, though unconscious, en-deavor designed to make others experience the relationship in a particular way. Some partners use each other as vehicles for containing emotions that are felt to be intrinsically dangerous. When the therapist enters the picture, he or she can become an even more convenient container for intolerable affects. On the one hand, the couple is challenging—even attacking—the therapist. On the other hand, one or both spouses are attempting to communicate through an unconscious transfer of emotion.

A chronic danger in treating borderline and narcissistic individuals and couples is the fatigue produced by the heavy demands made on the therapist. A tired therapist retaliates by losing interest and tuning out. Such countertransference responses preclude empathy, yet it is in such cases that evenhanded empathic attunement is most necessary. Therapists can become distracted and feel overloaded, not only because of the material being presented but also because the pain and suffering are unbearable to one or both partners. Therapists cannot attune because they find it hard to tolerate the primitive emotions that are thrown back and forth like a "hot potato."

In stressful situations emotional transmission is inevitable. The therapist may receive the couple's multiple projections and introjections directed toward each other, the therapist, and the treatment milieu. For example, a husband and wife may combine to attack and confuse the therapist, projecting their own feelings of inadequacy and despair. "This therapy isn't working. We don't think you can help us. We've been coming for six months and it's a waste of time. We're thinking of going someplace else." The therapist in such a situation may feel useless or inadequate when professional competency has been challenged. The countertransference feelings that arise can lead a well-intentioned professional to terminate treatment with a couple or an individual too soon, when what is really needed is to explore their sense of hopelessness and disappointment. Sometimes therapists don't want to know what patients desperately want known—the deepest, darkest core of the self. For therapists, as for patients, some things are simply too painful to endure.

USING THE COUNTERTRANSFERENCE AS A TOOL OF TREATMENT

Although much attention has been directed toward helping therapists avoid countertransference acting-out, less attention has been paid to the facilitative role countertransference can play when it is carefully acknowledged and incorporated into the treatment. Since a therapist's attunement to his/her own countertransference can be used as a communication tool to obtain important information about patients' emotional constellation, therapists need to examine their own reactions openly and honestly and, when it would be helpful, communicate certain aspects of their feelings to patients (Searles, 1979; Skynner, 1981). There are times when the therapist may feel pleasure or disgust while in a session with a couple. A colleague described feeling "possessed"—threatened with the loss of his identity and sanity—

when he did a double session with a particular couple. He tried to resolve it by limiting the treatment to individual sessions and sought consultation when the treatment was at an impasse. Skynner (1976) wrote that "the therapist may carry around such disturbing projections within himself for quite long periods before they suddenly disappear and return to the patient" (p. 79). In this process the therapist becomes a container (Bion, 1962) for toxic emotions that the patient cannot bear. It is part of the transmutative process of treatment: the therapist empathically attunes to the swirling emotions, internalizes and "holds" them for a time, returning them detoxified in a non-shaming manner by reframing them in a way that can be understood by both partners. In this way the emotions can then be reincorporated safely.

Addressing negative countertransference reactions in therapy may involve more than merely acknowledging them and expressing them in supervision. Sometimes countertransference reactions indicate important facets not only of the spouses' relationship when they came into therapy but also of the relationship created through therapy — that between therapist and the partners. Having accepted that the therapist temporarily becomes part of the couple's system, it is only a small step to recognize that the therapist occasionally becomes immersed — and even participates — in the pathology of the couple or the family. In participating in the system, but within the constraints ultimately imposed by therapeutic neutrality and empathy, the therapist may see events from a perspective otherwise unavailable. The following case vividly illustrates both the emotional dangers attendant on the therapist's role and the therapeutic leverage that sometimes comes with countertransference reactions.

CARL AND LORNA

In working with this couple, close scrutiny of my own negative reactions helped me find the key to helping them. The husband, Carl, was chairman of a conglomerate, a highly successful jet-setter. His wife, Lorna, was a thirty-something self-described "Southern belle," whose intelligence was hidden beneath a facade of baby talk and innocence. She felt bitter and betrayed when she discovered that her husband had been involved in an affair, and she was unwilling to forgive him. Withdrawing from their friends and family, she became extremely fragmented. She said that she felt like "running away from home" — she wanted to return home to the town in Georgia where she had grown up, even though no one in her family lived there any longer. She knew what she wanted no longer existed. Carl, surprisingly soft-spoken for a man used to giving public speeches to large crowds of people, seemed chagrined as he was repeatedly "bombarded" by his wife about what he called "a minor indiscretion." They continued the couples sessions for several months with no progress.

I had a strange experience of confusion that surrounded my work with them; I momentarily forgot names and lost track of facts. Although I usually trust my internal reactions, often responding intuitively without checking my every word, I was aware of feeling strong insecurities in connection to this couple, as though I were going to make some major error that would disrupt treatment. For some reason, I expected something to go wrong. I could not tell how much of this feeling was a reaction to their anxieties and needs and how much came from my own wish to be seen as capable of helping them. It felt important to prove my competence and be accepted by these interesting people.

I decided to share my concerns about whether or not I would be able to help them, and I suggested that we spend some time discussing this, because I did not want them to waste any more of their time and money. Lorna began by reassuring me. She was terribly afraid I would give up on them, "throwing them away," leaving them with no help. As Lorna related these feelings to her childhood terror of being abandoned, Carl said that he had also been wondering if I would really be able to understand. "I am a very complicated man," he said. "I send out signals designed to keep others off balance. I think I have been doing it to you, too. So you probably cannot help me."

As he spoke with a combination of pride and sadness, I was again besieged by questions and doubts. *Does he stay safe by always being alone? What is so dangerous that he must always maintain power over others? How does this encompassing need affect his marriage? Do I understand enough to help them?* I began to realize that I was feeling "thrown away" and feared that they would leave my office and never return. Indeed, I realized that *I* was experiencing the kind of confusion and fragmentation that was Lorna's chief complaint. When I recognized that Carl was much as he described—a master of the smoke screen but also brutally honest—I focused the sessions on that issue and what it meant to them, and my confidence returned.

All at once, I understood something about their union. Carl's daunting personal power had become a means for Lorna to recreate the feelings of loss and fear that had marked her childhood, and her symptoms confirmed his tragic sense of himself—that his power was an instrument for keeping from him the very things that mattered to him most. I no longer felt impotent and was able to share my insights with them. Carl seemed to relax and we were able to go on with the couples' work: their communication problems, discussion of sexual issues, the sense of disconnection that had left both of them feeling lonely and isolated. My ability to once again be empathic to the wound that each of them brought into the relationship made it possible for the change.

CONCLUSION

Once the concept of totalist transference is understood, the meaning of the therapist's strong affectivity can itself be examined in detail. Effective psychotherapy with individuals or couples depends on the therapist's ability to process empathically the events of the session. In order for empathy to be possible, it is necessary for the therapist to remain open to the emotional possibilities coming from within herself or himself.

The therapist brings human experience to treatment—not just training and previous experience treating couples but personal life experience. If this factor were not central, there would already be computer programs that successfully lead consumers through psychotherapy. There are none, and it is a safe bet that there will never be, because the capacity for empathic attunement to another requires some form of corresponding emotional experience with that of the patient or couple. This shared affective experience, with both its dangers and possibilities, is at the heart of psychotherapy, and countertransference provides the key we need to unlock the core issues of the partners in the relationship.

Through a process of empathic understanding of the unconscious or undeclared processes between husband and wife, the therapist can help spouses translate covertly transmitted messages and share with each other the underlying affects and defenses that each has felt necessary for self-preservation within the relationship. The goal is both to offer an environment that will enhance empathic understanding between the mates and to model for them a method of listening at a deeper level. Projections, introjections, and projective identifications are met with an empathic stance, as part of an investigation of the internal state of the partners. It is in the relational space where self and object meet that therapeutic work with the couple is most likely to lead to change in each of the partners and in the relationship. This process is greatly enhanced when the therapist utilizes the totality of the countertransference as an empathic tool to mirror the inner state of the mates and reflect with the couple on the dynamics of the relationship.

REFERENCES

Atwood, G. E., & Stolorow, R. D. (1984). *Structure of subjectivity: Explorations in psychoanalytic phenomenology*. Hillsdale, NJ: Analytic Press.

Basch, M. (1983). Empathic understanding: A review of the concept and some theoretical considerations. *Journal of the American Psychoanalytic Association, 31*, 101–125.

Bion, W. R. (1962) *Learning from experience*. New York: Basic.

Bollas, C. (1983). Expressive use of the countertransference. *Contemporary Psychoanalysis, 19*(1), 1–34.

Bollas, C. (1987). *The shadow of the object: Psychoanalysis of the unthought known.* New York: Columbia University Press.

Brown, S. (October 14, 1984). *Countertransference in marital therapy.* Presentation at UCLA, Los Angeles, CA.

Fliess, R. (1942). The metapsychology of the analyst. *Psychoanalytic Quarterly, 11*, 211–227.

Grayer, E., & Sax, P. (1986). A model for the diagnostic and therapeutic use of countertransference. *Clinical Social Work, 14*(4), 295–309.

Grotstein, J. (1981). *Splitting and projective identification.* New York: Jason Aronson.

Hedges, L. (1996). *Strategic emotional involvement.* Northvale, NJ: Jason Aronson.

Kohut, H. (1984). *How does analysis cure?* A. Goldberg & P. E. Stepansky (Eds.). Chicago: University of Chicago Press.

Main, M., & Weston, D. (1981). The quality of the toddler's relationships to mother and father related to conflict behavior and readiness to establish new relationships. *Child Development, 52*, 932–940.

Racker, H. (1968). *Transference and countertransference.* London: Hogarth.

Schafer, R. (1959). Generative empathy in the treatment situation. *Psychoanalytic Quarterly, 28*, 347–373.

Searles, H. F. (1979). *Countertransference and related subjects.* New York: International University Press.

Skynner, A. C. R. (1976). *Systems of family and marital psychotherapy.* New York: Brunner/Mazel.

Skynner, A. C. R. (1981). An open systems group analytic approach to family therapy. In A. S. Gurman & D. P. Kinskein (Eds.), *Handbook of family therapy* (pp. 39–85). New York: Brunner/Mazel.

Solomon, M. (1987). Application of psychoanalytic treatments for the nonanalytic practitioner. In J. Grotstein, M. Solomon & J. Lang (Eds.), *The borderline patient: Emerging concepts in etiology, psychodynamics, and treatment* (Vol. 2). Hillsdale, NJ: Analytic Press.

Solomon, M. (1989). *Narcissism and intimacy: Love and marriage in an age of confusion.* New York: Norton.

Stern, D. (1985). *The interpersonal world of the infant.* New York: Basic.

Stolorow, R. D., & Atwood, G. E. (1992). *Contexts of being: The intersubjective foundations of psychological life.* Hillsdale, NJ: Analytic Press.

Winnicott, D. W. (1971). *Playing and reality.* Middlesex, England: Penguin.

3

Countertransference
and Diagnosis
in Couples Therapy

SHEILA A. SHARPE

ONE OF THE FIRST couples I ever saw in therapy made me want to run away and hide about halfway through the consultation meeting. It was 18 years ago, but I remember this couple with crystal clarity, because they evoked such powerful reactions in me — primitive reactions way beyond what a dry, cerebral term like countertransference could convey.

They were quite a striking looking pair, Nora and Nathan. She had jet black hair, dead white skin, and most of her gaunt body was encased in a black cat suit. She wore an elegant pair of over-the-knee, black suede boots. I remember those boots very well, because I kept wanting to look at them instead of her chalky, mask-like face. Slashes of dark red glinting on her lips and talon-like nails completed the Vampira effect. Nathan looked more conventional, immaculately dressed in a perfectly tailored, expensive business suit. He was handsome, tall and dark, resembling Rock Hudson, but with a face even more devoid of animation. His dark eyes had an empty, robotic quality that made me feel like nobody was home. Just the look of this couple scared me. They seemed like unconnected, slickly costumed, brittle mannequins on the verge of shattering.

In retrospect, my initial image of the couple presentation was diagnostic, reflecting the empty, fractured, rageful quality of their relating and capturing the precarious state of a relationship in its death throes.

In a tight, little girl voice, Nora began by saying they had "a perfect marriage" except for occasional fights, which seemed to be getting more frequent and violent. Everything was fine now, but he had hit her so hard in the jaw last week that she had to have extensive dental repair. She smiled eerily while telling me this. Nathan interjected, without a trace of remorse, that he only hit her in self-defense. She had attacked him first, scratching his face with those long, vicious nails. He spoke in a careful monotone, presenting himself as "the rational one." Nora, he said, had become incensed because he wanted to go to sleep before she did. This "absurd, irrational" reaction on her part had been the preamble to other fights as well. In a petulant, challenging tone, Nora asked, "Do you want a divorce?" Nathan looked at her with cool disdain and did not reply. Suddenly she exploded in a vituperative rage, and an uncontainable, brutal fight took over the rest of the hour.

In the aftermath of this inauspicious beginning I considered the source of the referral. A psychoanalyst colleague of mine had almost begged me to see this couple. Although he treated an occasional neurotic, well-behaved couple, this pair's behavior (which he could not really describe) had made him feel so anxious and repulsed in the first session that he could not wait to get them out of his office. It appeared that I had the same initial intense reactions as my colleague. What we had experienced in this first encounter (which I only came to understand much later) was a beginning taste of how it felt to be pulled inside this couple's very primitive, hostile-symbiotic relationship system. Primitive fears were evoked: of being engulfed, of being overpowered by aggression and hate, of losing control, of being sucked dry by insatiable neediness. My wish to run from the couple, I also think, was stimulated by the partners' underlying profound fears of abandonment, which led them (especially Nora) to provoke abandonment and rejection.

As I gained more experience and saw other couples with fundamental similarities to Nora and Nathan, I found that very similar initial and subsequent countertransference reactions were often evoked in me, though with less and less intensity as these reactions became more familiar and I was able to make constructive diagnostic use of them. I also came to realize that other kinds of couples functioning at more mature developmental levels also induced characteristic countertransference responses. I have found it useful to consider these countertransference constellations within my classification of couples, according to their most prominent mode of object relating.

I have, to date, identified four basic kinds of couple relationships, distinguished by specific developmental themes, conflicts, and defenses that, taken in concert, reflect the couple's most prominent mode of object relating. (Object relating is here broadly defined to include internalized representations of self-other role relationships and their interpersonal expression.) The couple's characteristic relationship system stems from the partners' often shared attempts to rework the conflicts and themes from a particular early childhood phase in the development of self and object relations (Dicks, 1967). Progressing along a developmental continuum, these four kinds of couples are: the *symbiotic couple*, whose object relating reflects basic trust and primary dependency conflicts (longings for merger and fears of abandonment and engulfment); the *oppositional couple*, whose interaction is dominated by dependence-independence conflicts; the *gender competitive couple*, whose competitive interaction reflects gender identity and negative oedipal conflicts; and the *oedipal couple*, whose more modulated competitive interaction reflects unresolved positive oedipal conflicts.

The purpose of this chapter is to present the distinctive countertransference constellations and the allied pitfalls that I have found to be characteristically invoked by each of these four types. My aim is to provide an introductory guide to the kinds of transference-countertransference paradigms that the therapist can expect to encounter in treating couples at different developmental levels, with their distinctive object relations themes and conflicts. When one is forewarned, one is better able to recognize, manage, and use countertransference constructively.

I have found that countertransference reactions engendered in couples therapy are more potent, complex, chaotic, and unruly than those activated in individual treatment (or, perhaps in any other modality). The reasons for this greater intensity and complexity go beyond the obvious difference in numbers between treating one person versus two. Couples are a unique kind of dyad. Because couple relationships are "the nearest equivalent in adult life to the early bond between parent and baby," the treatment atmosphere is frequently charged with primitive emotion and chaos (Livingston, 1995, p. 428; see also, Dicks, 1967). The therapist must contend with the externalized, raw, in vivo display of the couple's conflicts. Being in the middle of a ferocious fight provokes far more intense reactions than hearing about the fight in individual therapy. Additionally, the triangular format of couples therapy exerts a powerful regressive force in the stimulation of intense rivalry and competition for a parent's love. The individual patient does not have to compete for the therapist, at least in an actual triangle. The couples therapist must contend not only with countertransference reactions provoked by the partners' competition for a position of preference, but also with rivalrous impulses toward the couple, which are more strongly activated in the triangle than in the dyad of individual therapy. As Winer (1994) has astutely noted, the couples therapist is also loaded to a greater degree with impossible expectations (like saving the marriage and fixing the partner), while bestowed with less authority than the individual therapist.

The kind of countertransference I consider here consists largely of those reactions induced in the therapist by the couple through the process of projective identification. I do not intend to imply that all countertransference is a product of projective identification or that other kinds of countertransference are not as important for the therapist to recognize and understand. The kind of countertransference induced by the couple is highlighted here because these are the reactions through which a deeper, experiential understanding of the couple can be gained.

Projective identification can be briefly defined as an intrapsychic and interpersonal mechanism of object relating and defense by which aspects of the self and internal objects are assigned to another person through projection or transference. The recipient (spouse or therapist) is then induced to identify with the projected/transferred role. The "induction" of assigned roles is achieved through behavior and communication patterns that tend to elicit certain responses. *Mutual projective identification* occurs when two persons, either patient and therapist or both partners of the couple, engage in this activity.

Those reactions engendered by the couple's expression of universally experienced object relations themes and conflicts cannot help but resonate to some extent with the therapist's own past and present relationship experience. Depending on the central conflict the couple is enacting, the therapist's own symbiotically based wishes, dependence-independence conflicts, gender identity issues, and oedipal conflicts will be activated to a greater or lesser degree, depending on the therapist's idiosyncratic experience.

While the therapist's own object relations experience is an important aspect of countertransference and will be a determining factor in the therapist's "role responsiveness"—how assigned roles from the couple will be received and played out (Sandler, 1976)—the focus of this study is on those aspects of countertransference that come mainly from the side of the couple. To that end, it is imperative that the therapist examine her countertransference to sort out which reactions are evoked by the couple (and can be used diagnostically and as a guide for therapeutic intervention) and which reactions come from, or are significantly amplified by, her own history or current life situation. As Renik (1993) has so persuasively demonstrated, countertransference enactments not only are unavoidable but are also the vehicle by which the therapist comes to recognize her countertransference, as will be illustrated in many of the subsequent case examples.

Each kind of couple will first be introduced by a brief description followed by discussion of the transference-countertransference paradigms characteristic of the couple type (see Table 3.1). The majority of case examples selected for discussion are couples who presented with clear-cut, rigidified, and entrenched projective identification systems, and hence represent the most difficult treatment cases of their kind, in part due to the strong

TABLE 3.1

Countertransference and Couple Diagnostic Profiles

COUPLE TYPE	OBJECTS RELATIONS PHASE/*CONFLICTS*	COUPLE REPRESENTATIONS	COUNTERTRANSFERENCE IDENTIFICATIONS WITH:		
			COUPLE'S SHARED SELF PROJECTIONS	COUPLE'S SHARED TRANSFERENCES	ONE PARTNER
Symbiotic • Hostile-blaming	**Primary Attachment** *Basic trust/mistrust* *Abandonment/merger/* *engulfment*	We are merged; we are fragmented. We are all good; we are all bad. I need you; I hate you. I am all good; you are all bad.	Abused victim-child	All-good, giving mother (the savior)	"Innocent" victim
• Pseudomutual		We are one. We are ideal twins.	Needy, deprived child	Transitional object All-bad, depriving, rejecting mother	Caretaker "Sick" Overgiving
Oppositional • Fusion-flight • Pseudo-independent • Ambivalent (push-pull)	**Attachment/** **Separation-** **individuation** *Dependence/* *independence*	We are (need to be) opposites. I am right, you are wrong. You can't make me be like you. Hold me close; let me go.	Unvalidated child	Benevolent, judgmental parent Critical, controlling parent	Cooperative partner
Gender Competitive *Gender identity* *conflicts* *Negative oedipal* *conflict*		We are fiercely competitive. I am superior; you are inferior. Admire ME! No, you admire ME! My gender is better than yours. I want to win you, but I'd rather defeat you.	Inferior, defeated boy or girl.	Idealized same-sex parent Devalued, inadequate same-sex parent	Same-sex, passive partner Admiring partner
Oedipal Competitive *Positive oedipal* *conflict*		We are special, lovable, the best. We compete "for fun." You are my ideal, but I am better. I, guiltily, want to both win you and defeat you.	Competitive, guilty child – • oedipal victor • oedipal loser	Idealized, desired oedipal parent Idealized rival parent	Seductive opposite-sex partner

countertransference reactions they evoke. I would emphasize that even though a couple may present for treatment most prominently displaying one object relations mode, other modes may operate in a mixed or layered fashion and come into the foreground at a later time. Progress and regression in the course of therapy, and in life, move the couple forward and backward on the developmental continuum. The diagnostic profiles are presented in a simplified "pure" form for clarity and purposes of comparison.

THE SYMBIOTIC COUPLE

The earliest, most primitive forms of object relating are expressed in the kind of relationship I have designated as symbiotic (Sharpe, 1981), following a modified version of Mahler, Pine, and Bergman's (1975) usage of the term. Although Mahler's description of the symbiotic phase of object relations development has been contested in several respects (Stern, 1985), her basic conception of the infant's early experience of a merged mode of object relating *in some form* remains pertinent and applicable to love relationships (Bader & Pearson, 1988; Pine, 1986, 1992; Sharpe, 1981, 1984).

Symbiotically entwined partners have not been able to integrate the most fundamental relationship capacity—the ability to trust oneself and the human world. This core deficit is probably due to very early and profound failures in developing a primary attachment to the mother, giving rise to a fragmented, inconstant sense of self and others. In their longing for a secure, loving bond with a mother figure to make them feel whole and safe from abandonment, the partners exhibit an extreme form of mutual dependency—a desperate searching for a primary dependent attachment, fueled by the fantasy of merging with an idealized, all-giving mother-spouse. Desires for merger are countered by profound fears of engulfment, which can lead to the erection of defenses, such as chronic blaming, to protect against engulfment. This core conflict is also usually collusively split between the partners. For example, Nora more strongly expresses abandonment fears and needs to merge and Nathan expresses fears of engulfment, as illustrated in his periodic attempts to rupture their symbiosis with abandoning, rejecting behaviors.

Although symbiotic wishes—the wish to merge with an idealized other, to be totally taken care of, to have the other act as an extension of the self, to have unconditional love, to always feel safe and secure—are operative to some extent in all relationships, fulfillment of these wishes is the dominant, life-sustaining aim of the partners in symbiotic relationships. When symbiotic wishes are frustrated in such a relationship, as inevitably they are, certain primary fantasies and affects surface or threaten to surface. Fears of abandonment, total isolation, annihilation, or self-fragmentation will emerge and threaten to overwhelm the disappointed partner with extreme anxiety, rage, neediness, emptiness, worthlessness, and depression. This process is exemplified in Nora's rage reaction and the couple's brutal fight precipitated by Nathan's separate need to go to sleep before she did, an act that threatened her fantasy of fusion. Going to sleep at all is often a problem for such couples, because profound fears of abandonment are provoked by this disruption of symbiosis.

To protect against these intolerable fears and affects, the couple develops certain primitive and characteristic defensive transactions. A rigid, entrenched projective identification system becomes crystallized and pervades the entire relationship. In the symbiotic system, the partner's fragmented sense of self or identity is sustained in a coherent form only through annexing the other in a sort of psychological cannibalism. Thus the boundaries between self and partner are blurred—the other is not perceived or treated as a real, separate person, but as a fantasy creation made up of split (idealized or denigrated) and projected aspects of internal self and objects. However, there is typically a rigid boundary between the couple unit and the outside world, producing a closed-cell syndrome, outside of which meaningful relationships with other people (beyond the family of origin) are minimal to nonexistent.

I have identified two basic subtypes of the symbiotic couple, distinguished by how the partners manage anger and their projective, splitting mechanism. The subtypes can be conceptualized to represent the extreme positions on a continuum of intense to minimal overt conflict and hostility. At the more openly toxic, conflict-ridden end is the *hostile-blaming symbiotic couple.* The interactions of these couples are dominated by ferocious blaming exchanges, the acting-out of "all-bad" self and object projections and transferences. At the pathological extreme, sadomasochistic blaming interactions are accompanied by the physical abuse of one or both partners (as in the case of Nora and Nathan). Milder versions of the hostile, blaming couple sound less sadistic, and their interactions appear more like chronically wounding, debilitating bickering.

At the other extreme is the conflict-avoidant *pseudomutual symbiotic couple*, whose pervasive aim is to sustain a fantasy of fusion that allows for no open expression of difference. The partners of this subtype tend to idealize the other as a twin of the ideal self, and displace anger, bad self and object projections onto a third party, e.g., a child, an ex-spouse, a parent, an institution, etc. Anger may also be defended against by physical or psychiatric symptoms, e.g., depression, eating disorder, phobia, or drug abuse.

Transference and Countertransference

In discussing the transference-countertransference paradigms characteristic of symbiotic and other kinds of couples, an expanded version of Racker's (1968) concordant and complementary countertransference identifications is useful. The therapist's identification with the projected aspects of the patient's self representations is termed concordant identification, while identification with aspects of the patient's objects is referred to as complementary identification. In the couple therapy situation, there are more possibilities for identification than in the two-person situation of individual therapy. The therapist may identify with those distinctive self and object representations of each partner, as well as those representations *shared* by both partners. Yet another important kind of countertransference identification is to the representation that the couple conveys of themselves as a couple unit. The Scharffs (1991) call this representation "the internal couple."

Most often it is the couple's conception and presentation of their couple relationship that evokes the first countertransference response in the therapist. In meeting Nora and Nathan, my first reactions were to the couple unit. They presented starkly conflicting, "split" images of themselves — striving to look like the perfect, immaculate, well-organized couple versus the opposite image of a destroyed, almost dead couple, pumped alive by rage. The extreme discrepancy between positive and negative images of the relationship is characteristic of symbiotic couples. The therapist's reaction of confusion — suddenly feeling unintegrated, disoriented, uncertain, and repelled upon briefly identifying with the couple's internal confusion and chaos — is also characteristic.

Because they convey such starkly polarized, split internal worlds, symbiotic couples of the hostile-blaming type tend to engender the most intense and disturbing initial countertransference reactions. In contrast, pseudo-mutual couples present a very tightly organized conception of themselves as a perfect couple, with the "bad" representations split-off and displaced onto a third party. Consequently, the therapist is not initially so invaded with the chaos and confusion of conflicting extremes, or assaulted with the sudden eruptions of blatant hostility.

Identification with the Ideal "Symbiotic" Mother

In the opening phase of treatment, symbiotic partners characteristically transfer to the therapist their shared yearning for the ideal symbiotic mother and try to induce the therapist to act out the role of the omnipotent, all-giving, all-wise, constantly available mother who is able to magically fulfill all needs. As a corollary to this shared transference, each partner expects the therapist to act as a narcissistic extension and magically fix the other partner who is, of course, the real problem. Falling for the idealized "you are the one and only" role is very tempting, yet leads to endless quagmires and problems in treatment. It is just this countertransference enactment that leads therapists to take cases they should not take, for example, to see the couple in therapy after having seen one of the partners in individual treatment. Every time I have succumbed to the joint plea, "It has to be you; you are the one and only!" I have deeply regretted it — usually for a long time, since treatment is long-term for most motivated symbiotic couples. Similarly, the grandiose countertransference, "I am the only one who can save this couple," may impel the therapist to take on a case that is beyond her capability or experience.

HOSTILE-BLAMING COUPLES: The desperate neediness of this kind of couple, combined with their initial idealized transference, can activate the therapist's own omnipotent, grandiose fantasies. Moreover, the feelings of repulsion and wanting to flee engendered by these couples may evoke guilt feelings and a resultant reaction formation, particularly in female therapists for whom the role of "bad," deserting mother is especially guilt-inducing. Thus, the female therapist may be more inclined to accept the role of idealized, omnipotent mother.

Assuming the role of maternal savior, however, is not a pleasant experience with hostile-blaming symbiotic couples. When heroic efforts to "be there" for the couple are not appreciated or inevitably not fulfilled and instead promote regressive escalation of their primitive demands, the therapist experiences a deflation of grandiosity and disappointment of her own symbiotically based wishes. One feels like a baby's transitional object, the special blanket that is screamed for when needed, mauled, sucked, shredded, and drooled over, and then cast aside and forgotten when the need passes, as when the spouses make up from one of their horrendous fights. I am reminded of one of my ruined weekends during the saga of my valiant, though misguided, efforts to treat/save Nora and Nathan.

About 6 a.m. one Saturday morning Nora called me, claiming an emergency, hysterically recounting a fight with Nathan, begun over her suspicion he had started using drugs again. She wanted to kill the weak, sniveling bastard. After hitting her, he had run out of the house in the middle of the night and not returned. The baby was crying and needed milk. She had no money to buy milk. What should she do? (Clearly, I was supposed to bring this intelligent, resourceful, wealthy woman money or milk! Instead, I suggested she call their nanny or Nathan's mother if she was unable to care for the baby.) A few minutes later, Nathan called me from his car phone. He had been driving around all night afraid to go home. His version of events was that Nora had started a fight over his being late coming home from work and had come after him with a knife, shrieking she was going to cut him to pieces. He was afraid to go home. What should he do? (I suggested calling the police.)

Nathan then called me again, saying Nora was crazy and he feared for the baby's life. He had sent his mother to the house to check on them, and Nora wouldn't let his mother in. (I suggested again that he call the police if he felt the baby's welfare was in danger or his life was threatened.) Then Nora called me again, screaming that Nathan had deserted her and the baby was starving. (I was beginning to feel pecked to death by a pair of vultures.)

Nothing I said or advised stopped the hysteria or the incessant phone calls until I suggested they come to the office for an emergency session. I rearranged my plans for the day and trudged into the office, dreading the session, wondering why I was sacrificing my treasured Saturday for this impossible couple. When I got to the office, there was a message from Nora on my answering machine telling me cheerfully that they didn't need to come in, after all. Nathan had come home, and they had made up. Everything was fine now.

As I sat there feeling like the most abused victim of our enmeshed threesome, I finally recognized that trying to be an all-giving, "savior" mother to this infant couple did nothing to heal their wounds but only fed their pathology and left me feeling bankrupt, exploited, and enraged (which of course was the aim of the "abused victim" aspect of their role assignments). The kind of good mother/therapist the couple really needed was one who would set more forceful limits on their destructive acting-out, while maintaining empathic attunement.

Without recognition of this transference-countertransference pitfall, the therapist can easily swing to the opposite countertransferential extreme and shift into an identification with the "all-bad" symbiotic mother—the couple's shared transference of the hated but desperately needed mother who angrily retaliates, rejects, deprives, and is unpredictable, unreliable, and unavailable. Just as the "all-bad" mother transference is activated between the partners when symbiotic wishes are disappointed, so it may go with the therapist. When the therapist's own symbiotically based wishes to be the couple's "ideal" mother (and so rewarded with everlasting love and gratitude) fail to be fulfilled, the therapist can become very angry and is prone to retaliate punitively by critically rejecting the couple or becoming avoidant and unreliable. The therapist thus enacts the partners' most feared expectations of exploitation, neglect, and abandonment in a repetition of their early life experience.

PSEUDOMUTUAL COUPLES: In contrast to the initial countertransference to hostile-blaming symbiotic couples with the exhausting need to fulfill insatiable conflicting demands, the countertransference with pseudomutual couples can be quite initially gratifying. In this constellation, the unconscious deal being offered is: "We will take care of you, admire you, make you feel special, if you will take care of us, make us feel special, and ensure the survival of our relationship by hiding our rage, disappointment, and hatred of each other, for these feelings would destroy our relationship and too painfully expose our terrible fears of abandonment." These couples can be very persuasive and creative in fostering this collusion, as is exemplified in the following case of Violet and Van.

Violet and Van, married 25 years, were a retired couple in their late fifties. Violet's depression and both partners' great distress over the current rejecting behavior of their "spoiled, selfish, self-centered" grown daughter were the presenting problems. (The daughter had moved out of town to live with an "evil scoundrel," of whom they totally disapproved.) Although they had a painful argument about this daughter (Violet wanted to cut off contact, Van did not), they considered their relationship very close, very happy, and usually untainted by disagreements of any kind. Both drank heavily and were overweight.

In the opening phase of therapy, this couple did everything in their power — and they were exceptionally creative — to seduce me into their pseudomutual admiration society. Their first gambit was the attempt to deny the fact they were in therapy and turn our relationship into a special friendship or make me one of the family. Therapy sessions became like visits to a beloved friend or daughter or mother. They brought candy, cookies, and baked goods to the sessions, enticing me to join them in a little snack. They did their best to take care of me, through careful observation or cleverly inducing me to reveal personal information. For example, they found out I liked chocolate, so they would bring me chocolate. Although I, for the most part, resisted eating their food, the therapy sessions began to seem like festive tea parties.

While I felt very cared for, I also felt increasingly uncomfortable with their rather driven attempts to meet my needs and in danger of losing sight of my job as their therapist. I was aware of my reluctance to disrupt the surface harmony, jolly atmosphere, and mutual idealization. I was hesitant to do anything that would make them feel rejected, angry at me, or disappointed in me, such as reminding them of the purpose of our sessions, exploring the meaning of their overgiving, or more aggressively tackling the reality of their deep anger and disappointment with each other. I was finally shaken out of our cozy symbiotic collusion by the following event.

One day — it happened to be my birthday — I listened to a message on my answering machine. The message was Violet and Van singing happy birthday to me. I was momentarily touched, feeling like a beloved, little child, then profoundly shocked that they had found out the date of my birthday. Aghast, I recalled that Violet had once mentioned the date of her birthday, and I had spontaneously responded that it was the same date as mine. Confronted with this lapse, I could no longer deny my active collusion in their seduction.

I had identified not only with the role of the longed for "ideal" symbiotic mother, but also with the "ideal" symbiotic daughter who would always lovingly comply (and never leave them as their ingrate of a real daughter had done). I recognized their wish for me to fulfill the role of their good, compliant child as a reaction to the loss of their daughter and as a reversal of their own childhood experiences with depriving, narcissistic mothers. I was particularly vulnerable to responding to the assigned child role because my own mother was dying when Violet and Van entered therapy.

With an understanding of my countertransference in terms of the couple's needs and our dovetailing losses, I could pursue appropriate treatment. Shortly thereafter, Violet and Van entered a long, stormy phase of separation-individuation, ultimately establishing (after three years of therapy) a truly mutual relationship.

Identification with One Partner

In addition to the characteristic countertransference reactions provoked by the shared self and object projections/transferences of the symbiotic couple, the therapist is also strongly induced to identify and form an alliance with one or the other partner. From the beginning, the partners are in competition to win the therapist as an ally. Although such competition is seen with most couples, symbiotic partners are often totally preoccupied with this endeavor. This is overt with hostile-blaming couples, but usually disguised with pseudomutual couples. Almost every early session with Nora and Nathan was dominated by their primitive competitive need for me to view him/her as the poor, innocent victim of the other's abusive craziness. With Violet and Van, the competition was covert and initially took the form of who could best take care of me. The underlying wish to prove the self as the good one and the partner as the bad one to be blamed for all the problems emerged only very slowly over time.

With hostile-blaming couples, neutrality is easier to maintain when abuse is perpetrated by both partners and neither one is convincing in the role of "innocent victim." However, in those symbiotic systems where one partner acts more clearly as the blamer and abuser and the other partner enacts the role of passive recipient of the blame and/or abuse, the therapist's identification with the "innocent victim" partner is much more likely and, perhaps, the most common countertransferential pitfall. The therapist enacting this countertransference begins to act out the rescuer/savior/ideal mother role in relation to the "victim" partner and turns against the abusive/blaming partner.

With pseudomutual couples, identification with one partner is most commonly evoked in two kinds of symbiotic partnerships. The one most commonly described in the literature is the relationship where one partner clearly carries the symptom and is the identified patient. The "sick" partner may have a phobia, an eating disorder, or a drug problem, or suffer from severe anxiety, depression, or other mental illness. This partner, characteristically, has also submerged his or her identity in that of the dominating, caretaking, more functional partner. The therapist's identification with the overfunctioning, caretaking partner as a co-therapist in the treatment of the "sick" partner is a common countertransference pitfall. Enactment of this countertransference serves to support the couple's pseudomutual defense and pathologically split role divisions. However, if the caretaking partner is excessively dominating and narcissistic and the "sick" partner actively struggles to individuate, the therapist is more likely to experience an identification with the "sick" partner and view the "caretaking" partner as an exploitative oppressor who is the real problem.

A related partner combination strongly evoking identification with one partner is what has been described as "the narcissistic/overgiving couple" (Nelsen, 1995). In this partnership, the narcissistic partner totally dominates and extracts servile caretaking from the passive, compliant, overgiving, usually masochistic partner. A strong preference for and identification with the overgiving partner is a most likely occurrence. The overgiving partner appears as quite saintly, responsible, fearfully insecure, endlessly giving, and compliant, with drastically low self-esteem, while the narcissistic partner appears as infantile, grandiose, dominating, endlessly demanding, and exploitative. Until one recognizes the collusive splitting of traits between the partners, it can be difficult not to overprotect the overgiving partner and unempathically suppress the narcissistic partner.

THE OPPOSITIONAL COUPLE

Reflecting a more advanced, differentiated mode of object relating is the oppositional couple (Sharpe, 1990), whose interaction is dominated by dependence-independence conflicts. Each partner strives for an independent identity within the relationship, an aim that is often in conflict with the regressive pull of symbiotic wishes as well as appropriate attachment needs. The couple's oppositional defense reflects the most prominent interactional theme, namely, to oppose—either to openly combat or covertly resist— whatever the other partner says, wants, feels, or values. Oppositional inter- action thus sets up rigid boundaries against dependency and intimacy be- tween the partners, in contrast to the merged, blurred boundary character of symbiotic relating. However, the boundary between the couple unit and the outside world is very diffuse, so that other relationships (parents, chil- dren, friends), activities, and work often take priority over the couple rela- tionship.

Partners entrenched in the oppositional mode of object relating have usually experienced great difficulty in the attachment/separation-indi- viduation phase (Lyons-Ruth, 1991) of object relations development, oc- curring in the second year of life and again in adolescence. Separation was often prematurely fostered, resulting in unmet dependency needs and the early structuring of rigid defenses against dependency longings. Such part- ners often share the internal objects of a critical, controlling, often narcis- sistic parent who did not support normal strivings for individuation but instead rewarded compliance. The shared internalized object relation most often played out in the marital transference takes the form of each partner perceiving the other as the reembodiment of a critical, controlling parent and experiencing the self as a small, ineffective, unheard cry against the other's omnipotent power. Concurrently, each partner's identification with the other's transferred role (and with the critical, controlling, narcissistic aspects of his or her own parents) serves to reinforce and entrench this projective identification system.

The mutual unmet developmental needs and wishes of the partners un- derlying their oppositional defense are the longings for validation and affir- mation of their uniqueness as individuals—particularly acceptance of the angry, defiant, differentiating but also dependent aspects of the self. Fears of being dominated, controlled, or used as a narcissistic extension and thereby losing a precarious autonomy are paramount, along with fears of dependency, which might also result in a similar loss. The oppositional defense also protects the partners against their fears of independence. The realization of autonomous, individuated strivings typically evokes fears of feeling abandoned, unloved, and guilty over separating from a disapprov- ing, needful parent (who is represented by the spouse).

The interaction of the oppositional couple looks less like pure blaming and more like push-pull power struggles or courtroom battles about who is right or wrong. However, the power struggle aspect is really a pseudo- power struggle, since when one partner succeeds in winning a point or getting his/her own way, strong fears of abandonment and guilt often arise, and the "winning" partner will usually abdicate in some fashion and throw the power back (unlike the truer power struggles of the gender competitive couple).

Collusive splitting of the dependence-independence conflict most commonly occurs in the form of one partner enacting the dependent, needy side of the conflict, in pursuit of the partner who looks more self-sufficient, wants more distance, and enacts the "independent" side of the conflict. The most common transactional role relationship (which reflects a re-enactment of the original parent-child conflict) is one partner acting as the critical, controlling, demanding parent of the other partner, who acts out the irresponsible, rebellious child or teenager.

I have identified three subtypes of oppositional couples based on couples' patterns of managing the dependence-independence conflict. At the more dysfunctional end of the continuum is the *fusion-flight couple*, usually unable to marry because one partner is phobic about commitment. The *pseudo-independent couple* is able to marry and sustain a relationship but manages the dependence-independence conflict by opting for a solution of great distance between the partners, who live parallel lives. The most functional kind of oppositional couple is the *ambivalent or push-pull couple*, who are more flexible, contained, and balanced in managing intimacy and distance.

Transference and Countertransference

In the opening sessions with an entrenched oppositional couple, their dependence-independence conflict is usually immediately transferred to the therapist in an oscillating fashion, characteristic of the couple interaction. The fears of being dominated, of being taken over, told what to do, or criticized, are expressed in initial and ongoing challenges to the therapist's authority. The therapist can easily feel the lure to engage in battles for control and domination. The bait often appears in the initial evaluative interviews as resistance over meeting time or one partner's attempt to take over the treatment plan.

The dependent side of the conflict (the feelings of helplessness, powerlessness, inadequacy, longings for affirmation and caretaking) are expressed in strong bids for the therapist to take sides as a parent-judge who will decide who is right or wrong. Requests for direction and guidance are frequent: "Tell us what to do!" or "Give us homework!" These behaviors tend to induce the therapist to identify with the couple's wished-for ideal parent—the all-wise, benevolent parent, who will take responsibility, make judgments, and give caretaking in the form of direction and advice in an identification with the benevolent, judgmental parent. However, when the therapist enacts this role and becomes too directive, the independent-negativistic side of the couple's conflict is activated, and the couple typically overtly or covertly rebels.

These challenges to authority, alternating with demands for parental guidance and inevitably followed by rebellious, discounting, spoiling behaviors ("Oh, we forgot to do the assignment, ha, ha!"), can engender a churning frustration and irritation in the therapist, typically evoking two kinds of identifications or role responses in the therapist. One is identification with the critical, controlling parent. Caught up in this reaction, one feels like an angry, thwarted parent who wants to discipline these incessantly quarreling and defiant siblings. The other common countertransference role reaction is identification with the partner's shared and projected sense of self as a small, unheard, unvalidated child angrily striving for affirmation of individuality through a negativistic form of independence — identification with the unvalidated child. In this mode, the therapist regresses and may occasionally act on the temptation to behave like a third two-year-old, competing to be heard, insistently arguing for his or her point of view, and stubbornly refusing to collaborate or compromise. When both of these countertransference reactions are rapidly oscillating, the feelings inside the therapist, often cloaked by rationalizations about the need to establish authority, are something like "I feel unheard, dismissed, unimportant, weak. I must show who is boss by stamping my therapeutic foot and having my way." These typical kinds of countertransference reactions evoked in the opening phase of treatment are illustrated in the case of Alex and Marla.

Alex and Marla, an attractive, professionally successful couple in their mid-thirties who had been married two years, came for couples therapy because of increasing alienation over their constant conflicts and Alex's threats to divorce. The oppositional stance invaded all aspects of their lives, personalities, habits, sexual preferences, and general likes and dislikes. Although the spouses disagreed about everything, the focus of their recent conflicts was the management of Alex's intrusive parents.

Marla began this fourth session with the accusation (mainly addressed to me) that Alex's parents were dropping by too often and without calling first. She complained in a repetitive, put-upon manner that her house no longer felt like her house, and she was particularly upset about the day they hung around for three hours when she was sick. She thought that Alex should do something about this intolerable situation, should "at least" speak to his parents about calling first. "Wasn't that the right thing to do?"

she asked me, disingenuously. As I began to respond, Alex interrupted, stating defensively that he had said something to them about calling first, but he resented the problem being dumped on him. Why should he be the one to hurt their feelings? "It's Marla's problem, right?" he asserted, looking to me for support.

I felt the weight of their joint expectation for me to act as a parental judge in their conflict and the pull upon me to rule in favor of each one. I both resented and liked the power of being elevated to the status of wise one whose judgment would be accepted as right. I could feel the impulse to give a lecture about marital boundaries. I resisted the impulse, knowing it would be viewed as taking Marla's side and would preclude exploration of the underlying shared issues. I aimed my intervention toward acknowledging their mutual need to be heard, understood, and supported.

However, as I began speaking, Alex interrupted me again, fearing that I was going to support Marla and not him. He launched into an angry diatribe. Marla was an adult, she should act like an adult, he insisted, self-righteously. She could tell them to leave if she wanted them to leave. She should "just get off her lazy ass, stop vegetating in the corner in her muu-muu and muk-luks and do something about something for a change!" Again I attempted to intervene, in the effort to contain his escalating anger, when Marla interrupted. Angrily, she retaliated, insinuating that Alex was a coward and insisting that it was his place to deal with his parents and not hers. "Wasn't that right?" She directed the question to me.

At this point, after having been interrupted and talked over three or four times, I was aware of feeling frustrated, discounted, and ignored. At first the couple seemed to elevate me to the status of King Solomon who would solve their dispute, but then they would shut me out, as though I were an insignificant bystander. I felt alternately like an ineffective parent who had no authority over quarreling siblings and like one of the siblings who was left out and couldn't get heard. I had the urge to shout, "Stop! Listen to me! It's my turn, now!" I also had the urge to bawl them out, take them to task for their lousy communication.

Knowing that these reactions of mine reflected their own feelings with each other, derived from family-of-origin experience, aided me in containing my reactions. Additionally, I was familiar from experience with these distinctive projective identifications. I also recognized as characteristic each partner's wish that the other act as the responsible parent who sets limits, a wish that is transferred to the therapist in the strong bids for taking sides, which is an expression of their deeper needs for validation, parental guidance, and nurturing. I could then take the role of a validating, affirming parent who fosters empathy and understanding, instead of passing judgment.

Identification with the "Cooperative" Partner

In addition to the countertransferential responses evoked by the couple's shared transference and projections, each partner individually stimulates countertransference reactions in the therapist, particularly by the specific kind of transference relationship each partner forms with the therapist. Because of the push-pull dynamic each partner plays out with the therapist (hold me close! — let me go!) and the strong bids to induce taking sides, the therapist tends to experience alternating tugs on neutrality, first feeling more empathic toward one partner and repelled by the other, then the opposite.

Although each partner of an oppositional couple initially views the therapist as a parental authority to be challenged or obeyed, one partner tends to respond to the therapist, at least superficially, in a more cooperative and compliant fashion. The "cooperative" partner may either enact the rebellious child role with the parental, controlling spouse, or be the more dominant, parental, responsible partner. In either case, it is the partner who cooperates with the therapist, supports the program, and validates the therapist who is most likely to win the therapist as a long-term ally. With the therapist's enactment of identification with the "cooperative" partner, the other partner tends to be viewed more or less negatively as the irritating, uncooperative one who is disturbingly rebellious and/or dominating.

For example, in the treatment of Alex and Marla, I found myself gravitating toward a stronger identification with Marla than with Alex. She was the less overtly narcissistic and less rigidly defended partner and therefore more consistently receptive to my interventions. Alex had a strong need to dominate and to defend himself against feeling passive or needy. For him, being a patient was experienced as a narcissistic injury. In the opening phase, he would frequently challenge my authority and the treatment plan by authoritatively proposing that they should shift to coming every other week because he was too busy (being an important workaholic), or that I should see Marla individually to work on her depression and sexual inhibitions. Therapists tend to find this kind of resistance irritating, and I am no exception.

The development of this constellation in the therapy is often a reenactment of the partners' and/or therapist's history with siblings and parents, wherein the parent(s) have fostered a good-bad role division between the children. In the above case, Marla was the "good," compliant daughter, who took care of her ailing mother and younger, "irresponsible" sister, while Alex had been the "black sheep" in his family because of his explosive temper, which had been directed at his favored, more compliant, but less achieving, younger brother.

Identification with the "cooperative" partner is probably the most common countertransference pitfall in working with an oppositional couple, and can lead to a therapy impasse or premature termination of the couple or the "uncooperative" partner. Although a more cooperative partner exists in most couples in therapy, the pull to identify with this partner is particularly strong with oppositional couples, because the therapist is vulnerable to reexperiencing her own separation-individuation conflicts and thus tends to be more in need of support and validation.

THE GENDER COMPETITIVE COUPLE

The mode of relating of the gender competitive couple reflects the central themes and conflicts originating in the gender narcissistic phase of self and object relations development (a term I have chosen over the traditional designation, "phallic narcissistic phase"). Partners have established core gender identity—they know and believe they are male or female—but a comfortable gender role identity has not been attained. Unhappy about their gender, the partners still harbor unconscious wishes to be the opposite sex or both sexes, with pervasive feelings of inadequacy about their masculinity or femininity. The unresolved gender role identity is often a result of the parents' inability to support and admire the gender role of the child, favoritism of an opposite-sex sibling, or to be adequate models of masculinity or femininity. Thus, the partners have been unable to comfortably identify with the same-sex parent.

The interactions of these couples are dominated by gender-related conflicts, most obviously expressed in each partner's pervasive need for admiration and competitive victories. The major aim of the competition is to prove superiority and to gain admiration of gender prowess, while exposing the partner as an inferior male or female. Unlike the oppositional couple, the gender competitive couple—while conflicted about winning—is really striving to win and can tolerate victory, though usually with a guilty aftermath.

In contrast to symbiotic and oppositional couples, gender competitive couples do not usually exhibit the extremes of marital boundary problems. Internal and external boundaries are more flexible, because the partners have usually attained a more individuated sense of self and stabilized object constancy.

In early therapy sessions, the partners characteristically compete with each other to appear more intelligent and ingratiating to the therapist. This behavior is in contrast to the less secure and individuated oppositional couple, who make strong bids for the therapist to take sides, or who are actively or passively negativistic and uncooperative.

The marital transference of gender competitive couples is often characterized by the partners' shared unresolved negative oedipal conflicts, i.e., unsuccessful aims to win the exclusive love and admiration of the same-sex parent, who has been experienced as competitive and/or inadequate, and to defeat the opposite-sex parent (or sibling). Their projective system usually involves the partners' inducement of each other to act out the competitive and/or inadequate same-sex parent role in relation to the childhood self, who is unsuccessfully striving for validation and admiration of gender adequacy. Disavowed feelings of envy, sexual inadequacy, and gender defectiveness are projected onto the spouse. Collusive splitting in regard to transactional roles typically takes the form of one partner acting out the dominating, overtly competitive, aggressive, exhibitionistic, "phallic" role, while the other partner enacts the flip side of the phallic defense and is passive, self-effacing, compliant, and self-sacrificing, but covertly competitive.

Transference and Countertransference

Gender competitive couples typically arouse the therapist's own unresolved gender identity issues in relation to family-of-origin internalized objects, which may include unmet narcissistic needs for admiration and confirmation, particularly confirmation of competence and gender adequacy. The spouses project their feelings of narcissistic injury and gender inferiority onto each other and onto the therapist. While initially these couples are often engaging and likable, they also characteristically induce in me feelings of insecurity, inferiority, the need to prove my competence, and wishes to be admired. Since this countertransference differs from my initial reactions to symbiotic, oppositional, and oedipal couples, I now think it is reliably diagnostic. While the couple's behaviors that invoke these reactions are sometimes hard to pinpoint, I think that the partners project their shared insecurities and competitiveness by certain subtle and not so subtle put-downs, concealed in the conflicting aims to be ingratiating and win my favor through admiration. For example, in the initial session with Tina and Gabe, these conflicting aims are evident.

Gabe began by praising my qualifications, stating that he had done extensive research to find the best therapist he could "in our back-water of a town." Not to be outdone in the art of polluting praise with insult, Tina quickly interjected that she had been very hesitant to waste her time on another mediocre therapist. However, she was impressed with a talk I had given and thought I might be the one couples therapist worth giving a try. Sighing, Tina continued to size me up with a bored gaze, while Gabe beamed at me eagerly and somewhat hungrily.

I felt hamstrung by my conflicting reactions to this opening gambit, a state that was to become painfully familiar and mirrored Tina and Gabe's entrenched state of impasse in their competitive warfare. In rapid, overlapping succession, I felt inflated by their praise, hopeful I could sustain a special position, anxious that I would have to struggle to prove my competence and would likely fail, burdened by impossible expectations, irritated about the deflating put-downs with an unwelcome wish to retaliate in kind, and a vague, depressing sense of defeat.

This opening transference-countertransference paradigm conveyed by the couple, which becomes the central theme of treatment expressed in many guises, can be summarized as follows: "We want to win your love/admiration and we want to defeat you; we will elevate you and then tear you down. That's what we do to each other, that's what was done to us, and that's what we will do to you!" The therapist reacts: "I want to win your admiration; I want to succeed with you. I will resist your efforts to defeat me (and the goals of therapy) and compete to prove my superiority. If you defeat me, I may reject you." In terms of projective identification, the therapist's countertransference to the couple's shared object transferences and self projections oscillate between identification with the admired, desired parent, identification with the devalued, rejecting parent, and identification with the inferior, defeated boy or girl.

As treatment gets underway, the couple characteristically transfers to the therapist at increasingly intense levels the negative oedipal marital transference. The therapist is both competed for as the desired, idealized same-sex parent and competitively defeated as the hated, rejecting same-sex and/or rival parent. In reaction to the idealized aspect of the transference, the therapist identifies with the role of admired, desired parent and may feel temporarily elevated by the couple's admiration. The therapist then may unconsciously support the couple's competition to win the therapist's preference by failing to interpret the couple's competitive behavior, failing to set limits on destructive aspects of their interaction, or by taking sides. However, as the spouses intensify their competitive interaction, the therapist's initial gratification is soon superseded by the wish to unload the burden of having so much power.

In reaction to the negative side of the couple's transference, the therapist experiences an identification with the devalued, rejecting parent and feels discounted, inadequate, impotent, and consistently defeated. These reactions are accompanied by wishes to competitively prove superiority through defeating and shaming the couple, often reflecting a repetition of the original parents' behavior.

In addition to the reactions evoked by the couple as a unit, there are ongoing strong inducements from each partner to prefer him or her and to expose, reject, and defeat the other. Scornful, humiliating attacks aimed at the tenderest of all places — the partner's sense of him or herself as masculine or feminine—are typical early behaviors of these couples, and evoke the therapist's own painful gender identity issues, including feelings and attitudes about both sexes. I have found, along with many of my colleagues, that it is more difficult to handle feelings evoked when the opposite-sex partner attacks and humiliates the partner of the same sex as the therapist, particularly when this partner is in the passive role. However, this early tendency to identify more strongly with the same-sex, passive partner can shift in the course of treatment. Identification with the more admiring partner can be quite compelling as therapy proceeds and the passive partner's wish to defeat the therapist becomes overt.

For example, in the opening phase of treatment with Tina and Gabe, I felt a stronger pull to identify with Tina than with Gabe. This occurred, in part, because of my gender. Tina's position as a woman trying to find a more assertive, confident gender role identity was personally familiar to me and evoked more empathy than Gabe's need to bolster his masculine identity through efforts to keep his wife in a passive, caretaking role, accompanied by frequent attacks on her "inadequate" sexuality. An additional factor was Tina's projective identification that beckoned—"Come join with me in teaching Gabe how to be a proper man and mate; let's gang up and deflate his macho masculinity." However, as the belittling, castrating aspects of Tina's competitiveness became more strident in the course of therapy and were aimed at me as well as Gabe, my countertransference identifications reversed. I, then, had to contend with stronger wishes to ally with and protect Gabe, who began to look like a struggling, emasculated underdog. The inducement of his projective identification became more and more seductive—"If you will admire, protect, and love me best, I will admire and love you best." At this point in the middle phase of therapy, reenactment of the couple's negative oedipal competition had reached a peak intensity. The sessions took on the following pattern:

Gabe would begin with a long-winded report of how awful things were, intermittently emphasizing the injustice of Tina's rejections of him and how hard he was trying. Tina would retaliate, attacking him for his biased, self-serving report and elaborate on his deficiencies, underscoring his preference for others over her. Gabe would reactively blow up in a dramatic demonstration of his injury and her cruelty. Tina would then withdraw and rebuff any of my repeated efforts to engage her, stating that Gabe clearly had the worse problem. I would feel pushed by Tina and pulled by Gabe to engage with Gabe, who would calm down when he got my full attention. Tina would then attack Gabe for taking all the time with his self-centered histrionics, or she would attack me for wasting my time on Gabe and forgetting about her. No matter what I tried, they remained inconsolable and unenlightened.

The competition for my attention and favoritism elevated me to a position of great importance, but I now felt immobilized by this role. Their earlier positively weighted joint transference to me as the admired parent to be wooed had now split into more focused, intense, and contrasting individual transferences. Gabe desperately clung to a crumbling idealized transference and the hope of winning my preference (in my role as his longed-for but hated father), while Tina enacted the disappointed, humiliated loser of the negative oedipal competition who was enraged at a rejecting, inadequate mother.

I felt most strongly the couple's collusion for me to reject Tina and ally with Gabe, and their collusion to defeat me, along with the goals of therapy. For a time I was seduced by this collusion into my assigned roles: I felt more and more allied with Gabe and angry with Tina to the point of wishing, at times, that I could just work individually with Gabe (who at least made a show of wanting to hear what I said). My increasing sense of defeat led me to want to shame and reject both of them. My dogged wish to succeed with this couple warred with my wish that they would decide to give up on the therapy or get a divorce. I would not be the one to admit defeat!

The recognition that my repeated sense of failure and narcissistic injury closely mirrored the couple's painful process with each other and me restored my empathic connection with them. I was then able to use my countertransference experience to work us out of this transference-countertransference stalemate by using the most potent therapeutic intervention — the countertransference-based interpretation. Interpretation of the marital transference had not worked with this couple without inclusion of my role and countertransference. The turning point of this session occurred as follows (edited for clarity):

Tina had just angrily accused me of ignoring her wounded feelings and deserting her in favor of Gabe.

SAS: (*to Tina*) I obviously, at times, do not foresee or pick up on your hurt, and I can understand that would feel bad to you. I think you're right to an extent, that I miss or overlook your feelings at times. I think something goes on between us that leads to the situation of things getting lopsided in here . . . that Gabe gets more attended to than you do. I think we have a triangle in here that gets going in a certain way over and over.

TINA: I don't mean to be blaming you. It just seems to go that way. His feelings take priority, and mine get overlooked.

SAS: I'm trying to figure out how this happens. I know one thing that happens is that I feel I receive a series of "stay away" messages from you . . . more so in recent weeks. Sometimes it's a response of "I don't want to talk about my feelings," and you'll then shift the focus to Gabe's problem. Sometimes your communication is more nonverbal, for example, a withdrawn "don't bother me" expression, or looking like you feel burdened if I ask you about something. And then you are often critical of how I conduct the session. I think I feel rebuffed when I get these reactions from you, and that leads me to turn away from you and toward Gabe, who welcomes my interest. As a result of this shift in my attention, you end up feeling I'm more responsive to Gabe and don't care about you.

Rather than apply this interpretation to the couple, where Tina induces Gabe to turn away from her and seek others with these rejecting behaviors, I interpret the transference/countertransference interaction between Tina and me, hoping she will make the connection or that I can later extend it to the marital transference.

TINA: (*thoughtfully*) I can believe what you describe happens . . . that I do those things. This is what happens to me. I get forgotten and left out. I know I'm sensitive to this. And when you get involved with Gabe over a period of time, or do something special for him, it reminds me of my family . . . when my mother turned so much of her attention to my father . . . I would be so important to my mother when my father was working or away, but when he returned I was . . . I wasn't special anymore.

Tina continues to speak about the painful situation of her mother's rejection of her in preference of her father, for whom she felt a mixture of longing and hatred. She makes the connection between the past triangle, her feelings in the relationship with Gabe and his father, and the repetition in our therapy situation. She is more focused on her similar feelings than on her role in creating the reenactments. But I feel she heard my input and may make use of it on her own. I then attempt to bring Gabe's role into focus by first addressing the transference/countertransference between us.

SAS: Gabe, I wonder if you can see what goes on between you and me that may contribute to Tina's feeling that there's a lopsided situation among the three of us.

GABE: Well, I know I talk more when Tina withdraws. (*to Tina*) I know you think I talk too much in any event—take more time than I should for myself.

SAS: I feel, at times, you have a way of commanding my full attention that makes it difficult to include Tina.

GABE: Oh? I'm not aware of that . . . really. I plead the unconscious. If I do that, it's unconscious.

SAS: I'd be the first to agree with the unconscious. I'm not suggesting any deliberate plot or meaning to cast blame. I think we all play a role in what happens in here, and it will help us to know what we do and feel. As I was telling Tina about the "stay away" messages I feel from her. I feel I get the opposite kind of messages from you that say, "Pay attention only to me." (*Gabe is looking tense and confused.*) What I'm talking about is your wish to win and be first, as we've discussed before.

GABE: Oh yes, I admitted that, didn't I? But I'm not really meaning to leave Tina out. (*looks uncomfortable; glances at Tina nervously*)

TINA: Well, you do. You hog the floor and play to her. I don't understand why you have to be the favorite. Is it because you felt your father favored your sister?

GABE: (*squirms*) Uh, maybe so. I know as a kid I was always competing with her . . . trying to get my father to notice me . . . to love me better. (*sadly*) I thought I was past all that.

In this intervention, I was far more successful in getting Tina and Gabe to consider their transferences and respective projective identifications when I first revealed my own responses to their behavior than when I had taken the more usual, objective position of confining myself to interpreting their transference roles with each other. This may be a more effective approach with this kind of couple when competitive defensiveness remains entrenched. By including my responses, I may level the playing field so that my interventions seem less like a critical pronoucements coming from a superior authority. Consequently, the threat to the partners' self-esteem is lessened, along with their need to defend with competitive behavior. Additionally, by revealing my responses with each partner I am taking them out of their usual competitive interaction with each other in a triangle with me and modeling a more constructive way to respond. These aspects of this kind of intervention may also have the effect of reducing defensiveness and creating a safer climate for self exploration.

The Oedipal Couple

The central relationship themes and conflicts of the oedipal couple reflect the oedipal phase of development and involve the unsuccessful resolution of the positive oedipal constellation. While competitive interaction is characteristic of the oedipal couple, the aim of the competition is not primarily to achieve admiration for the purpose of gaining confirmation of insecure gender identities, but to win the parental or sibling love object, who may be represented by the partner or an actual third party in a triangle or who may exist only as an ideal in fantasy. The partner often represents at various times the desired opposite-sex oedipal parent and the rival parent or sibling (Sharpe & Rosenblatt, 1994).

Motives underlying the need to defeat the partner stem from the partners' early oedipal experience and include: revenge to restore self-esteem from an unresolved oedipal defeat; pre-emptive protection to avoid another oedipal disappointment; fear and avoidance of intimacy in order to ward off guilt provoked by arousing the incest taboo; and fear of success that might provoke guilt and fears of retaliation from a rival parent or sibling.

In contrast to the presenting appearance of gender competitive couples, the oedipal couple presents a more subtle, individualized style of exhibiting masculinity or femininity. There is a broad range of well articulated and modulated expression of affects. Both partners usually have a well developed sense of humor, often used constructively to defuse hurt and anger rather than to humiliate or castrate the partner, as is more characteristic of gender competitive couples. The partners do not tend to project all of their inadequacies onto the spouse or blame the spouse for all that is wrong. A more secure achievement of object constancy is demonstrated in the partners' ability to discuss hurt, disappointment, and anger, while also being able to express feelings of concern and understanding for each other. The good is not forgotten when a bad feeling strikes. The capacity to usually experience loving and hating feelings toward the partner without resorting to splitting is a major and distinguishing strength of these couples.

The oedipal couple functions predominantly at the level of triadic object relating, while the gender competitive couple frequently regresses under stress to a dyadic level of object relating, wherein a rival is experienced unambivalently as an unwelcome intruder to be defeated and eliminated. In the context of a triangular constellation that provokes feelings of competition, oedipal partners are still able to sustain concern and caring for each other. Defeating the partner who is experienced as a rival evokes feelings of guilt along with triumph. This triadic level of object relating usually makes oedipal couples a pleasure to work with therapeutically, in part because their projective identification systems are open, flexible, and modulated in comparison to those of other couple types. Moreover, since their problems stem from unresolved oedipal triangles, the triangle of couple therapy is ideal for the working through of those conflicts.

Transference and Countertransference

In opening sessions, the relationship to the therapist tends to be warm, receptive, congenial, and curious, without the encumbrances displayed by other kinds of couples. There is neither the deep mistrust of symbiotic couples blended with omnipotent expectations of magical solutions from the therapist nor the defiant-compliant see-saw of oppositional couples, nor the rivalrous hostility cloaked by ingratiation characteristic of gender competitive couples. Like the gender competitive couple, the oedipal couple expresses competitiveness in this triangular situation by viewing the therapist as the desired oedipal object to be won. Thus spouses vie for the therapist's favor with impressive displays of charm, wit, knowledge, and insight. However, the wooing of the oedipal couple is quite distinct from that of the gender competitive couple.

The oedipal couple strongly wants to be admired *as a couple*, overshadowing at first their individual competition for favor. The partners' competitive interaction often has a playful quality, appearing as an entertaining show for the therapist. They come through to me as: "Look at how unique, witty, and lovable we are. We will be your favorite couple!"—and they usually succeed. In contrast, the gender competitive couple is too fiercely competitive to sustain a positive couple identity, and their competition is carried on in deadly earnest from the start.

In addition, the individual competition in the oedipal couple is between the partners, rather than with the therapist. Thus the transference is more engagingly positive, rather than tainted with hostile undercurrents. The therapist feels liked and admired for personal qualities rather than for trappings of power and status, the attributes most admired and coveted by gender competitive partners.

As may already be evident, the therapist's initial countertransference response to the idealizing joint transference of the oedipal couple is an elevated sense of unique and special importance that evokes a corresponding idealization of the couple. In terms of projective identification, this countertransference reflects an identification with the desired oedipal parent of both partners in conjunction with viewing the couple as "ideal" oedipal children. In this constellation, the couple becomes my favorite couple, my favorite children, whose gratifying idealization I want to sustain. Enactment of this countertransference leads to the therapist's reluctance to do the hard therapeutic work of uncovering the couple's underlying oedipal problems, for such work will be painful for the couple and may destroy their gratifying idealization. Therapeutic work stays superficial, perhaps at the level of improving communication, and everyone basks in the gratifications of acting out the wished-for outcome of the oedipal romance—that of the doting parent who encourages and allows the child to experience an oedipal victory.

Non-analytically oriented therapists are most likely to succumb to a protracted acting-out of this countertransference and are thus a poor match for a couple whose main problems stem from unresolved oedipal conflicts. The oedipal couples I have worked with have tended to be both deeply committed and highly motivated. Indeed, if the therapist dallies too long in this transference-countertransference stall, a highly motivated couple will often move the therapy out of this impasse or the couple will appropriately seek another therapist.

Although this countertransference resembles that evoked by symbiotic pseudomutual couples in the therapist's wish to sustain a mutual idealization with the couple, the motivations and the quality of the transference-countertransference idealizations are quite different. The pseudomutual couple longs for an all-giving, all-nurturing mother with whom to merge (as the partners try to do with each other). The wooing of the couple is expressed in basic nurturing and caretaking behaviors, like the bringing of food by Violet and Van, and the countertransference evoked in the therapist is at the oral-symbiotic level. The therapist identifies both with the needy, dependent baby who wants an "ideal" nurturing mother (represented by the couple) and with the role of the "ideal" nurturing mother longed for by the couple. All of this has very little to do with oedipal love. It is about feeding and being fed, and feeling warm, safe, cozy, and cared for. Under the sway of the pseudomutual couple's idealization, one can feel blissfully sated and shamefully adored, while in the grip of the oedipal couple's idealization, the therapist feels flushed, excited, and guilty.

This feeling of guilty excitement denotes the other characteristic countertransference elicited by oedipal couples. For the couple reactivates the therapist's own oedipal experience and unresolved longings. In this reverse aspect of the countertransference, the therapist views the couple as representative of her oedipally desired parents and identifies with the role of oedipal child—identification with the competitive, guilty oedipal child. In reexperiencing the oedipal child's central conflict, the therapist typically shifts back and forth from idealizing the couple as a parental unit (in the wish to sustain both partners' love) to the oedipal idealization of one partner (including the wish to win that partner away from the other). It is the positive oedipal constellation that is most strongly evoked, at least in my experience. This countertransference is illustrated in my work with Kendall and Julia.

Therapy was undertaken by this attractive, middle-aged couple in the wake of Julia's discovery that Kendall was having an affair (his only affair in their 15-year marriage). Although Kendall had ended his very brief affair and Julia forgave him, this devoted couple was sophisticated enough to recognize the affair as being symptomatic of problems in their relationship. They wished to understand why the affair had happened so it would not be repeated (an uncommon and, to me, exciting motivation for couple therapy). Both were deeply frightened that they were at risk of losing the other's love.

During an evaluation session, Kendall generously acknowledged that Julia was more introspective and insightful than he was. He then made a most insightful, interpretive remark in response to one of my questions. With twinkling eyes, he responded, "I just wanted to let you know that I can do this interpretive work too. I'm a fast learner, because I'm so competitive. You'll see, I may even surpass Julia." He flashed me a mischievous grin and then quickly turned to Julia, patting her on the knee.

She smiled and quipped, "We'll just see about that!"

"Oh, so, we're going to play who is smarter than who in here?"

"You mean . . . who is smarter than *whom*," Julia responded with mock primness, like a school teacher.

"No, I don't think so," Kendall replied. "The correct statement is, *who* is smarter than *who* when both of the *who's* are the subjects and have equal value." He grinned triumphantly.

Both laughed at their competitive antics. And I was delighted, especially by him.

Julia sighed, smiling, "As you can see, Kendall never quits until he wins."

"I wish that could be said about my career." He said this lightly but the sparkle went out of his intelligent blue-gray eyes.

I am aware of a gamut of feelings that are fleeting and vague during the session but become clarified upon later reflection. I want to keep the couple's admiration and affection, but a conflicting wish intrudes. I also feel particularly drawn to Kendall. I can feel his seductive pulling for an admiring, flirtatious response from me. He is such a charming, intelligent, and sensitive man with a sense of humor that reminds me of my father's. Lucky Julia, I think a little enviously. Later, I realize that my unconscious oedipal wish to win him away from Julia peaked out in my too admiring response to his display of insight, and I become uncomfortably aware that I did not respond to Julia with this degree of enthusiasm. Now I feel a little anxious and guilty. Unprocessed during the session, these feelings were expressed in my becoming oversolicitous of Julia, I supposed, in order to make up for my imagined crime. I like Julia very much, and I do not want to lose her affection or spoil their basically good relationship. On the other hand, there is the momentary competitive urge to do just that. The most potent of relationship brews is activated here.

The therapist's recognition of the reemergence of her own oedipal wishes in response to the couple should be sufficient to abort, or at least restrain, acting-out of this countertransference. However, as noted earlier, it is important for the therapist to sort out which reactions are primarily set off by her own personal history and which are largely generated by the couple through projective identification. There may, of course, be considerable overlap. In my initial countertransference responses to Julia and Kendall and observation of their interactions, I could discern certain themes of their oedipal experience that had been activated and were currently undermining their relationship.

First, in terms of diagnosis, it is worth noting that the arousal of the therapist's oedipal conflicts does not usually occur with other kinds of couples in the particular form described above. For therapists who primarily function at an oedipal-triadic level of object relating, a *persistent* romantic-erotic attraction to the opposite-sex partner is usually confined to a partner functioning at that same level. While I have felt liking, affection, sympathy, appreciation, and admiration for the male partners of other kinds of couples, they do not usually evoke sustained romantic-erotic fantasies in me. This is largely due to the quality and content of their projective identifications. For example, men in symbiotic relationships cast me in the role of a giving or depriving mother; for the men in oppositional relationships, I am the supportive-accepting or critical-controlling mother; and the men in gender competitive relationships perceive me as a maternal source of admiration for their prowess and masculinity or as the "phallic" castrating mother. In contrast, Kendall's modulated seductiveness evoked in me the feeling of being a desirable, admired, idealized mother *and* woman. When the men who began therapy relating in the symbiotic, oppositional, or gender competitive mode begin to stir in me romantic-erotic fantasies, it usually indicates that the couple (or the male partner) has developed into a triadic level of object relating with an activation of oedipal issues.

The direct, bold, competitive quality of Kendall's seductiveness and idealization and my strong response suggested to me that he was, historically, an oedipal victor (or a partial one). He conveyed an aura of self-confidence and narcissism that made me think he was used to competing for women and winning and *needed* to compete for women and win. In contrast, my countertransference to Julia suggested to me that she was, historically, an oedipal loser. Although Julia was a distinct personality and an engaging woman, I found myself noting a tendency to leave her out, or I would lose track of her reactions. In part, this reaction was evoked by her projected self-image of the left-out, rejected little girl. She conveyed this aura in subtle ways: in her plain, almost dowdy clothes, her soft-spoken, controlled manner of speech, her tendency to hold herself tightly, making herself as small and unobtrusive as possible, in looking to Kendall to take the lead. The presenting problem of Kendall's affair also suggested the oedipal victor-oedipal loser dovetail.

As their story unfolded, these hypotheses gleaned in part from my countertransference were verified. It became clear that Kendall's affair and the resurrection of the couple's unresolved oedipal conflicts had been provoked by a certain combination of circumstances.

Two years previously, Julia's ailing father, who had left the family when she was an adolescent for his long-standing glamorous mistress, had moved to town and required her care. Anger about her father's rejection was revived along with guilty fears about losing Kendall's love after winning him away from his first wife. She responded to these conflicts by withdrawing emotionally and sexually from Kendall and becoming more critically competitive.

Kendall, feeling in mid-life that he had failed to live up to his father's expectations and success, responded to her criticalness and withdrawal as a rejection and confirmation of his failure. As a child he was mother's "special little man," but would be literally kicked out of the bedroom when his successful father would return home from long business trips. Thus, once again with Julia, the oedipal winner became a devastated loser. To vengefully restore his deflated self-esteem, he provoked and succumbed to the idealizing attention of a younger woman and then guiltily made sure he was discovered.

Midway into therapy the oedipal transference-countertransference theme became exposed among the three of us in a way that forwarded and deepened the treatment process. Julia's perfectionistic overachievement had come into focus, and she had demonstrated her ability to laugh about this trait in herself. In response to a joke she made about her perfectionism, I made a joke intended to expand her awareness. This was all right with her and she laughed. Then Kendall made a joke, and we both laughed, but Julia did not. She suddenly looked injured and began to cry.

KENDALL: (*horrified*) What happened? I didn't mean to hurt you. I thought we were just kidding around.

JULIA: I know. I know. This is silly of me.

SAS: Obviously, you were hurt.

JULIA: (*trying to regain control*) Well, it was all right before Kendall made his remark and you both laughed. I'm not sure why. This is stupid.

SAS: Maybe our laughing made you feel ganged up on and left out.

JULIA: Well . . . yes . . . I guess so. I hate to admit that. It's a childish reaction. Just for a moment I felt that you and Kendall were laughing at me, you know, not with me, and that made me feel humiliated, stupid, and left out.

SAS: I can see how that happened . . . how you were hurt. Have you felt that way before in here?

JULIA: No, not really. Well, maybe a little bit. It's nothing you've done. But sometimes I have the feeling that a special connection exists between the two of you that I'm left out of. Usually, I can suppress that feeling. It's not based on anything, really, except maybe that Kendall is charming and funny and I'm not.

KENDALL: That's not true. You're plenty charming and funny. You're also more insightful than I am and deeper. As for this special connection with Dr. Sharpe . . . well, that surprises me. Actually, I thought it was the other way around. It's the two of you that get into this groove about interpreting the past. I'm not so good at that. I can hardly remember my childhood.

SAS: So you've felt left out as well.

KENDALL: Well . . . perhaps . . . at times, though I've never identified the feeling as such. It's not exactly a reaction I care to dwell on. (*chuckles*) I'm more aware of feeling competitive, being competitive, but I'd guess you'd say that's a more palatable companion to feeling left out. Actually, you might even say I compete to avoid *being* left out.

JULIA: Oh, that's interesting. I think I do the same thing, but I guess I'm not so sure I'll succeed.

At this moment, I feel torn. I want to follow up with both of them. I am, once again, seduced by Kendall's way with words and nondefensive willingness to examine himself. Momentarily I have the urge to put Julia on the back burner and carry on with Kendall. I then realize there is a competitive element to his astute self-examination, and that Julia has been the one to initiate exposure of her painful left out feelings and lack of confidence in succeeding. It is clearly more important to first continue with her. My reluctance to pursue her feelings no doubt has something to do with my distress about the mistake I made and the nagging guilt that she has divined my attraction to her husband.

SAS: From what you were saying earlier, it sounds like you're worried that I like Kendall better than you . . . or is it the other way around?

JULIA: Both, actually, if I'm totally honest (*she smiles wanly*), but then again not really. I know these fears are coming from inside me. I know I'm insecure because of my childhood and my father; we've gone into that. But I still worry about losing Kendall's love, that he'll want another woman, or regrets that he left his first wife for me . . . that I'm not a big enough prize for what he lost. (*begins to cry*)

KENDALL: Oh nonsense, nonsense. (*hugs Julia*) I don't feel that way. I've never felt that way. I've always loved only you. I've never regretted for a moment marrying you. It was the best thing I ever did.

As I watch the couple lovingly embrace, I realize, ironically, that I am now the one who feels left out.

CONCLUSION

Successful treatment of couple relationships depends upon diagnosis of the couple's developmental mode of object relations. The thrust of my previous work has been on the objective assessment of the couple through observation, history-taking, etc. Countertransference reactions received a paragraph or two, here and there. What I have come to realize in recent years, and I hope this chapter demonstrates, is that the royal road to understanding the couple is through the therapist's countertransference. However, in order to use this most valuable of therapeutic tools, the therapist must be willing to enter experientially into the couple's conflictual system, step into the assigned roles, and then be able to step out of the role enough to objectively analyze the experience. This is no easy task. In allowing the subjective experience of an assigned role, the therapist runs the risk of being swamped, of being taken over by the role and rendered helpless and ineffective.

In this state, one is suddenly no longer directing the therapy. The couple is directing and you are playing an unfamiliar part in an unknown drama. The content of your reactions is also powerfully disturbing, for you are thrust into reexperiencing (in identification with the couple) the gamut of conflicts from your own relationship history, conflicts you think you have overcome or, at least, left behind. The couple becomes, at once, your parents, your children, your siblings, your spouse.

Given the content and intensity of these reactions, it is not surprising that couples therapists want to resist this kind of experience, stay out of the emotional fray, and seal themselves off from countertransference, if at all possible. The proliferation of programmatic approaches to couple therapy is, in part, a testimony to this resistance. It is also not surprising that relatively few therapists really want to do couples therapy, and those who do often give up this aspect of their practices sooner or later. I think this resistance to doing couples therapy is, in part, due to the great intensity and complexity of countertransference reactions, as I have tried to demonstrate.

While there are compelling reasons for the therapist to want to run from countertransference, I have found that escape is not really possible. A blindness to countertransference usually means one is playing out an assigned role without knowing it and without the crucial information that examination of the experience can yield. In that event, the likelihood of the couple's premature termination or the occurrence of protracted impasses and unwarranted treatment failures is very high. The facility of being able to dance in and out of the couple system, in and out of countertransference enactments, takes years of experience to develop. This way of working is extremely emotionally and intellectually demanding, but for those of us who keep reentering the fray the results still seem to be worth it . . . at least on some days.

REFERENCES

Bader, E., & Pearson, P. T. (1988). *In quest of the mythical mate: A developmental approach to diagnosis and treatment in couples therapy.* New York: Brunner/Mazel.

Dicks, H. (1967). *Marital tensions.* New York: Basic.

Livingston, M. S. (1995). A self psychologist in couplesland: A multisubjective approach to transference and countertransference-like phenomena in marital relationships. *Family Process, 34*(4), 427–439.

Lyons-Ruth, K. (1991). Rapprochement or approchement: Mahler's theory reconsidered from the vantage point of recent research on early attachment relationships. *Psychoanalytic Psychology, 8*(1), 1–23.

Mahler, M. S., Pine, F., & Bergman, A. (1975). *The psychological birth of the human infant.* New York: Basic.

Nelsen, J. (1995). Varieties of narcissistically vulnerable couples: Dynamics and practice implications. *Clinical Social Work Journal, 23*(1), 59–70.

Pine, F. (1986). The "symbiotic phase" in light of current infancy research. *Bulletin of the Menninger Clinic, 50*, 564–569.

Pine, F. (1992). Some refinements of the separation-individuation concept in light of research on infants. *Psychoanalytic Study of the Child, 47*, 103–116.

Racker, H. (1968). *Transference and countertransference.* New York: International Universities Press.

Renik, O. (1993). Countertransference enactment and the psychoanalytic process. In M. J. Horowitz, O. F. Kernberg, & E. M. Weinshel (Eds.), *Psychic structure and psychic change: Essays in honor of Robert S. Wallerstein* (pp. 135–158). CT: International Universities Press.

Sandler, J. (1976). Countertransference and role-responsiveness. *International Review of Psycho-analysis, 3*(43), 43–47.

Scharff, D. E., & Scharff, J. S. (1991). *Object relations couple therapy.* Northvale, NJ: Jason Aronson.

Sharpe, S. A. (1981). The symbiotic marriage: A diagnostic profile. *Bulletin of the Menninger Clinic, 45*, 81–114.

Sharpe, S. A. (1984). *Self and object representations: An integration of psychoanalytic and Piagetian developmental theories.* Unpublished doctoral dissertation. The Fielding Institute, Santa Barbara, CA.

Sharpe, S. A. (1990). The oppositional couple: A developmental object relations approach to diagnosis and treatment. In R. A. Nemiroff & C. A. Colarusso (Eds.), *New dimensions in adult development* (pp. 386–415). New York: Basic.

Sharpe, S. A., & Rosenblatt, A. D. (1994). Oedipal sibling triangles. *Journal of the American Psychoanalytic Association, 42*, 491–523.

Stern, D. N. (1985). *The interpersonal world of the infant: A view from psychoanalysis and developmental psychology.* New York: Basic.

Winer, R. (1994). *The impossible profession.* Unpublished paper.

4

Countertransference Reactions to Borderline Couples

EDA G. GOLDSTEIN

THERAPISTS WHO WORK with couples with borderline qualities know all too well the strong emotions that are typically aroused. The specific nature of borderline dynamics and behavior stimulate fluctuating, disturbing, contradictory, and sometimes seemingly irreconcilable reactions. It is likely that the borderline couple's urgent needs, turbulent interactions, and flagrant behavior make couples work more fraught and potentially hazardous than is the treatment of borderline individuals (Slipp, 1980). Consequently, couple therapists are vulnerable to lapses in empathy and countertransference feelings, which, if not understood and managed well, can obstruct or derail the treatment. After briefly describing the dynamics, treatment, and countertransference issues in work with borderline couples from both object relations and self psychological perspectives, this chapter will discuss and illustrate some of the countertransference reactions that arose in the initial phase of work with a borderline couple seen by the author.

THE DYNAMICS OF BORDERLINE COUPLES AND THEIR IMPACT

Borderline couples who come for treatment generally show a history of chronic disharmony that has escalated. They are often locked in angry interactions. Sustained intimacy is a problem and they may show alternating periods of closeness and distance or repetitive clashes that keep them enmeshed and frustrated at the same time. One or both members of the couple may be highly impulsive, sometimes engaging in food binges, substance abuse, infidelity, financial mismanagement, suicidal threats and acts, or other types of self-destructive behavior. The couple may have attempted to end their relationship, only to reunite.

Borderline couples often display primitive defenses such as denial, splitting, and projective identification. Blaming, power struggles, competition, verbal aggression, and even physical violence may dominate the relationship. Conflicts around autonomy, dependence, and validation, as well as fears of rejection, separation and abandonment, are commonplace. The partners cannot live together in peace and harmony but are unable to live apart. Offspring become triangulated into the couple interaction and borderline families tend to show overinvolvement and enmeshment or neglect and rejection (Goldstein, 1981; Grinker, Werble, & Drye, 1968; Gunderson, Kerr, & Englund, 1980; Schwoeri & Schwoeri, 1981, 1982; Shapiro, Zinner, Shapiro, & Berkowitz, 1975; Shapiro, Shapiro, Zinner, & Berkowitz, 1977; Zinner & Shapiro; 1972, 1975; Walsh, 1977). "Few cases will present the intensity, power, manipulativeness, and drama found in borderline families" (Everett, Halperin, Volgy, & Wissler, 1989, p. 2).

Even in therapy sessions, it is difficult to help borderline partners to listen to and really hear one another. This stems not only from their heightened degree of conflict but also from the fact that each member of the couple has a fixed view of and is unable to empathize with the other. They interpret one another's behavior in terms of their own reactions and cannot understand or accept that a partner may have different motivations and feelings than they have themselves. Even if they show an accurate perception of the unique ways a partner thinks and feels, they do not respect these differences and label them as "wrong" or "stupid."

While all authors concur that borderline couples develop mutually frustrating interactive cycles, these patterns are not all the same. For example, a couple in which a more narcissistic individual is paired with someone who is borderline will show different dynamics than will two overtly borderline individuals. Solomon (1985) suggests that those individuals on the narcissistic end of the spectrum tend to seek fusion or sameness with their partners and have difficulty tolerating any degree of difference, while those who are on the borderline end of the developmental spectrum are more caught in a conflict between their wishes for autonomy and their fears of disapproval or rejection. Adler (1985) argues that the narcissistic individual is more sensitive to blows to self-esteem, while borderline persons fear loss and abandonment. Lachkar (1992) suggests that the borderline member of a couple views the narcissist as calming, while the narcissist finds the borderline partner's expressiveness exciting. She agrees with others that the borderline partner fears abandonment but observes that the narcissist fears being invaded and taken over by the borderline's demands. While most writers about borderline disorders describe their alternating merging and distancing behavior, Kohut (1977) emphasizes the borderline's need to protect against fragmentation by avoiding closeness to potential selfobjects, in contrast to the narcissistic individual's need to seek selfobject experiences.

THEORETICAL PERSPECTIVES

Object relations theory views couples as sharing problematic patterns of internalized object relations (Scharff & Scharff, 1987, 1991; Siegel, 1992; Slipp, 1988; Stewart, Peters, Marsh, & Peters, 1975). Displaying intense transference reactions to one another, members of a borderline couple often experience themselves as victimized children in relation to powerful parents. Each partner denies and splits off undesirable traits in himself or herself, projecting these onto the other partner, then reacts negatively or punitively to the object of the projections. As each partner projects selected split-off traits onto the other, the other collusively accepts what has been projected and acts in accordance with the projection. Each may complain of feeling "set up" to respond in a particular way by the mates, only to be criticized or rejected for his or her reactions. Sometimes, it appears as if one member of the couple carries all the "badness" and the other all the "goodness," even if they sometimes exchange roles.

Because of the use of primitive defenses, each partner lacks an accurate perception of the provocative ways he or she behaves. In some situations, couples take on the appearance of possessing only "good" or idealized qualities so that their partnership seems "perfect," while they split off and project "bad" qualities outside the relationship, including onto offspring. As long as the splitting and projective identification continue, neither member of the dyad is forced to confront his or her own "unfavorable" traits.

Alternatively, Kohut's (1971, 1977) self psychological theory views both partners as having selfobject needs, that is, needs for others to fulfill functions that they themselves cannot provide, that are archaic, urgent, and extreme (Schwartzman, 1984; Solomon, 1985, 1989). They tend to live out their earlier unfulfilled parental relationships quite dramatically when they mate, since fantasies of wholeness, total acceptance, and approval are activated (Solomon, 1985, p. 144). Selfobject failures and traumas at the hands of parents and significant others in childhood are reawakened. When selfobject needs are not met as a consequence of one or both partners failing to function as a mirroring or idealizing selfobject for the other, rage, depressive reactions, injured self-esteem, and fragmentation of the self may result (White, 1984).

The repetitive lack of recognition and failure to gratify one another's selfobject needs lead to mutually frustrating interactions. Each partner utilizes sometimes primitive defenses to protect him-/herself from narcissistic injury and to preserve self-esteem and self-cohesion. Conflict, power struggles, and feelings of victimization result as one partner, for example, withdraws in order to preserve his or her autonomy and the other provokes a fight in order to maintain contact.

THE TREATMENT OF BORDERLINE COUPLES

Despite important differences, object relations and self psychological couple treatment share certain common features. Both models require a therapeutic atmosphere that is safe and facilitating and aim at helping the partners to perceive and relate to one another in terms of their "here and now" qualities rather than as representatives of their troubled development. In order to ensure an optimal therapeutic "holding" environment it is suggested that the object relations couple therapist: (1) create a clear, firm, and consistent structure with boundaries against destructive acting-out, show acceptance and neutrality, tolerate intense and unpleasant affects, and limit aggression so as not to permit excessive blaming, scapegoating, or loss of control; (2) help the partners to identify their difficulty in supporting and providing "holding," the distortions in the way they perceive and relate, and the repetitive and rigid behavioral sequences that thwart sustained intimacy and harmony; (3) actively foster the partners' ability to provide more optimal "holding" for one another through suggestion and example; (4) help partners accept traits and feelings in themselves that they have denied, disavowed, and projected onto one another, thereby lessening their distortions of one another; and (5) identify the transference component of certain reactions by connecting them to past family-of-origin experiences, thereby helping the partners to separate the present from the past in order to free them to interact in terms of their "real," rather than their transference, characteristics. Because the partners are entrenched in their feelings, attitudes, and behavioral patterns, even the therapist's most tactful interventions may be experienced as confrontational and arouse considerable resistance.

While sharing some similarities to the object relations model, the self psychological treatment of couples has some major differences in emphasis and ways of intervening. Self psychological treatment relies more on the use of the therapist's empathy and attunement to each partner's subjective experience and on interpreting and repairing selfobject failures, in contrast to the exposure and interpretation of primitive defenses and collusive behavior that are employed in object relations therapy. The self psychological therapist attempts to: (1) be attuned to both partners' subjective experience through empathic immersion, acknowledge their individual and sometimes conflicting selfobject needs, and in some instances function as a selfobject; (2) sensitize each partner to the other's needs and ways of thinking and feeling, thereby expanding the capacity for empathy; (3) empathically comment on and relate to the needs underlying the dysfunctional interactions and the defensive patterns that are established; (4) interpret the connection between past and present in order to help the partners understand and appreciate the origin of their own needs and fears, lessen the hold that developmental failures have on their relationship, and find better ways of gratifying their needs; (5) help the partners learn to repair and restore their own positive connection when disruptions in their relationship occur; and (6) nondefensively examine and acknowledge his or her own empathic failure in order to repair and restore the selfobject transference between the couple and the therapist. When empathy is not sufficient to contain destructive behavior, the therapist may need to be more active in setting limits and providing structure. This should be done, however, with an attitude of empathy and in collaboration with the couple rather than in a rigid and authoritarian manner (Goldstein, 1990).

PERSPECTIVES ON COUNTERTRANSFERENCE

Object relations theory and self psychology embody different views of countertransference and its management. A major emphasis in object relations couples therapy is on the therapist's role as a container for denied and disavowed feelings in the partners that are projected onto one another and onto the therapist in order to relieve internal conflict. During the treatment, the therapist becomes the object of the couple's projective defenses, which, because of their intense nature, stimulate strong feelings—what has been termed "induced countertransference"—in the therapist. It is thought that such reactions can be used to inform the therapist about the nature of internalized self and object representations that manifest in interactions with partners and other family members (Siegel, 1992, pp. 103–108). The therapist uses his or her own countertransference in understanding the couple. He or she may sit with these feelings or use them to interpret the couple's defenses and dynamics.

The provision of optimal "holding" and "containment" necessitates that the therapist understands and uses his or her countertransference positively; however, there is a tendency for therapists who work with borderline couples to experience feeling out of control and to become highly reactive. Anger, feelings of being shut out, rejected, devalued, and abandoned, retaliatory impulses, taking sides, and avoidant behavior are common. Frequently therapists may feel totally overwhelmed by the couple or are swept up into the unfolding drama, thereby losing their ability to intervene effectively.

The thrust in self psychological treatment with respect to countertransference involves the therapist's ability to remain empathically attuned to each partner. Rather than viewing the patient as responsible for "inducing" reactions in the therapist, self psychology sees both therapist and patient as shaping all aspects of the therapeutic situation. Some writers (Brandchaft & Stolorow, 1984a, 1984b) have gone so far as to argue that the borderline structure does not really exist per se and that seemingly borderline behavior is iatrogenically stimulated in certain individuals when the therapist or others do not respond to their archaic selfobject needs adequately. The therapist must strive to understand how his or her own personality, belief systems, and needs influence therapeutic understanding and responses. For example, a therapist, by virtue of his or her family-of-origin issues, relationship preferences and experiences, communication style, gender, age, ethnicity, values, personality, and archaic selfobject needs, will probably be better able to empathize with one partner than the other. The therapist may have difficulties tolerating and accepting, let alone empathizing with, the attitudes and behavior of one or both of the partners.

Even if the self psychological therapist is able to empathize equally with each partner, one or both may become upset if the therapist seems too understanding or supportive of the other or when the therapist is empathic with a partner who has conflicting needs or polarized perceptions. Striking a balance between helping each partner feel validated without appearing to be taking sides is a major therapeutic task. This is especially difficult with borderline couples, since they are so extreme, needy of affirmation, competitive for nurture, and volatile.

In contrast to the object relations approach, self psychologists argue that a major countertransference pitfall is the therapist's interpretation of apparently aggressive or provocative behavior as a manifestation of resistance or primitive defenses. Instead the self psychological therapist must relate empathically to the archaic selfobject needs and defenses against them that members of a couple show. Thus he or she must understand that individuals' needs for constant affirmation, feelings of rejection and disillusionment, outbursts of rage, sullenness and withdrawal, non-involvement, glibness and superficiality, devaluation, missed appointments, non-payment of fees, self-destructiveness, and acting-out are understandable reactions to actual failures in attunement, inabilities to meet selfobject needs, or anticipation and fear that such needs will not be met. This knowledge enables the therapist to refrain from reacting to patients in counter-therapeutic ways as he or she helps the partners identify their own selfobject needs, how these are frustrated, and how dysfunctional patterns result.

PROBLEMS IN SEEING ONLY ONE MEMBER OF THE COUPLE

Because of the extreme one-sidedness of both partners' views of themselves, their marked inability to view themselves or the other realistically, and their lack of empathy for the needs and feelings of the other, seeing only one member of the couple in therapy is problematic. Most borderline individuals do not lie about themselves or the other partner but they are unable to tell the whole story. Denying or disavowing their own provocative behavior, maintaining distorted perceptions of the other's motivations and feelings, or being insensitive to the ways in which they frustrate or disappoint their partner, they convince the therapist of the correctness of their vision of the relationship. In these instances, it often is a shock and an embarrassment when one has the opportunity to meet the partner and realizes that one has "missed the boat" completely. For similar reasons, seeing one partner in treatment while a second therapist sees the other often creates conflict between two therapists, each of whom experiences only one part of the relationship and is sure that his or her perceptions and assessment are accurate. This situation may be particularly acute if there is little or no collaboration between therapists, who may begin to replay the couple dynamics between themselves.

Some borderline couples display such unrelenting and destructive interactions, particularly in the beginning phase of treatment, that the therapist decides to see each partner separately. By structuring the sessions this way and by being able to show more empathy for each member of the couple, the therapist may be able to calm the system. Working in this way, however, necessitates that the therapist help the partners manage their tendency to use their experience of the therapist as an ally against one another outside of sessions.

USING ONE OR TWO THERAPISTS

Whatever the therapeutic framework, because understanding and managing one's countertransference to a borderline couple is fraught with difficulty, the use of two therapists who work as a team has sometimes been suggested. Co-therapists can serve as a check on each other and stay outside of the interaction with greater ease. This may have advantages if both therapists truly understand the dynamics of borderline couples and their impact, have a positive working relationship, and spend time discussing the case with one another or in supervision. All too often, however, even experienced co-therapists become entangled in disagreements about their understanding of and treatment strategies with borderline couples and demonstrate a parallel process to that of the couple, sometimes even triangulating a supervisor or consultant into the drama.

CASE EXAMPLE

Phil and Judy, a Jewish couple, ages 42 and 34 respectively, were referred by one of my colleagues, Dr. A, a woman therapist who had seen Phil individually for treatment some years earlier. They had been married three years. Phil called Dr. A in desperation, requesting that she reach out to Judy and try to involve her in treatment. Dr. A saw Judy once, but Judy refused to continue, agreeing to see a couples therapist only reluctantly. When Dr. A called me, she indicated that Phil had "one foot out of the marriage" and really wanted to leave, but felt unable to do so because Judy was six months pregnant. She felt that Judy was in denial about the seriousness of the couple's problems, out of touch with her feelings, and unwilling to take any responsibility for her role in causing them. Dr. A said I would enjoy working with Phil, whom she described as having made considerable progress in individual treatment. She felt he should never have married Judy, since she was "impossible."

When I met with the couple, Phil sat on the edge of the couch and launched into an angry litany of accusations against Judy, who appeared tearful and depressed. When she did try to defend herself, Phil talked over her, saying, "You just don't get it," and looked as if he were on the verge of physically attacking her. I was unprepared for this opening and was aware of feeling anxious. I tried unsuccessfully to help Phil contain his aggressive attack on Judy in order to create a calmer and safer environment. Despite my repeated and varied efforts to empathize with his anger and desperation, to request that he allow Judy to speak, to explore his inability to stop venting his rage, to draw Judy into some dialogue with Phil, and to confront his unwillingness to let Judy or myself to get a word in edgewise, I had little impact on him. Increasingly frustrated, at one point I heard my voice rise, almost telling Phil to keep quiet. I felt mortified that I was beginning to act the way Phil described Judy as responding.

Nevertheless, Phil did not appear bothered by my reaction and continued to seek my approval for his point of view. He repeatedly asked, "What do you think of a person who acts the way Judy does?" He never waited for an answer, however. In response to my comment that he seemed to feel like he was "at the end of his rope," but that his continuous attack on Judy was preventing us from sorting out the issues between them, Phil said that he knew his attitude "stunk," but he did not care anymore. He wanted Judy to know how it felt to be yelled at and criticized all the time. "I'm not going to take it anymore." He thought he was a nice and easygoing person, but that Judy had driven him to act like a lunatic and he knew she now would say, "I told you so." Looking at me and pointing at her, Phil said, "It's not my fault I'm acting this way; it's hers."

Phil's basic accusations were that Judy had no sense of what it meant to be part of a team and could not deal with reality. "She does not know how to be a partner and does not understand that our situation is urgent." By this he meant that he had told her repeatedly of his increasing business and financial difficulties, that there was no money, and that he was considering declaring bankruptcy. He felt she did not hear him since she kept spending as usual and asking him for money. "She won't look for a job or ask her father for a loan, but she talks to him every day about how rotten I am." Phil angrily explained that when Judy begrudgingly agreed to work in his office some months earlier, he had to fire her because she was so arrogant and insulting to the other employees. He went on to say that he did not know what she did with her time — that she certainly did not clean the house and rarely cooked. "Forget sex! I haven't been laid in weeks." Phil felt that all Judy, like her father, knew how to do was criticize and yell, that she offered no emotional support, and was cold, critical, and a perfectionist, just like her mother. He felt she also undermined him with her parents. "I'm working as hard as I can to keep everything together for us and I never once get a word of encouragement or appreciation from you or your parents."

Despite my impulse to tell Phil to shut up, his frustration and neediness were palpable. I was able to comment that it was clear that Phil felt totally unsupported in the relationship, but that Judy obviously had needs, too, and that it was important for us to establish an atmosphere in which they could begin to hear one another. Before I could get the words out Phil began to talk over me. This pattern continued until the end of the session, which went on longer than was scheduled. I tried to bring it to a close unsuccessfully several times and eventually actually got up from my seat and firmly said that I had to stop. I remember being surprised that Phil and Judy agreed so readily to return the following week.

I must confess that I was not sure that I wanted to see Phil and Judy again, although I was sympathetic to their plight and felt a sense of urgency given their financial situation and Judy's pregnancy. I felt totally ineffectual and disappointed in myself for feeling so out of control in the session, annoyed at Dr. A for sending me the case, and surprised that despite the seeming legitimacy of Phil's complaints, Dr. A did not realize that Phil was "impossible" in his own way. She had seen Phil as a mature, insightful, ambitious, and creative entrepreneur, and Judy as irresponsible, angry, selfish, and denying. In contrast, I experienced Phil as out of control, abusive, and controlling and Judy as his helpless and passive victim.

Fortunately, before reaching for the telephone to call Dr. A, I had some time to reflect on what had occurred. I realized that my feelings were just as intense, one-sided, and distorted as I thought Dr. A's were and that both of our reactions, taken together, likely were diagnostic of complex dynamics within each partner and in their interactive pattern.

In our second session, Phil continued with his diatribe against Judy, but finally attempted to give her some opportunity to talk when I commented that I could see that he was obviously under enormous financial pressure, was feeling alone, and needed to get a lot "off his chest," but that it was important that he let Judy share her feelings and perceptions. Judy then began to systematically rebut each of Phil's accusations in a rather rehearsed way and to attack him for being irresponsible, sneaky, reckless with money, totally undisciplined, too trusting of, and secretive about, and generous with his business associates, who were taking advantage of him, while he gave her no priority at all.

Judy vividly recounted examples of his impulsive spending sprees, his lack of planning for the future, his extravagance with others financially, and his tightness with her. "You can buy a new sound system. Why do I have to keep asking you for the rent money?" Phil replied angrily, "Judy, there is *no* money." To which Judy responded, "I've heard that for two years. What's different? How do you expect me to believe you when every time I look at your American Express bill, I see more charges for dinners, compact discs, clothes, and car rentals because of another accident? I need clothes and furniture for the baby. You say I'm not dealing with reality. What about you?" Phil retorted that he was trying to save his business; Judy looked like she wanted to kill him. "You only think about your business but never about me and the baby. Do you ever ask me how *I'm* feeling? Do you ever try to get involved in the fact that you're going to be a father? You'll never be a success. You have great ideas, but you don't know how to follow through. You deal with your business the way you do everything else. You should just get a job. We don't have to make a lot of money."

Turning to me, Judy said, "He's a total slob. He leaves his clothes all over the house. He's always losing his keys. He doesn't care how fast he's going when he's driving. Now he doesn't even have his license or own a checkbook. On some days he comes home early and watches television until he falls asleep. If he's so concerned about his business, why doesn't he work harder? I try to be there, but he completely shuts me out. Yet he talks to my father endlessly."

Phil could not contain himself and said, "All I get is lectures from you about how I'm fucking up. That's not listening." Judy replied that Phil wasn't telling me about how he sabotages his own business by making completely wrong decisions. "If I try to help him he gets furious at me. Then he tries to punish me by not talking to me and I'm supposed to want to jump into bed with him." At points when Phil yelled over her, Judy would also turn to me for approval, saying in an exasperated and pliant tone, "This is what it's like to try to talk to him. Yes, I do yell too much and I am critical, but do you blame me? How am I supposed to work right now? I'm expecting a baby in two months. He thinks that I don't worry about money, that I enjoy not working, and that I'm not looking for a job deliberately." During this session my repeated attempts at empathizing with their feelings and trying to create a safe space fell on deaf ears, but when Phil got up and started pacing in an agitated fashion, my suggestion that we stop the session for a few minutes in order to cool things down resulted in a temporary deescalation of the battling.

I was exhausted after this session and felt agitated and overwhelmed. I felt an urge to rescue Phil and Judy but inadequate to do so. Concurrently I wanted to shake both of them and tell them to stop their fighting. While I experienced Judy's description of and complaints against Phil as equally as compelling as his were against her, I also found her to be as cold, critical, and contemptuous of him as he described. Further, she did not seem to register the urgency of their situation nor did she show any empathy for what Phil was going through. She not only revealed a different side of herself but also another side of Phil, which helped to explain his contribution to their problems.

Thinking in object relations terms, I observed that Phil's self presentation was of a hardworking, well-organized businessman who was trying to provide for his wife, whom he portrayed as a selfish, denying, entitled, withholding child who had not the vaguest idea about how to provide any support or be a partner. In contrast, Judy's self-presentation was of a mature, responsible, reasonable, and concerned expectant mother who was frustrated in her attempts to be a partner to an irresponsible, undisciplined, self-indulgent, insensitive, and punitive husband. Each seemed unaware of the non-idealized or unacceptable parts of themselves that they perceived in one another and each seemed to behave in ways that justified the other's point of view.

I wondered if my shifting and somewhat contradictory sympathetic and judgmental attitudes toward each of them were in response to the couple's fluctuating, contradictory, and split-off parts of themselves that they were projecting onto me. I also speculated that my feelings of being overwhelmed might reflect just how out of control, needy, alone, and powerless Phil and Judy were feeling and how much they wanted to be rescued. At the same time I wondered if by experiencing their "badness" I was relieving them of feeling any sense of responsibility or remorse for their behavior or, alternatively, whether my role was to punish them for being "bad."

I soon realized, however, that all my formulations put the responsibility for my intense reactions on what Phil and Judy were inducing in me rather than what I was bringing to the situation. Thinking more self psychologically, I began to consider the role my own background and experiences were playing in my responses to the couple. I acknowledged to myself that witnessing such intense, overt, and physically threatening aggression between partners who seemed totally insensitive to their impact had the potential of triggering my own anxiety-ridden memories of watching my grandparents verbally slug it out when I was a child. Perhaps my intervening so quickly to diffuse Phil's rage and my sense of urgency stemmed from my own family-of-origin issues and was not attuned to his need to ventilate. Further, I wondered how the feminist in me reacted to Phil's overbearing behavior and to Judy's initial passivity and depression. It seemed likely that I was responding to them in terms of how I would react to the situation rather than in terms of who they were. I also speculated that my conflicted response to Judy's rebuttal of Phil's accusations might have reflected a reaction formation, since I was aware of having felt angry at him and wanted Judy to fight back in the first session.

I then considered whether the frustration of Phil's and Judy's selfobject needs by one another, coupled with my lack of attunement to them and to my not yet being a reliable selfobject, was causing them to behave in extreme and negative ways. In this connection, it seemed possible that Phil's uncontrollable rage might be related to his loss of self-esteem as a result of his business problems, to his not being sufficiently mirrored by Judy, and to his feeling abandoned by her. He felt fearful of a business collapse, burdened that he had to do everything by himself without validation, disappointed in Judy as a partner, and perhaps fearful of becoming a father. Likewise, it seemed possible that Judy's demeaning and critical attitude toward Phil and her seeming denial of their financial problems reflected her deidealization of and disappointment in Phil, her fear of the future, her awareness of her dependence on him at this stage in her pregnancy, and her feelings of abandonment.

I decided that it would be a mistake to actively confront and interpret Phil and Judy's dysfunctional interaction and seemingly primitive defenses. I thought this would contribute to their feeling unresponded to and would stimulate rather than diffuse their aggression toward one another. Instead, I concluded that attempting to be as empathic as I could to each partner, while trying to establish some common ground, was a better approach. It also seemed important for me to take a step back, to slow down, and to react with less of a sense of crisis.

I felt more relaxed in the next two sessions and began by commenting on how frustrated, alone, and fearful both Phil and Judy were feeling. I also said that each seemed to feel quite disappointed in the other and that perhaps we could talk about the beginning of their relationship and how they got to the place of mutual frustration, as well as a little bit about their backgrounds. Each session was calmer initially until their battle reescalated when they began to disagree about their perceptions of one another. I learned that, in addition to their sexual attraction to one another, Phil found Judy's independence and admiration appealing. He thought she would be a steady and supportive force in his life and would not be too needy. She was working at the time of their dating and Phil thought she would not expect him to take care of her the way other girlfriends had. Further, he was aware that her parents were well-off financially and that her father, a successful businessman, might take him into the business or help him in other ways should the need arise. Judy was excited by Phil's ambition, creativity, and energy and responded to his attention and willingness to share his ideas and feelings with her.

It was clear that Phil and Judy had very specific and highly charged expectations of one another that stemmed from their own families of origin. Their relationship began to sour for Phil after he dissolved what had appeared to be a successful business partnership with his oldest brother, with whom he had a irreconcilable feud and who, he felt, robbed him financially. Then Judy's father reneged on his offer to take Phil into his business and he had to struggle on his own. Meanwhile Judy had stopped working and had difficulty finding another suitable job. Working in Phil's business at his request was highly stressful for both of them, as Judy saw a different side of Phil and his dealings with others that distressed and frightened her. Admittedly, she became more vocal in offering him advice, nagging him about his lack of organization and his relationships with his associates, less supportive, and more critical of him. Depressed about the business and his relationship with Judy, Phil became uncommunicative and watched television endlessly. After Judy stopped working for Phil, at his insistence, they hardly spoke. Judy became more demanding and argumentative and Phil became secretive, withholding, and punishing. Nevertheless they agreed to try to have a child and Judy quickly became pregnant.

While space considerations do not permit a full description of the couple's families of origin, the following picture emerged. Phil was the youngest of three sons and a daughter and grew up in their shadow, always feeling like a "fuck-up." Due to his perseverance, however, he became a successful athlete until he suffered a knee injury. His father, a successful entrepreneur whom Phil admired, never gave him positive attention. He went bankrupt when Phil was an adolescent and the family experienced severe financial reversals. While they eventually recovered with his mother's help, Phil had to struggle financially and he lost faith in his father. He was closer to his mother and sister, who were sources of companionship and encouragement.

Judy never got along with her mother, who was extremely critical and self-involved, but idealized her father, who was very successful in business. Although they fought a great deal, he would discuss his business concerns with her endlessly and taught her a lot about the "tricks of the trade." While Judy's mother was highly emotional and volatile, her father was the steadier one in the relationship and catered to her mother. Judy was still quite dependent on her father and had an angry and charged relationship with her mother. Both of her parents were quite intrusive in her present life.

Because of the persistent blaming and arguing that was occurring in the sessions, I asked Phil and Judy what we might do to try to structure the sessions to ease their tension enough so that we could begin to sort out their difficulties and move forward. Interestingly, each suggested that I meet with them separately, an idea to which I readily agreed. Showing empathy for their ways of viewing one another and providing some selfobject functions for each of them, I used these sessions to help Phil talk through his business options and his anger at Judy, to help Judy share her concerns about disappointment in Phil and deal with her parents more effectively, and to help both of them become more attuned to what each was looking for in the relationship, how their needs were being frustrated by one another, how their reactions were creating further obstacles to their supporting one another, and how some of their individual and couple problems stemmed from their families of origin.

After Judy gave birth to Michael two months later, I reinstated couple sessions and we were able to talk about ways they could deal with their financial and relationship problems more constructively. Each partner accepted me as a good selfobject despite times when he or she attempted to use me to support his/her point of view and undermine my relationship with the other. It was necessary for me to deal with Phil and Judy's skillful attempts to triangulate me into their fighting and with their disappointment in me when I failed to respond as they wished. Fortunately, they brought up these issues spontaneously and I was able to repair disruptions that occurred in our relationship by exploring, understanding, and acknowledging how I had failed them. In order to do this successfully, I had to resist acting out my own negative reactions to their behavior and labeling their expectations of me as inappropriate.

While the partners' relationship with one another was stormy and included one separation just prior to and after the birth of their son, they were able to make considerable progress over the period of a year of treatment with respect to establishing a sense of teamwork, managing finances, planning for the future, mutually supporting one another, dealings with their in-laws, and parenting their son. These outcomes are more than adequate when the nature and degree of borderline dynamics are fully understood.

REFERENCES

Adler, G. (1985). *Borderline psychopathology and its treatment*. New York: Jason Aronson.
Brandchaft, B., & Stolorow, R. D. (1984a). The borderline concept: Pathological character or

iatrogenic myth. In J. Lichtenberg, M. Bornstein, & R. Silver (Eds.), *Empathy II* (pp. 333–358). Hillsdale, NJ: Analytic Press.

Brandchaft, B., & Stolorow, R. D. (1984b). A current perspective on difficult patients. In P. E. Stepansky & A. Goldberg (Eds.), *Kohut's legacy: Contributions to self psychology* (pp. 117–134). Hillsdale, NJ: Analytic Press.

Everett, C., Halperin, S., Volgy, S., & Wissler, A. (1989). *Treating the borderline family: A systemic approach*. Boston: Allyn & Bacon.

Goldstein, E. G. (March, 1981). *The family characteristics of borderline patients*. Developmental Deficits in Adolescence panel chaired by Bertram S. Cohler at the 58th Annual Meeting of the American Orthopsychiatric Association, New York.

Goldstein, E. G. (1990). *Borderline disorders: Clinical models and techniques*. New York: Guilford.

Grinker, R. R., Werble, B., & Drye, R. (1968). *The borderline syndrome*. New York: Basic.

Gunderson, J. G., Kerr, J., & Englund, D. W. (1980). The families of borderlines: A comparative study. *Archives of General Psychiatry, 37*, 27–33.

Kohut, H. (1971). *The analysis of the self*. New York: International Universities Press.

Kohut, H. (1977). *The restoration of the self*. New York: International Universities Press.

Lachkar, J. (1992). *The narcissistic/borderline couple: A psychoanalytic perspective on marital treatment*. New York: Brunner/Mazel.

Scharff, D. E., & Scharff, J. S. (1987). *Object relations family therapy*. Northvale, NJ: Jason Aronson.

Scharff, D. E., & J. S. (1991). *Object relations couple therapy*. Northvale, NJ: Jason Aronson.

Schwartzman, G. (1984). Narcissistic transferences: Implications for the treatment of couples. *Dynamic Psychotherapy, 2*, 5–14.

Schwoeri, L., & Schwoeri, F. (1981). Family therapy of borderline patients: Diagnostic and treatment issues. *International Journal of Family Psychiatry, 2*, 237–251.

Schwoeri, L., & Schwoeri, F. (1982). Interactional and intrapsychic dynamics in a family with a borderline patient. *Psychotherapy Theory, Research, and Practice, 19*, 198–204.

Shapiro, E. R., Zinner, J., Shapiro, R. L., & Berkowitz, D. (1975). The influence of family experience on borderline personality development. *International Review of Psychoanalysis, 2*, 399–411.

Shapiro, E. R., Shapiro, R. L., Zinner, J., & Berkowitz, D. (1977). The borderline ego and the working alliance: Implications for family and individual treatment. *International Journal of Psychoanalysis, 58*, 77–87.

Siegel, J. (1992). *Repairing intimacy*. Northvale, NJ: Jason Aronson.

Slipp, S. (1980). Marital therapy for borderline personality disorders. *American Journal of Family Therapy, 8*, 67–70.

Slipp, S. (Ed.). (1988). *The technique and practice of object relations family therapy*. Northvale, NJ: Jason Aronson.

Solomon, M. F. (1989). *Narcissism and intimacy*. New York: Norton.

Solomon, M. F. (1985). Treatment of narcissistic and borderline disorders in marital therapy: Suggestions toward an enhanced therapeutic approach. *Clinical Social Work Journal, 13*, 141–156.

Stewart, R. H., Peters, T. C., Marsh, S., & Peters, M. J. (1975). An object relations approach with marital couples, families, and children. *Family Process, 14*, 161–172.

Walsh, F. (1977). Family study 1976: Fourteen new borderline cases. In R. R. Grinker & B. Werble (Eds.), *The borderline patient* (pp. 158–177). New York: Jason Aronson.

White, M. T. (1984). Discussion of G. Schwartzman's "Narcissistic transferences: Implications for the treatment of couples." *Dynamic Psychotherapy, 2*, 15–17.

Zinner, J., & Shapiro, E. R. (1975). Splitting in the families of borderline adolescents. In J. Mack (Ed.), *Borderline states in psychiatry* (pp. 103–122). New York: Grune & Stratton.

Zinner, J., & Shapiro, R. L. (1982). Projective identification as a mode of perception and behavior in the families of borderline adolescents. *International Journal of Psychoanalysis, 53*, 523–529.

5

Oedipal Countertransference in Marital Therapy

JUSTIN A. FRANK

In this our life there are no beginnings but only departures entitled beginnings, wreathed in the formal emotions thought to be appropriate and often forced. Darkly rises each moment from the life which has been lived and which does not die, for each event lives in the heavy head forever, waiting to renew itself.

—Delmore Schwartz, "The World Is a Wedding"

ANCIENT LOVES AND HATES, thoughts and desires, pains and griefs remain alive inside every adult, no matter how much they seem forgotten. And what each marital partner brings to a marriage is an internal psychic model that comprises childhood events and fantasies about his or her own parents and their relationship. These internal parents are never wholly realistic because they are always filtered through a multitude of complex unconscious feelings such as idealization, envy, sexual longings and rivalries, primal scene fantasies (universally held images of parental intercourse), contempt, hostility, and dependent yearnings. Each partner also brings to a marriage sets of expectations about how he or she will be treated by the other. These expectations—well described by Klein's (1959) idea of the psychic law of talion (an eye for an eye)—are based on how each individual treats his internal parents and family units. Thus, while every marriage has newness and freshness, each union contains numerous preconceptions that also affect the relationship.

The fundamental organizing principle determining "the final shape of [adult] erotic life" (Freud, 1923), both in terms of object choice and how the marital partners relate to one another, is the Oedipus complex. How this complex gets resolved in childhood is central to psychosexual development and becomes a cornerstone of marital success or failure. As in psychoanalysis, the process of identifying, exploring, and understanding derivatives of oedipal issues, such as sexual identity, murderous aggression, incest, guilt, and obsession with triangular entanglements, is essential in any psychodynamic marital therapy. Yet too often marital therapists fail to explore oedipal issues, focusing instead on alleviating problems of narcissistic injury and rage, identifying fears of abandonment past or present, or even exposing the pathological projective identification mechanisms that drive and distort a marriage. I think such avoidance often has its origin in countertransference anxieties unique to marital therapy—namely, oedipal countertransference. In this chapter I focus on the oedipal countertransference both as resistance to therapeutic work and as a potential source of information about marital dynamics.

AN OEDIPAL OVERVIEW

Freud (1926) felt that the oedipal myth was a universal source of anxiety in children—anxiety about wanting to kill their same-sex parent, while at the same time sexually possessing the other. The conflict that develops between yearnings and the consequences of their gratification—even in fantasy—leads to inhibition of erotic desire and subsequent rechanneling of genital sexuality into more regressed forms of psychosexual satisfaction. The reverse is also present as the "negative" Oedipus complex—most clearly described by Nagera (1969). Here the child loves the same-sex parent, while feeling rivalry toward the opposite-sex parent.

These complex feelings are universal, and the particular way they are resolved determines not only adult object choice and how one loves and hates but also how the superego develops. Oedipal anxieties and conflicts exist regardless of the particulars of family structure. Thus, when one attempts to understand actual or external ("real") family events, one must be aware that they are perceived, experienced, and ultimately refracted through an oedipal lens.

There are other aspects of the oedipal myth that should be mentioned. First, Freud (1912–13) wrote in *Totem and Taboo* that killing the primal father is inevitable and that every human being is an "Oedipus in germ" (p. 265). Second, anticipation of the primal scene is also universal, according to Freud, whether actually viewed or not. The impact of parental sexuality on the child is ultimately what matters when considering primal scene fantasies. Recently Ron Britten (1989) has elaborated some ideas about this impact, namely that the child, aware of parental intercourse, feels alone and excluded. The child then becomes aware that he exists not only in material fact but also in the minds of his parents, who have independent thoughts about him. Mastering oedipal anxieties involves recognizing and tolerating this fact. I find Britten's (1989) ideas particularly useful in my work with regressed or primitive couples, illuminating the way they refuse to tolerate independent thought on my part, while they actively encourage me to participate with them in their pathology.

A third aspect of the Oedipus complex that must be discussed is the child's unconscious hatred and envy of the parental couple from which he is actually excluded. A fourth component, as described by Bion (1958), is arrogance. It is reflected in the oedipal prisoner's relentless search for the truth—a search that continues at all costs, even if the cost be total destruction (in the play, it is the destruction of Thebes itself). A fifth Oedipal factor was introduced by Melanie Klein (1945), who described envy of parental intercourse and subsequent attacks on mating and fertility. These attacks, when unconscious, can undermine sexual satisfaction in the marriage.

COUNTERTRANSFERENCE: OEDIPAL AND OTHERWISE

Countertransference has to do with unconscious processes in the therapist, which, when recognized, can help the work with the couple in several ways: by helping the therapist understand marital dynamics, by shaping specific interpretive content, and by preventing potentially countertherapeutic enactments. When unrecognized, countertransference feelings can interfere with treatment, leading to, among other things, taking judgmental positions (identification with superego elements in the couple), therapeutic impasse, or acting-out by the therapist. For example, an unrecognized oedipal countertransference may keep a young therapist from openly discussing the couple's sex life—his own childhood prohibitions against sexual curiosity about parental intercourse inhibiting here and now exploration.

Oedipal countertransference is present in any therapeutic relationship, so in some sense it must be regarded as normal. At times, previously resolved oedipal conflicts can get stirred up within the therapist. Some therapists, no matter how well trained or well analyzed, are surprised when this happens; they seem to think that conflicts resolved are conflicts eliminated. On the contrary, oedipal situations play a consistent part in everyone's daily life. Transference is at its greatest when the couple's treatment begins, since it is unmodified by the patients' experience of the person of the therapist. The therapist's oedipal expectations get activated as he or she enters the privately shared culture that exists within the couple. It is as if the therapist is suddenly being born into a preexisting structure within which communication codes and private cues abound.

Therapists may counter potential feelings of helplessness or anxiety by becoming experts, authorities about the unknown. Or we might be hard on ourselves for not understanding, persecuted by the pain of our natural limitations — limitations that are in some ways greatest at the first couple interview. Later in treatment we can defend against this pain by blaming the couple, seeing them as impossibly difficult and destructive of any treatment efforts. I think that these anxieties are strikingly similar to those an oedipal child may have in relation to his parents — a similarity that often results in affixing blame to the spouse who is of the same sex as the therapist. It is not uncommon for a countertransference-based impasse in marital therapy to develop when the therapist gets stuck blaming one marital partner or seeing one partner as having all the pathology. At times we see the opposite, a defensive reaction against this kind of blaming (projection of the therapist's superego), when the therapist continually strives to balance every bit of pathological behavior evenly between the partners.

By virtue of being labeled as the "helper," the therapist is naturally prone to conscious and unconscious parental and reparative feelings. These tendencies comprise what Money-Kyrle (1956) calls "normal counter-transference." He writes about the reparative drive, which "counteracts the latent destructiveness in all of us." This natural reparative urge evokes, in my view, childhood feelings of wanting to undo oedipal attacks against the parental couple. The urge may also be a direct repetition of a childhood need to fix a marriage that is perceived as bad, whether depressed or violent. It is when the dynamic therapist is under the sway of such feelings that he or she begins to offer suggestions to the couple, rules to live by. These generally fall on deaf ears. John Zinner (1990) has written about the dangers of getting caught in the manifest content — something I think is more likely when the therapist does not recognize his oedipal countertransference. The second aspect of the wish to be a helper is the parental drive, more easily understood than the reparative drive. While both drives express the wish to help, one takes the vantage point of the child; the other, of the adult. In working with couples the parental drive often leads the therapist to set himself up as the wise settler of disputes and giver of perspective. Most couples covertly undermine this stance — which I think of as oedipal reaction formation — while they overtly seek the comfort and understanding that the therapist so willingly offers.

Obviously, oedipal countertransference varies with the therapeutic setting. When we are doing co-therapy, there are often parallel transference configurations between the "therapist couple" and the patient couple. Several recent papers out of the Tavistock Institute of Marital Studies (Ruszczynski & Fisher, 1993, 1995) explore these phenomena. Age difference between the therapist and the couple is another factor determining (although at times obscuring) countertransference. For example, a young therapist treating an older couple may have unconscious prohibitions against childhood curiosity about his own parents' sex life that might prevent an open exploration of the couple's sexual relationship. A third setting variable affecting oedipal countertransference is, in my experience, the location of the treatment. A therapist who works within an institution often feels more comfortable denying his or her own oedipal anxieties, because the therapist has the illusion of institutional protection against anxieties of exclusion and childhood experiences of powerlessness. A final setting variable is supervision. Often the newer therapist may evoke the supervisor as a marital counterpart to help deal with oedipal anxieties about the couple, especially anxieties of being overwhelmed. Anxiety, while at times crippling, is usually a source of information about the couple's dynamics — so I am wary of the therapist who feels too comfortable in the consulting room.

IDENTIFYING THE OEDIPAL COUNTERTRANSFERENCE

In my experience three types of oedipal countertransference manifestations occur once treatment is underway. The most obvious is same-sex rivalry — the therapist unconsciously competing to appear to be the better, more understanding spouse. A second type, rather than being the "negative Oedipus" complex, occurs when one member of the couple reminds the therapist of his own parent imago from childhood. This type of association is more likely to be evoked in the couple setting than in individual work. Third is primal scene anxiety, which is manifest in a variety of ways. I have supervised many cases in which the therapist's fears of spousal abuse in the couple don't fit with the material. While the couple is evoking the therapist's fantasy, the degree of concern is often greatly exaggerated. The supervisee becomes controlling and even judgmental, which often inhibits free exploration of marital dynamics.

When one has a typical way of thinking, working, and responding to couples, deviation from that pattern indicates countertransference trouble. This deviation can be seen when the therapist changes his/her style uncharacteristically (for example, suddenly scolding the couple), feels unfamiliar anxiety (suddenly anxious about something in his/her personal life), avoids looking at obvious clinical material (the couple has a series of associations that beg interpretation, but the therapist changes the subject or remains silent), or in fact acts out (inadvertently or even willfully extending the session).

In my own work, I prefer to look at any unexpected fantasies and associations I have, as well as changes in my behavior, as evidence of countertransference phenomena. With one couple, for example, I found myself remembering a recurring fantasy from my own psychoanalysis—a conscious daydream I used to have of breaking into my analyst's consulting room and interrupting him and his patient, hoping that he would excuse himself and attend to me. It was only after I had had this image several times that I realized I was dealing more with siblings stuck in a rivalrous transference relationship to me than with a married couple whose fighting was overtly about marital trust. What they didn't trust was their projection onto each other of their greedy, needy selves who wanted all my attention and love. After examining my countertransference, I had a deeper understanding of their regressed state and also felt better able to work with how and why they relinquished their parental roles and responsibilities.

Case Example I

A supervisee presented a couple she was treating, complaining that the wife, a 40-year-old woman without a particular career, who had spent her adult life raising her children, kept seeming to press for individual sessions. The husband wanted his wife to spend more time with him than just going on family holidays together. He was a powerful corporate executive who envied his wife her leisure time, yet feared her having an independent life outside the family. I said what any supervisor would have said, namely that for some reason the wife is uncomfortable with triangles and needs a woman ally. I also felt that the supervisee had an unconscious identification with the husband, pushing the wife back toward him as an accommodation.

Then the supervisee said that she was pushing the wife to get back to interacting with the husband because she strongly objected to the wife's shifting the focus away from the marriage. I felt that what the supervisee was experiencing must be worked with in terms of her countertransference, not merely as a natural response to keep the couple in a couple treatment format. I asked her if there were something about the wife that she didn't want to see, or if she knew whether the wife's mother had been someone who didn't want to know her daughter's mind. Yes, she said, the wife was sexually abused as a child by her father and older brother. Then the supervisee admitted to strong reluctance to talk about the abuse in any detail. She identified with the wife's reluctance to talk. Once we recognized this, the supervisee said that her own parents used to have violent quarrels and that her mother often tried to talk to her about it. She remembered not only how much she hated to hear her mother's complaints, but also how she prayed that both parents would just go away and leave her alone. So what at first appeared as a natural wish to keep the couple working together rather than as individuals—something necessary in a couple therapy training program—was in reality a countertransference enactment based on oedipal fears.

Case Example II

Oedipal jealousy is often tinged with envy—Riviere (1932) felt, for instance, that Iago represented the split-off, envious aspect of jealous Othello. This is a case of Tom and Nora, two married physicians in their mid-forties with a 14-year-old daughter. The couple came to treatment when the wife was on the verge of leaving her husband for their best friend.

As an only child, Nora was always included in her parents' lives. She was much loved, and her parents seemed to have a deep commitment to each other in what looked like an ideal relationship. On further exploration, I learned that her parents did occasionally fight about money, but rarely more than that. In her own marriage, Nora was childless for ten years and was thrilled to finally become pregnant and give birth to a girl—repeating the configuration of her own family of origin. Tom, Nora's husband, was a decent but distant man, tolerant of Nora's hysterical behavior, although entirely ignorant of the multiple affairs she had had early in the marriage. He came from a relatively nonverbal family with two brothers, both of whom were politically "red neck" racists. Tom was a philanthropic, liberal physician, devoted to inner-city work despite his relatively reserved personality.

Nora and Tom were best friends with another couple, Rita and Richard. Rita was a doctor practicing the same specialty as Nora. In fact, Rita had been a senior resident when younger Nora transferred into the program. When Nora suddenly became chief resident Rita was stunned and angry. Rita, Nora told me, was an envious, vicious woman who was also quite brilliant. But early on what attracted Nora to Rita was Richard—an often sullen but occasionally witty, perceptive man. Eventually she became Richard's best friend, confidant, and supporter when he was depressed. Their friendship was accepted by all four people. This year, however, it turned into an affair. Nora felt no guilt about betraying Rita per se, but was disappointed in herself because she had been proud at having been a loyal friend, defending Rita against her many detractors.

Nora unconsciously arranged to be found out and when she confessed to Tom, all hell broke loose and the couple arrived for immediate problem-solving treatment. They were in a crisis and about to separate, although, interestingly, Tom still wanted to keep the marriage intact. It was hard to move from the crisis into a thinking mode: even when we tentatively succeeded I found myself focusing on Nora's behavior rather than on Tom's controlling and near-schizoid approach to his married life. I found myself exploring oedipal rivalry with women — with Rita and with Nora's mother. We soon got stuck in what I had initially felt were useful discussions of Nora's behavior. Furthermore I found myself at the same time thinking that Nora's affairs made sense in some way, for Tom really was reserved, aloof, and wrapped up in both his career and his philanthropic investments.

When I found myself thinking about my own mother I was alerted to other possible interpretations of Nora's behavior. I began to remember — at first seemingly at random, and then recognizing that it was only when I was with Tom and Nora — thinking that my mother should leave my father, that he was always so critical when he was home, and that his career came first. I remembered how my sister and I would eat dinner before he got home and my mother would wait for him and they'd eat together at 8 or 9 p.m. I realized that I was superimposing my own fantasies about my parents' unhappiness onto Tom and Nora and wishing to rescue her from terminal boredom. Once I understood this a bit, I began to think about Nora's long history of affairs not as evidence of oedipal rivalry but as something else. I started remembering that my parents often went out and seemed to have genuinely happy times together. There was more to their lives than arguments. I began to wonder if I hadn't seen their marriage as more unhappy than it was as a defense against anxiety about being excluded from that kind of intimacy, protecting myself from jealousy and envy. It became clear that I was siding with Nora's view of her marriage because of my own countertransference.

What I discovered was that Nora was not simply attacking her marriage in particular, nor was she having affairs as rivalrous assaults on Rita and other women — she was attacking the institution of marriage. She could not tolerate her parents' happiness together and unconsciously attacked all marriages — her own and then Rita's. She wanted to spoil them all because of her envy. She even spoiled her own. Tom was not that bad, we both realized. And she chose him for good reasons, consciously and unconsciously. Part of what she was doing also kept her from ever having to mourn her internal parents, because she never fully left her childhood, never having recognized that it was her relentless unconscious attacks on the parental couple that kept her from having what she wanted in her own marriage. Conscious idealization masked unconscious hate. And much of that hate was driven by envy — the deep pain of not getting what she wanted. From the beginning of her own marriage, Nora's denied envy of her parents kept her from feeling the sorrow that Elvin Semrad (1980) called "the vitamin of growth."

Case Example III

When Max and Mary arrived at my office, their marriage was in acute crisis. Max was on the verge of leaving and Mary was in a state of deep passive withdrawal. He railed against her from the beginning of the session about how cold-hearted she was, and also how sadistically she could treat him—that she viewed him as a male pig, as someone who was always the cause of their problems. Their long and stormy marriage had survived a stillbirth, a protracted affair (Mary's), and violent rages (Max's). They had married after Mary—who was then a married mother of three—seduced Max, whom she had met while on a family holiday.

Mary, while being physically similar to Max—slight and almost petite—was quiet and overtly sweet. I felt a warmth in her, a tolerance for all his ranting mixed with profound guilt about the pain her affair had caused him. Still, that was long ago (a year after the stillbirth) and she felt there was no point in discussing it now. What brought them to treatment was Max's fear that Mary was again about to embark on an affair with a much-admired mutual friend.

I found myself, over time, unable to work with the couple in a reasonably balanced way. Almost all my efforts were aimed at calming Max down, keeping him from storming out of my office screaming hateful venom at his wife and at me. The force of his rage dominated my thoughts and feelings, and I remember at times cringing in childlike fear during his rampages. The mornings I had appointments with the Newmans became filled with dread, making it hard for me to concentrate on the patients who preceded them. Treatment choice at this point was not about anything other than whether or not I could tolerate being in the same room with them. This itself became a source of information about the marriage, as I discovered that the Newmans themselves could not tolerate being at close quarters.

Work with Max and Mary continued over several years with many vicissitudes and some considerable gains. What I am here going to describe is a period of impasse that was improved only after I recognized a paralyzing oedipal countertransference rivalry with Max. Until that time, what follows is how the sessions typically went:

MAX: I've got it all figured, Doc. She always had to do things that were exciting, secret, like getting guys and sleeping with them in the room next to her husband. When she decides she wants something she just goes for it. And now she wants you to be her special friend. I just want things to run more smoothly at home, and already we're not speaking except in here. I can't stand to be with her. She's sick. She can't help it, but she doesn't know when she is suddenly going to want something.

JAF: I think you (Mary) don't speak because you feel it's too dangerous. (*In retrospect, some of my comments are obviously my own projections.*) Can you share your thoughts now?

MARY: I'm not thinking. I'm just listening to everything Max is saying, but not thinking about anything.

JAF: It's too dangerous to think independently anymore because Max gets enraged if you do anything independent—it scares him and he superimposes your ancient affair on everything. (*to Max*) How are you going to be able to sit through all this (discussion of the affair)?

MAX: Maybe I should leave? I know what you should say.

JAF: What should I say?

MAX: Why don't you leave, Max?

JAF: I think you can't stand Mary talking to me if you feel excluded from the discussion.

MAX: (*to Mary*) What do you think about that?

MARY: What's the question?

MAX: (*getting suddenly enraged*) See? I just asked a question, can't you answer it? (*slowly*) WHAT DO YOU THINK? She does exactly this to me all the time. You never get a straight answer to anything. And the whole purpose is to get me mad and then to say she can't talk because I'm too angry and she hates fighting. It works. My last therapist was paranoid about me. He kept thinking I was going to sue him, and I'm not even a lawyer. Do you think I'm paranoid? He kept talking about my suing, so I think he was paranoid.

JAF: Maybe he felt about you the way your wife does—afraid you'll attack.

MAX: So, I get mad. The fear is their problem, not mine. I never attack, just yell. (*to Mary*) You disgust me. There, is that an attack? It's just a fact.

MARY: It's too risky here.

JAF: You want guarantees that Max won't attack back or interpret what you say independently of what you think you mean. No one can guarantee that, not even Max.

MAX: I know what she'll say, anyway. (*in mimic tone*) "I feel so bad, empty, life is not worth living. I'm worthless. If it weren't for the children, I'd kill myself."

MARY: Well, that is one of the things I was going to say. I'm not depressed, but just feel worthless. That I don't do anything worthwhile. I'm just a caretaker, a nothing. And now my world has become so small and constricted I've no life in me, no interests. I have no energy to do anything.

MAX: I'm so sick of hearing this. She always blames me for her emptiness and bad feelings.

JAF: You have to insert yourself into her every discussion.

MAX: I've had it with you, too.

At this point the session ended, rather typically — Max storms out and Mary trails behind. I often hear them quarreling in the street. Yes, that became the secret behind my paralysis. I had always felt identified with Mary, that she needed protection against Max's tyranny. I feared being like Max, and that any effort at investigative work with Mary might be turned by her into persecutory attack. But it was the weeks of hearing quarreling outside my window that led to a countertransference breakthrough. I began to remember a period of my own childhood when I heard my parents quarrel behind closed doors. It was so loud that I needed loud music to drown out the noise. My room was not safe, just as my office was invaded before the sessions by feelings of dread and after by actual quarreling voices.

Oedipal boys often see their fathers as extremely dangerous — they feel castration anxiety, which is fear of retaliation for their often unconscious wish to kill and replace their fathers. I felt only the fear — some of which Max made easy for me to feel — and then the wish to escape. Because of this I was unable to see Mary's provocation or think about why Max might have been so tyrannically enraged. Eventually, upon analysis of my countertransference defensiveness I became better able to set limits on Max, whose rages I discovered were aimed at actually keeping Mary from talking. He, in fact, didn't want to know what she might say, despite all appearances to the contrary. Until this time I had felt that much of my reaction was an identification with Mary. Because of my own unconscious oedipal feelings I was unable to empathize with Max's pain and fears of abandonment. I could heretofore only regard Mary as the victim who needed to get away from the destroyer Max. After differentiating this couple from my own internal couple I began to recognize that I had colluded in not letting Mary talk, that I too was cringing, but cringing only consciously, like Mary. The unconscious cringing was by a frightened Max, a Max living in dread of Mary's telling him she didn't love him after all. Facing these fears allowed the work to continue.

SUMMARY

Analysis of oedipal countertransference, particularly when it involves aggression, same-sex rivalry, and fears of primal scene fantasies is essential when working with couples. Oedipal feelings in the therapist are inevitable, and exacerbated in all couple cases. In this chapter I have given examples of how unrecognized oedipal issues can block treatment. Part of our struggle as therapists involves facing these troubles — re-facing them, if you will — and paying attention to the ways in which our consulting-room behavior might reflect unconscious oedipal troubles. While these troubles are evoked by the couple transference, they risk being blocked by countertransference blinders.

REFERENCES

Frank, J. A. (1990). Listening with the big ear: A Laingian approach to psychotic families. In A. Silver & M. Cantor (Eds.), *Psychoanalysis and severe emotional illness*. New York: Guilford.

Frank, J. A. (1988). Who are you and what have you done with my wife? In J. Scharff (Ed.), *Foundations of object relations family therapy*. New York: Jason Aronson.

Freud, S. (October 15, 1897). *Letter 71*. In J. Strachey (Ed. and Trans.), *The standard edition of the complete psychological works of Sigmund Freud* (Vol. 1, pp. 263–266). New York: Norton.

Freud, S. (1926). Inhibitions, symptoms, and anxiety. In J. Strachey (Ed. and Trans.), *The standard edition of the complete psychological works of Sigmund Freud* (Vol. 20, pp. 87–174). New York: Norton.

Freud, S. (1912–13). Totem and taboo. In J. Strachey (Ed. and Trans.), *The standard edition of the complete psychological works of Sigmund Freud* (Vol. 13, pp. 1–161). New York: Norton.

Freud, S. (1923). Two encyclopedia articles. In J. Strachey (Ed. and Trans.), *The standard edition of the complete psychological works of Sigmund Freud* (Vol. 18, p. 245). New York: Norton.

Heimann, P. (1950). On countertransference. *International Journal of Psychoanalysis, 31*, 81–84.

Klein, M. (1945). The Oedipus complex in the light of early anxieties. *International Journal of Psycho-Analysis, 26*, 11–33.

Klein, M. (1952). Origins of transference. In M. Klein, *Envy and gratitude and other works 1946–1963*. London: Hogarth.

Klein, M. (1959/1975). Our adult world and its roots in infancy. In *The writings of Melanie Klein* (Vol. 3). London: Hogarth.

Klein, M. (1932/1975). The psychoanalysis of children. In *The writings of Melanie Klein* (Vol. 2). London: Hogarth.

Money-Kyrle, R. (1988). Normal counter-transference and some of its deviations. In E. B. Spillius (Ed.), *Melanie Klein today: Mainly practice* (Vol. 2). London: Routledge.

Nagera, H. (Ed.). (1969). *Basic psychoanalytic concepts on the libido theory*. London: Karnac.

Rako, S., & Mazer, H. (Eds.). (1980). *Semrad: The heart of a therapist*. New York: Jason Aronson.

Riviere, J. (1932). Jealousy as a mechanism of defense. *International Journal of Psychoanalysis, 13*, 414–424.

Ruszczynski, S. (Ed.). (1993). *Psychotherapy with couples*. London: Karnac.

Ruszczynski, S., & Fisher, J. (Eds.). (1995). *Intrusiveness and intimacy in the couple*. London: Karnac.

Schwartz, D. (1978). The world is a wedding. In D. Schwartz, *In dreams begin responsibilities and other stories*. New York: New Directions.

Sophocles. *Oedipus Rex* (Richard Lattimore, Trans.).

Zinner, J. (1990). *Listening with the third ear in couple therapy*. Unpublished manuscript.

6

An Intersubjective Perspective of Countertransference in Couples Therapy

JEFFREY L. TROP

MODERN RELATIONAL theories have significantly changed our conceptualization of the process of psychotherapy. While most attention in the field has been devoted to the application of relational theories to individual therapy, increasing efforts have been made to integrate new relational concepts into clinical work with couples. Several authors (e.g., Lachkar, 1985; Solomon, 1988) have discussed the use of self psychological concepts in the psychotherapy of couples. Solomon (1994), building on Kohut's concepts of self psychology, has reconceptualized issues related to dependency that contribute to conflictual elements in couples. Ringstrom (1994) has used intersubjectivity theory to detail a comprehensive treatment approach to couples.

The purpose of this chapter is to describe the application of the theory of intersubjectivity to conjoint therapy. Here the emphasis will be on the concept of countertransference within an intersubjective framework. I contend that disjunctive interactions within couples can uniformly be illuminated by understanding the principles unconsciously organizing the inner experiences of both parties. Countertransference within an intersubjective framework can be conceptualized as the unconscious organizing principles that shape the therapist's experience in relationship to the couple and to each partner. Before clinically illustrating this thesis, let me first review the theoretical framework of intersubjectivity.

In a paper I co-authored with Atwood and Stolorow (Atwood, Stolorow, & Trop, 1989), we delineated the theory of intersubjectivity:

The intersubjectivity concept is in part a response to the unfortunate tendency of classical analysis to view clinical phenomena in terms of processes and mechanisms located solely within the patient. Such an isolating focus fails to do justice to each individual's irreducible engagement with other human beings and blinds the clinician to the profound ways in which he is himself implicated in the phenomena he observes and seeks to treat. From an intersubjective perspective, phenomena that have been the traditional focus of psychoanalytic investigation are seen not as products of isolated intrapsychic mechanisms, but as forming at the interface between interacting subjectivities. In our previous work, we have shown that an intersubjective viewpoint can illuminate a wide array of clinical issues, including transference and countertransference, resistance, conflict formation, and borderline and psychotic states. (p. 555)

Whether or not . . . intersubjective situations facilitate or obstruct the progress of therapy depends in large part on the extent of the therapist's capacity to be aware of his own organizing principles. When such reflective self-awareness on the part of the therapist is reliably present, then the correspondence or disparity between the subjective worlds of patient and therapist can be used to promote empathic understanding and insight. (p. 556)

Central to the theory of intersubjectivity is the concept of an organizing principle. Atwood and Stolorow (1984) have proposed " . . . that the need to maintain the organization of experience is a central motive in the patterning of human action" (p. 35). Each person thus has unique organizing principles that automatically and unconsciously shape experience. For example, a person invited to an event where there are unfamiliar people may enter a room and someone in the room may immediately turn his back. One person may organize this to mean that he or she is undesirable and repugnant. Another person may conclude that he/she is better than anyone at the event and assume a haughty indifference. A third person might interpret the other's turning away as a random occurrence; it would not be assimilated as having a personal meaning regarding his/her entrance into the room. Thus, persons will automatically organize experience according to the unique psychological principles that unconsciously shape their subjective world. Atwood and Stolorow (1984) further describe their concept of organizing principles:

The organizing principles of a person's subjective world are themselves unconscious. A person's experiences are shaped by his psychological structures without this shaping becoming the focus of awareness and reflection. . . . In the absence of reflection, a person is unaware of his role as a constitutive subject in elaborating his personal reality. The world in which he lives and moves presents itself as though it were something independently and objectively real. The patterning and thematizing of events that uniquely characterize his personal reality are thus seen as if they were properties of those events rather than products of his own subjective interpretations and constructions. (p. 36)

Their description of intersubjective theory has applicability to the dyadic interactions that occur within couples. Thus, the focus of the couples therapist should be the multiple intersubjective fields that occur in conjoint therapy. The area of investigation of the couples therapist is the interaction between the subjective worlds of the two partners, as well as the meanings that occur at the interface of the interacting subjectivities of the therapist and each partner.

Atwood and Stolorow (1984) define the concept of an intersubjective disjunction as applied to individual therapy: "Disjunction . . . occurs when the therapist assimilates the material expressed by the patient into configurations that significantly alter its meanings for the patient. Repetitive occurrences of intersubjective disjunction . . . are inevitable accompaniments of the therapeutic process and reflect the interaction of differently organized subjective worlds" (p. 47). Thus, an understanding of countertransference must include the therapist's awareness and capacity for reflection about the unconscious principles that automatically structure inner experience.

The case to be presented was previously discussed (Trop, 1994) in an article describing intersubjectivity theory and its application to conjoint therapy. The emphasis in the present material concerns a countertransference disjunction that arose from the mobilization of the therapist's organizing principles in response to the clinical material of the couple.

JOHN AND LINDA

John and Linda came into treatment after they had been married three years. Their treatment occurred over a six-month period and they were seen one time per week. John, 50, had been promoted six months previously to an executive position of great responsibility in a large public corporation. He had worked in the company all of his professional life and had risen through the hierarchy to this position. His father had also worked in this firm and had retired several years earlier. His father had actively promoted John's entrance into the company. Linda, 38, was an Asian woman. She had quit her secretarial post at the same corporation when they had married. They had a one-year-old son, Paul, who had been very much desired and was treasured by both of them. They both had been previously married, and John had two children, a girl, 16, and a boy, 14, who came to visit them on weekends.

They came into treatment at Linda's insistence and were referred by Linda's family physician, who felt she had been depressed at her last visit.

John was opposed to coming for help because he believed that people should be able to fix their own problems. He said, however, that he wanted to improve their relationship and would try to be helpful. Linda said that she felt that their problems had begun soon after they were married. She felt that the zest and excitement that had brought them together were increasingly diminishing in their marriage. She said that her husband had been spirited and fun-loving when they had met and that now he was withdrawn and increasingly angry at her. She also felt that he had previously been very generous in his financial dealings with her and had now become restrictive and penurious. She felt that the marriage was in grave jeopardy and that there was a real crisis between them. John seemed shocked and was clearly taken aback by her sense of urgency. He said that he felt that his wife previously had been very supportive of his job demands and that she was now unrelenting in her demands that he spend more time with her. He said his experience of his wife was that she was always trying to control him. He added that previously she had not been materialistic, but that he now regarded her as increasingly superficial.

I continued over the next several sessions to explore the history of their relationship. John recounted that they had met about four and a half years ago when Linda was a secretary at the same firm. She was single at the time and John was married. He had been very depressed (about his marriage) for many years. His first wife was very unaffectionate, and he was attracted to Linda's obvious warmth and spontaneity. However, he always valued loyalty and had never even considered leaving his wife. John said that Linda had been assigned as a secretary for a project he directed and so they had spent many hours together. He was not comfortable telling me the details of their beginnings and seemed ashamed as he related them to me. I pointed out that he seemed apprehensive about how I might feel toward him.

John seemed surprised by his own response when he acknowledged that he felt I might look down on him for leaving his first wife. He hastened to add that he tried to talk to his first wife about his feelings of alienation but she dismissed his concerns as a mid-life crisis. She was devastated when he finally left the house. I could see John's pained facial expression and his concern about how I perceived what he was articulating. I clarified for him that he apparently did not feel that I would be able to see health in his wish to feel alive and vital in a relationship. I also said that I understood that he had no wish to hurt his first wife's feelings and that her pain was certainly her reaction to his leaving her and not to his intent. While this interaction with me was not central to the problems between them, it established much greater trust between John and me.

I then commented on the divergence between their two assessments of the gravity of the situation and wondered with each of them about this. Linda immediately said that she was prepared to leave the marriage. I asked what her feelings were about this, since she seemed hopeless even though we had barely begun to try to understand what was happening between them. She said that she did feel hopeless; she didn't think the situation would improve. Her husband, while listening to her, looked puzzled; I noted and commented on this, and he confirmed that he had not seen their problems as so serious and grave.

I then asked Linda if she felt that something had become extremely altered for her and perhaps she felt that he didn't care about her anymore. She began to cry and said that she indeed felt that way, that he didn't really love her. I asked him if this were true and he said absolutely not, that he certainly did love her very much.

Linda at this point looked quizzically at her husband. I said that it seemed hard for her to believe that he did really love her. I commented that if she had come to believe he did not love her, then, of course, she would feel there was a crisis in her marriage. John, however, apparently retained a conviction that both of them remained in love. He agreed and said that he sorted out problems in his job and hoped they could sort this out together.

I inquired if, in the light of this comment, he had any theory about how his wife had acquired this perception of how he felt about her. He was not sure how this had come about and asked me if I had an idea about this. I replied that I was not sure, but that we could figure it out together. At this juncture, Linda felt some relief and became warmer and more relaxed with John.

In the ensuing sessions, I continued to explore what they experienced about each other and to attempt to identify the central issues. Linda complained incessantly about her husband's increasing attention to his work and his increasingly late hours.

At this early juncture in the therapy, I became aware that my experience differed from my usual feelings about the couples I was seeing. I usually felt that I was able to identify with the struggles of both parties, to enter into their inner worlds and have an empathic grasp of their longings. In this situation, however, I felt very connected to the husband's experience of feeling impinged on at work by his wife's demands. I also began to experience the wife as shrill and demanding.

I made a mental note of my inner response and resolved to try to understand it. In the next few weeks, however, I continued to experience the wife's needs as insistent and demanding and to feel increasing sympathy for the husband. More and more my sense of affiliation with the husband seemed to be based on an accurate and objective view that the wife was immature and unable to fend for herself. I began to think of her as envious of her husband's career with an underlying motivation to thwart his ambitions. While I tried to maintain an affiliation with both parties, I found myself tilting toward rationalizing how the wife's background contributed to her need to be special.

At this time, I was having an incidental conversation with a psychiatrist friend. The friend asked how my practice was going, and I replied that it was going fine. I said that I was working too hard and intended to cut back my schedule. My friend spontaneously started laughing uproariously. I was taken aback. I asked why he was laughing, and he said that ever since he had known me he had heard my intentions to reduce my schedule and that it never happened. On this topic I sounded like a broken record.

Over the next several days, I began to think about my own attitude toward work. I gradually remembered many times when my own father was away working at night and I missed him. My own attitude toward work seemed heavily influenced by my relationship with my father, who was anxious about success and dealt with his anxiety by working very long hours. As I pondered this issue, I began to think about my own organizing principles and my own feeling of being driven. I began to be open to the possibility that John and I organized our reactions to work and ambition similarly. I began to painfully consider that I was falling short of my own articulated ideal of working less to cover over an apprehension about my own self-differentiation from my father. I felt more and more certain that this issue had shaped my tilt toward John's experience and my inability to consider the legitimacy of Linda's experience.

Thus, this interaction with my friend provided me with a perturbing perspective on my own self-definition. I reconsidered my "objective assessment" of Linda. As I painfully contemplated how this had occurred, I realized that I was in the grip of a chronic conflict between a stated wish to have a more balanced life and an underlying, archaic anxiety about taking time away from work. This was most probably the same underlying unconscious anxiety that held sway over my own father.

My awareness emerged over several weeks' time with much contemplation and considerable psychic turmoil. Once I saw my role in co-constructing my experience of Linda, I was able to be intensely interested and attuned to her experience. I clarified for her that she seemed to feel that John was more involved with his work than with her. She confirmed this and stated that when they had met they spent much more time doing activities and being together. She now felt shut out of his life. I told her that she seemed to feel that John did not care very much for her and had given her a baby to pacify her. I said that she longed for her loving husband to come back, but feared he was gone forever.

It seemed that Linda was convinced that her husband's increasing work demands meant that he did not care about her. I told her that I regarded her concerns about her husband's preoccupation with work and lack of attentiveness to her as entirely legitimate issues.

Linda began to describe a long-standing feeling of deficiency and lack of confidence. She was the only child of elderly parents. She described her mother as critical and undermining and as needing to be the focus of attention. This was particularly prominent in her mother's relationships with men. Linda said that when she began to date in high school, her mother would monopolize conversations with her boyfriends.

Her father was a businessman who was preoccupied with work. She remembered a few interactions with her father when he talked to her with energy and enthusiasm. Such conversations often concerned a business negotiation or the stock market. Even though she did not understand the details, she listened raptly and recalled her enjoyment at his aliveness in her presence. As she continued to describe her family, it became clear that, when both her parents were present, her father would focus exclusively on her mother; any deviation from this would arouse her mother's anger. Linda remembered feeling increasingly empty and devitalized when in the presence of both her parents.

It was evident from Linda's description of herself that her self-esteem had always felt precarious. She had been drawn to John because of the enthusiasm he directed toward her. John's attention had served to counteract her underlying feelings of deficiency. One of Linda's organizing principles was that she was inherently unappealing as a woman. John's initial responsiveness had evoked a hope for transforming this deficit. Her evolving inner experience was one of increasing panic and subsequent rage at her husband when she experienced him as neglecting her. She yearned for his mirroring responsiveness to her, but her interactions with him became demanding and controlling as she became increasingly hopeless. She focused on a need for material possessions as concrete proof of his interest. He reacted to these demands for material goods by becoming more withdrawn and stubborn, further reinforcing her view that he did not care for her.

I directed my comments describing my understanding of her unconscious organizing activity to both of them. I said that his wife had felt that he was spending less time with her and had interpreted this automatically as an indication of his increasing disinterest with her. Since this experience recapitulated the central and most painful themes of her childhood, she felt increasingly worthless. I told him that what he experienced as controlling and demanding was a disguised expression of a primary longing for responsiveness to her femininity. He listened intently and understood that she felt seriously undermined by him. I asked him if he had ever thought about their situation in this way and if he had any ideas how he might have exacerbated these feelings in her.

John replied that it had always been hard for him to take seriously his wife's feelings of insecurity because he, in fact, found her so attractive. His response was to joke about these feelings. He acknowledged that he had not understood how desperate she felt because *he* knew that he loved her. I asked him if it was difficult for him to express his loving feelings directly, and he quickly said yes, that expressing feelings was not the easiest thing for him. I asked him more about his family background. It emerged that his father had been a businessman like himself and that his parents' marriage was very similar to his own first marriage. He sensed the joylessness of their marriage and on one occasion remembered talking to his father about it. His father stressed that what was important in life were values like loyalty and tenacity and that marriage was work. His father said firmly that if a person made a choice, then it was his responsibility to make it work. His father was a harsh man who was always convinced that his way was the right way. John had admired his father for his power and strength and had always aspired to be strong just like him. As John talked, I experienced painful feelings regarding the similarity of our backgrounds.

I wondered with John if leaving his first marriage had been difficult because he had deviated from the concepts that had shaped his life previously and had clearly diverged from his father's moral stance. It was difficult for him to talk about this, but he said he still felt tormented about having caused his former wife and children so much pain by pursuing his own aims. He confided that recently he had begun to ruminate that indeed he might have made a mistake by marrying Linda, since she was becoming more and more angry with him.

Over several sessions, I began to explore in greater detail his work history. John's supervisor, the chief officer of the company, had begun piling more and more work on him as time passed. His hours at work had become gradually extended. I asked him how he felt about this and whether this was acceptable to him. He actually seemed shocked and puzzled by my question. I pointed this out to him and told him that he seemed confused. He said that this was a hard question for him to answer, since he did not really think about his feelings very much. He did, however, know that he did not feel that his work hours were something about which he truly had a choice.

At this juncture, I felt vitalized and emboldened as I sensed that John and I were both dealing with similar conflicts about work. I pressed him on this point and asked why he did not have a choice. He could not answer, but then spontaneously said that he did not know what he was feeling. He missed spending time with his wife, but felt stuck in his job. He felt that there was truly nothing that he could do about this situation. Thus, the unconscious principle that organized John's experience pertained to his work supervisor. His organizing principle was that he must do whatever was required to comply with the wishes of his supervisor and perform his job and sacrifice his feelings for his wife. His organizing principle of dutiful loyalty was an expression of his idealizing relationship with his father. While my difficulties in his attitude toward work had a different origin, the outcomes for me and John were similar. Both of us felt apprehensive about deviating from an old inner design when we surrendered to states of vitality outside of work.

I offered an interpretation of his underlying state, directing it to both of them, but primarily to Linda. I said that I thought that John was raised to be loyal, hardworking, and in particular to go along with whatever his superiors wanted. I also said that, as part of this configuration, John had been influenced by his father to devalue the importance of feelings of joy and excitement. I said that an organizing principle that shaped John's sense of self was that self-differentiation from his father's values was prohibited. Thus, when John fell in love with Linda, he had begun to make contact with important aspects of himself that had been prohibited within the context of his relationship with his father. It had been difficult for John to sustain confidence in the importance of these new aspects of himself when work demands began to escalate and he began automatically to comply with the demands of his supervisor. John nodded enthusiastically and said my comments were absolutely correct.

This interpretation was of great importance to both of them, but especially relieving for Linda. She said that it was essential for her to hear that his increasing preoccupation with work was a product of a conflict he had about his own ideals for himself. She began to understand that he truly wanted to be with her, but that being able to refuse his superior's request for more work was a source of wrenching conflict for him. She was able to decenter from her initial response and became more attuned to her husband's underlying struggle.

Over time, John continued to work on the issues related to his differentiation from his father. He requested individual therapy and was referred to another therapist. He ruefully confided to me that he knew he was not the most likely candidate for therapy when I had first seen him. Gradually, he was able to free himself of the need to comply with the demands of his supervisor and was able to assert his own needs at work. This involved an intense inner struggle, because he knew that limiting his work time would impede his advancement in his company. He also worked at feeling more comfortable articulating loving and affectionate feelings toward his wife.

Linda was increasingly able to see her husband's turmoil as a manifestation of his own conflicts. She also gained greater awareness of her tendency automatically to organize any inattentiveness on his part as an indication of her unacceptability as a woman. She understood that her feelings of unattractiveness did not correspond to *his* experience of her. Her feelings were instead a remnant of the repetitive rejection of her needs for responsiveness from her father. John also was able to see clearly that his wife's attempts to control him were expressions of panic about not being found lovable and he tried to be more directly affirming and affectionate. They mutually decided to end the therapy because they both felt they had revived the spirit of their earlier time together.

Discussion

During the early moments of this conjoint therapy, I found myself deviating from a stance of mutual understanding. I felt judgmental and disdainful toward the wife's concerns and driven to pathologize her experience. Through an inadvertent exchange with a colleague, I became aware of the dynamics that underlay my reaction. My countertransference arose because of an unconscious organizing principle about feeling safe and secure by throwing myself into work. This organizing principle arose in the context of a relationship with my father but led to a constriction of my own capacity for joyful use of leisure time. Thus, countertransference from an intersubjective vantage point involved the automatic mobilization of an unconscious organizing principle similar to the husband's. It was only by engaging in a painful process of self-reflection that I was able to recapture an empathic perspective toward both parties.

As a consequence of my understanding of countertransference, both spouses in this treatment were helped to become aware of the unique, unconscious, and invariant principles that organized their own experience and that of their partner. Thus, each partner developed significant understanding of the interacting organizing principles that co-determined their marital problems.

Linda's organizing principle was that no man would find her enduringly appealing. When she met her future husband, his warmth helped her temporarily to overcome her organizing principle and feel more vitality as a woman. John's subsequent withdrawal into work was automatically assimilated by her as an indication of her flawed self. In her efforts to repair her narcissistic injury, she became critical and controlling.

John's primary organizing principle was a product of his difficulty in differentiating from his father's ideals. He automatically complied with demands of authority figures at work and ignored his own needs to feel vital and alive. His father's ideals involved being dutiful and hardworking and valuing loyalty and compliance. Hence, for John, experiences of joy and excitement were unconsciously experienced as a threat to his tie with his father. Linda's vitality and humor had awakened in him a buried capacity for an intense attachment. Thus, Linda initially had helped him transcend his archaic organizing principles and begin to resume his emotional development. However, in the face of increasing work demands by superiors, his newfound and precariously established capacity for affective vitality began to be eroded.

In addition, I became aware of a central conflict in my attitude toward work. From a systems perspective, all three parties reformulated aspects of developmental longings that had previously been disowned in order to maintain the stability of original family systems.

References

Atwood, G., & Stolorow, R. (1984). *Structures of subjectivity: Explorations in psychoanalytic phenomenology.* Hillsdale, NJ: Analytic Press.

Atwood, G., Stolorow, R., & Trop, J. (1989). Impasses in psychoanalytic therapy: A royal road. *Contemporary Psychoanalysis, 25,* 554–573.

Lachkar, J. (1985). Narcissistic/borderline couples: Theoretical implications for treatment. *Dynamic Psychotherapy, 3*(2), 109–125.

Ringstrom, P. (1994). An intersubjective approach to conjoint therapy. In A. Goldberg (Ed.), *Progress in self psychology* (Vol. X). Hillsdale, NJ: Analytic Press.

Solomon, M. (1988). Self psychology and marital relationships. *International Journal of Family Psychiatry, 9*(3), 211–226.

Solomon, M. (1994). *Lean on me: The power of positive dependency in intimate relationships.* New York: Simon & Schuster.

Trop, J. (1994). Conjoint therapy: An intersubjective approach. In A. Goldberg (Ed.), *Progress in self psychology* (Vol. X). Hillsdale, NJ: Analytic Press.

SECTION II

Countertransference in Practice

7

Transference and Countertransference in Clinical Interventions with Divorcing Families

JUDITH S. WALLERSTEIN

TRANSFERENCE AND COUNTERTRANSFERENCE responses significantly shape process and outcome in all psychological interventions. These responses are especially salient in clinical interventions with a divorce population, where displacements from the present crisis as well as from the past profoundly influence the reactions of both clinician and patient. Although families in the throes of divorce constitute a substantial portion of the population in treatment, the special nature of the perceptions and relationships that emerge at this critical time remains largely unexplored. Yet, it has been informally acknowledged for several years that there are aspects of these relationships that inflict a heavy emotional toll on the clinician.

The observations that provided the basis for this chapter came from my clinical supervision over an eight-year period of experienced clinicians working with families at a freestanding divorce counseling center in Northern California. My purpose here is twofold: (1) to turn the searchlight on the therapist in order to identify some of the common countertransferences that occur during the immediate aftermath of the marital rupture and to delineate their intrapsychic and interpersonal parameters; and (2) to show that these countertransference responses are not merely rooted in the idiosyncratic past of the therapist, or even primarily responses to transferences that draw on the patient's early experiences—rather, they can and often do reflect reactions to the patient's crisis-driven transferences, as well as to the specific nature of the divorce crisis. These interactions, which derive pri-

marily from the present, can evoke intense anxieties and unexpectedly powerful feelings in the clinician.

This expanded view of transference to include displacements from the
present, and of countertransference to encompass the sum of the clinician's
responses to the patient, is in keeping with advancing formulations of psychoanalytic theory. It is clearly in line with the widened dyadic conceptualization of the transference as realized by Gill (1955), in which the patient's
transferences, fueled by the experiences of the past, are shaped by the
perceptions of the clinical experience into a plausible construal of meanings
and affective responses in the current interaction. It is in keeping as well
with Sandler's (1976) emphasis on the clinician's countertransference urge
to assume a role that will play out the predetermined scenario of external
and internal object relationships that are held within the patient's unconscious transference expectations. Making an analogy to the transformed
perceptions of the transference, originally considered to be a hindrance and
now recognized as the central vehicle of treatment, Sandler noted that
countertransference, which had originally been regarded as a hindrance,
has now become widely recognized as an important aspect of the therapist's
understanding and capacity.

In Orr's (1954) now classic formulation of the range of countertransference responses, three main areas were demarcated: (1) the specific responses
of the therapist evoked by the patient's transferences or, as he put it, "countertransference proper"; (2) the responses to the patient generated out of
the therapist's experiences and disposition as a whole — the therapist's transferences to the patient; and finally, (3) the specific responses of the therapist, also generated out of his or her experiences and disposition, to the
therapeutic activity itself, namely, the variety of controlling, competitive,
voyeuristic, sadistic, exhibitionistic, or nurturing impulses gratified in the
therapist by virtue of playing the central role in someone else's life. Related
to this last set of responses are the reactions of the therapist evoked by the
particular circumstances of the patient population. (An impressive example
is Eissler's [1955] delineation of the characteristic interplay of transferences
and countertransferences specific to therapy with dying patients.) This third
aspect of countertransference has particular relevance to psychotherapy
with families in the throes of marital breakdown.

COUNTERTRANSFERENCES TO THE MARITAL BREAKDOWN

All human relationships are echoed to some degree in the clinician's own
life experiences. It is, in fact, precisely out of the clinician's capacity to
resonate to the patient's experience that the psychotherapeutic bond is created. Nevertheless, the relationships between men and women, the passions

of love, hate, sexual jealousy, and fear of loneliness, are particularly likely to engage the emotions of the clinician who works with divorce. The paradigm situation in this work is the spectacle of two adults who may still be legally married to each other, one (or both) of whom is trying to hurt or even destroy the other. The reversal of love into hate, the collapse of the idealized good object and the emergence of the bad object in its place are frightening to observe at close range. Moreover, there is little evidence that one becomes inured to the pain of witnessing a marriage as it draws to its unfortunate end. As one supervisee put it, "Here are two people who at one time loved each other, had sex together, touched each other, caressed each other, and all of this has turned now to hating each other. It makes me despair that there is no enduring love in the world, nothing to count on, no reliability in human relationships."

Such observations inevitably evoke anxiety in the clinician. For who among us is immune to the mundane conflicts of marriage, the difficulties in sustaining intimacy, the minor and major lapses in all marriages that inevitably threaten the continuity of relationships? Although the roots may extend far back into childhood, the problems that the divorcing person brings are by their very nature problems that all of us address daily—the love/hate, dependence/independence issues in relationships between adult men and women. The concerns that they raise, whatever their childhood roots, are the questions of adulthood: Will love endure, and under what conditions? Will I be alone or will we be together? Can I trust him (her)? Will he (she) betray me? Will he (she) be there when my need is the greatest? And from common questions such as these, as in those questions that arise in work with the bereaved, the therapist has no inherent defense and inevitably remains open, vulnerable to suffering and beset with anxiety.

Moreover, the clinician inevitably has had personal experiences that bear directly on these concerns. Observing the unhappy couple can evoke childhood memories of conflict between the clinician's own parents. It can inflame fresher wounds, closely related to the patient's experience in the present: an unhappy love affair, a troubled marriage, a recent or ongoing divorce, a divorce within the close family, related experiences of separation, prolonged illness, or bereavement. It can reinforce as well an existential sense of the limits to life and to all relationships. In my experience over the years, there was no single supervisee in divorce work who did not contemplate his or her own relationships with new, typically intense anxiety. Resolution varied for each of these clinicians according to his or her history and circumstance. Sometimes a clinician would address the anxiety by affirming personal ties. One supervisee volunteered, "I feel much more secure about my own marriage since I have been working here." Others emphatically denied anxiety or even connectedness. One therapist told me, "I'm glad I'm not married, so I don't have to worry. I'm not even in a relationship." My supervision of a clinician who was undergoing her own divorce while working with this population was for her, and for me, a most painful professional experience.

In trying to understand these common responses, one is struck by the extraordinary lack of psychological distance between therapist and patient, and the ease with which identifications move back and forth across the therapeutic interface. One is constantly aware of the oscillations taking place within the clinician — the fluidity, the transitory resting of these identifications with child, with mother, with father, with parts of former and present self. It is inevitable that the person who comes seeking help, whether bruised or suffering from abandonment and betrayal, who is feeling rejection, loneliness, or even relief, is experienced by the therapist as a potential double. "There but for the grace of God go I" is the perception of the therapist in this psychological pas de deux. On a primitive level, the countertransference can be phobic: "Will I catch it? Will it happen to me?" On a more sublimated level, the response follows a more logical sequence, but the outcome is the same: "If indeed such a tragedy can happen to this attractive, well-educated competent man (or woman), why not to me?"

There is a further aspect to the countertransference response of the therapist. However one resolves the conflicts that have been evoked, there are psychic consequences that soon become evident in the countertransference. Therapists who achieve psychological distance by counting their blessings may have achieved resolution at an unexpected price, finding that they feel newly vulnerable to the possibility of future loss, to the guilt of being emotionally well fed among the hungry, to the patient's transference envy, to the primitive "evil eye." Alternatively, the therapist who overidentifies with the suffering patient may become depressed and continue to relive past or current personal losses.

These conflicts, along with defensive maneuvers that are brought into play by them, are likely to endure throughout the entire course of the intervention. They constitute the core countertransference responses to this work and to this population as a whole.

COUNTERTRANSFERENCES TO THE DIMINISHED PARENTING

I turn now to countertransferences specific to circumstances in the divorce population, i.e., those evoked by the striking deterioration in parent-child relationships that follows so frequently in the wake of divorce. At the height of the crisis the clinician confronts many instances, such as those described by Wallerstein and Blakeslee (1989), of diminished parenting among previously devoted parents. These changes often elicit a combination of anguish and impotent rage in the clinician. Their emotional impact is powerful because clinicians who choose to work with families are especially sensitive to the suffering of children. For reasons often rooted in their own early histories, they are eager, sometimes driven, to rescue the child. This work often intensifies their inner conflicts by reinforcing the rescue fantasy, at the same time rendering it painful to sustain and almost impossible to implement within acceptable roles.

In one common scenario, a parent who was close to the children during the marriage turns abruptly away, refusing contact out of a need to escape painful feelings, out of the excitement of a new love affair, out of anger at the other parent — out of a complex mixture of conscious and unconscious motives. The children are, of course, bewildered and frightened by this sudden rejection. Lacking ways of assuaging their hurt or of defending themselves against the threat of abandonment, they typically locate the cause of their loss in their own imagined unlovableness.

Recognizing the psychological source of the parent's behavior, which may include a severe underlying depression, does not prevent the therapist from identifying with the grieving child and suffering on his/her behalf. Inevitably, the clinician experiences intense anger at the parent along with compassion for the child (and sometimes compassion for the parent as well). These feelings draw on early identifications and archaic feelings of love and hate that the clinician experienced as a child with his or her own parents. In the complex morality play that is enacted within the clinician's inner world, the therapist becomes simultaneously both the victim child and the "good parent" who rescues the child. For each protagonist, the therapist takes on in heroic fantasy the role that has been lost. The therapist speaks for the child who cannot speak for herself and for the "good parent" in lieu of one or both of the real parents who are failing to perceive or relieve the child's suffering.

Intense internal countertransference conflicts are generated in all clinical work with children who are neglected, exploited, or abused. In many instances, legal and protective resources are available, however insufficient these may be. But, in the threatened emotional and physical abandonment that is part and parcel of divorce, the therapist is entirely dependent on clinical skill (Wallerstein, 1985). Perhaps of even greater moment is the fact that, in the general population, most poor parent-child relationships that come to therapy show long-standing difficulties. In divorcing families, the rejection of the child is more likely to represent an abrupt change, which the clinician experiences as occurring before his or her eyes. Thus, once again, the clinician is brought face to face not only with the inconstancy of human relationships — even in the parent's attachment to the child — but also with the enactment by a parent of that core childhood terror, the threat of abandonment. Often the clinician is burdened with what may be the accurate realization that he or she is the only one in this situation who is aware of the child's suffering and the risks posed to the child's future psychological development.

Such issues are commonplace in this work. Their power to move the therapist does not necessarily diminish with experience, and in fact the reverse may occur: the therapist may experience cumulative anxiety, irritability, and depression, intensified by physical fatigue and a sense of depletion that can provoke a strong impulse to take flight and avoid further professional contact with this demanding population.

COUNTERTRANSFERENCES TO THE PATIENT'S TRANSFERENCES

Here, I want to consider the significance of the divorcing patient's transferences and the linked countertransferences of the therapist. By Sandler's (1976) definition, transference constitutes a major resistance to psychological change, representing an unconscious attempt to manipulate the therapist into taking on a particular role relationship within the clinical encounter. This phenomenon has been more difficult to isolate, or even to discern, in divorce work because of the conscious, sometimes very vigorous, efforts of many patients to enlist the therapist as an ally both in and outside of the therapeutic arena. These conscious agendas can obscure the unconscious transference.

There are many transferences that are characteristically brought into the interaction with the therapist at the outset. Perhaps the most troublesome transferences for the clinician are those evident among patients whose primary response to the marital rupture is ego-syntonic rage at the former partner. Many of these patients have been severely traumatized by the events of the separation. Haunted by memories and flashbacks of humiliation, they are driven to a continued replaying of the divorce scenario in the hope of regaining mastery and rewriting the last act. In many instances they feel truly helpless to control or modulate their anger or to alter the fixation of their projections. Intense fear of their own aggression, as well as the projected or real aggression of the other, propels them along a destructive, and self-destructive, path. In one common countertransference phrase that is used widely, they have been called "hostility junkies."

The responses of one senior clinician under my supervision sheds light on the deep-seated and primitive countertransference fears that are triggered in response to the irrationality, the severe psychopathology, and the hidden violence of the patient's transferences.

Mr. R., the patient, an attractive man who was competent in many domains of his life, had been in and out of litigation for many years over his children. He was referred by the court after court-mandated mediation continued to fail. His history was both tragic and familiar. He had returned home after a routine business trip and was astonished to find that his wife and child had vanished. He located them only after a frantic search of several weeks' duration. This patient's persistent rage, his inability to consider compromise, and his search for retribution were rooted in his consuming need to master the enduring wretchedness of that homecoming, to repair the severe narcissistic injury that he had sustained, to reestablish control, and ultimately, as the supervisee said, "to become whole again." Never one to temporize, after his wife's abandonment he became locked for years into a rigid combative stance.

From the outset of his contact with the clinician, Mr. R. barely tolerated her uttering a single word, while he recounted his "story" in detail at each meeting. The implicit threat conveyed by his loud, agitated tone and bearing was "Watch your step! You can be my ally as long as I am in control. As soon as you take an independent position, you are the enemy."

The supervisee speaks: "I was scared. I know that his anger, which had not diminished over the years, scared me. The irrationality scared me, and the fact that he was flushed and physically agitated. I probably responded to the erotic quality of the flushing, and I tried to be charming, hoping that he would calm down. I know that I tend to deny physical danger, but unconsciously I'm sure I felt threatened by the always present possibility that he would explode and become violent. But what bothered me most was that I felt he had wiped me out. All the time I was with him, I felt threatened with annihilation — that was the central issue. He kept conveying in his entire manner that I was worthless as a person, and helpless as a professional. I guess this is my problem, but I couldn't help but wonder if he was right.

"I tried to cushion my anxiety by including his wife and children in some of our interviews. There was some benefit to this, although I worried all the time about his insensitivity to his children. But the truth is that it was easier for me to have them there, so that I was not his only target. I was eventually able to help him, and them, quite a lot, but even so he could accept my help only by denying my role. He agreed to a very different kind of arrangement with the children, out of court, which was not bad at all, but he rudely ordered me out of his life at termination. I think, now, that once he saw his wife in a better light, I became the bad object, and he retained control."

The transferences are already in place as the patient enters the consulting room. A fantasy, triangular conflict shapes the transference and defines the clinician within it: "Are you for me? Or are you for him (her)? Will you judge for me, or for him (her)? And, if you are for me, will you do as I say?" Although the therapist is inevitably perceived as judge, this provides very little leverage because the patient cannot conceive of neutrality and is therefore incapable of perceiving it in the transference. Or, if it is perceived, neutrality is associated with impotence. Sharp dichotomies dominate the patient's field of vision and the relationship with the therapist: control or be controlled, triumph or be vanquished, and ultimately, at its most primitive level, prevail or die.

The central countertransference of the clinician, namely, the fear of annihilation, provides the key to the primitive psychological roots of the transference and illuminates the highly disturbed psychological functioning of the patient. For the clinician is not reacting with the kind of anxiety that is aroused in a relationship with a neurotic patient, but with a much greater, far more primitive fear of personal and professional annihilation. The transference bears a striking resemblance to the malevolent and persecutory transferences that are projected by paranoid characters and psychotic patients. Such transferences pose a potent threat to the psychological stability and integrity of the clinician. They are often perceived in the countertransference as threatening psychic annihilation. The severe psychopathology in the patient is not readily apparent to the clinician, because the patient's history often provides a logical accounting for the attitudes and feelings that are expressed. In many such instances, the psychopathology becomes visible most clearly through the prism of the countertransference.

The irrationality of so much of the patient's thinking is especially frightening when it is coupled to intense ego-syntonic anger. However much the clinician may deny fear — and in my experience, such denial is common — irrationality is inevitably associated with the possibility that the patient will lose control. The experienced clinician knows that this is a realistic aspect of divorce work — that the anger not only serves to ward off the patient's depression, but also to diminish the voice of conscience. It can also impair both the patient's and clinician's capacity for reality-testing and judgment. There is in all of this work a potential for violence, either turned back upon itself, aimed at other members of the family, or turned against the community. Moreover, as the clinician also knows, the patient may well embark on violence with full recognition, even a full embrace of the consequences, as in murder followed by suicide. Inevitably, considerable anxiety and intense anger are attached to the realization of this potential violence. Typical countertransference defenses are the repression or denial of these realistic fears and anger. As a result, their influence may be even greater. It is not surprising, considering the power of these conflicts, that many therapists feel drawn to join in the fray, in order to resolve the anxiety of being caught at midpoint between dangerous antagonists and feeling safe nowhere. Indeed, the impulse to take sides is one of the major countertransference hazards in divorce work with high-conflict families, especially because the courts can provide a legitimate arena for their struggles.

Paradoxically, both the anger and the fear, if acknowledged and kept within limits, represent the clinician's accurate and appropriate responses to the patient's projections and reflect a realistic assessment of the patient's transferences. Without these countertransferences, the clinician's ego boundaries and reality-testing would be even more severely shaken. As Winnicott (1958) has suggested, one rarely noted benefit of the countertransference is that anger and fear can be helpful to the clinician in maintaining his or her psychological stability and capacity to work effectively in the face of the severe psychological assaults of threatening transferences.

GENDER AND TRANSFERENCE

The gender of patient and therapist has particular relevance in this work, as becomes apparent in the transferences of the patient and the countertransference responses of the clinician. This is so because one response to the anger or disappointment of the failed marriage is to generalize from this man to all men, or from this woman to all women, so that the patient's certainty becomes, for example, that women betray, men abandon. Or men betray, women abandon. Such transferences can be simultaneously infused with erotic, hostile, and vengeful elements. They are unconsciously designed to evoke countertransferences that will reinforce the transference expectations of being hurt and the hope of being healed. Sometimes the patient is seeking to recapture the capacity to experience any emotion or sexual excitement, to remedy the sense of "feeling dead inside" that is often reported in the aftermath of divorce.

I note here only a few instances, drawn from my supervisory experience, of the importance of the gender of the therapist in this work, especially in understanding the transferences and countertransferences that dominate the relationship at the outset. One supervisee, a young, attractive man, was taken aback at the number of women patients of all ages who made seductive overtures to him. He told me that, while he was initially flattered by the open invitations, the coy messages left for him on the telephone, the intrusive questions about his weekend plans, he was inevitably put off by his sense that these advances were neither loving nor genuinely erotic, but were, in fact, hostile, demanding, and controlling. He felt angry at being punished for something another man had done while being called upon, at the same time, to undo the patient's hurt and reverse the scenario. He also reported that he was very anxious in response to what he felt to be the desperation underlying the seductive gestures, and by his sense that after they left his office, these women, especially the older ones, were acutely embarrassed by their own behavior, which they experienced as ego-alien, but which they felt helpless to control.

Both in the men and in the women seen at the Center, the need to seek restitution in the therapeutic relationship for the narcissistic hurt of the divorce was a powerful element of the transference. The response of male patients to the women clinicians, however, was somewhat different from the response of female patients to men clinicians. Whereas some men flirted, their behavior, even when mocking and demeaning, generally lacked the same harsh undertones. Their approach was less driven, less overtly sexual, and less hostile, although no less needy. Many men who had been rejected by their wives, or who felt guilty about leaving the marriage, were especially responsive to what they perceived as the gentleness and acceptance of the woman clinician. This was particularly important for men who were unaccustomed to talking about their feelings and for whom the expression of sadness was alien.

A particular kind of interaction that takes place between women patients and women therapists has specific relevance in divorce work. There is often a sense of close kinship, of "sisterhood is powerful," an expectation that another woman will quickly understand the hurt and join the phalanx against "men who misuse women." This very quick "sisterly" transference provides the woman clinician with a point of immediate entry, a straight "woman-to-woman" tone that can be extremely effective, although the hazard of reinforcing hostility toward men is a serious one and the general danger of consolidating the patient-therapist bond on an anti-men basis is a critical countertransference issue. (It should also be noted that, although a degree of camaraderie can be achieved between a male clinician and a male patient, the same kind of instant, intense "brotherly" transference and countertransference responses are relatively rare between men.)

There is, however, often a strong negative underside — whether conscious or unconscious — to these sisterly transferences. It is not unusual for the woman who feels helpless and abandoned to indicate, in subtle or direct ways, that in her (fantasy) view the female therapist has a man, a good job, children, and a secure social position, while she has none of these. Although these transferences are rooted in early relationships between mother and child, and in both positive and competitive sibling relationships, they also are governed by the triangle — a perception of the therapist as "the other woman" who has, or will take, what the patient has lost. Moreover, they are also embedded in the painful betrayal experiences of the present crisis. "You look just like the woman he left me for," said one woman angrily.

The countertransferences to these transferences are no less powerful. The identification with the therapist as a comrade in arms decreases the distance between clinician and patient and increases in the clinician the power of the hazardous notion, "There but for the grace of God go I." The fantasy in the transference, that the clinician possesses what the patient has lost, increases the countertransference guilt and anxiety over having too much or the countertransference fantasy of triumph, of being secure, of indeed having what the patient has lost.

CONCLUSION

The relationship between the clinician and the individual patient or family is shaped by transferences and countertransferences that have their roots in the divorce matrix of the present as well as in the respective developmental histories brought by the protagonists to the clinical interaction. The final scenes of the failed marriage are played out in the consulting room not only in the painful content of the verbal interactions but, just as importantly, in the transference reactions of the patient caught up in the crisis and in the subsequent countertransference responses of the clinician. Despite all efforts, the clinician cannot easily maintain the professional and personal equanimity that is more readily maintained in a psychotherapy that proceeds at a more measured tempo.

In working with divorcing families, the clinician is engaged emotionally from the start, not only because of the intense and sometimes archaic transferences of the patient but also by virtue of the fact that divorce work necessarily touches central issues in the clinician's own life. The relative unfamiliarity of clinicians who currently work with many of the special subgroups of this population (due to the fact that much professional training does not include them within its scope and also because psychological knowledge is still limited) increases the clinician's vulnerability to countertransference responses.

Central to our understanding is the full appreciation of how transferences and their linked countertransferences derive so importantly from the here and now of the divorce crisis, however much they also build upon earlier life experiences. It is in this context that the displacements that I call "transferences from the present" take their place conceptually. They are, perhaps, always in force to some degree and are not unique to the divorce experience, but it is certain that their intensity and ubiquity are at the core of the divorce experience. Similarly, the clinician's countertransference responses can be seen as plausible constructions of a present situation impinged upon by dispositions and vulnerabilities that derive from the past. It is this broadened conception of the nature of the transference-countertransference matrix that is crucial to our understanding of the special experience of divorce and to the fashioning of our clinical stance and intervention strategies.

REFERENCES

Eissler, K. R. (1955). *The psychiatrist and the dying patient*. New York: International Universities Press.

Gill, M. M. (1955). *Analysis of transference* (Psychological Issues Monograph No. 53). New York: International Universities Press.

Orr, D. W. (1954). Transference and countertransference: A historical survey. *Journal of the American Psychoanalytic Association, 2*, 62–670.

Sandler, J. (1976). Countertransference and role-responsiveness. *International Review of Psychoanalysis, 3*, 43–47.

Wallerstein, J. S. (1985). Changes in parent-child relationships during and after divorce. In E. J. Anthony & G. H. Pollock (Eds.), *Parental influences: In health and disease* (pp. 317–347). Boston: Little, Brown.

Wallerstein, J. S., & Blakeslee, S. (1989). *Second chances: Men, women and children a decade after divorce*. New York: Ticknor & Fields.

Winnicott, D. W. (1958). Hate in the countertransference. In *Collected papers: Through pediatrics to psycho-analysis* (pp. 194–203). New York: Basic.

8

Envy in the Countertransference

JOEL JAY WEST   JOAN SCHAIN-WEST

ENVY IS frequently viewed by many as an insidious, pernicious, and destructive emotion. Its consequences are obvious, but its subtlety is not. Many of the emotions underlying defenses such as idealization, avoidance, denial, devaluation, and contempt are rooted in envy. In this regard, the therapist is not spared. However, because envy of patients, when acted upon, is considered so shameful and unprofessional, there is great reluctance even on the part of supervisors to routinely consider its role in the treatment relationship. The association of envy with shame and guilt likewise contributes to the therapist's reluctance to raise the issue in consultation, supervision, or even self-discovery. The unconscious nature of most envious feelings adds to the difficulty in bringing them to light. These issues should alert us to the importance of considering and confronting countertransference envy as a routine aspect of self-awareness. When contaminating the work with an individual or a couple, it can set one partner against the other or even destroy the relationship.

It has been said that a patient's psychological development rarely goes beyond that of his therapist. Why should this be so? Therapists are aware of many healthy and desirable traits that they are unable to attain for themselves. Is it possible that they do not promote, support, or encourage such traits in patients in a conscious or unconscious attempt to ward off their own feelings of envy? We believe that, as therapists, we are insufficiently alert to the ways in which our own envy in the countertransference can derail or limit therapeutic effectiveness.

LITERATURE REVIEW

There is a notable dearth of literature focusing specifically on countertransference envy, although a great deal has been written about both envy and countertransference. Winnicott's seminal article "Hate in the Countertransference" (1949) was ground-breaking, in that it described this therapist's feelings of murderous rage toward a young boy about whom he had the best intentions. Winnicott is open and honest in the article; more importantly, he is open and honest with the boy. He states that he would have lost his temper and hit the boy had he not known about his hate; he let the boy know about it as well. Here we have an early description of a therapist reaching down to very primitive feelings in himself and using them to preserve the treatment relationship. Although Winnicott is not addressing the emotion of envy per se, the shame and guilt associated with hateful feelings toward a patient make this article relevant and timely for our purposes.

Allphin (1982), in "Envy in the Transference and Countertransference," is equally self-revealing, in that she describes envying her patient's ability to stamp her foot and do whatever she wanted, even threaten to throw over the therapy after the therapist had worked so hard to help her. Allphin goes on to describe a dramatic change in the treatment process resulting from the therapist's awareness of countertransference envy. The awareness enabled her to listen to the patient more empathically. This allowed the patient's rage to surface in the therapy, thereby becoming accessible to interpretations.

In his early book on transference and countertransference Racker (1968) points out that the therapist can be alerted to countertransference envy by the "invariable sign of neurotic reaction—anxiety." He suggests to the therapist, "postponing communicating any interpretation, if possible, until he has analyzed his state and overcome it."

In *Between Analyst and Patient: New Dimensions in Countertransference and Transference*, edited by Helen C. Meyers (1986), McDougall addresses envy as it relates to the female analyst's psychosocial development, but she does not address it as it relates to the treatment relationship. In the same text, Kernberg focuses extensively upon the impact of the patient's aggression toward the therapist but not the reverse. Kernberg (1992) later addresses the issue of envy in "the couple" and makes an interesting link between envy, aggression, and sexuality, believing that spouses' ambivalent feelings toward each other can be expressed sexually, thus protecting their love relationship. This concept can be very useful in couples therapy; however, he does not directly address countertransference concerns. Nevertheless, envy of a couple's sexual activity can blind a therapist to underlying issues, such as using sex as a defense against intimacy and closeness.

In "Countertransference Triumphs and Catastrophes" Giovacchini (1989) describes countertransference as a "ubiquitous phenomenon," but he does not address the issue of envy specifically. Nor does Natterson (1991), although his excellent discussion of the true and false self suggests that any form of aggression that is "split off" and disavowed results in an "essentially a reduced self." This implies a reduction in the capacities of any of us who are unable to integrate negative as well as positive feelings — envy is usually considered a negative emotion.

There can be positive value in the therapist's envy, provided he or she seeks the value of it and does not just act on it thoughtlessly. Recognizing our feelings of envy can alert us to what we are doing to ourselves. For example, when we feel envious, we are attacking our capacity to enjoy the satisfaction of our role in treatment (West, 1995). It can also help us understand what we are doing to or withholding from the patient, such as making poorly timed interpretations, lacking focus, or withholding support or encouragement. It can deepen our understanding of the patient, as pointed out by Spero and Mester (1998), who note that envy is frequently stimulated by needs in the patient that resonate with similar ones in the therapist.

Searles (1979), in working with severely regressed patients at Chestnut Lodge, frequently encountered envious feelings in himself in response to patients' lack of concerns, their "delicious freedom," and "inordinately unrepressed fantasy life." At times, he states, he felt like a totally responsible nursemaid to an utterly carefree child, but "this child of his, unlike other children, is of adult size and playfully assaults him with not only small child demands, but also the demands of, at times, a most lustful and aggressive fellow adult." Searles is ruthlessly open with his readers but, curiously, not with his patients. Likewise, Epstein and Feiner (1979) suggest "keeping a low profile" with patients in order to avoid stimulating their envy, but they do not recommend reporting one's own envious feelings.

It is interesting that two leading intersubjectivity theorists, Stolorow (Stolorow, Brandchaft, & Atwood, 1987) and Natterson (Natterson, 1991), have not listed envy in their subject index. Natterson (Natterson & Friedman, 1995) implies the arousal of his own envy when he discusses the impact of his childhood poverty on his work as well as his awareness when a patient's "sophistication in areas of art, music, and theater" exceeds his own. Natterson states, "This asymmetry has often been felt by me, and, I am sure, by him." In this case, it is unclear how the asymmetry was handled in the therapy. Since intersubjectivity includes all the feelings that are aroused between patient and therapist, it is surprising that little appears in the intersubjectivity literature.

Kernberg (1992) has written extensively about aggression in the couple relationship, relating it to oedipal competitiveness as well as preoedipal jealousy and envy. He notes the "rivalry and activation of reversed triangularization"—that is, "the fantasy end wish for oedipal revenge by introducing a third party into a love relationship and thus threatening one's love object with a rival." We can hypothesize that the potential for triangular oedipal jealousy and preoedipal two-person envy can easily be stirred up in working with couples; feelings like "I would like to have what he is giving his partner," or "Does he really deserve all that patience and attention?" or "I would be nicer to him than that." Needless to say, such feelings interfere with focus on the couple at best and are competitive and destructive at worst.

It is our belief that unconscious countertransference envy may be responsible for certain unexplainable treatment failures. Envy is so noxious to us that denial is often operative.

ISSUES CREATING ENVY

The most obvious issues that can arouse or generate envy in the therapist are the patient's youth, beauty, intelligence, wealth, fame, friends, children, possessions, or creativity. Less obvious sources of envy are the patient's relationship capacities, such as the ability to be connected, involved, and committed, as well as to be loving and lovable. The patient's ability to be dependent, to be playful, frivolous, flexible, carefree, or free to be irresponsible (unlike the very responsible therapist) can also be envied, along with the patient's capacity for fun. Other common traits that may stimulate envy are independence, autonomy, assertiveness, and ease in standing up for oneself. Envy can be particularly insidious when the patient's goals for his life are different from those of the therapist for the patient or the therapist for himself.

CLINICAL EXAMPLE

Dave and Erica, a newly married couple, both 26 years of age, came for therapy because of difficulty agreeing on a major life-style decision confronting them. Dave thought he wanted a "low-key job" outside of the city in which he could escape "the rat race" he saw his father running. Erica was confused and unable to offer the support her husband needed in his quest.

Dave had performed well in college and orginally had plans to pursue a professional career like his father. However, after graduation he began to adopt an alternative lifestyle. He explored oriental religions, meditation, and Buddhist philosophy. Therapeutic investigation uncovered his lifelong feeling of pressure to conform to his father's controlling attitudes. His mother, brother, and he had all struggled with the obsessional and self-righteous style of his professionally successful father. His brother had been diligent and was viewed as the good son, while the patient had always seemed to his father to be lazy and insufficiently disciplined. His mother had been more emotionally attuned to him, but seemed incapable of defending him against his father's contemptuous attitude. Much of his personality appeared to be based on angry opposition to his father's pressure.

While Erica did not overtly reject her husband's wishes, she urged him to try the well-paying job his father had lined up for him "so he would really know" what he wanted. Upon exploration, her stance proved to be largely a result of the long-standing feelings of insecurity and anxiety originating in her childhood. She had been a compliant child with a seriously depressed mother who required frequent hospitalizations. The mother's chronic illness had imbued the household with a sense of gloom, doom, and imminent disaster. There were financial problems, frequent separations, and guilt induced by the harried father whenever his daughter expressed needs or opinions of her own. The father explained that he was "only trying to hold it together." His daughter felt like anything she did "out of step" would not only rock the boat but capsize it. Thus, in her marriage, Erica was unable to overcome her own anxiety about security and offer emotional support to her husband.

During our work together Dave began conventional employment with encouragement from Erica and myself. However, it soon became evident that he chaffed under the pressure to perform to the expectations of his superiors. Despite numerous interpretations that the anger he felt at his father's pressure was now being transferred onto his bosses, his wife, or me, he continued to question why he should have a lifestyle that he resented. I began to wonder whether his stance should not be given more serious thought. I had to question whether I was attempting to impose a set of values and a life-style that suited his professional father, his wife, and myself, but did not suit this patient. Was I envious of his freedom to lead a more relaxed life without the demands for achievement and recognition that I had expected of myself? Was I envious of his freedom to not conform to the expectations of his father or of society? After considerable soul searching and conferencing, I felt I had to support the development of a self that was uniquely the patient's, even if it did not meet with my own ideas about fulfillment of his potential. I was then better able to explore issues with Erica that needed attention. Did she want to be a strong supportive partner? If so, as she claimed, what obstacles stood in her way? She recognized the origin of her need for security at all costs, as well as her tendency to be passive and compliant instead of forceful in supporting the choice that would make her husband happy. She was then able to better manage her anxiety and modify her response to her husband's decisions.

A year after leaving therapy, Dave wrote with pride that he was now the caretaker of a nature preserve and felt pleased with his life. He added that he felt quite satisfied with the self-realization he had achieved in therapy and that his wife was enjoying their lifestyle as much as he was.

In this instance considerable self-examination led me to the awareness that what I might consider realization of this patient's potential may have been an envious undermining of his desire to lead a life that was not so "productive" but fulfilled his desire for a more relaxed existence. The recognition of the envious component to my attitude led me to question the appropriateness of my initial stance and to realize that it interfered with my ability to help these spouses give each other the support for which they clearly yearned. Dave's wish to be at one with nature needed to be respected by me and by Erica as an expression of his individuality and selfhood.

FURTHER CONSIDERATIONS

A frequently overlooked source of envy is the patient's relationship with the therapist. The therapist's own availability, reliability, care, and concern for the patient can be envied by the therapist. In other words, the therapist can envy the patient's role as a patient. The therapist can also envy the role someone else may take in the patient's life. This is particularly risky when a previously dependent patient develops a new relationship in which he transfers his dependency from the therapist to a new object choice. For this reason, it is usually unwise for a therapist to see a couple in therapy when one partner has been a patient in individual treatment. Transference as well as countertransference issues become extremely complex.

When any of the issues creating envy touch needs, weakness, or vulnerability in the therapist, a variety of therapeutic mishaps can occur. The therapist may attack the patient's thinking by presenting his/her own ideas as the only truth. Or, he may need to prove he has the right answers and knows more than the patient; he may need to prove he is better at analyzing than the patient.

CLINICAL EXAMPLE

Martin and Jessica, a couple married for ten years, presented with marital difficulty caused by the husband's recent affair and the wife's threat to leave him. Exploration revealed an intellectual relationship without passion, with vague feelings of boredom and years of dissatisfaction and unfulfillment on the part of both. This was Martin's first infidelity and he expressed remorse, regret, and a desire to work out the problems and keep the marriage together.

Martin was a 45-year-old professional who had been brought up by a mathematics professor father and an artist mother. As a child, he sought the approval of his father, who was focused on intellectual achievements and demanded a very high level of perfection from everyone. The patient felt that, while he was academically quite successful, he had never lived up to his father's expectations. He added that he and his father had little respect for his non-intellectual mother, but that he had always had great respect for his accomplished and successful wife.

Jessica, a 41-year-old professional, was raised by a dominant mother who "ran the show" and a weak, passive father, whom the family viewed as "a loser." Although she believed that she was her father's favorite child, her and her mother's contempt for him rendered his approval unimportant. She was identified with her highly competitive mother, whom she admired for what she perceived to be intelligence and strength. Another feature of her childhood was the absence of warmth or closeness between the parents and the lack of support or sensitivity to feelings evidenced throughout her family. She described her siblings as combative, competitive, and always trying to "one up" each other.

Our work in therapy focused on the ways in which Martin used his intellect to invalidate and disregard his feelings and desires and how he failed to share them with his wife. He quickly realized that he could not tell his wife what his needs were when he didn't even know them himself. Jessica pointed to that as an inadequacy of his about which she could do nothing. I suggested that she might be able to help him by seizing upon any expression of his effort to communicate a need to her and exploring it with him. I questioned whether her view of a man, exemplified by her mother's view of her father, might interfere with her being supportive of her husband's efforts in this regard. Would she see him as "a loser" if he stumbled in his first efforts at expressing feelings?

Three months into the therapy, Martin brought in a dream: he was in an office that was like a home and a lot of people were there. There was an earthquake and he moved under an arch. He found a platinum blond woman there and he hugged her and they fell over a couch. He said he felt okay about it.

Martin interpreted the dream with considerable insight. He realized that the blond stood for an attractive movie star who resembled his wife. He recognized now that he had never acknowledged the depth of love he felt for his wife because he was so unable to talk about feelings. I noted that the "falling" sounded like falling head over heels in love. At that point he became very emotional. He had never allowed himself to feel how much in love he was. He had kept the relationship at a more intellectual and dispassionate level.

I questioned him about the arch in the dream. It was in the middle of the room with couches and chairs in groups that faced away from the arch and away from each other. I suggested the earthquake symbolized the change (the "shake-up") in the relationship between his intellectual and emotional selves. He was now able to find a place between the two positions his father and mother represented. As a result, he concluded that he could connect to his passionate self without contempt for his feelings and without fear that his feelings would be taken over by his wife, as they had been with his overly emotional mother. I then *added* to his understanding of the dream the fact that the couches were facing away from each other, suggesting that as a reflection of the contempt his intellectual mind had for his mother and for his own emotionality.

The dream interpretations were well received and increased Martin's self-awareness and self-acceptance. Jessica responded very positively and said she felt cared about in a way she never had before. However, on reflecting about the session, I realized that by elaborating on the significance of an additional detail of the dream (the part about the couches facing away from each other), I had shifted the focus away from the patient's thoughtful analysis of his dream. He had spent years trying to prove his competence to his perfectionistic father and dismissive wife and now he was showing me how competent he could be at a therapeutic task. My effort to further the investigation of the dream obscured a discounting of the value of his efforts and could be seen to emphazise what was wrong rather than what was right with his efforts, similar to his childhood experiences. Martin needed recognition from me, and I had missed an opportunity to affirm him. This alerted me to my need to be more aware of those hidden desires in my patient, but particularly to an unconscious competitiveness in myself. I had not been able to let his interpretation stand as complete; I needed to "one up" him. Did I envy the patient's clever and perceptive analysis? Did his wife do something similar?

In the session following the dream interpretation I explained my findings about myself. Jessica was surprised that I would see this as in any way unsupportive of her husband. She thought he needed insight more than affirmation. I suggested that she ask him if that was so. His response was that he needed both. Then he changed his mind. He said he needed insight from me but support from her. To my surprise, Jessica was able to see that she does to Martin what I had done—that is, "one up" him by countering his ideas with ones she thinks are "a bit better." Her understanding of how this subtly undermines his feelings of self-worth and power led her to conclude that how he felt should be the most important issue. Martin commented that it was quite possible that her ideas were not necessarily "a bit better."

We had worked together long enough at that point for Jessica to make the link between her present behavior and her childhood experiences, particularly the model of a marriage her parents had represented. Martin also realized not only that had his father been critical and dismissive but that, as a dependent child, he was not in a position to counter his father's comments. The circumstances with his wife were different; now he could stand up for himself.

The incident with this couple brought me to a deeper realization of the presence of my own internal envious agent, a representation of the maternal imago of my childhood (West, 1995). The resulting competitiveness has been the subject of my formal and informal psychoanalytic investigations. This incident underscored the fact that I will need ongoing attention to unconscious envy in my future interactions. The incident also led me to wonder if I overly protect my ideas (and not share them, at times) due to an unconscious avoidance of the risk of the critical dismissal I experienced with my mother, similar to what this patient experienced with his father and wife. I was left with the awareness of feeling vulnerable and inadequate when colleagues presented their ideas with confidence. Did this lead me to sabotage my own? Perhaps I isolate myself to preserve my thinking from a feared envious attacker? Thus, this couple's growth led to my own growth as well.

IMPLICATIONS FOR TREATMENT

While the therapist's need for admiration is usually seen in narcissistic terms, it can also be a way of keeping the patient dependent on the therapist or of devaluing the patient. The therapist's need for agreement can be in the service of avoiding his own envy of the patient's ability to understand himself, as well as a way for the therapist to be admired; such disparate motives are not mutually exclusive. Also, the need for admiration or idealization from the patient can also go hand in hand with envy of the patient's partner as a recipient of that admiration. This can put a couple's relationship in jeopardy.

An envious countertransference reaction can cause a variety of other problems. The more obvious forms of attack, criticism, or authoritarian posture are not common, but do occur. More frequently, empathic listening may be impaired; optimal responsiveness may not be forthcoming; validation, approval, encouragement, or support in all and any of its forms may be withheld and subtle undermining of autonomy and independence can result.

Mingling of unconscious envy with a conscious desire to be helpful is not uncommon. It is frequently experienced by the therapist as confusion, ambivalence, or uncertainty about the direction of the treatment. This situation is particularly intense when the therapist needs to be a selfobject to one or both partners in therapy and is unable to "let go" at an appropriate time. Such therapists feel fine when needed but feel badly when not needed, complicating their own emotional investment in the treatment with the couple's newly developed ability to do well without it. The conscious feelings of loss experienced by the therapist may then be expressed by envious undermining of the couple's progress.

When the therapist reveals his/her own envy to the couple, undertaken in the service of the therapy, it can have useful therapeutic effects. Perhaps the most important is that the therapist serves as a model for comfort with negative feelings and is not ashamed of human emotions that could be considered by the spouses to be "unacceptable." The clients can have the experience of negative emotions that do not lead to the unfortunate results that they may have experienced in childhood. When the therapist is able to "contain" his/her envy by reporting it, and is not derailed by it, the spouses can look at the value of talking about such feelings instead of acting them out against each other. This is particularly valuable in the intimate relationship, where unconscious envy can result in a destructive form of competition. Thus, awareness can be used intersubjectively in the therapy to assist the intersubjectivity in the marriage.

An additional positive treatment result of reported countertransference envy is the verification of the treatment itself. For example, if a couple is told that the therapist envies their experience of being in therapy to air their issues, it can reinforce the positive experience they are having. Likewise, envy of an aspect of a particular patient can contribute to his good feelings about himself. If the therapist envies the patient's *joie de vivre*, the patient obviously has something worthwhile, something enviable. This accentuates the patient's value to his partner.

CONCLUSION

Issues of countertransference envy are usually not developed in the literature. This is probably because of the difficulty and shame therapists have in acknowledging their irrational feelings. In addition, it is reminiscent of that most difficult subject to address, that is, the parent's envy of the child. How dangerous it is to envy the ones we are here to help and protect, whose welfare we are supposed to promote, and whose development we aim to foster. However, our children (and our patients) can relight awareness of our own missed or misused opportunities, as well opportunities that we will never have. The ambivalence resulting from this state of mind can be integrated more successfully when realistic adult choices can be made based on self-awareness. We believe that the inability to deal with our own unconscious ambivalence can lead to otherwise unexplained failures in therapy.

However, recognition of countertransference envy and its consequences is an extremely difficult and sometimes impossible task. We have our human nature to contend with. The ability to be open to those uncomfortable aspects of ourselves requires more honesty and astuteness than we sometimes have at our disposal. Recognizing countertransference envy requires vigilant alertness; frequently an outside observer sees what we cannot. Ongoing consultation or conferencing may be the best method to achieve recognition of envy. Small, safe peer groups can also be a practical solution for the experienced but otherwise isolated therapist. Although scrupulous self-awareness is helpful, countertransference envy can *still* be insidious and resistant to change. When we are unable to resolve such feelings on our own, we might consider sharing them with our patients. It is possible that just such a discussion will provide the necessary opportunity to explore countertransference envy and to make appropriate control of it possible. Such resolution could facilitate therapeutic effectiveness as well as contribute to the emotional growth of the therapist.

References

Allphin, C. (1982). Envy in the Transference and Countertransference. *Clinical Social Work Journal, 10*, 151–164.

Epstein, L., & Feiner, A. H. (Eds.). (1979). *Countertransference*. New York: Jason Aronson.

Giovacchini, P. L. (1989). *Countertransference triumphs and catastrophes*. Northvale, NJ: Jason Aronson.

Jones, J. M. (1995). *Affects as process: An inquiry into the centrality of affect in psychological life*. Hillsdale, NJ: Analytic Press.

Kernberg, O. F. (1992). *Aggression in personality disorders and perversions*. New Haven, CT: Yale University Press.

Meyers, H. C. (Ed.). (1986). *Between analyst and patient: New dimensions in countertransference and transference*. Hillsdale, NJ: Analytic Press.

Natterson, J. (1991). *Beyond countertransference: The therapist's subjectivity in the therapeutic process*. Northvale, NJ: Jason Aronson.

Natterson, J., & Friedman, J. (1995). *A primer of clinical intersubjectivity*. Hillsdale, NJ: Jason Aronson.

Racker, H. (1968). *Transference and countertransference*. New York: International University Press.

Schain, J. The new infant research: Some implications for group therapy. *Group: The Journal of the Eastern Group Psychotherapy Society, 13*, 112–121.

Searles, H. F. (1979). The analyst's experience with jealousy. In L. Epstein & A. H. Feiner (Eds.), *Countertransference*. New York: Jason Aronson.

Searles, H. F. (1979). *Countertransference and related subjects*. New York: International Universities Press.

Spero, M., & Mester, R. (1988). Countertransference envy toward the religious patient. *American Journal of Psychoanalysis, 48,* 43–55.

Stolorow, R. D., Brandchaft, B., & Atwood, G. E. (1987). *Psychoanalytic treatment: An intersubjective approach*. Hillsdale, NJ: Analytic Press.

West, J. J. (1995). *Signal envy: The relationship between envy, greed and shame*. Unpublished manuscript.

Winnicott, D. (1949). Hate in the countertransference. *International Journal of Psychoanalysis, 30*, 69–75.

9

On Love and Lust
in Therapeutic Treatment

MARION F. SOLOMON

Caring is the term most often used for clinical concern, but the word *passion* better transmits the deep-running sense of interest and often outrage that must infuse difficult and persistent clinical efforts.

— L. Havens, *Making Contact*

EXCEPT FOR THE WORK of a few pioneers (Field, 1989; Samuels, 1985), the professional literature has been remarkably silent on the subject of erotic countertransference feelings. Hate in the countertransference is much better understood than the feelings of love or eroticism that may emerge in treatment (Searles, 1959; Winnicott, 1965). Typically, when therapists write about their own sexual feelings for patients, they echo the traditional advice to control the feelings, go back into analysis, and terminate the treatment if there is any possibility that the feelings might spiral out of control. Because the issues of countertransferential love and lust are rarely discussed in couples or family therapy literature, the investigation here begins with individual therapy and analysis.

In 1907 Freud called psychoanalysis "a cure by love." What did he mean? Where did sexual love fit into his formulation? If a patient "falls in love" with a therapist, are the feelings the patient experiences as "real" as the feelings experienced by a couple in an intimate relationship? What, then, of countertransference love? Do we speak of "caring" about a patient, a "kind of affection," because we don't have the courage to call it love? Is there a place for genuine love on the therapist's part? These questions reflect central issues of concern to psychotherapists dating back to the earliest analytic relationships.

For therapists, as for patients, there are different forms of love. The therapist working optimally will experience, at times, feelings of passionate attachment and intense emotion. As the therapist listens, with appropriate attention, to erotic, sexual, or loving feelings expressed by the clients, he/she may be aware of thoughts, fantasies, and images that do not differ in any essential way from those that arouse these emotions outside the office. Even though the therapist wishes to maintain therapeutic neutrality, his/her feelings *are* part of the relationship. If the purpose of therapy is to help patients be involved in a passionately committed relationship, it is no surprise that the therapist experiences powerful emotions. The problem is not in the emotions themselves but in their unconscious, unhealthy enactment.

More than one of the pioneers of psychodynamic treatment engaged in sexual adventures with patients. Among those who are known are Jung's sexual entanglement with his patient, Sabina Spielrein; Horace Frink's disastrous divorce and short marriage to one of his patients; Otto Rank's affair with his patient, Änais Nin; and August Aichhorn's affair with his patient, Margaret Mahler (Tansey, 1994). The indiscretions of these eminent men are entries in a long list of notorious stories about therapists whose countertransference acting-out included sexual involvement with their patients.

Although Freud wrote little about desire and lust, he considered such feelings impediments to be overcome. His communication with Jung regarding his protégé's sexual enactments is shockingly clear:

> Such experiences, though painful, are necessary and hard to avoid. Without them we cannot really know life and what we are dealing with. I myself have never been taken in quite so badly, but I have had a narrow escape. I believe that only grim necessities weighing on my work, and the part that I was ten years older than yourself when I came to psychoanalysis, have saved me from such experiences. *But no lasting harm is done.* They help us to develop the thick skin we need . . . to dominate the "countertransference," which is, after all, a permanent problem for us; they teach us to displace our own affects to best advantage. They are a blessing in disguise. (McGuire, 1974, pp. 230–231)

In his frank acceptance of the possibility of an affair with a patient, Freud demonstrates how much less seriously he took such behavior than psychotherapists do today. The difference is all the more impressive when we take into account the great increase in sexual freedom since the turn of the century. Today, as we understand the uniqueness of the therapeutic relationship, such a liaison automatically engenders an array of serious questions about the therapist's ethics.

Some analysts believe that there is no dynamic difference between love in the transference and ordinary love, or between transference love and countertransference love.[1] The state of being in love, which makes its appearance in the course of individual treatment, has the character of genuine love (Gabbard, 1992). The transference love of a patient for a therapist has perhaps a degree less freedom than the love that appears in ordinary life between intimate partners and is called "normal love" (Gabbard, 1994). Understanding the regressive pull of the transference adds clarity to feelings of love and desire and explains why love creates surges of emotions that are powerful, immediate, and compelling in their tendency to override reason and reflectiveness.

Beyond the legal and ethical issues, erotic countertransference feelings raise some knotty problems both in relation to the process of therapy and the reality of the therapist's life. Here we have a situation for which there is no model in ordinary life: therapists are expected to treat their emotional reactions to patients, and patients' to them, as something unreal, analyzing their reactions and using the interpretations to facilitate treatment. There are three crucial issues to be evaluated in situations of countertransference love: (1) whether the countertransference assists or hinders the treatment; (2) how the therapist addresses feelings that are defined as illicit; and (3) how such issues are played out and dealt with in the therapy. While certain emotional reactions have negative ethical implications (when they are realized in action), that does not mean that those reactions are *invalid*.

Gabbard (1994) warns of the danger that "sexual and loving feelings, in particular, are likely to impel us into action" (p. 1085). There is, however, another danger. *Denial* of the existence of countertransference love or erotic reactions may leave large holes in the treatment. Being willing to allow oneself to become immersed in unconscious patterns of patients in an attempt to reexperience and repair old wounds — including sexual wounds — is not always inappropriate. How do we deal with the risk in order to achieve the benefits?

Perhaps the difficulty can be illustrated best by reversing field relations. It is important to understand the significance of a *lack* of problematical countertransference responses because it means that either patient or therapist is coming close to material that feels dangerous. In couples therapy,

---

[1]The 1992 annual conference of the American Psychoanalytic Association was focused on "Love in the Analytic Setting," and in 1993, a meeting on the same theme occurred at the American Psychological Association. Analysts including Otto Kernberg, Estelle Shane, Glenn Gabbard, Irwin Hirsch, Jody Davis, and Michael J. Tansey presented detailed clinical vignettes involving erotic countertransference. Gabbard (1993) acknowledged that "sexual and loving feelings are powerful, immediate, and compelling in their tendency to override the steady reflectiveness of the analyst" (p. 1085).

when the spouses seem to talk in circles, fight over nothing, and have no sexual interest in one another, the clues to their complex reactions can often be found by considering sensations and emotions *within the therapist*. If a particular countertransference reaction is a rare occurrence for a therapist but arises repeatedly in a single case, it is likely a signal of some sort, even a request from one or both partners for attention to a problem that cannot be addressed consciously. Such "unthought knowns" (Bollas, 1987) provide a shortcut across unconscious processes. The task of the therapist becomes utilizing the information to identify the processes in play. If there is no effort to make some sense of the affect pushing into the treatment, then it may be enacted in a way that is destructive.

When dealing with preoedipal sensual yearnings that remain unexpressed by the mates, the therapist can focus the partners' attention on their physical sensations and, at the same time, attune to his/her own internal signals that may be connected to erotic feelings. Allowing these feelings to unfold and be held, understood, and accepted may quickly uncover the core issues of the couple. As the swiftly flowing currents of the sessions take the form of intense emotional states associated with infantile representational worlds and unconscious defenses that interfere with current relationships, the role of the therapist as a container of emotions increases in importance.

MATERNAL EROTIC TRANSFERENCE AND COUNTERTRANSFERENCE

The urgent desire for actual bodily contact—a desire for maternal envelopment along with a terror of being lost, engulfed, or smothered within the maternal orifices—motivates many patients (Kumin, 1985; Wrye & Wells, 1994). Wrye and Wells (1994) describe the "preoedipal maternal erotic transference-countertransference": both analyst and patient may experience simultaneous terror of, and longing for, fusion with the other. The primitive wish for merger can be especially frightening for male therapists. The termination phase is a particularly high-risk time for sexualized countertransference enactments, as the impending loss of the relationship triggers a painful mourning process and powerful defenses in both (Gabbard, 1994).

The problem, according to Wrye and Wells (1994), is "less one of behaving oneself than of allowing oneself to participate . . . where even speech can be eroticized, yet, nevertheless, experienced as strangely inadequate" (p. 127). What is desired by the patient (and, in some instances, the therapist) is bodily contact in which there is no boundary; patient and therapist, in essence, share the same skin. There is the longing for oneness and yet a terror of the urge to be one. Without words to explain this preverbal desire, the yearning is translated into the advanced equivalent of the wish to merge: the sexual experience. (Many people who repeatedly display sexually provocative behaviors may actually be seeking a much more primitive form of contact in which boundaries are blurred in a kind of primitive narcissism described by Grunberger [1979].)

This transformation of the infantile need to merge into expressly sexual terms is often especially clear in couples therapy. Preverbal bodily desires are typically enacted in the intimacy of a couple's relationship. It is possible to understand what is occurring as an unconscious collusive pattern between partners by observing its enactment in the treatment (Brennan-Pick, 1985; Carpy, 1989; Wrye & Wells, 1994). Each partner separately and the couple dyad will attempt to draw the therapist into an oedipal or preoedipal (archaic, nameless, and wordless) reenactment of precognitive experiences that have been an underlying driving force in their relationship.

Therapists can discern the operation of this dynamic when they experience intense emotional, psychological, or physiological countertransference reactions. It is the work of therapy to translate primitive experiences into some kind of narrative coherence that helps partners *think* about unconscious feelings. To give words to nameless dread, to hold and contain what is experienced as intolerable, and to perceive realness and sanity beneath what feels like "craziness" are transformative experiences. Even when failures occur in the process, the mending of these failures in the present can be deeply reparative of old wounds. When the therapist is able to experience immersion in the transference, allowing the countertransference to arise — and, at the same time, retain or quickly regain solid boundaries — therapeutic progress is often noteworthy.

Therapists may face an inordinate challenge: that of being aware of feelings of love or desire, being able to think about the feelings, and, yet, avoid the pull into the dangerous emotional currents of intense, lustful sensations. Since maternal erotic sensations are the residue of very primitive responses to the mother's body, these bodily sensations can be intensely felt without accessing words or thought. The ability to think about the feelings as they emerge enables the therapist to connect with oedipal triangles as well as more primitive sensations. This is especially true in the course of intense treatment. If therapists are afraid even to *think* about such reactions because they are defined as unhealthy or unhelpful, it may not be possible to deal with the feelings in a way that is constructive for patients. In denial of the sexual feelings or in awareness of the erotic undercurrent but not of its transferential nature, there is a true danger of being pulled into unethical sexual acting-out.

Another undesirable possibility is being so frightened of becoming overwhelmed by lustful sexual feelings or maternal erotic sensations that there is a failure to acknowledge what is occurring between the partners or between either of the partners and the therapist. From this perspective, it would appear that when oedipal and preoedipal erotic countertransference feelings remain unconscious and cut off from awareness, it may greatly impair and even derail the treatment.

In the Shadow of Eros

Sexual dramas often infuse therapeutic relationships, and a few practitioners and theorists are beginning to address this reality. Some therapists have openly examined the dyadic and triadic erotic feelings that emerge in couples and family therapy. Freida Fromm-Reichmann (Tansey, 1994) reported her experience with a patient that resulted in termination: "You see, I began to analyze Erich, and then we fell in love, and so we stopped. That much sense we had!" (p. 480). Robin Skynner (1976) has described how he used his own sexual arousal in a family session to help understand the sexual tension between mother, father, and adolescent son.

The process of putting old faces on new relationships — of reexperiencing archaic feelings in the current situation — occurs in all intimate relationships. There is a strong tendency to respond to any encounter that sparks old memories — be they conscious or unconscious, cognitive or somatic — as if here and now is there and then. Whatever projections, introjections, and projective identifications are occurring between partners constitute an integral part of the unconscious processes that couples bring into therapy. The therapist's countertransference responses can provide important clues to the underlying unconscious processes of the couple, including libidinal and/or aggressive feelings that are ongoing in the relationship. Having learned to tune into the psychological and physical reactions that influence responses to patients, the therapist can then recognize that a nonreaction may correspond to the internal deadening of libidinal or aggressive feelings in the patient as well as oneself.

In 1914 Freud wrote that "working through" requires repetition in the treatment situation; repressed desires can be remembered only after they have been felt within the transference. Winnicott (1958) noted that permanent changes can only be brought about when new reparative experiences occur in the transference neurosis of an analysis. Countertransference responses provide clues to what cannot be said in words. Sometimes erotic feelings in the countertransference signal intense, primitive, unthought, and unthinkable affect. Kumin (1989) has noted that "many of the regressions encountered in both outpatient and hospital practices are, in fact, defenses against, and symbolic expressions of, the emerging eruption into consciousness of sexual desire concerning the person of the therapist" (p. 10). Almost any symptom—whether neurotic, borderline, or psychotic—can serve as a screen for erotic transference feelings. It is necessary to develop fine-tuned receptors for the signals of erotic countertransference, and then seek to differentiate whether they are a response to what patient or therapist brings into the sessions. Further, it is important to recognize whether a countertransference response is based upon unresolved problems from the past, or issues such as gender roles and power, which are part of the socialization process in our culture.

Because we are indoctrinated in gender roles long before our training as therapists, our countertransferential pulls may strongly reflect traditional sexual roles. As children develop, the trait of dominance is encouraged in males, while submission is fostered in females (Benjamin, 1988). Erotic love may thereby become erotic *domination* for some males. Male therapists tend to be better able to see themselves as the object of sexual feelings than female therapists. They are caught in the cultural pull of male dominance and societal view of powerful males as sexually attractive. Men tend to stifle their responses, consciously and unconsciously, because of the regressive forces and vulnerability that may arise along with sexual feelings. Masculinity requires "ever-vigilant defenses against succumbing to the pull of merging again with mother," which limits erotic expression (Stoller, 1975, p. 149).

Female therapists may be somewhat better able than males to recognize eroticized early bodily longings and to tolerate the regression required to work within preoedipal erotic transferences. At the same time, female therapists may be psychologically and culturally inhibited from allowing the erotic transference to develop fully—especially if the patient is considerably younger. Instead, there is a denial of feelings, a projection onto the patient, or a numbing of affect in the session. When the therapist is female, the therapeutic dynamic is the reverse of what men and women ordinarily experience—the male is in a less powerful position than the female. A male patient may be less likely to feel erotic impulses toward female therapists because of a fear of the power of women.

The tendency is to revert to the other way males and females know how to relate—as mother and child. Female clinicians may be tempted to take on a maternal stance and reenact the early nurturing relationship, but confusion inevitably arises as the therapeutic bond deepens and intensifies. Empathy and mothering may then become conflated. Concomitantly, the female therapist, unconsciously fearful of losing boundaries or being violated or made somehow weaker, may view the emergence of sexual feelings from either herself or her patient (male or female) as anathema.

"It isn't occurring," "I feel nothing," "This is your resistance to treatment," were the responses of a woman therapist who sought consultation when, in her work with a lesbian couple, one of the partners insisted that she saw signs of a sexual interest on the part of the therapist. Perhaps it was purely projection; perhaps there was something the patient gleaned that was out of the therapist's conscious awareness. As the therapist withdrew in a cloud of denial of having any reaction at all, the patient became increasingly aggressive and resistant to the couple's therapy. Certainly there were feelings on the part of the therapist—if not erotic feelings, than anger, anxiety, shame, or rage.

Erotic elements in the countertransference cannot simply be put aside. That much is obvious. Maintaining equanimity while being aggressively pursued or accused by a patient is impossible. If these issues are not raised by the therapist, underlying feelings that affect the treatment may remain unconscious, unthought, and surely unstated. Just as a therapist restrains judgment about the patient's feelings and behavior, so it is crucial to restrain judgment about his or her own reactions, and sometimes about his or her own behavior. If given complete precedence, ethical reflexes can obstruct the larger goals of psychotherapy, because even an attempt to "follow the rules" can lead to disaster.

An example: A male therapist, who was in the midst of a divorce and lonely and depressed, attended a singles dance. To his surprise, he discovered that one of his patients, an exquisitely beautiful woman who was divorcing her husband, was at the same event. He asked her to dance without considering the repercussions. Upon realizing his attraction to her and what it could mean to their work together, he left the event after that one dance.

Not surprisingly, the patient brought up the encounter during their following session. She was extremely agitated and confused, uncertain about what the interaction had meant. She wanted him to be attracted to her, to love her, but knew it would be dangerous. Acting in what he thought was an ethical manner, seeking consultation, the therapist mulled over his alternatives. In their following session, he explained to the patient that he had behaved inappropriately and that he was having personal problems that had muddled his thinking the night of the dance. He assured her that it was in no way her fault but that, because of his mistake, their therapeutic relationship had been irretrievably damaged. Therefore, they could have no further relationship, therapeutic or otherwise. He then referred her to another male therapist for treatment.

Although this therapist did not act out unethically, his reaction to his lapse in good judgment appears not to have included a careful weighing of the damage termination might cause. The costs of this decision to the patient's treatment were, in fact, enormous. He did not, it would seem, fully consider either the needs of his patient or her own self-recrimination for dancing with him — her guilt and shame for "the problem." The fallout from this rupture is still being addressed in her current therapy.

Certainly, therapists must remain aware of the critical importance of self-restraint. But this therapist added to his indiscreet behavior a greater wound: the emotional disconnection so dreaded by his patient and the validation of the feeling that her sexual needs were destructive, as she had experienced in her family of origin. Rather than dealing directly with how he was acting out his feelings of loneliness, depression, and burnout with this patient and possibly others, he applied the simple solution seemingly prescribed by the rules. Quite probably, it was *he*, and not his patient, who would benefit from referral to a new therapist!

There is no easy solution to the problem of erotic countertransference. As it happened, the new therapist in this case also found himself in a dilemma with respect to this patient's transference feelings. She professed her sexual desire for this second therapist, and he responded by telling her that not only his professional bonds but his marriage bonds precluded such an involvement. He began receiving gifts and letters from this admiring and very lovely patient. Acknowledging the patient's sexual attractiveness, the therapist reasoned that he could be sending unconscious, inviting messages to her. He addressed her belief that only through seduction would he consider her worthy and lovable. Her fear of being once again dismissed by her therapist encouraged her to employ the tactics with which she believed she had kept her family of origin together: allowing herself to be used sexually by her father. By seeking help with his own countertransference responses through supervision, this therapist understood how he was being pulled into a reenactment of his patient's old, frightening scenario. With this understanding, he was able to focus on her underlying fears and her past and present experiences, even as he managed his countertransference feelings. The therapy was successful.

This account illustrates the complexity of the problems engaged when the issue of erotic countertransference arises. The mere possibility that such feelings are in play can produce reactions that appear extreme only in retrospect. In addition, the feelings at issue are undoubtedly among the most powerful and complex of all affective responses.

Partners who enact their unresolved preoedipal issues in the couple relationship may be seeking resolution of primitive developmental problems. Therapists can recognize that primitive defenses underlie the presenting problems by attuning to the countertransference reactions that they elicit. The first task for the therapist is to actually recognize when such preoedipal bodily sensations emerge. The next task, even more difficult, is to tolerate the feelings without acting on them.

The complexity of the couple's relationship naturally affects what is evoked in the inner experience of the therapist. The countertransference challenge in this context is one of maintaining a quiet, open attentiveness without feeling pressured into prematurely "doing something" or forming an alliance with either mate. Sometimes the reactions come as a surprise, as they did in one of my own cases several years ago.

JOSH AND ELLEN

Josh and Ellen were a couple in their forties who had been involved in an intensely loving but chaotic relationship for almost two years when they sought couples therapy. They both functioned very successfully in the business world and were surrounded by friends and acquaintances who respected them as accomplished leaders in their respective media-related professions. I was very fond of Ellen and had great admiration for the way she had overcome a history of abuse and forged a successful life for herself. I felt less attuned to Josh. He admitted to a penchant for abusive behavior, and although he had never physically hurt Ellen, I felt that I must put extra effort into being even-handed with this couple.

A very charismatic figure and a leader in his field, Josh was accustomed to exercising enormous power — but he was also very needy and demanding. He often called for therapeutic help when he and Ellen were in a crisis. Several times, after one of their breakups, he called to request that I contact Ellen and intercede so that she would reestablish their joint therapy. Ellen always welcomed Josh's invitation to reconnect and work through their problems. The therapy continued in this way for almost a year.

When things were going well between them, for weeks or months, they would begin to talk of marriage. Then, without warning, a seemingly insignificant issue would blow up into a huge argument. Often, in the midst of such an argument, Josh's voice resonated loudly and could be heard outside my office. Ellen would turn to me for help and understanding. Josh would stop, turn to me, and earnestly say, "I want you to be on my side." While his responses to Ellen seemed emotionally abusive, it was clear that Josh, too, was suffering. I tried to stay focused on his pain: his experience of growing up with a physically abusive father who often beat his mother and occasionally bloodied Josh when he attempted to intervene.

Josh's memories were filled with conflated images of sexuality and violence and intertwined feelings of anxiety and anger. He recalled a Friday night ritual in which his father would go out drinking, and his mother would take a bath with the bathroom door open. He recalled being given baths by his mother, long after he was too old for such intimacy to be appropriate. But he never spoke to her about his discomfort or guilt, because he liked the sensations and fantasized about them. He blamed his father's many violent beatings of his mother on his own sexual feelings and his wish to have his mother for himself.

He wanted the love of both his parents, but was torn apart by their struggles. He was always part of a triangle. He wanted to love his mother, but she was weak and incapable of providing a safe environment for him. He wanted to be close to his father, but protecting his mother meant that he must align with her. In this family triangle, he felt forced to take sides with his mother, which resulted in denial of a relationship with his father and an underlying anger that could not be expressed. He grew up with an image of maleness as abusing and degrading females. At a conscious level he rejected this "legacy" and was determined that he would "never lay a hand on a woman." However, in some cases, the desire to harm or degrade another at an unconscious level is at the center of erotic excitement. The hostility that generates sexual excitement is an attempt, "repeated over and over, to undo childhood traumas and frustrations that threatened the development of one's masculinity or femininity" (Stoller, 1979, p. 60). Stoller recognized a continuum of hostility, at one end of which love coexists with hostility.

Instead of expressing angry feelings directly, Josh learned the subtleties of indirect manipulation and sabotage. Whenever things were going well, or when there was a special outing, he would do something that spoiled the pleasure for his mother and himself. He would dawdle, despite her urgings to hurry, and they would miss the bus; or he would provoke a fight with his sister and upset the whole family. "I wanted to ruin it," he said, without understanding the reasons for his behavior. This behavior served as an outlet for his repressed anger. Only after the destruction was done did he allow himself to have a pleasant time.

A pattern of triangulated relationships has followed Josh throughout his life. He has often found himself either caught between the demands of others or demanding others to be on his side. Josh's manipulative handling of interpersonal dynamics has frequently provoked anger in the people involved, both toward one another and him. His vulnerability has manifested itself in his tendency to draw what I call a "narcissistic shell" around himself to protect against pain and loss. But his protection also has kept him from being fully engaged in life and able to give freely of himself.

Ellen recognized the historical antecedents of her part in their problems as a couple. At the core of her personality structure was a sense of betrayal. Her childhood memories consisted of being beaten, when she had done nothing wrong, by a father who claimed he was only doing the mother's bidding. "If that was true," she said, "he didn't have to beat me so hard." Ellen felt a betrayal then, and later, as an adult, when her parents bluntly refused to acknowledge that they were in any way responsible for this abuse. Nor did they accept blame for Ellen's difficulties in trusting other people and unwillingness to be in a dependent position. She had channeled all her energies into her career, enlisting the help of several men who were mentors, even though she continually feared betrayal.

As Ellen described it, she had also been betrayed by a therapist several years before. Ellen explained that she had succeeded in getting an appointment for a single consultation with one of the most respected analysts in the city. After their meeting, this therapist agreed to see her at a reduced rate if she would enter daily analysis. Ellen had been in treatment for four years when she met Josh and decided it was time to cut back on the individual analysis. Her therapist began telling her, perhaps correctly, that the relationship with Josh was damaging and potentially dangerous to her.

"I felt like I was in some kind of love triangle with Dr. A and Josh," Ellen explained. "I was flabbergasted when, one day, Dr. A said that what I was doing was self-destructive and that he didn't think he could work with me if I continued to see Josh. We ended the therapy that day." Once again—this time with her therapist—a key relationship ended in disaster, leaving Ellen feeling hurt and abandoned.

Soon after they began couples therapy, Josh and Ellen made plans to move in together. Josh then promptly became irritable and withdrawn, frightened by the reality of their growing intimacy. As in the past, the closeness that he desired also felt constricting and smothering. He pulled back and provoked arguments. Ellen once again felt betrayed. She said that she must end the relationship—and she did, for a few weeks. Shortly thereafter, Josh, realizing how much he wanted to be with her, contacted Ellen and talked again about buying a house, living together, and someday marrying. They spent a wonderful weekend together, but on Monday morning he became angry, unfairly accusing Ellen of being distant and unavailable. As he became angrier, she sought reassurance that they indeed would go ahead with the plans they had made over the weekend to move in together. Josh misinterpreted this as her "looking for an argument" and completely withdrew. Again, the old unresolved issues of each were recreated in the relationship. Again, the pattern of disruption and reconnection recurred. When I later asked how they had resolved this particular fight, Ellen replied, "We made love—that's how we always resolve things."

Responding to Ellen's comment, Josh said, "I like sex. I like it a lot, so Ellen can always win me over, even when I'm so angry that I don't feel at all sexual. But," he added, "there is something more that I want, something that is always elusive—that wish to have her arms around me, to hold me ever so tightly and never let go of me." He began talking about how they had made love the evening before, describing his fantasies in very sensual terms. Even as he spoke to Ellen, he turned to me, seemingly imploring me to understand feelings that were quite beyond words.

I became aware of my body responding, knowing at some deep level the sense of sexuality and blissful merger that he desired. My initial impulse was to push the feelings away, as they were much too intense for comfort. I was aware of feeling pulled deeply into someone else's mind. I know that to work at this deep level, I must stay clear-headed.

Shortly after this session, I had a dream that Josh had sneaked into my bed while I slept, and, as I awakened, was attempting to force himself into me. He had a very powerful thrust, and although I felt frightened, I did not resist. When he entered me, however, he continued to thrust forward and soon his entire body was completely inside me. I woke up suddenly, upset and thinking that I must stop working with this couple. At the same time I was shocked to feel a surge of warmth at the idea of carrying Josh in my womb. I knew that I would continue to work with them.

Several days later Josh called to say that he and Ellen had had a terrible fight. "I can't figure out what happened," he said. "I'm so confused, and I need your help. Please see us as soon as you have an opening."

I called Ellen, as I had in the past, but this time she said that they had had their worst argument – one that was dangerously close to erupting into physical violence. "Even though he didn't lay a hand on me, I'm frightened." She didn't want to continue in couples therapy. "The relationship is over," she said. I agreed to see Josh the following morning to help him sort out his own fears about what had happened.

In time, Josh convinced Ellen to reestablish their relationship. But, as he told her his view of the therapeutic experience – that I had chosen to see him and not her – Ellen's sense of betrayal came out full force, her anger very intense. She felt what, in truth, was happening – that I had become focused on the needs and feelings of Josh. My countertransference response with Ellen was one of a parent occupied elsewhere. Her rivalry for attention and her rage towards me was a natural response to my empathic failure.

Once again, Josh felt caught between two powerful forces – a position that recreated his childhood drama. For Ellen, the therapist had become part of the problem – another parental figure who was betraying her. Her initial response was refusal to continue the couples therapy and uncertainty about continuing the relationship with Josh.

Josh came to the next session and related a dream from several years ago. "I am in a strange city, giving a lecture at a university. I watch one of the co-eds going back to her dorm. I think of ways I could seduce her to get her to let me come to her room. I follow her and see her entering a room upstairs. Her face seems to shine and I want to be with her. I wait until night and sneak into the dorm. I guess which room must be hers. It is just luck that I find the right door. I open the door and see her. I take off my clothes and climb into her bed. Then she wakes up and tells me to get out of there, and I go. I didn't mean to hurt her. I just wanted to be close to her and have her hold me." He said that though he had dreamed this years ago, he had been thinking about all the dangerous risks he took with women, things that could have gotten him into serious trouble.

"Perhaps you feel you have sneaked into my bed," I said. Josh sat very still and said nothing. "You think you have seduced me into seeing you alone," I continued.

"I have," he replied.

"And you're afraid that I will wake up and throw you out of therapy."

Josh said nothing.

I wondered what I was doing with Josh. And what do I do with him now? What about Ellen, who also had been my patient in the couples therapy?

"It was very important for you to win, to have me on your side," I said. "But now that you think you have what you wanted, you don't know what to do with me. . . . It is important that we sort this out," I added.

Josh was silent for a long time.

"Ellen is the one I love," he said, "I can't have a relationship with you."

"The relationship with me is not a true relationship but a transference from your past," I said. "The real relationship is with Ellen, who can and wants to be part of your life."

"I want Ellen back," he said finally, after a long silence.

"I know," I replied.

"There is something about the relationship with Ellen; it's heaven, and then it's hell. She's part of it. It can't just be me," he said.

"She is part of it," I agreed. "And I'm part of what happened in the therapy, Josh. I fell into the trap of allowing you to change our work by seeing you without Ellen. You experience me just like all of the other women in your life, from your mother onward. But that doesn't change the reality of what you do in each of your relationships. You keep finding yourself caught in these impossible situations. If Ellen is close and loving, you push her away or you provoke fights. You want someone to always be there with you, as if you are attached to each other. So you push for emotional closeness with me, and if I respond, you push me away. If Ellen lets down her guard and shows you her love, you push her away. Distance frightens you; closeness frightens you. You cannot get what you need."

Josh nodded, and I was silent. Then he related another dream. He said that he was back in the home where he had grown up. He was frightened and trying to get comfort from his mother. "She reached out and drew me close to her—pulling me to her—I remember her hugging me so tightly with her enormous breasts. I couldn't breathe." Josh didn't know how to be close to her without being smothered. "I think both of my parents were very sexual," he said, "but not with each other. I think my father turned to other women and my mother turned to me."

"And you are afraid that I will pull you toward me, playing on your yearning for closeness, and then smother you with my enormous breasts, never letting you go. You think that you have succeeded in seducing me, and it terrifies you."

"Yes," he whispered.

"If I have succumbed to your charms, then I cannot be strong enough to help you. I'd be like your mother, who couldn't give you what you needed."

"That's right," Josh added, "and I would have only contempt for you."

"You would have seduced me and hated me for it," I concluded.

We talked about Josh's anger and aggressive feelings, which are part of his sexuality. He saw that his pattern of doing things to upset his mother — for example, disrupting their outings — was now repeated with Ellen and in the transference with me. Triangles were what he knew; he knew how to draw people into crazy-making relationships. He knew also how to charm people and to get under their skin.

That is what Ellen said when she came back into the couples therapy with a diamond ring on her finger. We began talking about her sense of mistrust and feelings of betrayal. When I acknowledged that I had caused her pain by agreeing to see Josh without checking with her and by making her feel that she had been dropped by me, she seemed to relax a bit but remained cautious. Discussing the problems that we had together, allowing her to express her hurt, disappointment, and anger, seemed to be the beginning of a new phase of our work.

In the interaction among Josh, Ellen, and myself, Josh reenacted the behavior that was part of his most distressing childhood experience. His own sexual arousal as a child and his guilt and self-denigration for being the "cause" of his parents' bloody battles were recreated in the therapy. They were played out in the eroticized transference and the rage that Ellen felt toward me, while Josh, who had provoked her anger, stood by as like helpless child, hoping Ellen and I could work it out.

Ellen's repeated experiences with her abusive mother, her competition with her mother for her father's affection, and the later betrayal by her father, who professed to be her ally, were also reenacted in countertransference and through the therapeutic triangle. She became enraged when she saw herself as abused by Josh and betrayed by me. But instead of disconnecting and running away, she confronted the abusers in therapy sessions, recognized her part in the interaction, but did not blame herself as she had done so often in the past.

I raised the issue of sexual triangles and the experiences in their families of origin that were being replayed with me. Josh came to understand how the love that he yearned for inevitably led him into a relational trap. If he allowed himself to depend on a woman—any woman—his need might be so great that she would take control of him. His history had imprinted a lifelong fear of being engulfed and smothered. Recognizing that he created triangles as a protection against intimacy, Josh could choose, at last, *not* to act out his fear. Instead, he confronted his own dangerous expectations of what might happen in an intimate relationship. He began to observe and analyze how, in such triangles, he would project responsibility onto others and disclaim his own feelings and desires. Together we were able to examine how he had repeatedly duplicated an old pattern. His response was once necessary to protect himself from being overwhelmed by premature expectations that he do something to resolve his parents' problems. With analysis of these issues, he became better able to understand how his habitual interactional patterns often cause him to experience intense pain with those he loves.

Ellen had an opportunity to feel the reemergence of old wounds and the lifelong sense of betrayal she felt whenever she allowed herself to depend on anyone. She also came to recognize the intensity of her anger in such situations and to contain the emotion rather than acting on it. While using her rational mind to clarify and "hold" these difficult emotions, she increasingly learned to tolerate what had been too painful to endure. She used the situation to change her lifelong pattern of breaking off relationships the moment she felt betrayed or hurt. She chose not to end the relationship with Josh but to try to understand her part and his in their recurring battles. Nor did she terminate the therapy, despite feeling intensely angry at what she perceived as yet another betrayal.

What Josh did in his relationships and in therapy was to pursue and then frustrate women in the way that he had experienced frustration and guilt as a child. Ellen, used to abuse, fit perfectly into a chaotic collusion. They reenacted their expectations in an unhealthy alliance of connections and disconnections. It was not until we had recreated the painful patterns in the therapeutic situation, and then maintained a strong enough therapeutic bond so that they could reexperience the painful emotions of love and hate, that these partners could begin to unravel the threads of past and present and reconnect in a less destructive way. What they each brought to the relationship, both in real qualities and unconscious agendas and needs, did not change. But their old defense patterns began to crumble.

Josh learned to put words to his fears of being smothered when he allowed himself to be close and to tell Ellen when he needed to retreat instead of acting it out. Ellen began to reevaluate instead of instantly reacting when she felt anxious or threatened as Josh turned his attentions elsewhere. This relationship will never be calm or smooth, but they have survived two years of marriage.

DISCUSSION

Although this case contains a lesson in the potential danger of countertransference reactions, the turbulence also provided an opportunity for the couple and therapist to see how the hidden expectations included in early representations of relationships can erode a current relationship. The patterns of
each partner were being replayed in the therapeutic triangle. Once I became
aware of how I was being drawn into each partner's worst-case scenario, I
was able to extricate myself and provide a corrective experience.

Examining what occurred, acknowledging that there was a break in the
therapeutic alliance, and not putting the fault on patients' projections or
other pathology became part of the healing. Fortunately, the therapeutic
alliance with Josh and Ellen was strong. When they brought their anger and
disappointment into the sessions, they were able to get from me what they
could not get from their parents — recognition that their needs were the
priority and the failure did not lie solely with themselves.

By being willing to accept the feelings projected into me — the seductive
mother to Josh and betraying father to Ellen — I was able to confront the
issues that arose between the two of them and between each of them and
myself. This is not a short-term process. The work is still ongoing.

CONCLUSION

Sometimes the therapist's erotic impulses toward a patient may signify the
presence of sexual abuse in the patient's history. The countertransference
of the therapist, in deep empathy and communication with the eroticized
transference, gives access to the unconscious fantasies and images associated with sexual trauma. Some abused people behave seductively in their
relationships but have great ambivalence about real sexual involvement.
They love, but also passionately hate, the person who prematurely aroused
them sexually, and they tend to give both feelings to anyone who elicits an
erotic response in them. These ambivalent love-hate relationships include
lovers, spouses, and, by extension, the therapist. The drama is kept alive by
enlisting new partners in the sexualized love-hate encounters. The therapist's countertransference provides clues to repressed material. The patient's
defenses require the therapist to stay connected with the disowned reactions
to premature sexuality without fearing engulfment and without rejecting
the patient.

In drawing a distinction between therapists whose loving or sexual feelings are enacted, causing harm to patients, and those who do not enact, a
caution is in order: this line may be crossed unexpectedly in times of great
personal stress. In the context of divorce, death of a loved one, major
professional adversity, or even adult developmental crises related to aging,

any therapist can potentially succumb to the fantasy that a patient may satisfy his or her intense emotional hunger. Maintaining gratifying personal relationships should be a high priority for those working in the mental health professions.

Ultimately, the result of all countertransference responses depends upon the therapist's ability to recover his or her bearings after feeling pulled toward a variety of enactments. The danger on the other side is to maintain an overly cautious stance and remain above the swiftly flowing currents of the couple's emotional turbulence. When that occurs, the therapy remains superficial.

The countertransference provides clues to the unconscious contract between partners. The willingness to risk immersion into the dangerous countertransference provides the path to change. Allowing emotions, thinking about feelings instead of suppressing them, separating emotions from action so that there is time to reflect on them—this is the process that enables healing. Discussions about sex and aggression, erotic anxieties, and pre-oedipal desires and terrors become part of the treatment. Framing the interpretations so that spouses can hear what they otherwise live with in unconscious collusion often resolves not only sexual issues but a myriad of maternal, sensual, bodily desires, as well as fears and defenses that are part of transference collusions between partners.

Failure to recognize the flow of loving, sensual, and/or erotic feelings that couples bring into the therapeutic situation may feel "safer" and less chaotic, but in such cases the deeper collusions cannot be touched. Therapists must ascertain that they are comfortable discussing sex, aggression, erotic fantasies, anxieties, preoedipal stirrings, terrors, and feelings of love with their clients. Countertransference can be used like a magical divining rod, leading the therapist to a wellspring of unconscious riches. Suppressed, it can do nothing to stave off a drought.

REFERENCES

Benjamin, J. (1988). *The bonds of love: Psychoanalysis, feminism, and the problem of domination*. New York: Pantheon.

Bollas, C. (1987). *The shadow of the object: Psychoanalysis of the unthought known*. New York: Columbia University Press.

Bollas, C. (1983). Expressive use of the countertransference. *Contemporary Psychoanalysis, 19*(1), 1–34.

Brenman-Pick, I. (1985). Working through in the countertransference. *International Journal of Psychoanalysis, 66*, 156–166.

Bowen, M. (1978). *Family therapy in clinical practice*. New York: Jason Aronson.

Carpy, D. V. (1989). Tolerating the countertransference: A mutative process. *International Journal of Psychoanalysis, 70*, 287–294.

Dicks, H. (1967). *Marital tension: Clinical studies toward a psychological theory of interaction*. London: Routledge and Kegan Paul.

Field, N. (1989). Listening with the body: An exploration in the countertransference. *British Journal of Psychotherapy, 5*, 512–522.

Freud, S. (1907). Delusions and dreams in Jensen's Gradiva. In J. Strachey (Ed. and Trans.), *The standard edition of the complete psychological works of Sigmund Freud* (Vol. 9, pp. 1–95). New York: Norton.

Freud, S. (1914). On narcissism: An introduction. In J. Strachey (Ed. and Trans.), *The standard edition of the complete psychological works of Sigmund Freud* (Vol. 14, pp. 109–140). New York: Norton.

Freud, S. (1915). Observations on transference love. In J. Strachey (Ed. and Trans.), *The standard edition of the complete psychological works of Sigmund Freud* (Vol. 12, pp. 159–171). New York: Norton.

Gabbard, G. (December, 1992). Meeting of the American Psychoanalytic Association Panel on "Love in the Analytic Setting."

Gabbard, G. (1994). Sexual excitement and countertransference love in the analyst. *Journal of the American Psychiatric Association, 42*(4), 1083–1104.

Grunberger, B. (1979). *Narcissism: Psychoanalytic essays* (J. S. Diamanti, Trans.). New York: International Universities Press.

Gurman, A. S. (1978). Contemporary marital therapy: A critique and comparative analysis of psychoanalytic, behavioral and systems theory approaches. In T. J. Paolino & B. S. McCrady (Eds.), *Marriage and marital therapy*. New York: Brunner/Mazel.

Havens, L. (1986). *Making contact*. Cambridge, MA: Harvard University Press.

Kohut, H. (1977). *Restoration of the self*. New York: International University Press.

Kumin, I. (1985). Erotic horror: Desire and resistance in the psychoanalytic situation. *International Journal of Psychoanalytic Psychotherapy, 11*, 3–20.

Main, M. (1983). Exploration, play, and cognitive functioning related to infant mother attachment. *Infant Behavior and Development, 6*, 167–174.

McGuire, J. (1974). *The Freud/Jung letters: The correspondence between Sigmund Freud and C. G. Jung*. New Jersey: Princeton University Press.

Samuels, S. (1985). Symbolic dimensions of Eros in transference/countertransference. *International Review of Psychoanalysis, 12*, 199–207.

Searles, H. F. (1979). *Countertransference and related subjects*. New York: International University Press.

Searles, H. F. (1959). Oedipal love in the countertransference. *International Journal of Psychoanalysis, 40*, 180–190.

Scharff, D., & Scharff, J. (1987). *Object relations family therapy*. Northvale, NJ: Jason Aronson.

Skynner, A. C. R. (1976). *Systems of family and marital psychotherapy*. New York: Brunner/Mazel.

Slipp, S. (1984). *Object relations: A dynamic bridge between individual and family treatment*. New York: Jason Aronson.

Solomon, M. (July, 1985). Treatment of narcissistic and borderline disorders in marital therapy: Suggestions toward an enhanced therapeutic approach. *Clinical Social Work*, 141–156.

Solomon, M. (1989). *Narcissism and intimacy: Love and marriage in an age of confusion*. New York: Norton.

Solomon, M., & Weiss, N. (Winter, 1992). Integration of Daniel Stern's developmental theory into a model of couples therapy. *Clinical Social Work, 20*(4), 124–137.

Spence, D. P. (1982). *Narrative truth and historical truth: Meaning and interpretation in psychoanalysis*. New York: Norton.

Stern, D. (1985). *The interpersonal world of the infant*. New York: Basic.

Stoller, R. J. (1975). *Perversion: The erotic form of hatred*. New York: Pantheon.

Stoller, R. J. (1979). *Sexual excitement: Dynamics of erotic life*. New York: Pantheon.

Tansey, M. J. (1994). Sexual attraction and phobic dread in the countertransference. *Psychoanalytic Dialogue, 4*, 139–152.

White, M., & Epston, D. (1990). *Narrative means to therapeutic ends*. New York: Norton.

Winnicott, D. W. (1965). *The maturational process and the facilitating environment: Studies in the theory of emotional development*. New York: International Universities Press.

Wrye, H., & Wells, J. (1994). *Narration of desire*. Hillsdale, NJ: Analytic Press.

Zajonc, R. (1980). Feeling and thinking. *American Psychologist, 35*, 151–175.

10

Love's Labour's Lost: Countertransference with a Terminating Relationship

KENNETH MANN

THE FOCUS of this chapter is on Ellen and Evan,[1] who have been working with me in couples therapy for the past year and a half. My private practice is a general practice that comprises equal numbers of homosexual and heterosexual individuals and couples. Most of my homosexual clients believe that seeking a gay-identified therapist eliminates the possibility of bias and prejudice that would make the therapeutic situation toxic for them. Clients often state that they seek a gay-identified therapist because they feel this choice will facilitate psychotherapeutic growth in a way that working with a heterosexual therapist would not. Isay (1993) warns that many therapists might be less than supportive of gay clients without necessarily being conscious of this bias.

Ellen and Evan were clear about what type of therapist they sought. They were seeking a gay-identified therapist who was involved in a long-term relationship. The switchboard operator at a community referral service for gay, lesbian, and bisexual people suggested they interview me. These types of referrals often do not support an analytic framework that is built psychotherapeutically on a classically defined transference. Ellen and Evan began their work with me knowing more about me than I did about them. Clients I begin working with in this way sometimes present in an overly social and casual manner. It takes effort to create a serious and focused context for

---

[1]This case is a composite of many I have seen.

work. While the tone needs to be made less casual, care is required to ensure the communication of support and common goals necessary to establish a meaningful therapeutic alliance. Cornett (1995) discusses the importance of the gay therapist as role model and as a facilitator of a twinship selfobject experience that many gay clients have not experienced before with others. He also evaluates the challenge in providing this and yet being able to create the atmosphere necessary to promote intrapsychic change.

When a couple begins therapy with personal knowledge about the therapist, the therapeutic context that is created promotes utilization of the real relationship throughout the work (Greenson & Wexler, 1969). When aspects of the real relationship become a focus in therapy, countertransference issues become even more vital to the processes. As Ellen and Evan had come to treatment with a developed perception of who I was as a person, they were receptive to the incorporation of my thoughts, feelings, and reactions to them in our work. Since I met the criteria they had established for a good enough therapist, they were more than willing to hear my subjective experience of them. They liked me before we began; this allowed me to easily engage them in a process where I was very much a real presence. The challenge became being able to say things that were difficult for them to integrate and accept while remaining a good enough therapist in their view. This was due to the specific nature of their intrapsychic issues as well as the general issues that emerge when clients perceive confrontation as rejection.

Over the past year and a half, a plethora of material and a myriad of clinical situations have emerged in which my most effective interventions were rooted in the context of the real relationship and enhanced by my understanding of countertransference. When I utilized countertransference as projective identification and as a way to access the influence of my own values and beliefs, a challenging case became more manageable and ultimately more enriched. My objective here is to show how these countertransferential themes emerged for me via the clinical material and how I attempted to utilize them psychotherapeutically.

CASE BACKGROUND

Ellen and Evan had lived together in a middle-class suburban community for 20 years. Evan was 44 years old and Ellen was 54 years old when we began our work together. Ellen had been married for several years when she was in her twenties and had two children. Ellen had custody of these children, who were in local colleges at the time Ellen and Evan began therapy. Ellen noted that her ex-husband and father of her children had abandoned the family many years previously and had had no contact with the children since their early childhood. When Evan met Ellen, they moved in together quickly. This was Evan's first serious long-term relationship. Over the years, Evan and Ellen had co-parented Ellen's two children and they seemed close to both of them.

Evan and Ellen took an active role in groups that were either political or psychologically supportive of parents who are members of the gay and lesbian community. They emerged as role models for others and seemed quite open to advising and supporting others. Their experiences allowed them to play an important role for other gay and lesbian individuals with children, particularly those dealing with the stresses unique to a suburban setting. In the gay and lesbian community they were a high-profile family. Their request for couple therapy was the first psychotherapy experience they were engaging in as a couple. Ellen and Evan had both participated in individual psychotherapy prior to their living together. Both had focused on themes of sexual identity and coming out in their treatment. Their focus was now on their relationship with each other.

CONGRUOUS COUNTERTRANSFERENCE THEMES

In thinking about the totality of this case I begin here with the realization that I have always been a little more excited about beginning my work with gay and lesbian couples and individuals than with heterosexuals. I begin the work with a feeling that I am on familiar ground and that I am going to be able to empathize and apply special insight. This usually wears off rather quickly. I am, of course, colluding with those clients who believe that only a gay therapist can understand them. I am in touch with that voyeuristic side of myself that enjoys meeting and working with gay and lesbian couples, learning about how other couples live and work together in the community. I guess, quite simply, these are my people on both a sociopolitical and emotional level.

With Ellen and Evan this presented me with countertransference dilemmas that needed to be worked through. Ellen and Evan had been together for a longer period of time than any other lesbian or gay couple I had met. I was very taken by this; I felt they were special just by virtue of the longevity of their relationship. I began our work with a conscious need for them to be a couple and to fulfill my fantasy of the potential of long-term homosexual relationships. In the first few sessions I caught myself moving away from exploring the darker and more problematic aspects of their dynamic. It was a few sessions before I pushed myself to delve into what exactly their "fighting" looked like. I did not want to think of them as fighting. I had a sense that what was beneath the surface was very toxic and I could feel myself turning away from the potential that this couple might not be so ideal, so high-functioning or, worse, they might not necessarily be able to maintain themselves as a couple. On a personal level, I was being asked to let go of my own fantasy and need to have a role model, a need that echoes throughout the gay and lesbian community. Cabaj (1991) has delved into the need for gay-identified therapists to be alert to times when their overidentification with their clients causes them to deny what needs to be analyzed. In my work with most couples I usually delve into psychopathology and have to remind myself to remain oriented to the couple's and individuals' strengths. Here, I was avoiding an analysis of what their "fights" were about. About eight sessions into our work, I was able to use my own feelings in a way that would ultimately help Ellen and Evan better understand what had begun happening to them in their own psychosocial context.

When couples are in a prolonged difficult period characterized by tension and conflict, they experience a shifting of allegiances and alliances with their friends. Usually several friends become aligned with one partner, while different friends support the other. As Ellen and Evan described the shifts in their friendship networks, it seemed that most people were distancing themselves from both of them. I believe that my initial pull to deny the intensity of the pathology that they presented as a couple parallels their friends' need to move away from them during this crisis. (Months later, I was working with one of their friends, who revealed that she could not stand to be around them because it was so depressing watching them argue and thinking about the possibility of their not being a couple any longer.) Losing their network served to make them more isolated during a difficult period. As they were both exquisitely sensitive, they experienced people moving away from them as a narcissistic injury, which served to deepen their sense of loss and abandonment.

I was able to use my countertransference to help them understand the experiences of those around them. I acknowledged that I, too, reacted to them as role models and felt myself denying the extent of the conflict that existed between them. As I had avoided this material in the beginning of our work, so, too, were their friends avoiding witnessing Ellen and Evan's possible breakup. This enabled them to reconsider their perceived abandonment and start to experience the underlying loss of their own relationship. As they began to mourn the loss of what once was, they were able to openly share the sadness of their conflict with each other. This helped to shift the affective tone of the sessions from intense, hostile bantering to a more authentic and ultimately painful realization of how much the relationship had deteriorated. They moved from being able to express only anger toward each other to being able to discuss how alone, how disappointed, and how frightened they felt.

As I began evaluating and analyzing the dynamics of their "fighting" with them, I learned more about what I had initially been trying to avoid. In the first sessions Ellen dominated the history-telling while Evan quietly and passively looked around, seemingly detached and apathetic. My attempts to stop Ellen, in an effort to allow Evan a chance to talk and to create a working alliance with me, were met with considerable resistance. Ellen insisted that it was only from her that the real and true story would emerge. As I began to set limits, manage behaviors, and establish rules for how they could talk and present material in the session, Evan was ensured more time to present her thoughts and feelings. My limiting Ellen in this way prompted her regularly to threaten to abandon the therapy. Only the thought of leaving Evan unsupervised with me propelled her to comply with the external structure that I imposed. By approximately the thirteenth session, Evan was able to articulate that she was scared of Ellen. Evan gradually disclosed the degree to which violence dominated their relationship. The intensity of the stories that were revealed to me over the next month affected me far more than any other domestic violence case I had treated.

Most of the fights that Ellen and Evan had over the previous year had ended in violence. Although Ellen was only slightly more robust than Evan, it was Evan who would consistently be physically hurt. On several occasions her injuries had required medical attention, including stitches and a brace for a fractured finger. On a superficial level, the pattern of events began with Ellen experiencing something that Evan had done as being provocative and purposely directed against her. Ellen's anger would then escalate and intensify to the point where she would strike out against Evan. Evan would run away and return several hours later to find a calm and contrite Ellen, who would then apologize for having become violent. Although this was not an unfamiliar pattern in domestic violence, I was disgusted and enraged with Ellen in a way that I had not experienced with other people with whom I have worked. I needed to evaluate these countertransference reactions in order to allow the work to proceed therapeutically. My self-analysis would ultimately help them learn about the dynamics that perpetuated this pattern.

What Ellen and Evan had done was shatter my fantasy of what a long-term lesbian couple would look like. I was operating at first from my wish for them to be together and to be a model couple for myself and others. As the first months of therapy proceeded, the level of psychopathology and violence was so difficult to process that it made me sad, angry, and also ashamed. I remember many years ago listening to my grandmother's gossip in the kitchen about some neighbor; her tirade had ended with the incredulous exclamation, "And they're Jewish, too!" I had never had a problem working with violence in heterosexual couples, but now these issues were stimulating intense thoughts and feelings for me. As with my grandmother gossiping in the kitchen, this one was a bit too close to home for comfort.

During one session Ellen and Evan described an argument they'd had in a department store that followed the usual pattern—Ellen's perception of Evan as being insensitive to her needs became a catalyst to rage. While listening to this description, all I could focus on was how angry I was at both of them. They had probably confirmed the most biased stereotypes of homosexual relationships for the surrounding heterosexual suburban audience. How could they risk such sociopolitical damage? My model couple was disintegrating in front of an audience, an audience that I feared would generalize their negative reactions to them as a couple to me and my partner.

The complicating factor in the countertransference dynamic was that I was resonating with my own homophobia. Although therapy and experience have brought me much freedom, here I was regressing. My irrational reactions contained my own powerful need to prove how normal I really am and my own fear of rejection by the larger society.

It was my homophobia that led me to generalize from Ellen and Evan to all homosexual couples and to my own relationship. I found myself asking if these relationships are bound for failure. It was my homophobia that fed the need to have Ellen and Evan be the role models I craved—and I was left angry and disappointed with them for having so many problems together. Ironically, I never thought for a moment that the problems of heterosexual couples indicated fundamental crises that threatened the future ability of men and women to create meaningful intimacy. There was still something within me that colluded with the belief that same-sex relationships are inherently neurotic and will inevitably break down at some point. Ellen and Evan reawakened this within me and it scared me. I, like their friends, had withdrawn from the salient issues of violence and aggression that needed to be addressed. In retrospect, I was hoping not to face some of the darker realities of this relationship and the possibility of its ultimate dissolution.

These countertransference issues influenced me in another way that needed to be thoughtfully analyzed. Because Ellen was the aggressor and seemingly the catalyst to their explosive conflicts, I came to view her as being more responsible for the dynamics of the relationship than Evan. My countertransference had temporarily blinded me to the contributions each made to their domestic violence.

This displacement of blame paralleled what Ellen and Evan were doing with each other. Ellen saw Evan as being responsible for the problems in the relationship. Evan, I came to learn, saw Ellen as being responsible for the problems, a position I reinforced. Everyone was looking to blame someone else rather than look within himself or herself. For me, it was easier to work with a violent lesbian client than with a dysfunctional lesbian couple, both of whom were involved in perpetuating and maintaining the violence between them. Once this issue was clear to me, I was free to explore how they were both a part of a system of violence. We began by facing the reality that they were both physically and emotionally unsafe in the relationship and that if the violence did not stop, they would have to consider separating while we worked together. Sure enough, each session started with details of major conflicts the night or day before that had culminated in Evan's getting hurt in some way. We began to process the material they presented from a more multidimensional view as Evan's role in the cycle of violence was recognized. As I directed this shift, I began to move out of the protected shadow of being able to blame the violent one for what was wrong in the relationship. This was not an emotionally healthy lesbian woman being victimized by an out-of-control, unhealthy lesbian woman but two women who were bringing out the most negative and dysfunctional elements of each other's emotional life. My fantasy had been that this was not a dysfunctional couple but that everything would be just fine if we could get Ellen on some major tranquilizer; then the relationship could keep going.

To direct this shift, I needed to accept the significant pathology that existed in this couple and the possibility that Ellen and Evan might not be able to do the work needed to move toward a healthy intimacy. Once I was able to contain my fears of this couple failing and learned to tolerate being with a long-term lesbian couple in so much distress, the therapy became manageable. What I needed to accept was the dismantling of my own fantasy and values.

Projective Identification Themes

The focus over the next couple of months became the mutual exploration of the dynamics of their past relationships, specifically with their families of origin. Together we evaluated how these dynamics created a dysfunctional and cyclical pattern in which each was gratified by aspects of the violence that had become commonplace between them. As we analyzed how Ellen and Evan influenced each other, I learned more about their families and childhood histories. Together we worked to illuminate the source of the current problems between them. We acknowledged that the goal would be to establish new patterns of being together that would allow them to sidestep their repetitive pathological dance. As we made connections between their histories and the present, I was able to use myself as a source of important information relating to how they were experiencing each other in the present and how they experienced unresolved relationships from the past.

For the first time, Ellen and Evan began to understand each other's histories and how past experiences were influencing what was happening in the here and now. Ellen described a safe, protected, and idyllic early childhood that was shattered by the unexpected death of her mother when she was a young girl. Her father, overburdened and depressed, withdrew from her. Her older brothers became very controlling and rigid and did not allow her to express herself or process her feelings. They were also habitually physically abusive.

Evan described the chaos and tension typical of alcoholic families. Her mother actively drank and would physically abuse Evan's younger sister and sometimes her brother — but never her. Evan had mastered how to assuage her mother's wrath and would avoid being the target. She would most often accomplish this with passivity and compliance. Evan would also play a peacekeeping role between her mother and father, with the goal being to decrease the intensity of their arguments. Ellen and Evan came to realize that their current problems replicated some of the dynamics that existed in their families growing up.

Ellen, who was never allowed to express her pent-up rage, had found a forum to express it. She identified with the aggressor when she acted out physically. We discussed how this was an attempt, in the here and now, to both master and avoid the pain she experienced as a child. Ellen also began to take more responsibility for her overall separation anxiety, which invaded her intimate relationships. We discussed her sensitivity to abandonment and loss and how this was triggered when Evan was passive and withdrawn. Her experience of an empathic failure took her back to a far more primitive, intense, and pervasive experience of loss.

Evan came to understand her continuing need to live in the shadow of someone else's menacing anger. A crucial element of the dynamic was Evan's experience of power when she was able to ignite Ellen's rage. In this way, Ellen's rage had come to be exciting to Evan. Its release ultimately allowed Evan to feel some mastery over her own aggression. Evan came to understand that as a child she spent enormous amounts of intrapsychic energy putting out fires and that she still welcomed the opportunity to watch the flames from as safe a distance as possible.

These projective identification themes became the focus of the work for the next couple of months. In the process the couple developed better communication skills and at times acknowledged feeling understood by each other. I also became more central to the couple's stability and became the recipient of individual and dyadic projections. As we began isolating the psychogenic roots of Ellen's sadness and fear of abandonment, she put me in the position of being the bad object. Despite my clarity about our appointments, Ellen would show up at my office alone on the wrong day and at the wrong time. Tearfully, she would turn and walk away when I explained that I was working with other people that evening. She denied that she was looking for a chance to work with me alone and turned down opportunities to work outside of the couple sessions.

I was very frustrated on these occasions and thought how impossible she made it to take care of her or help her feel important. I was able to see Ellen as the rejected, neglected, and unwanted burden that she felt herself to be ever since her mother's sudden death. This was a role she would play with Evan as well. With exquisite sensitivity, Ellen was always searching for anything that would show how Evan could not or would not respond to her needs. I was also able to feel Evan's frustration with this pattern. It would be impossible to nurture Ellen or provide for her emotional needs.

In our couples therapy sessions, Ellen had begun threatening to leave the session when she did not like something that Evan said. This threat hung over our sessions together. It was only after I introduced my countertransference to them as a couple that they were able to identify the meaning of this theme in their lives together. I shared my feelings of being unable to provide for Ellen and how frustrating it was for me to fail her in this way. This experience compared to Evan's role in the dynamic between them.

Evan's devalued self took the form of not allowing herself the right to her own voice. She had learned from an early age that being invisible was equated with safety. One of the most anxiety-provoking affects she could potentially express would have been anger, particularly as she experienced it in her relationship with Ellen. Ellen was as unsafe an object for such expression as her mother had been. In her relationship with me, I felt Evan would reveal just enough of her emotional life to be understood, only to then withdraw into a passive and uncommunicative stance. On these occasions I would feel angry at her and think to myself, What a dependent, childlike attitude to take when there is such serious work to be done. I also felt a pull from Evan to speak for her, whether to set limits on Ellen's aggressive behavior or to explain some aspect of her emotional life in an effort to sidestep the projective identifications that complicated their relationship.

While Evan's withdrawal was certainly a well-developed safety mechanism, my anger was a key to understanding its passive-aggressive aspect. Although Ellen was impulsive and needed to develop self-control, she was also being provoked. I could now feel it in my work with Evan. I introduced this into our work when Evan had become quiet after she had said something of significance and Ellen had actually listened to her for a minute. My experience of frustration and anger allowed Evan to better understand her role in the couple's difficulties and confirmed Ellen's experience as well. This helped Ellen to be less defensive about taking responsibility for her anger and how she expressed it. We identified together that it was Evan's childlike position that reinforced Ellen's dominant, authoritative manner and cast her in the role of the mother. We agreed that reenacting these roles would never allow them to be equals, a prerequisite to a safer and more authentic relationship.

As a couple, Ellen and Evan catalyzed thoughts and feelings within me that eventually facilitated understanding more about the projective identifications active in their relationship. For me, the primary affect dominating the sessions at this time was anxiety. My anxiety held within it clues to conflicts that existed in their representational worlds. As we began to untangle the dynamics of their conflict I became more sure of what was happening between them but less sure that they would remain in therapy long enough to work it through. With Evan's emotional withdrawal and Ellen's threatening to leave the session, I was the one feeling the fear of abandonment and loss. Working with them brought a sense of imminent loss and danger. I felt anxious juggling the demands of keeping Evan from her defensive position of passivity and Ellen involved and working but not so threatened that she would terminate.

I came to feel that I was responsible for maintaining this balance and that if one of them left the session, literally or figuratively, it was because of my incompetence. They, of course, bought into this and in covert ways reinforced my thinking and feeling. They were psychologically gratified by the amount of anxiety I had been willing to absorb; this helped them both to feel safer, although it did not facilitate psychological growth. There was less reported violence at home but just the same amount of disappointment, sadness, and hopelessness. They felt as a couple that they had come a long way and were ready to talk about termination. Joan Lachkar (1992) has identified this phenomenon as prevalent in couples where borderline and narcissistic pathology prevails. The countertransferential risk, as she views it, is to agree with them and terminate the therapy.

My objective was to move beyond the stagnation by empowering them with insight I was gaining through my countertransference. We discussed how I had become the one carrying the anxiety for them, and explored how my feeling the pressure of maintaining their anxiety levels paralleled how they felt with each other. Ellen and Evan both verbalized the incessant threat of abandonment by the other and their fear that mistakes would push the other away. Because of their history of loss, these current themes escalated the unresolved issues from their past and intensified their fear of each other. Ellen's mother's sudden death had shattered an idyllic world; would Evan do the same to her? Evan's parents had slipped away from her via either alcohol or apathy; would Ellen similarly abandon her?

My experience of them as a couple and direct introduction of my countertransference helped them fully appreciate the impact of their anxiety.

Slowly, they began to show empathy and nurturance toward each other. They began to think and talk about their need to separate. The separation was presented as one where they could maintain a friendship and effectively co-parent Ellen's children. For me, it is still sometimes difficult to think of this long-term lesbian couple not being a couple anymore. However, I have been able to use my expanded self-awareness to guide me and keep my own needs and values separate.

A few weeks ago I was waiting for Ellen and Evan, who were to be my first appointment that afternoon. As I walked to the door to let them in I noticed that I had put on shoes from two different pairs. They were both casual boat shoes and looked very much alike but with slightly different coloring and stitching. I thought in that moment about what a wonderful metaphor that was for my coming to terms with their being a mismatch. On the surface there looked to be harmony, but a closer and careful inspection revealed that they did not truly belong together. I felt this had meaning for me and Ellen and Evan in the here and now, as I had always been able to dress myself appropriately before. As I let them in, I knew we had something potentially rich to work with. If they did not notice my sartorial error, then I would bring it up in the same spirit and with the same goals with which I had shared my thoughts and feelings in our past work.

REFERENCES

Cabaj, R. (1991). Overidentification with a patient. In C. Silverstein (Ed.), *Gays, lesbians and their therapists* (pp. 31–39). New York: Norton.

Cornett, C. (1995). *Reclaiming the authentic self: Dynamic psychotherapy with gay men.* Northvale, NJ: Jason Aronson.

Greenson, R., & Wexler, M. (1969). The non-transference relationship in the psychoanalytic situation. *International Journal of Psychoanalysis, 50,* 27–39.

Isay, R. (1993). On the analytic therapy of homosexual men. In C. Cornett (Ed.), *Affirmative dynamic psychotherapy with gay men* (pp. 23–43). Northvale, NJ: Jason Aronson.

Lachkar, J. (1992). *The narcissistic/borderline couple: Psychoanalytic perspective on marital treatment.* New York: Brunner/Mazel.

11

And Baby Makes Three

JUDITH P. SIEGEL

BEFORE THE HOPE of having children came into my life I had not fully realized the extent to which the therapist's life circumstances impact on the therapy. Professional objectivity and neutrality had been stressed throughout my training, and I naively believed that my private life could remain such during the time I spent with clients. This belief was challenged when I went through a divorce and overidentified with one of my clients who was also going through a divorce. Although our life circumstances were quite different, I often listened to her with a voyeuristic ear, for she was months ahead of me in the legal and emotional process. When we terminated I disclosed my own divorce and thanked her for in some way helping me through my own difficult moments. She was touched by the disclosure but also relieved that I had not told her during her therapy with me. The boundary between professional and private self had been maintained, and therapeutic objectivity had prevailed.

A CASE OF INFERTILITY

I was six months into my second marriage when I had my first appointment with Beth. She was in the process of being divorced by her husband of one year and had been referred by her internist because of psychosomatic abdominal pain. Beth was significantly depressed about both the failed marriage and her lost opportunity to have a baby, which she seemed to be miscarrying psychogenically. Gordon, who was almost twenty years older, had four young adult children from his first marriage. The couple had dated for a few months when Beth decided to end the affair because, at age 38, she knew she wanted to have children and Gordon would probably not. He had surprised her by confessing to a deep love for her and a willingness to have children with her, providing his vasectomy could be reversed. After a successful operation and settlement of a prenuptial agreement, the couple married.

Beth admitted that she had become obsessed with getting pregnant and that she could tell she was alienating Gordon. She was surprised, however, when he announced that the marriage was a mistake and that he was moving out. Shortly after, her abdominal pain developed. Beth used our sessions to get in touch with her profound anger and sorrow. As the only child of parents who had been in their forties when she was born, she had been doted on throughout her childhood. Her parents had nevertheless placed high expectations upon her and assumed that she would excel academically and athletically. Beth had been emotionally closer to her father than her mother and felt an unambivalent love from him that was a source of inspiration and strength. Her relationship with her mother was more complicated. Beth believed that in some ways her mother was envious of her success and perhaps resentful of the close relationship between her husband and daughter. The family rarely acknowledged emotionally charged issues, and the tension between mother and daughter had not been discussed or resolved.

A few months into our individual sessions, Gordon told Beth he wanted to reconcile and asked to join our sessions. Gordon had been depressed since the separation and felt he had acted in haste. He had been attracted to Beth because of her high level of energy, her intelligence, and her *joie de vivre*. She made him feel like the most important thing in her life, and he became dependent on her to lift his spirits and make him feel important. Beth was attracted to Gordon's calm demeanor and sophistication. She needed a man who would not be intimidated by her business success and vitality. I noticed that Gordon could also pamper Beth like a special child, and both seemed to enjoy this parent-child kind of interaction. There were many narcissistically vulnerable components to their relationship, as they tended to experience either a blissful connectedness or a cold distancing precipitated by Gordon's rage. This state was stimulated primarily by Beth's focus on becoming pregnant, which left Gordon feeling excluded and unloved. Beth avoided recognizing Gordon's mild displays of irritation and tried to believe that Gordon held the same desires and level of commitment as she. Therapy entailed providing a holding environment where the splitting could be addressed and each could learn to communicate his or her needs and feelings without fearing a rageful reaction.

Our work progressed smoothly until the couple agreed to attempt pregnancy again and Gordon's sperm count was found to be low. Beth was referred to an infertility clinic for assisted reproduction, a process that at the time I knew relatively little about. The couple had started to look at terminating couples treatment, but decided to stay on for support with the stress of trying to conceive.

In my own life I was also trying to conceive and, although my gynecologist reassured me that there was no reason for alarm, I believed that I, too, was going to have to face unknown obstacles. I listened carefully to Beth's descriptions of the impersonal clinic, the disparaging statistics for women our age, and the endless phone calls with insurance companies. Beth's treatment included pergonal injections, which she learned to give herself daily. Gordon was supportive of his wife's efforts, but sheepishly admitted to being afraid to give needles. I remember feeling angry at him, despite Beth's insistence that she understood and accepted his limitations. Therapy was a safe place for Beth to talk about her frustrations and anxiety. In her childhood she had accomplished the family's needs for perfection, and she was the "golden girl" to both of her parents. The cost of her success was premature emotional self-sufficiency and repression of all unacceptable feelings, such as anger. She had particular difficulty accepting her loss of control over conceiving and tended to blame herself in ways that led to depression and exhaustion. Gordon experienced Beth's sadness as a withdrawal of narcissistic supplies and tended to respond with passive-aggressive anger that sabotaged Beth's chances of successful fertilization. Both began to use me to provide acceptance and support of their underlying feelings and help them relate to each other with greater tolerance and empathy.

Beth had gone through four unsuccessful cycles when my own nightmare began. Preliminary tests verified my own fertility problems, and my doctor referred me to the same infertility clinic that Beth attended. On my first appointment I had as much anxiety about running into Beth as what the test results might be. I decided I had to disclose my own effort to conceive and the fact that we were mutual patients.

Beth seemed stunned by the news. Her first response was that I was several years younger and would probably have no problem conceiving. I found myself silently agreeing with her and experiencing a sense of victory. As I processed my reaction I realized that in fact I was not much younger than Beth at all and that my sense of competition was very out of character. When I asked her what she thought it might be like for her if I got pregnant quickly, her silence contained hatred. She could not talk about her reaction in greater depth, but canceled our next appointment. I wondered about the source of my competitive reaction to Beth and how I would feel if her insemination was successful while mine failed. I was aware of my bitterness toward all real and imagined pregnant women and could not imagine how this would not be communicated to her.

The therapeutic alliance was irreversibly strained. Beth denied having any reactions to our shared patient status: the more I tried to focus on it the more silent she became. Within a few sessions, Beth had withdrawn from me and was increasingly self-sufficient. She had less and less to talk about, and became a "realistic optimist" about all aspects of the infertility clinic. I was no longer able to serve as a good enough object and my efforts to provide a holding environment, acceptance, or insight were rebuffed. My observations of the changes in our relationship and their connection to our shared infertility seemed to create frustration for her, and she continued to deny that my situation affected her in any way. Beth spoke of finally accepting her lack of control over her own infertility and the strength she felt from letting go of her belief that she was responsible for the outcome of the inseminations. As these were issues we had worked on together prior to my self-disclosure, I felt trapped: how could I support her growth while questioning whether it was real? Gordon, relatively pleased with the quality of their relationship, also seemed annoyed by my interest in processing the impact of my situation. Gordon's narcissistic vulnerability made it frustrating for him to feel peripheral in the session and he was content with Beth's resumed optimism and energy. Beth and Gordon decided to end their couples treatment with a flight into health and, although I believed that breaking through Beth's denial would ultimately have enabled her to discuss envy, anger, and other feelings that to her were unacceptable, I could not reverse their decision.

A CASE OF IMPASSE OVER PREGNANCY

Two years later I had an interesting consultation appointment with a lesbian couple. Jean and Sharon had been together for six years and were co-parenting Jean's two adolescent children. Although Sharon had initially been content with this family constellation, she experienced the urgency of the "biological clock" when she turned 38 and realized that she wanted to have a baby of her own. Jean, now 42, was just finishing graduate school and was firm in her resolve to devote herself to her new profession, Sharon, and unencumbered traveling. Despite their mutual respect and affection, each became increasingly entrenched in her separate position and felt unloved by an unresponsive partner.

My reaction was complicated by the fact that I had just learned that I was five weeks pregnant and that there was some degree of risk. Under normal circumstances I would not reveal my pregnancy to clients for several weeks more. Once I understood the nature of this couple's underlying conflict I told them that I did not think I was an appropriate therapist for them, but would refer them to someone whom I thought they would easily connect with. They both insisted that they felt very comfortable with me and my style and needed to know why I couldn't work with them. When I explained my pregnancy, they both insisted that my life was my own business. I replied that even though I liked Jean, I felt I would unconsciously overidentify with Sharon and that would not be a helpful experience for either of them. Jean was especially vocal in trying to persuade me that we could monitor that situation together. Reluctantly, I agreed to help them with their predicament.

The early work in therapy focused on the projective identifications underlying their tense mode of interacting and the difficulty each had expressing anger directly. Jean grew up in Brooklyn as the younger of two children born to Jewish immigrant parents whose lives had been dramatically affected by World War II. Although neither of her parents had been confined in concentration camps, they had both suffered extensive discrimination and loss before they were able to escape. Like many children of her generation, Jean described tremendous pressure to achieve and a family culture where nothing she did was good enough. Because of her family's limited financial resources, she had been denied the college education provided to her brother, and she married at a young age to escape the family tension and control. She found herself attracted to a female neighbor after she had been married ten years and had two children. She initiated a divorce in order to pursue that relationship; since then she had had three significant partners. Jean suffered with anxiety that surfaced when she needed to speak publicly or when she experienced strong feelings, and at those times she felt like running out of the room. She had no interest in psychotherapy to work on these issues except as they affected Sharon.

Sharon grew up in a relatively stable family as the middle child of three. She had a particularly close relationship with her mother, and was in that way was triangulated into her parent's marriage. Sharon had married a fellow graduate student, but divorced two years later. Her sexual preference was not fully revealed until she was in her early thirties, and she had been involved in only one intimate relationship before she met Jean. Letting go of that attachment had been extremely difficult for her, and she stated that she dreaded the thought of having to date again. Sharon had a job that provided stimulation and adequate financial compensation.

For many years the relationship had been satisfying for both. Each partner felt extreme gratitude to the other for helping her pursue a meaningful career and supporting her through difficult life crises. Sharon's father had died shortly after she moved in with Jean, and Jean had helped her through her mourning. Jean's son had learning problems, and Sharon provided tutoring and support. The two had rarely fought before Sharon's desire to become pregnant surfaced. Their discussions began calmly, and they both could empathize totally with the other's situation, but without changing their own position. The resulting anger was not expressed directly, but surfaced over quarrels around household chores, such as uncleaned messes, and money. At the root of every quarrel, however, was the need for one partner to sacrifice her life's dream, and their shared refusal to do so. At the same time, they were deeply attached to each other, and neither wanted to take action that would lead to dissolution of the relationship.

Sharon decided to go ahead with artificial insemination, hoping that Jean would change her mind once she got pregnant. Jean hoped that with any luck Sharon would not get pregnant and they could continue to share their lives. Underneath this was a growing resentment toward me and my expanding belly. The relationship tension continued to escalate as Sharon began to turn to old and new friends to share her insemination experiences and be supported when a cycle failed. While Jean felt jealous and excluded, she was unable to tolerate listening to the details of Sharon's cycle and insemination experiences. When Sharon's menstrual period confirmed another failed attempt, Jean could not hide her pleasure. I felt trapped in my work at this point, as it was impossible to be supportive to one partner's concerns without in some way violating the other partner's belief in my care and validation of her position. I interpreted this to them as a shared projective identification, as we all felt polarized and fearful of irreversible damage.

There was a growing but unarticulated tension building between Jean and me. I could empathize with Jean's lament that this was the first time she felt like her life was her own and I understood how her imposed childhood sacrifices magnified her feelings of being betrayed and overlooked. In the session, however, I often felt that Jean needed me for the singular purpose of changing Sharon's mind; if I could not do that, I was useless to her. I also experienced Sharon's appeal to me for help in changing Jean, a project she tried to ensure through friendship and humor. I felt manipulated in a different way by each, and because I was unable to produce what either wanted, increasingly devalued. My most intense countertransference, however, came from being pregnant.

My pregnancy affected my work in several ways. Pregnancy to me was blissful, partly because it had been wanted so desperately and partly because of the miracle it truly is. I was introduced to the alliance of motherhood, strangers for the most part, who would smile at or touch my stomach and volunteer their own pregnancy stories without even being introduced. I knew that not all women felt that way about their pregnancies, and yet I found it hard to comprehend how Jean, who had given birth twice, could fight to deprive Sharon of the joy I had in my life. Sharon's own drive and determination helped me contain my overidentification, but there were many times I secretly applauded her pursuit of pregnancy in ways that must have been perceived by both.

Therapy with this couple also helped me develop an awareness of how my pregnancy created a tension between my professional and personal life. I often felt like my baby was becoming a target for this couple's anger and most often sat with my hands folded over my stomach in a protective and concealing way. Becoming aware of my competing roles as therapist and mother, I worried that my unborn baby might be suffering from the stress of my work. Jean acted as if my pregnancy were goading Sharon on, that she would have abandoned her quest for a baby if she were not constantly reminded by my pregnancy. Rather than express anger at Sharon, Jean was becoming increasingly angry at me. Sharon would arrive early for their appointment and quickly tell me about her latest medical developments. Jean would arrive late and in a surly mood, denying her anger and blaming her lateness on her studies or the traffic. My efforts to talk about the pregnancy and how they each felt about it were responded to with polite inquiries into my health and well-being and denial of its impact on their therapy.

I gave birth prematurely and was not available to see Jean and Sharon for almost a month. When they returned to treatment, Jean's anger was no longer masked. She was angry at me for abandoning her, but also denied having any need for me at all. My interpretation of how my "no win" situation struck me as similar to her childhood experience of feeling like the family failure, despite her hard efforts to win praise, only increased her wrath. Sharon took a protective stance toward Jean, which aided Jean's detour of anger from her to me. It occurred to me that she, too, was angry at me for having achieved what she was deprived of, and that Jean's anger served a purpose for her as well. Jean announced that because of her now due student loans, unemployment, and financial stress magnified by her child's special summer schooling needs, she was no longer willing to pay for couples treatment. Sharon returned for one subsequent session to terminate with me; although she was willing to work with me on an individual basis, she recognized that it would preclude Jean's ever returning for couples therapy in the future. I spoke to Sharon one year later to give her a referral to a psychotherapist specializing in infertility, as her inseminations had not been successful and she was depressed about giving up her dream to have children.

DISCUSSION

In both cases, my reactions contained aspects of all three forms of countertransference. My need to be needed, my grandiose decision to persist despite my awareness of therapeutic complications that contraindicated my suitability to provide the therapy, and my active voyeurism all speak to classical countertransference themes that were insufficiently addressed.

Other reactions were clearly projective identifications that enabled me to understand the individual and relationship dynamics more completely

(Ogden, 1979; Siegel, 1992). In the case of the infertile couple, my competitive reaction to Beth and my initial anger at Gordon for not giving her the pergonal injections were good examples of concordant countertransference, where I accepted and experienced Beth's reactions as my own (Racker, 1953). Only later did I understand that my sense of frustration when I failed at working through the impact of my self-disclosure was also in part Beth's reaction to failing to become pregnant in spite of doing everything in her power. My sense of inadequacy and powerlessness undoubtedly mirrored her own situation and most likely reenacted internalized object relations. Beth's flight into self-sufficiency was also an important transference, which revealed aspects of her relationship with her mother. Although I had appreciated from the beginning that Beth's need to control and excel had narcissistic roots, her reaction to my perceived lack of availability was very similar to a false-self compliance, with aggressive components (Hanna, 1992).

In the case of the couple at impasse over pregnancy, there were many examples of countertransference as projective identification. My sense of being needed for only one purpose was a concordant countertransference to Jean, who had been manipulated and devalued in her own family. My impulse to protect Sharon reflected a complementary countertransference, as she elicited in me the kind of support she formerly received from her mother.

Complicating this was the reality of my infertility and, later, my pregnancy, and the impact of these life events on my work. In general, too little attention has been given to the life circumstances of the therapist and the ways in which these affect the therapy. Only recently have issues other than pregnancy been thoughtfully addressed, although therapists experience illness, marital stress, and a host of personal life events that affect their work (Gerson, 1996; Gold & Nemiah, 1993). The traditional analytic position advises against disclosure. Because transference requires that the analyst be a blank screen upon which the patient can create revealing themes, personal information about the analyst can contaminate the therapy. Greenson, for example, noted that problems in an analyst's personal life could make him more susceptible to countertransference and advised the analyst to cancel appointments for a few days (Aaron, 1974).

More recently, some therapists have advocated sharing personal information, especially in instances when the therapist's situation is not one that can be sufficiently resolved in a short period of time (Weiner, 1983). This seems obvious in instances where the therapist's life event is public knowledge. Because the establishment of a transference, which is vital to analytic treatment, is not necessary in successful couples therapy, the argument of contamination seems almost irrelevant.

Goldstein (1994) has suggested that the therapist's disclosure should be prompted by the client's needs and best interest. She argues that when this happens the resulting sense of mutual honesty and openness leads to a more connected way of relating. However, when the information that is revealed changes the meaning of the therapist to the client, many unanticipated pitfalls are created. In addition to imposing a burden or creating a sense of responsibility that impedes treatment, the realities of the therapist's situation can dramatically change the way in which the therapist is experienced by the couple. The partners may feel undeserving of the therapist's time and attention and reluctant to add to the therapist's stress or pain. Because the therapist is now viewed as preoccupied or depleted, his/her perceived capability to provide needed resources to the couple may be sharply diminished. Scharff and Scharff (1987) have discussed the importance of contextual transference and countertransference, which they conceptualize as a vital aspect of therapy. They suggest that one of the therapist's most important functions is to provide a holding environment in which the needs of the client can be recognized and responded to.

I believe that because of my infertility Beth experienced me as a rival to her, as someone she could no longer trust. Her flight into health was in part precipitated by the fact that in her eyes I was no longer capable of holding her emotional experiences and safeguarding her well-being, a contextual transference that most likely mirrored childhood experiences with a rival, emotionally distant mother. My perceived unavailability propelled her to become strong and self-sufficient.

In a similar way, my pregnancy stimulated anger in both Jean and Sharon, although my overidentification prevented me from seeing Sharon's indirect hostility at the time. While the occurrence of anger stimulated by the therapist's pregnancy has been documented in other kinds of treatment situations (Genende, 1988), my pregnancy held specific meaning for a couple struggling with the issue of conception. I became a target and receptacle for anger that was too dangerous to be confined within their relationship, as my pregnancy was a real reminder of their polarized differences. The more I came to symbolize their conflict, the less able they were to see me as useful.

In both cases I decided to share my parallel life situation early in its development and tried to process the consequences by focusing on the changes in the therapeutic relationship informed by observation as well as countertransference reactions. While I was prepared to look at the countertransference themes revived by my own unresolved internalized issues and the projective identification themes, I had difficulty working with the reactions in my work precipitated by my pursuit of and experience of pregnancy. Nadelson et al. (1974) have spoken about the identity changes that occur in the therapist in her first pregnancy. While there was undoubtedly some element of preoccupation and fascination with my changing body, my stronger feeling was one of resentment regarding the invasion of my privacy. The time that I needed to recover from both my infertility and later a precarious pregnancy was compromised by my professional responsibilities. I felt compelled to share personal information that I was not ready to disclose and to assume a composed posture around events that were still raw, unprocessed, and difficult to manage (Meyers et al., 1995).

While neither case had an ideal outcome, I believe that the disclosure was necessary. What I am left questioning are the functions of the therapist that are contaminated when parallel life situations enter the treatment room and the ways in which both the therapist and clients must struggle together in order to move beyond. Childbearing is a particularly sensitive subject to couples experiencing infertility, and the therapist's personal situation is bound to have an especially profound impact. I am also cognizant of the ways the therapist grows through these life experiences (Ruderman, 1986), so that he/she is ultimately better able to be responsive and empathically available to future clients who experience similar situations. The challenge, however, is to find a way to utilize concurrent parallel life situations so that their effects on the therapy can be safely examined and made clinically palatable. By processing the different kinds of countertransference reactions, the therapist has an opportunity to gain a richer understanding of complex relational themes and to manage potentially nontherapeutic responses.

REFERENCES

Aaron, R. (1974). The analyst's emotional life during work. *Journal of the American Psychoanalytic Association, 22,* 160–169.

Genende, J. (1988). A therapist's pregnancy: An opportunity for conflict resolution and growth in the treatment of homosexual men. *Clinical Social Work Journal, 16,* 66–77.

Gerson, B. (1996). *The therapist as a person.* Hillsdale, NJ: Analytic Press.

Gold, J. H. & Nemiah, J. C. (1993). *Beyond transference.* Washington, D.C.: American Psychiatric Press.

Goldstein, E. G. (1994). Self-disclosure in treatment: What therapists do and don't talk about. *Clinical Social Work Journal, 22,* 417–433.

Hanna, E. (1992) False-self sensitivity to countertransference: Anatomy of a single session. *Psychoanalytic Dialogues, 2,* 369–388.

Meyers, M., Weinshel, M., Scharf, C., Kezur, D., Diamond, R., & Rait, D. (1995). An infertility primer for family therapists. *Family Process, 34,* 231–240.

Nadelson, C., Notman, M., Arone, E., & Feldman, J. (1974). The pregnant therapist. *American Journal of Psychiatry, 131,* 1107–1111.

Ogden, T. (1979). On projective identification. *Journal of PsychoAnalysis, 60,* 357–371.

Racker, H. (1953). A contribution to the problem of counter-transference. *International Journal of Psychoanalysis, 34,* 313–324.

Ruderman, E. B. (1986). Gender related themes of women psychotherapists in their treatment of women patients: The creative and reparative use of countertransference as a mutual growth experience. *Clinical Social Work Journal, 14,* 103–124.

Scharff, D., & Scharff, J. S. (1987). *Object relations family therapy.* Northvale, NJ: Jason Aronson.

Siegel, J. (1992). *Repairing intimacy: An object relations approach to couples therapy.* Northvale, NJ: Jason Aronson.

Weiner, M. F. (1983). *Therapist disclosure.* Baltimore, MD: University Park Press.

12

Pitfalls in Couples Therapy around Issues of Parenting

BONNIE S. MARK

MULTIFACETED COUNTERTRANSFERENCE feelings arise when working with couples on parenting problems. Helping a couple enhance their parenting skills potentially creates a transference-countertransference pattern that can easily degenerate into resistance and frustration. Countertransference feelings are especially pronounced in couples treatment if the parenting issues in the therapeutic situation correspond to the very issues therapists have been unable to work through in their own lives. Winnicott (1953) described the need for frequent reexamination of issues in the therapist's personal history or current life, particularly when a therapeutic impasse arises: "I have had to learn to examine my own technique whenever difficulties arose, and it has always turned out in . . . resistance phases that the cause was in a counter-transference phenomenon which necessitated further self-analysis" (p. 280). According to Kernberg, "The analyst's insight into the meaning of his countertransference reaction does not itself help the patient. What helps the patient is the analyst's using this information in his transference interpretations" (1965, p. 53).

In the initial consultation with the parental couple, the therapist may begin with consideration of aspects of the family and home atmosphere that might lead to improvement of the child's problems. Suggestions may involve communication techniques or behavior changes, such as structure setting, developing firm boundaries with follow-through and consequences, and providing consistency in the home. When there is no unconscious agenda, the parents' complaints about their children and their family life can often be dramatically improved with a few concrete changes in the home environment. When problems have deeper roots, the work changes from parent counseling to psychotherapeutic treatment of the couple. In such situations, although there is generally an expressed wish to work toward creating a more appropriate, adequate, or structured environment, the unconscious processes may undermine what initially appears as progress and family behavior may revert over time.

The organization of the dysfunctional family system exists in part to protect parents or other family members from facing their own pathology. In the cases presented in this chapter, the couples did not have the ability to implement or follow through with the changes they initially agreed were necessary. Even when the parents consciously recognized the importance of the physical and emotional tone of the home, they appeared to resist change and were unable to implement any of the recommendations suggested. Therapy seemed ineffective. When such impasses occur, understanding the missing links in the home environment and family dynamics is often facilitated by attention to the countertransference issues that arise.

In working with the Johnsons, parents of a 15-year-old "tagger" (a teen who uses spray paint to put messages on walls and buildings), I was aware of growing frustration, resentment, and a feeling that the parents were not using the time in our sessions effectively. Some of my feelings were due to my own sense of impatience and my tendency to focus on specific actions that need to be taken. Therapy was at an impasse. At first, the parents did not verbalize their own upset and vulnerability. Their son, who perceived himself as a graffiti artist, was acting out by disobeying all rules and structure in the home, stealing spray cans, and eventually getting arrested. The Johnsons came regularly to the sessions, but did not implement the changes we discussed. At one point, I stated, "It seems that little has changed." They agreed, yet continued to perpetuate the same pattern of failing to establish a stable home environment or to provide clear structure and consequences for transgressing boundaries. I began to express to the couple my feelings that my time and their money were not being well spent. They seemed to respond to my sense of being anesthetized, and it paved the way for refocusing the sessions on the emotional deadness that enveloped this family. Issues that the couple had systematically refused to acknowledge now emerged. As they began to express their own feelings and I was able to mirror their emotions through my own internal experience, their ability to respond to their son changed and his acting-out behavior diminished.

THE MISSING PIECE OF THE PUZZLE

A suggestion to the parental couple to explore and examine new areas can cause resistance in many covert and overt forms. A therapist's discomfort, frustration, or anger that cannot be accounted for by anything that has transpired outside of the session can be a sign that this is happening. Reflecting on these countertransference feelings can initiate the search for answers and enhance the therapist's ability to intervene in the family system. The therapist serves at once as an observer and participant in the dynamics of the family. I compare this process to looking for a missing piece to a jigsaw puzzle. By recognizing the feeling that something is missing or incomprehensible within the family interaction, I can utilize curiosity to complete the puzzle. At times, the missing piece is a conscious omission, which comes to light when the parents are ready or when I have created a secure environment for them to reveal whatever was previously buried. With other parents, the missing piece may remain hidden for a long time because of unconscious anxieties about the issues concerned.

I pay particular attention when my sense of bewilderment arises for no reason that I can discern. I might say, "I hear your words, but something seems missing." I then suggest that we might want to search for the missing piece. Sometimes we must begin with issues about the safety of the therapeutic situation. It does not help to make interpretations based upon a particular theory in order to fill in the missing piece. Theory is experience distant (Kohut, 1977) and is unlikely to have an impact on the treatment.

Moreover, rummaging only through well-lit places causes us to miss the less illuminated areas. Using a metaphorical flashlight, we must shine a light into the darker crevices. By focusing on our own countertransference issues, as well as what they are presenting, we can look without shame or blame at the emotional issues evoked.

This search for the missing piece is illustrated by the treatment of a couple living with the secret of the illegitimate birth of their first child. Jon and Barbara endeavored to evade recollecting the grievous secret that haunted and reminded them of their forced marriage, difficult economic situation, and general ambivalence toward their oldest child. The couple decided not to tell their son and were confident that the secret was well maintained among the aunts, uncles, and grandparents. No mention was ever made of this secret. When Jon accused Barbara of never wanting their now 13-year-old, rebellious adolescent, Barbara withdrew from the session and eventually from the room.

Solving the puzzle with Jon and Barbara began with the awareness that some crucial element seemed to be missing. The first part of the process was for me to recognize my own sense of frustration and anger at their elusiveness. As Barbara withdrew, I recognized her shame, her devastation, and her effort to protect some hidden element from coming out. Even though I could see that this was not the time to prod, I had a sense of what she must be feeling. First, I had to be sure that these elicited emotions were indeed hers and not my own. This necessitated my performing a rapid self-assessment during the session and in the time following the session.

A missing puzzle piece is the antithesis of "knowing." Bollas (1983) describes this as the "unthought known." Overcoming the need to account rationally for the missing element in the analysis permits examination of the unknown. Recognizing and interpreting some of the feelings that came to me when Jon confronted Barbara, I shared my experience with them. This seemed to unlock a door to their shameful feelings. In the following session I learned the secrets that housed the pivotally suppressed origins of their marriage. Broaching the issue with a discussion of my response to Jon's confrontation, Barbara was able to discuss her experience and eventually to uncover the shame, guilt, and helplessness that she had carried for so many years. This paved the way for Barbara to express the anger at herself, at her husband, at her parents for forcing her to marry, and at her religion, which had told her that she had no choice but to have the baby. With this family, the key to unlocking the fundamental issues that caused tension and conflict in their family system was the expression of my countertransference feelings. Accessing these countertransference issues first depended on my not insisting upon a specific treatment model to offer a solution, but instead listening to my own emerging feelings and being willing to share them with the couple. Through this process, the parental and family issues were opened up for examination.

REFLECTING ON FAMILY COMPETITION

Sibling rivalry can crucially affect the tone of the home environment. With the Davidsons, the need for their children to compete with and surpass their cousins' achievements was a message conveyed covertly and understood by all in the family. Without an overt declaration, this manifested itself in showing off to the extended family, impressing the grandparents, scoring higher than the cousins on achievement tests, and so on.

As pronounced as the drive for the children to excel was the denial that the sibling rivalry of the past generation continued into this one. In working with this couple, it became clear that their resistance to acknowledging this kept the topic from being raised; the children, aged 10 and 12, were so accustomed to their competitive way of life that they did not challenge it. Instead, the children's rivalry with their cousins led to fierce and violent fights with each other. In this situation, the Davidsons did not know, at least consciously, how the family process was enacted and thus consistently failed to admit how pervasive and disruptive the sibling rivalry was. The use of the missing piece analogy gave them a chance to deliberate on what might be transpiring and thus drove us to look for answers.

It became clear to the Davidsons that their burning expectations and pressure created an explosive family dynamic, which manifested itself in the inability to go on family vacations. Even dinner at a restaurant was an anxiety-ridden experience. The couple kept asking for direction to make surface changes in the family's behavior, such as the imposition of disciplinary consequences, but refused to recognize that the problem with their children was itself rooted in a larger family system.

When the children joined in a family session, I very quickly felt the competitiveness for attention. Everyone, children and parents, wanted to be at center stage. At first, I did not recognize or acknowledge my own discomfort, but soon I identified my feelings of being pulled in several directions at once. At the same time I felt anger toward the parents. They seemed to be refusing to explore the family issues by keeping them submerged beneath the constant noise in the room. Everyone was talking, and even when family members heard each other, no one seemed to listen to what was being said. It was clear that all of the family members, including the parents, were struggling, but there were no silences, and no room for anything significant to be discussed. I began to feel overwhelmed as the chaos resonated inside me.

In the midst of a session, Mrs. Davidson threw her hands in the air and asked, "Are we getting anywhere tonight?" I felt challenged. Suddenly I felt a need to prove to the family that I was adequate to help them. I realized that I was carrying the feelings of the entire family. My need to prove myself, arising at that moment, was in tune with their underlying dysfunctional family pattern. When I was able to recognize what I was feeling and differentiate those feelings from issues in my own life, I could resonate with the feelings the family was having. With this clarity came the ability to help the family understand the process, and in particular to work with the parents, helping them recognize how they were perpetuating roles and behaviors that they disliked. This focus on countertransference issues was the critical tool, the "missing piece," that enabled us to penetrate to the heart of the problem.

I AM SHOUTING AS LOUD AS I CAN: COUNTERTRANSFERENTIAL HATE IN COUPLES THERAPY

The countertransference Pandora's box was opened when Winnicott (1958) discussed the fury he felt towards an incorrigible adolescent boy in his seminal article, "Hate in the Countertransference." His work helped clinicians to recognize and accept the underside of their responses to clients, including judgment, disdain, or discomfort. Winnicott (1949) discusses the therapist's options of remaining silent and containing the hatred or communicating it to the patient in order to further therapy. The main thing, of course, is that through his/her own analysis the therapist becomes free from the vast reservoirs of unconscious hate belonging to the past and to inner conflicts. Sometimes the sense of frustration about both the progress of therapy and the commitment of the patient(s) to therapy can nearly overwhelm the therapist. Rather than interfering in the process, these feelings can also be taken up and interpreted as part of the therapeutic relationship.

I worked with Jill and Joseph in couples therapy while their son, 16-year-old Jake, was in treatment with a colleague. Jake became the primary focus of treatment as Jill and Joseph became increasingly frustrated, impatient, and angry at their child, as well as at the therapy because of the lack of change in their child's behavior. Neither I nor their son's therapist could help them accept the severity of their son's involvement with illegal drugs. Jill and Joseph felt they could help their child heal through love and support and refused to recognize that they were enabling the child to continue to fall deeper into his drug-dependent behavior by not setting definite limits.

As treatment progressed, Jill and Joseph consistently resisted taking any steps that they felt could be interpreted by Jake as throwing him out or not loving him. The couple took this position despite his poor grades, numerous unexplained school absences, and his having been caught selling marijuana at his high school. Recommendations for a therapeutic boarding school that might address his low self-esteem, learning issues, and drug use were refused because Jill and Joseph feared that Jake would experience this as rejection. Jill believed that her son would never forgive her if she sent him away. Other suggestions of ways to help him attain some level of self-control, such as denying him the privilege of driving his car until he had a series of clean drug tests and requiring him to get a part-time job, were not implemented.

Even when it seemed that headway was being made and the couple appeared to understand that a job would give Jake a sense of purpose, encourage responsibility, and promote his self-esteem, the parents could not let him take any initiative on his own to get a job. After the first day of unsuccessful job hunting, Jake informed his parents that his appearance (his long hair and earring) made it hard for him to get hired, and he didn't intend to change the way he looked. Instead of pushing their son to contend with these obstacles, his father found a job for him at a friend's office.

On the one hand, Joseph's action gave Jake an opportunity to work. In the long run, however, the parents' and teen's choices created a setup for failure. Their son did not want the job, did not want to change his appearance, was not motivated to keep the job, and was fired. Moreover, Jake was earning more money from marijuana sales at his school than from his licit employment. From their viewpoint, the couple felt they had implemented the ideas generated from the parenting sessions; therefore, they were rather perturbed when I pointed out that their efforts to rescue their son could not help but backfire. I felt exasperated that they seemed to sabotage efforts I made to offer constructive ways of dealing with their son.

I recognized that I was angry and frustrated and deemed myself unable to clarify my feelings to them. I knew from the child therapist that their son complained of feelings similar to my own with respect to his parents. In fact, I assumed that much of his acting-out behavior was his attempt to be heard and seen as he was, rather than as his parents wanted him to be. At certain moments, I had the desire to scream at them and in some way shake them up into "seeing." This was precisely how they described experiencing their relationship with Jake. Acknowledging my countertransference feelings, I realized that the dynamic in the office duplicated what the family system was like for their son, who felt unheard and misunderstood, as well as for them.

When I began to delve into these countertransference feelings, a significant breakthrough in the therapeutic work was finally possible. I had to recognize that my own anger was due to my conviction that Jill and Joseph had robbed their son of the opportunity to discover some important truths necessary for his growth. Moreover, I felt that they were interfering with his ability to help himself, just as they were constraining my ability to help them. My inclination to reverse the downward spiral in the family simply perpetuated the same patterns that existed between them and their son.

Jill and Joseph were unable to validate and recognize their son's feelings until they were recreated in the therapeutic milieu. Treatment enabled them to examine their role in the family conflict and learn new means of communicating their thoughts, feelings, and expectations, as well as disappointments. As they learned to understand and process these issues on an ongoing basis, a positive shift in the family relations and consequently in Jake's behavior resulted.

A similar situation is described in the following case. The Kleins' marriage had deteriorated over the years because of their disagreement regarding their learning-disabled, delinquent daughter, Julie, now 14. Brad and Amy Klein sought my help because Julie refused any treatment for herself. The couple expressed their hopelessness and helplessness, and conflicts emerged between them as they felt increasingly powerless—even to get her into treatment.

This couple had relinquished their authority, holding on to the feeling that love, acceptance, and becoming "friends" with their child should be paramount. The parents failed to realize that, as much as parents desire to be friends to their children, their children need them as parents. In their child-centered world, Brad and Amy's primary goal was exposing their only daughter to "the world and all its pleasures." For this family, their affluence, their need to do things differently from their own parents, their need to avoid conflict, and their desire to perpetuate the illusion of a well-functioning family in their country club community worked adequately until Julie's adolescence, when she began to get failing grades in her classes at school. This was the critical factor that brought this couple in for treatment.

Despite my encouragement to explore aspects of Brad and Amy's current relationship or history that may have been part of the problem, the only question the couple consistently raised was what to do about Julie's school problems. Addressing the school issue, I proposed a private school option that would meet Julie's learning needs while providing more structure and a therapeutic milieu. I gained insight into the power the daughter had over Brad and Amy when the parents did not follow through with the school choice, reportedly because the girl stated she wanted to attend her local public school with her friends. By acquiescing to the child, these parents had put themselves in a bind. They could not attend to Julie's wishes and also enforce a more appropriate school choice. They decided she would do better if she were at the school she desired. When I suggested that the parents were catering to Julie's demands to avoid conflict, they did not disagree, but they would not insist that she change schools unless she chose to do so. I felt helpless to help them.

With this family, I was constantly repressing my own frustration because I felt a need to help, despite the fact that they rendered my attempted interventions useless. I felt both empathy and rage toward their daughter for being so difficult and creating this unworkable situation. Through recognizing the impossibility of the situation, I could see how I had also been trapped within the family dysfunction. Moreover, just as I needed to feel potent, they sought acknowledgment by being seen as successful in the community and would do anything to avoid looking at their own helplessness. Our problems resulted in a complementary collusion. This was the pattern that had to be broken.

Heimann (1950) has suggested that countertransference is a tool for understanding patients because the therapist's unconscious can sometimes link better with the patient than the rational mind can. Even when the emotions are negative, a deep relational connection can emerge through the feelings of the therapist. With Brad and Amy, I at first empathized with their helplessness as their daughter's performance continued to degenerate. I felt badly for the parents, yet I also recognized a sense of "I told you so" within myself. Acknowledging the part of myself that felt ignored by these parents, I ascertained that my own ego needs, in particular my hope that they would acknowledge that I was right, were interfering with my ability to communicate. I had to put my ego aside as they blamed the public school—and everyone but themselves—for Julie's behavior. For them, accusing others replaced taking responsibility, taking action, and making their daughter accountable. I realized that waiting for them to take a fall to prove that I was right about the school situation had begun to replace other aspects of effective intervention.

Eventually I reflected with the parents on the extent of the helplessness we all felt in the situation. I recognized and shared their impotence, feeling angry, frustrated, and powerless to do anything, just as they did. When I acknowledged this, they asked what they could do, and I asked in turn, "What thoughts do you have about how to handle the problem?" They were no longer like children, rebellious to authority, but equal partners in seeking a solution. It did not take them long to regain their authority as parents to their daughter.

WHEN THE COUPLE NEEDS PARENTING

Although childrearing is often described by couples as their greatest joy, they can also experience the raising of children as their greatest frustration and sorrow. When the balance shifts and parents are filled with emotions ranging from frustration and anger to helplessness, they seek the supportive network provided by their mate, their family, and their friends. Stern (1985) has suggested that a significant role of the father at infancy is to be there for the mother. In many ways, parents seek the therapist as an extension of this role. This is particularly the case if they have feelings of frustration, anger, or shame or feel overwhelmed, since these emotions contribute to a sense of pronounced isolation. This feeling of pervasive loneliness can be experienced irrespective of whether one or two parents are raising the child, in married or divorced families. Even the presence of extended family may not mitigate the isolation. Clients coming to couples therapy presenting problems with parenting may feel that the therapist becomes "the parent they never had," subsequently providing them with the inner resources to parent their own children.

The benefits and drawbacks of such transferential roles are demonstrated in the case of Liza and Bobby, two 30-year-old "kids" who had three young children. Liza expressed her fantasies of "doing parenting right" and her wish to raise children differently from how her parents did. Liza experienced the therapeutic hour as a safe place to talk about her fears that she and Bobby had failed and her ensuing feelings of disillusionment and disappointment. As this couple developed insights and skills as parents during the first months that we worked together, both Liza and Bobby experienced great relief and both placed me in a position of power as the "expert" with regard to parenting their children. Despite the fact that at that time I had no children of my own, in their fantasy I had three "perfect" children. Of course the idealization served to build my sense of self-esteem. I could easily take the expert role, providing them with answers. I looked forward to our sessions because I noticed that while working with them I felt empowered, almost omnipotent.

However, I quickly began to see the counterproductivity of my "expertise" as enabling this couple to stay dependent and insecure. This was a place of familiarity, as both had a great deal of insecurity and low self-esteem, which endured since childhood. Using supervision to understand my part in perpetuating this couple's helplessness, I slowly was able to modify my interventions and function in a more effective manner, giving fewer suggestions and assisting as they developed their own abilities individually and as a couple within the family. It is all too easy to fall into the role of "rescuing parent." It feels at first rewarding and fulfilling. Recognizing that these feelings serve unconscious needs and can interfere with patients' developing their own skills reopens the therapeutic process.

Throughout our work, I had to monitor feelings of wishing to parent Liza and Bobby in place of the sympathetic family or support network they so needed and desired. Reflecting upon these rescue fantasies, I could see that in part I was motivated by feelings of guilt that their life was comparatively far more difficult than my own. Identifying these sentiments was the first step in working with the countertransference, therefore enabling me to monitor my wish to rescue. Searles states, "I used to feel guilt at finding myself powerless to help patients experience and express grief; then I gradually came to realize that in situations in which the patient is beginning to deal with grief nothing is required of me except not to interfere" (1979, p. 31). With Liza and Bobby, the therapeutic process was facilitated by my recognizing and revealing my own feelings of wanting so very much to be there for them—"Perhaps too much," I said. This was followed by their naming aloud their wish to be taken care of. This was a desire that neither had expressed to the other. Indeed, these feelings were so deeply buried that they could acknowledge their existence only when they arose in the transference-countertransference relationship. As we looked at these wishes—to be taken care of and nurtured—feelings that from time to time all parents experience to a greater or lesser extent, I was able to help them learn to provide nurturing to each other.

CONCLUSION

Couples therapy is particularly challenging when addressing parenting issues, because it presents so many difficulties in terms of the multiple overlaps with the therapist's own childhood experiences, parenting experiences, and childrearing values, as well as specific feelings towards patients. A range of emotions can be evoked when working with couples around parenting issues. Sometimes these feelings can be put to work through their introduction directly into therapy. Other times it is necessary to know what is being evoked, but to keep one's counsel or share it only with colleagues. Whether shared with patients or not, awareness of the countertransference feelings helps to keep the treatment on course. An advantage of using the countertransference therapeutically is that it enables the therapist to participate simultaneously in the dynamics of the couple's relationship and in the dynamics of the larger family system, while maintaining the objectivity of an observer. The challenge is to find ways to maintain an observing stance while at the same time immersing oneself into the relational milieu. Ongoing supervision and consultation are important for understanding, identifying, and utilizing countertransference to effectively increase the value of therapeutic interventions.

REFERENCES

Bollas, C. (1987). *The shadow of the object: Psychoanalysis of the unthought known.* New York: Columbia University Press.

Heimann, P. (1950). On countertransference. *International Journal of Psychoanalysis, 31,* 81–84.

Kohut, H. (1977). *Restoration of the self.* New York: International Universities Press.

Kernberg, O. (1965). Notes on countertransference. *Journal of the American Psychoanalytic Association, 13*(1), 38–56.

Racker, H. (1968). *Transference and countertransference.* New York: International Universities Press.

Searles, H. (1979). *Countertransference and related subjects.* New York: International Universities Press.

Slakter, E. (1987). *Countertransference.* New York: Jason Aronson.

Stern, D. (1985). *The interpersonal world of the infant.* New York: Basic.

Winnicott, D. W. (1949). Mind and its relation to the psyche-soma. In D. W. Winnicott, *Clinical notes on disorders of childhood.* London: Heinemann.

Winnicott, D. W. (1953). Transitional objects and transitional phenomena—A study of the first *not-me* possession. *International Journal of Psychoanalysis, 34,* 89–97.

Winnicott, D. W. (1958). Hate in the countertransference. In D.W. Winnicott, *Collected papers: Through pediatrics to psychoanalysis.* New York: Basic.

13

In Sickness and in Health

ROBERT CARROLL

Countertransference is all we've got.

—Carl Whitaker

I work the way I do because it's the way I know how to help.

—Carl Whitaker

ABOUT FIFTEEN years ago, I became increasingly aware of illness, not as a doctor is professionally aware of illness, but personally aware of physical mortality, the role illness had played in my family, and my personal reactions to the patients I had treated over the years, particularly those who were meaningful to me. I ascribed it to becoming middle-aged, some recent knee reconstruction I had, my father's precarious physical health, and other factors. I began to feel I needed to know more about illness. I was aware of my own vulnerability and that I had not had to confront death in my own family in many years.

I began looking for and welcoming referrals of people and families in which physical illness played an important role. I did an informal study of physicians who had developed life-threatening illness and had gone from the doctor's side of the bed to the patient's side to see what they had learned. I became aware of the predicaments caused by illness both for the sick individual and for families in which someone became sick. I concluded that as a physician I had a dual relationship to illness, both professional and personal, and I began exploring how they must both be brought into play in the service of the therapeutic task.

It was in this context that Allen and Lenore were referred to me about eight years ago.

CASE PRESENTATION

When I first met Lenore she frightened me. Illness surrounded her. Disease permeated her emaciated body and her life depended on breathing oxygen from the portable tank she wheeled into my office.

Her head ached with severe, intractable pain. Her face contorted as she clutched her forehead with her hand. She coughed unrelentingly—a horrible, hacking spasmodic cough that filled the room with the spectre of contagion.

She was with her husband, Allen, and together they told me their story:

Lenore had been in reasonable health until about three years previous when she had her thymus gland removed after a tumor had been discovered. She was recovering well when she became pregnant with Sara.

When Sara was born her head was small and her development was delayed. The possibility of cerebral palsy was raised. At eight months Sara developed cancer of the adrenal gland and had it removed. At thirteen months her bowel obstructed from adhesions. A section of intestine was removed and then another a few weeks later. She was now almost two years old and there was no recurrence of the cancer. Allen and Lenore even hoped that she might be okay.

Soon after Sara's third surgery, Lenore developed a severe pneumonia. She had an unclassifiable autoimmune disease that destroyed her lungs. She needed to be on a respirator to keep her alive, and then a skull x-ray, done because of increasingly severe headaches, revealed what was thought to be a brain tumor in the region of her pituitary gland. Intracranial surgery found no tumor.

After the head surgery, her headaches worsened. Her lungs were shot. She might live a few more years, but there was no hope of recovery. When she became addicted to morphine and frantically took more for relief of the pain, the doctors cut her back. She could no longer bear to live. She overdosed in an attempt to kill herself, but she didn't die. Instead she ended up on the respirator again and then back home, all her pills now hidden by her husband and a housekeeper who doled them out in daily measure.

She had seen several psychotherapists and psychiatrists during this time. She saw her husband's psychotherapist, a colleague of mine who referred them to me. Finally, when the initial history was complete, I asked them why they had come to see me.

Lenore said, "I don't know. I want to die."

Her husband said, "I don't want her to die, but I don't want her to live this way either."

They both asked, "Can you help?"

I didn't know, but I did know that in order to even try I would have to acknowledge and deal with my own issues. Lenore had a chronic, debilitating, terminal illness. What if I were sick like Lenore? What if my wife were? Our child? Would I have the strength? Would I want to die? Allen and Lenore's relational rift following Lenore's suicide attempt left them at odds, not knowing what to do. Would I help my wife take her life if she wanted me to? What do I owe my family and how is my life not only my own?

These were the questions Allen and Lenore were living, but they were stuck, and they asked if I could help. I didn't know. We would have to find out.

The first thing I did was to suggest that I see them at their home. It was too difficult a trip for Lenore to come to the office. I didn't want the treatment to pose an unnecessary burden, and it was something I knew I could do to help. Lenore's mother agreed to underwrite the expense of the treatment. She also wanted to find a way to help. It was something she could do.

I arrived at the house late one afternoon the following week. It was in the Upper Valley, and it was hot. The landscape was wilted and dry. The paint was peeling from the gutters, sills, and eaves of the modest ranch house. I knocked on the door. A dog barked.

The Filipino voice of Christina, the housekeeper, rose above the barking as she opened the door. Lenore was sitting at the dining room table breathing medicated oxygen from a mask over her nose and mouth, punctuated by coughing and gagging and vomiting and moaning. A long tube coiled its way from the table around the kitchen through the den down the hall and into the bathroom where the oxygen pump putt-putted like the aerator in a fish tank. I walked over to Lenore and said, "Hi." Standing next to her mother was one of the most engaging, angelic little girls I had ever seen.

"Hi," I said.

"Hi," she responded and then, again, "Hi."

"What's your name?"

"This is Sara," said Lenore through the coughs.

"Hi," said Sara.

"Hi, dok-tor," said Christina, mimicking and encouraging the little girl.

"Hi," said Sara.

"I'm glad to meet you, Sara. I came to see your Mommy."

"Hi," said Sara.

And then I noticed her eyes askew, her strange voice and awkward gait, standing on her toes extended, the two-year-old who looked barely one. Yet, somehow, she was radiant.

"Hi," said Sara.

"Hi," I said. "Hi."

Lenore and I sat in the bedroom to talk. She sat on the bed, while I sat in a side chair. She was coughing, and I was listening and sipping lemonade and trying to figure out what I could do. When we were done I reached for my empty glass and headed toward the kitchen.

"I'll take care of that." Lenore intercepted the glass just as she began another coughing fit. She was still trying to hold up her end of things. I waited a few minutes until the coughing subsided and then made my way to the door. Sara was in the hall.

"Hi," said Sara.

"Goodbye, Sara," and I was out the door. The heat was stultifying.

The experience of seeing patients in their home—the smells, the spaces, the people who live there, who come and go—make the reality vivid and thick. This was a sick-house. As soon as I walked through the door, I was hit by the stench. By the time I left, I could barely breathe. What if she's contagious? What if I've caught it? I called her pulmonary specialist. I needed reassurance.

When Allen appeared for his appointment several days later, he was anxious and agitated.

"Doctor, I gotta tell you, I'm feeling overwhelmed. Three years ago I was a 33-year-old adolescent, hang loose, hang-out, have a good time, no responsibility, nothing, and now this. I don't know how to manage it. I run day to day, minute to minute, doctor to doctor. Between Lenore being sick and Sara, I just do the best I can."

"Allen, I'm doubling Lenore's dose of morphine. She needs some relief from the pain."

"I know, doctor, she told me. We tell each other everything."

"Tell me what you know about her suicide attempt."

Allen's face tightened.

"I never told anyone this. When Lenore took the pills, when she wanted to die, she told me. She told me this was it. She couldn't go on. She thought it would be better this way, better for me and Sara. She didn't want to live until Sara was five or six years old and then have Sara lose her. I told her,

'No! I want you to live,' but she insisted that this wasn't living. She said there was no hope for her and she couldn't stand the pain. Anyway, later that day she took the pills, a whole handful. When I came home she was already groggy. She told me what she'd done. I didn't want her to die, but that seemed selfish. Finally, I decided it was her life, and I should help her in any way I could. No one should be in that position, but I made the decision. I told her I would help her die." And with that Allen began sobbing.

"I tucked her in. I couldn't sleep. I stayed on the couch and told Christina the coughing was keeping me up. I must have checked her a hundred times. Each time I would go into the bedroom, I hugged her and kissed her and then I had to leave. I thought I was losing my mind. I didn't know if it was really happening. The next morning I opened her door, expecting it would be over, but Lenore was still breathing. I still had to go through with it. I dressed Sara and spent the morning playing with her. I told Christina Lenore had a rough night and just to let her sleep. The hardest part was when my mother dropped by, but I just acted normal, told everyone Lenore was sleeping and shouldn't be disturbed. I was scared to check her, but by afternoon I had to. She was moaning. She wasn't going to die. I called the ambulance. You know the rest."

I was stunned by the depth of Allen's commitment to Lenore. I admired the way he struggled to do the right thing when there was no right thing to do. He inspired me to continue my efforts in the face of what was to come. Allen and Lenore's destinies were inextricably bound and interwoven into the life of their marriage. I respected that.

When I next came to see Lenore, she was in the middle of a coughing spasm. About ten dry hacking coughs brought up a small amount of thick green sputum followed by ten more coughs and a dozen more. During the last bunch, her gag reflex was triggered, and she vomited into a tissue and onto her lap. She apologized and wiped it up.

We finally settled in.

"So," I said, "how do you feel today?"

"Terrible, my head hurts."

"You look a little brighter."

"Yeah, I think the increase in medicine helps, but I can't live this way. I want to die."

"What about Allen and Sara?"

"That's just the point, Dr. Carroll. Sara hasn't even bonded to me yet. She's closer to Christina than to me. She even calls her Mommy sometimes. I've been in the hospital for half of her life. I'm going to die one way or the other. There's no real hope for me getting better. Allen is a young man. It makes so much more sense for Allen to be free now and Sara before she can miss me when I'm gone. If I live another five years it will be worse for them both. Allen would never admit it, but it's true. Besides, this is not a way to live. I'm in pain all the time. I can't stop coughing, and it's only going to get worse. What's the point? I'd rather be dead."

"Allen wants you to live, Lenore, even if it's worse for him. He's only worried that it's impossible for you, but first we have to do something about your pain. It's hard to be with anyone, even people you love, when you're in this much pain."

I found Lenore's reasoning compelling. I didn't know I wouldn't feel the same, but Lenore was alive. I needed to find a way to help make her life more bearable, and that was best done medically.

It was clear that in order to help Lenore, I would have to find ways to help her with her pain and depression, two factors that increase suicidal desire in terminally ill patients (Chochinov, Wilson, Mowchun, Lander, Levitt, & Clinch, 1995). We investigated pain control programs, and she found one she liked.

Most people kill themselves because they don't know what else to do. Lenore was not a quitter. Given a real option, she seemed willing to take it. Parenthetically, Lenore did not ask me to help her die. That would have posed yet another set of predicaments.

She was admitted to a pain control center as an inpatient and treated with biofeedback, guided imagery, acupressure, massage, and medication. I started her on large doses of antidepressants. Eventually she was able to cope with the pain well enough to oversee Sara's second birthday party. It was the first time the family had invited nonfamily guests to the house in over a year.

Later, when Lenore and I spoke of the party and the cake and the family and friends, she was quick to point out that it changed nothing. She still wanted to die, but she was less insistent when she said it, and she stopped bringing it up herself. It had become less important. It was the first time that I knew I could, in fact, help. We were about three months into treatment and we were working together. I was very relieved.

During Lenore's absence from the house, Allen, with my encouragement, removed all the old wall-to-wall carpeting, refinished the floors, and painted the walls. When Lenore returned, the house seemed transformed. Everyone breathed a little easier.

Now that Lenore had some relief from the pain and the house was more livable, life settled more into a routine. I came to see Lenore about twice a week. Each time we talked, Sara became more the focus of our discussions. When Sara was there, we would all sit outside in the yard. Sara would play, sometimes alone, sometimes with us, sometimes with the dog. She was walking better now.

One day, I came to the house, and Lenore greeted me at the door hacking and coughing and excusing herself to go to the bathroom. The inhalation therapist was there to give Lenore her breathing treatments three times a day. Allen gave her the last one before bed each night. Sara was in the living room on the couch next to the inhalation therapist. They were both watching TV.

"Hi, Sara," I said as I plunked myself down next to her.

"Ha wa ya da-in?" she said and started giggling. I turned to the inhalation therapist. "Did you hear that?"

"Oh yes," she said. "'How're ya doin?'"

Lenore came down the hall, and we went outside. I told her what happened. She seemed pleased, but not that surprised.

"Has she been talking?" I asked.

"Well, no, not exactly. Sometimes I think she says a couple of words. The thing about Sara is how she relates to other people. When we go to the mall, she can be in the stroller and people come up to her. They want to know her, and she wants to know them. She doesn't have to talk for that."

"Have you seen the movie *My Left Foot*?" I asked Lenore.

"Allen and I were just talking about it. He didn't think I should go; he thought it might be too difficult for me. You know, it might be depressing. Maybe he's right."

"Oh no, it's a movie of triumph, very uplifting."

"But it's about illness."

"Yes, it's about a man who has cerebral palsy who was so incapacitated that he couldn't express himself with his muscles. As he grew up, he was aware of everything, he felt everything, but he hadn't learned to speak. He was kind of like Sara."

"Sara doesn't have cerebral palsy!" Lenore's voice was raised.

"It doesn't matter what you call it. She has the same problem. She can't control her muscles. People thought this man was stupid, that he didn't understand. Sara understands more than we think."

"That's what I think!" Lenore exclaimed.

"She needs you while you're alive, Lenore. No one understands her better than you. You're her mother."

"Don't you think I want to see my child grow up?" Lenore's voice was quaking. "The older she gets, the harder it's going to be for her when I die."

"You're alive now."

"I can't do anything. I can't even pick her up. I'm too weak. She calls

Allan 'Da,' but when she calls me, she just clears her throat, like she's coughing. It's too much. What can I do?"

"Just be here for her while you're alive. There are lots of hands to do the work. You understand her. She needs you. You're two of a kind."

A few weeks later Lenore had a dream:

"There was an earthquake. I was running. I was scared. I was trying to get home . . . here. I was scared a building was going to fall on top of me. I'd be crushed. I was scared I was going to die. I didn't want to die." Lenore paused.

"I heard you, Lenore."

This set of events was the turning point. Sara, trapped by deficit, stigmatization, and circumstance, made a developmental step both individually and relationally. She said her first sentence: "How wa ya da-in?" It was a real question, and she was asking me. I was amazed. She was delighted.

I became excited. I felt there was real hope. Sara needed to be believed in, reached out to and understood. Lenore could do that, but Lenore needed something too, a reason to live. Sara had the life and Lenore had the understanding. It was a way to be mother and daughter together. It was a breakthrough for us all, a breakthrough of something Lenore had known all along about Sara, but was scared to feel—how alive Sara was, and how wonderful. I talked with Allen the next day. He sensed a difference, too. As always, Allen and Lenore shared everything. We were all working together now.

Lenore's dream was a perfect metaphor for the predicament of her life, and I was her witness (Zuk, 1966). It took a few weeks until Lenore could integrate the meaning of her dream into her concious understanding. Finally, for the first time since I'd known her, she cried.

"I want to live so bad," she said. "I want to live so bad." I cried, too. It was a moment of communion between us.

From there, life went on. My presence at the house was no longer as necessary, and I began coming weekly or less.

Spring became summer, and the heat was rising. The blooms were filling the crepe myrtles again, just as they had almost a year ago when I first met Lenore and Allen and Sara. I hadn't been to the house in several weeks. One day the phone rang. It was Allen.

"Lenore died today."

Our conversation was brief. Allen and I arranged a meeting. After the funeral and the shiva, Allen came to my office. He began, "It all started last weekend. Something was strange. She wasn't coughing. We just stayed at home together, Lenore, Sara, and me, laughing and playing. She called it a 'family weekend.' We loved it. Then her breathing got weird. It was deep and slow and she seemed out of it, and then she would drift back in, and she wasn't coughing. I asked her if she wanted to go to the hospital and she said no, and that's when I knew she was dying.

"That night we slept together. We were close. In the morning I got up early and called the ambulance. I wanted it to come before Sara got up. I didn't want a scene in front of Sara. In the ambulance her mind cleared and she knew what was happening. She told me no respirator. She hated the respirator. She was okay about dying; it was the pain she couldn't stand. I asked if she trusted me, and she said yes. I told her I loved her and she told me. She told me to say goodbye to Sara, and that she'd always love her.

"When we arrived at the hospital, the doctor met us, and I showed him the living will that said, no respirator. He said that we had a problem. The will was invalid because she chose to go on the repirator during a sinus operation. That was different, I told him, and if he wasn't going to honor her wish, I would carry her home. The doctor finally agreed.

"We made her comfortable and gave her fluids through the IV. I held her hand and told her over and over again how much I loved her and that everything would be all right. Eventually, she just stopped breathing. There was no pain. She was at peace.

"I went home. It took me a couple of hours before I could tell Sara. I didn't even know if she would understand, but somehow I think she did. I told her that Mommy died and wasn't going to come home. I told her Mommy lives in our hearts, and I put her hand on her chest, and now when we go out for a ride and head home, I ask her if Mommy's home, and she says, 'No.' Then I ask her where Mommy is, and she puts her hand over her heart and I think she feels sad. I think she knows. Thank you for giving my wife back to me."

And with that we were both crying. We hugged. I made arrangements to come out to the house to see Sara one last time, and I told Allen that Lenore and I had talked about writing all of this down. I asked him if he wanted to read it. He told me that he did. He said it would help.

DISCUSSION

My work with this family was one of the most meaningful experiences of my professional and personal life, but I had no idea that it would be when Allen and Lenore first came to my office. What impelled me to undertake this difficult, complicated case, and what kept me involved?

I was strongly identified with Allen as a husband in the predicaments he faced. I admired his devotion to Lenore, and I wondered how and if I would have the strength to carry on as he did. Allen's commitment to Lenore and his family led me to renew my own commitment both to their family and ultimately to my own. I saw in Allen an example of how I might hope to be, but he was weakening, and he needed help.

Lenore's willingness to undertake yet another round of treatment, specifically the effort she expended in the hospital to learn new mechanisms of coping with pain, showed a depth and strength of character. I responded to that. Also, her concern with the details of our social interaction at her home — offering me lemonade, walking me to the door, etc. — was evidence to me that she still wanted to be engaged. If she could only get some relief, there might be hope.

But it was Sara who carried the real hope for this family. As children are always our hope for the future, frequently they are also our impetus into it. Sara, disabled and stigmatized by her illness, was able to transcend her circumstance in the way she related to others and to me in particular. She made both an individual and relational developmental leap. She showed us all what hope there might be to rise above ourselves.

My identifications, reactions, motivations, and choices came from my own history. I grew up in a house where my younger sister was ill much of the time. She preoccupied my parents. When my own son was born premature, he was sick and almost died. My wife went through a prolonged postpartum depression. I had to hold my family together during that time, and by having done it, I got a taste of what this family might be experiencing. It frightened me, not only because I *could* relate to their experience, but because I *did* relate, and their predicament was so much graver and more complex than mine was.

Their circumstances were also different from mine. My wife and son recovered completely; Lenore had a terminal illness and was going to die. Sara's medical condition was still guarded. She was disabled and her motor skills were developmentally delayed. I had to face issues with them that I had not had to face previously.

Whether or not I could help had everything to do with how I committed myself — my personal experience and my professional expertise — to the task of doing what needed to be done to heal the relational rifts created by illness in this family. It also had to do with this family's willingness to commit their own resources to the job and all of our ability to work together.

When I present this case at conferences, I still cry at times as I reexperience the emotional flux of my participation in the events that occurred. Occasionally, I have been asked whether I became overinvolved with this family.

As therapists we are always walking the line of involvement with our patients, and no matter whether we draw the line here or there, it will always be tested by the patients and our own intuitions about what might help. I do not know how to evaluate whether or not I was overinvolved except to say that the degree of my involvement seemed required by the situation if I was to help. The quality of my involvement was determined by the relationships that developed between us, and this was determined as much by Lenore, Allen, and Sara as by me.

The rule of thumb taught to psychotherapists in training is that therapists should not reveal our personal lives to our patients. This is not possible. Everything we do, who we are, who we purport to be, from our office decor to the inflections in our voice to our participation in the detailed enactments of therapeutic relationships is suffused with personal revelation. We are continually engaged in relational dialogue with our patients. The question is not whether or what to reveal but how to reveal by involvement and participation in the therapeutic process.

I both revealed a great deal of myself and became intimately involved with this family. We created and participated in a therapeutic relationship that facilitated a relational healing. I tried to do it responsibly and respectfully, but in the end I did it the way I did because it was the way I knew how to help.

THE RELATIONAL BASIS OF ILLNESS AND HEALING

Each of us follows dual developmental imperatives — to individuate and to be connected to others through intimate relationships (Bergman & Surrey, 1992; Carroll & Carroll, 1986; Jordan, 1989; Miller, 1986, 1987). Becoming someone in particular while remaining a part of a larger whole is termed differentiation. As used by Bowen (1978), the term "differentiation of self" embodies the dual imperatives of individuation from and connection to our families of origin. Buber's I-Thou, (1958), Winnicott's holding environment and transitional space, (1965, 1975), Stolorow's intersubjective field (Stolorow, Brandchaft, & Atwood, 1987), Friedman's dialogue of touchstones (1985), and Boszormenyi-Nagy's contextual therapy (Boszormenyi-Nagy, 1980; Boszormenyi-Nagy & Krasner, 1986; Boszormenyi-Nagy & Spark, 1973) are among the examples of attempts that have been and are being made to describe what exists in the realm between people as individuals and also as part of relational systems and the larger ground of our relational world.

Lenore may have had the right to end her own life, but how she did it and when and why had huge implications for those who were committed to her and in whose lives her death would have meaning. The implications of

Lenore's death as a mother to Sara or a wife to Allen were different from the implications of an individual who wants to end her own life. How we weigh and balance these considerations (Allen, 1988) will determine to a large extent what we believe is relevant to the therapeutic enterprise.

All psychotherapy has a relational basis, no matter what the theoretical orientation. It is something we, therapists and clients, do together. Therefore it makes sense that we utilize our relational knowledge in therapy.

One set of circumstances we all experience is illness in ourselves and family members. In these circumstances our relational knowledge comes from what we've learned as sons, daughters, mothers, husbands, caretakers, doctors, patients, etc., when someone is sick.

Psychiatrist/anthropologist Arthur Kleinman (1980) makes a distinction between a disease and an illness. Disease is a breakdown in the anatomy, physiology, or biochemistry of an individual, but the illness is the manifestion of the disease in people in the relational/social world. In other words, illness has a relational dimension as it manifests in individuals and between family members. A person with a serious disease may not be very ill, and significant illness may result from little disease (Jaffe, 1980; Levine, 1987; Remen, 1988; Siegel, 1986; Simonton, 1980).

Lenore had both horrible disease and debilitating illness manifesting in the lives of everyone who cared about her and was committed to her. Sara also had serious disease, but after the acute phases, increasingly less illness.

It was by overcoming the relational rifts between Lenore and Sara and Allen that healing took place. Of course, it is critical to eliminate or minimize disease whenever possible, as it was necessary to minimize Lenore's pain and depression, but even with incurable disease, healing can occur (Levine, 1987; Remen, 1988).

Allen and Lenore had reunited, transcending the illness that separated them. Sara and Lenore had bonded as mother and daughter, and when Lenore died, Sara and Allen went on together with hope instead of remorse.

A number of years ago I heard Naomi Remen (1988) speak on "Healing through Dying." When I first heard the title, I couldn't imagine what she meant. After hearing her talk, I knew she meant something akin to the healing that was to take place in this family during those last weeks before Lenore's death.

A RELATIONAL VIEW OF COUNTERTRANSFERENCE

In psychotherapy the manifestations of relational knowledge that we bring to therapy are termed transference when evoked in a patient and countertransference when in a therapist. As therapists, how can we use this evoked relational knowledge, i.e., our countertransference, in the service of the therapeutic task?

Because countertransference is a manifestation of our relational knowledge, first learned and later evoked in relationships, it is reasonable to assume that whatever we learn relationally will inform any countertransference that may manifest. Experiencing illness and solving the individual and relational predicaments posed will inform a therapist in new illness situations. However, how are we to be in situations where we have little previous experience?

In these situations we must give ourselves to the treatment in the real relationships we share with our patients (Greenson, 1971), participate in them, and become a function of them in ways that may evoke our anxiety (Devereux, 1967). This anxiety can then become the impetus for creative developmental growth. No one can go through the situation described in this case without being changed. Being committed and involved requires a willingness to become something new.

The practice of therapy is just that, a practice, something that must be done and accomplished. We do it together with our patients. When we encounter something new, we must figure out what we might do and how we might do it together.

Schutz (1951) compares making music together to creating relationships, in that our egos must be subordinated to the task at hand, although we have not lost our selves. Indeed, our selves must be fully committed to the task of participating in the flux of the music, our relationship through the flow of our lives together.

Viewed this way, therapy becomes a much different enterprise. We no longer focus questions on whether countertransference is a good thing or a bad thing, but we understand it is the only thing we've got to give to the task. We give it as professionals with any expertise we might have as medical doctors or pain control specialists or psychological analysts, but the greater task is to allow ourselves as people with relational history to participate in the lives of one another so that healing might occur.

CONCLUSION

I could not have been any help to this family or brought my expertise to bear if I had not been willing to commit myself to the relational issues between Allen and Lenore, a husband and wife whose relationship had gotten stuck, and between Lenore and Sara, a mother and daughter who hadn't bonded. In that process I learned something about what it means to live a commitment through sickness and health because I had done just that as a family psychiatrist and as a husband and father in my own family. What I learned about a husband's devotion to his wife, a mother's to her daughter, and the meaning of family are now part of my relational experience, and in that I became changed.

As another young man, whose wife had become ill, once said to me, "When we promised to love each other through sickness and health, we didn't know what we were talking about until there was some sickness."

REFERENCES

Allen, D. (1988). *Unifying individual and family therapy.* San Francisco: Josey Bass.
Bergman, S. J., & Surrey, J. (1992). The woman-man relationship: Impasses and possibilities. *Work in progress, No. 55.* Wellesley, MA: Stone Center working paper series.
Boszormenyi-Nagy, I. (July, 1980). Contextual therapy. *American Journal of Psychiatry, 137*(7).
Boszormenyi-Nagy, I., & Krasner, B. (1986). *Between give and take.* New York: Brunner/Mazel.
Boszormenyi-Nagy, I., & Spark, G. (1973). *Invisible loyalties.* New York: Harper and Row.
Bowen, M. (1978). *Family therapy in clinical practice.* New York: Jason Aronson.
Buber, M. (1958). *I-Thou.* New York: Charles Scribner's Sons.
Carroll, S., & Carroll, R. (1986). *The functions of symbiosis.* Paper presented at UCLA Self in Context Conference, Los Angeles, CA.
Chochinov, H. M., Wilson, K. G., Mowchen, N., Lander, S., Levitt, M., & Clinch, J. J. (1995). Desire for death in the terminally ill. *American Journal of Psychiatry, 152,* 1185–1191.
Devereux, G. (1967). *From anxiety to method in the behavioral sciences.* The Hague: Mouton and Co.
Friedman, M. (1985). *The healing dialogue in psychotherapy.* New York: Jason Aronson.
Greenson, R. (1971). The real relationship between the patient and the psychoanalyst. In M. Kanzer (Ed.), *The unconscious today.* New York: International University Press.
Jaffe, D. (1980). *Healing from within.* New York: Bantam.
Jordan, J. V. (1989). Relational development: Therapeutic implications of empathy and shame. *Work in progress, No. 39.* Wellesley, MA: Stone Center working paper series.
Kleinman, A. (1980). *Patients and healers in the context of culture.* Los Angeles: University of California Press.
Levine, S. (1987). *Healing into life and death.* New York: Doubleday.
Miller, J. B. (1986). What do we mean by relationship? *Work in progress, No. 22.* Wellesley, MA: Stone Center working paper series.
Miller, J. B. (1987). *Toward a new psychology of women.* Boston: Beacon.
Remen, N. (1988). *Healing through dying.* Presentation at the Cancer and the Family Conference, Los Angeles, CA.
Schutz, A. (1951). Making music together. *Social Research, 18*(1), 76–97.
Siegel, B. (1986). *Love, medicine and miracles.* New York: Harper and Row.
Simonton, O. C. (1980). *Getting well again.* New York: Bantam.
Stolorow, R., Brandchaft, B., & Atwood, G. (1987). *Psychoanalytic treatment: An intersubjective approach.* Hillsdale, NJ: Analytic Press.
Winnicott, D. W. (1965). *The maturational processes and facilitating environment.* New York: International Universities Press.
Winnicott, D. W. (1975). Transitional objects and transitional phenomena. In *Through pediatrics to psychoanalysis* (pp. 229–242). New York: Basic.
Zuk, G. (1966). The go-between process. *Family Process, 5,* 162–178.

14

Countertransference in the Storying of a Child's Suicide

SHARON MCQUAIDE

IN THE LOCAL PAPER there had been two obituaries side by side. One was for a man in his eighties who died after a long bout with cancer. The other was for a man of twenty-five; no cause of death was given. Both had the same last surname.

Several weeks later there was a message on my answering machine requesting that I please call to schedule an appointment. When I called, a trembling child, or so I thought, answered the phone. "Could I speak with your mother?" I asked tentatively.

"I am the mother, or, I was the mother. I guess I must sound how I feel."

The woman, Sally, then began to tell me about the suicide of her son, Peter, two days after the death of his grandfather. She and her husband, Bob, were heartbroken, bewildered, and in shock, and were following others' advice to call and get professional help for their sorrow.

When Sally and Bob entered the office the grief that they were carrying was so great and so palpable I felt as ashen as they looked. Their love for their lost child was enormous and the pain was seeming unbearable to them. They had read that a tragedy like this often tears a couple apart and, after thirty years of marriage, they did not want their marriage to fall apart. Life seemed frightening and unpredictable to them now, they said, and they found themselves clinging to each other and to their remaining son, Tom.

With great detail their minds kept replaying the night they got the phone call, the visual picture of the other's reaction when the stranger delivered the news that Peter—who had been living three thousand miles away from them—had ended his life, asphyxiated in a car with a bag of his favorite cookies beside him. Bob could not chase away the image of his wife dropping to the floor and rocking in a fetal position. Sally could not get used to seeing her husband sobbing uncontrollably. Accustomed to his being unemotional and rational, she could not recognize this man she was now living with who could not stop crying and who described feeling depersonalized. They were both frightened that they would feel this deep sorrow forever.

For Sally and Bob, the details related to the suicide, the funeral, and their initial shock reactions kept returning with the insistence of an obsession. They seemed traumatized. In addition, their guilt and self-blame were enormous. Although they did not know why their child chose to end his life, they assumed they were to blame—that there had been something terribly wrong with their parenting. Assuming as fact that they could have prevented his suicide, they were storying his death as if they had full responsibility. In this guilty state they were reviewing Peter's childhood, second-guessing everything they could have done differently, analyzing, criticizing, and regretting all that they could remember about the times when they were together. They both assumed that Peter chose death over life because of something they did or didn't do.

To one witnessing this process, their guilt appeared to be distorting—in a harshly critical way—what seemed to be normal parenting experiences. If they continued to reinterpret their time with their son in such a guilt-saturated way, privileging only times that could have been potentially damaging to their son, they would end up with a narrative that would prevent their recovery from trauma.[1] As Roth and Chasin (1994, p. 189) have noted, "The stories we create about our lives and relationships both arise from and shape our experience." The stories we choose to write are both our creations and our creators. Peter's suicide would script the story of their lives and they would be actors playing roles shaped by this tragedy.

CHOICE OF TREATMENT TOOLS

The most salient features of Sally and Bob's presentation were the trauma, the guilt, and the problem-saturated narrative they were constructing of their time with their son. These three facets of their presentation are, respectively, the centerpieces of distinct theoretical approaches—the trauma model (as described by Herman, 1992), psychoanalytic theory, and the

---

1. I have borrowed the notions of narratives being problem-saturated or solution-saturated and of certain narratives being privileged over others from White and Epston (1990).

narrative metaphor. This suggested that selected concepts from these three approaches might provide useful insights for working with Sally and Bob and would help me organize my thinking and my work with them.

It should be added that, due to the time-limited nature of the work, the goal was to help the couple "get on track" again. Total "recovery" from the loss of one's child seemed unrealistic in the short amount of time allotted to us.[2] Character change and exploration of certain feelings were triaged out as we stayed focused on trauma, guilt, and the permission to construct a new narrative.

Trauma Theory

Traumatized by the unexpected suicide of their son, Sally and Bob were secondarily traumatized by watching each other's grief reaction, as well as by "losing" — at least temporarily — the protective predictability and familiarity of the other. My assessment of the couple was that they were not only bereaved but that they also met criteria for having suffered trauma.

> Traumatic events call into question basic human relationships. . . . They shatter the construction of the self that is formed and sustained in relation to others. They undermine the belief systems that give meaning to human experience. They violate the victim's faith in a natural or divine order and cast the victim into a state of existential crisis. (Herman, 1992, p. 51)

For Sally and Bob, the self schemata that were constructed around the parenting role, which was a core part of both of their identities, were shattered, leaving them in existential crisis. Family members function as selfobjects (Unger & Levene, 1994), and loss of this child selfobject brought the threat of internal fragmentation at the same time that their belief system and sense of order were externally fragmenting.

In *Trauma and Recovery*, Herman (1992) describes how the fundamental assumptions about the positive value of the self, the safety and trustworthiness of the world, and the meaningful order of creation are destroyed, leaving the individual with life events that cannot be assimilated into his or her "inner schemata" of self in relation to the world. Feeling fragile for the first time in their lives, Sally and Bob felt the reliability of the world had been destroyed. They described feeling anxious and vulnerable, and especially terrified during times of separation from each other or from their surviving son, Tom. Bob described starting to have panic attacks at times when his inner state was too different from the outer states of the people

---

2. In the beginning of our work, six months of weekly sessions had been certified by their managed care company.

around him, for instance, at cocktail parties where people appeared happy in marked contrast to the inner sorrow that never left him.

In Herman's model, the fundamental stages of recovery from traumatizing experience are: establishing safety and a therapeutic alliance, remembrance and mourning, and reconnection with ordinary life. In the remembrance and mourning stage, the reconstruction of the trauma transforms the story so that it can be integrated into the individual's life story.

> The reconstruction of the trauma requires immersion in past experience of frozen time; the descent into mourning feels like a surrender to tears that are endless. . . . After many repetitions, the moment comes when the telling of the trauma. . . . no longer arouses quite such intense feeling. It has become a part of the survivor's experience, but only one part of it. The story is a memory like other memories, and it begins to fade. . . . grief, too begins to lose its vividness. (1992, p. 195)

In session, Sally and Bob would need to make the "descent into mourning," to "surrender to tears," and to reconstruct and deconstruct the story of their son's life and suicide.

In the reconnection stage the task of constructing a future is faced. The old self and old beliefs that the trauma destroyed are mourned and a new self and new beliefs must be developed. Herman describes this work as reclaiming the world. I hypothesized that in our work together Sally and Bob would travel back and forth through these three stages.

Guilt

In addition to seeming traumatized by their son's suicide, the harshness of Sally's and Bob's superegos was hitting them with full force. They were experiencing intense guilt that they had not foreseen and prevented their son's suicide. They were telling themselves that they were failures as parents and, as their new view of their parenting was so far from their ego-ideals as parents, they were experiencing a drop in self-esteem. Guilt, depression, lowered self-esteem, and punishment through loss of the enjoyment of life dominated their present condition. They expressed fear that they would never be happy again. I feared that, if their now relentlessly attacking superegos were not "subdued," they would be right.

Bob, in particular, seemed to be feeling he no longer deserved the life and happiness he had before Peter died. Loving his lost son and feeling too guilty to acknowledge that he had any anger at Tom's decision to take himself away from the family, Bob expressed his anger as self-hatred and superego attacks. In "Mourning and Melancholia" (1917), Freud described depression as a response to loss in which the person's sorrow and rage in the face of that loss are not vented but remain unconscious, thus weakening the ego. This anger turned inward—which may have been an anger toward his son that Bob felt too guilty to express—could predispose him to developing depression.

The psychoanalytic concept of the superego seemed especially relevant to helping this couple. Regarding the functions of the superego, Edith Jacobson (1964) proposes that the superego: regulates narcissistic and object cathexes; regulates mood, including guilt and depression; raises or lowers self esteem; and distributes reward or punishment.[3] I hypothesized that as we traveled through Herman's three stages to recovery, interventions aimed at challenging the harshness of the superego would allow for a less self-punishing story about Peter, would aid in the restoration of self-worth, and would allow for the acknowledgment of the possibility of feeling anger toward Peter. This would reduce the likelihood that depression would follow bereavement.

So, my early assessment joined Judith Herman's trauma model to psychoanalytic theory, in particular to the concept of the superego as a target for psychotherapeutic intervention. If the benign and loving aspects of the superego (Schafer, 1960) could be activated in treatment, and if the harshness of the superego could be quieted as the psychotherapy relationship developed and strengthened, then Sally and Bob could begin to story their relationship with their son in a way that would not retraumatize them or condemn them to a life of superego-inflicted self-punishment and self-hatred.

Narratives

My hope, then, was that Sally and Bob could construct a narrative that would enable them to live their lives fully, despite the tragedy that had occurred. As it was, they were storying their son's life in a very restricted way. Their search for a reason for their son's death had been limited to the parenting arena—looking for mistakes they had made, communications they might not have heard, family interactions they should have prevented. Sally even called herself "manipulative" for taking her son to sports events as a child. When asked if her son had wanted to go to those events she replied that he did.

Regarding the goals of treatment, White and Epston (1990) write:

> Insofar as the desirable outcome of therapy is the generation of alternative stories that incorporate vital and previously neglected aspects of lived experience,

---

3. If Jacobson were writing today, she might add that, in addition to regulating mood and self-esteem, the superego allows rewarding or punishing stories.

and insofar as these stories incorporate alternative knowledges, it can be argued
that the identification of and provision of the space for the performance of these
new knowledges is a central focus of the therapeutic endeavor. (p. 31)

If we were able to deconstruct the post-suicide, guilt-saturated narrative,
my hope was that alternative stories would be "generated" and "performed"
in session.

Combs and Freedman (1994) see the work of therapy as "facilitating
experience of new stories—life narratives that are more empowering, more
satisfying, and give hope for better futures" (p. 69). They do this by what
they call "deconstructive listening," in which clients are invited to relate to
their life narratives as actively constructed stories rather than as passively
received facts, and to choose stories they prefer and that enable them to
make meaning. Questions with a deconstructive intent allow clients to see
their stories from a different perspective and notice that their stories are
constructed, that these stories may have limitations, and that other narratives are possible.

Combs and Freedman give the example of working with a couple whose
story is organized around the disappointment they feel with each other.

> One of us (Combs) asked this question: "Has disappointment kept you from
> responding to some things and encouraged you to respond strongly to others?"
> My intention in asking this question was to invite the couple to consider how the
> story of disappointment may have directed their attention toward disappointing
> events. . . . As a narrative takes shape, it powerfully influences the selections a
> person makes about what further events should be storied. (p. 73)

An identical process seemed to be operating for Sally and Bob. Guilt was
allowing the memory, understanding, and storying of some events but not
of others. The superego was "editing out" the construction of alternative
stories for their narrative. The "story of guilt" was their creation but would
also be their creator if it were not deconstructed.

An Integrating Metaphor

In addition to trauma and psychoanalytic models, then, the narrative model
was used for concepts to organize the work. These models, however, are
usually seen as mutually competing, even as contradictory. They implicitly
or explicitly contain different notions of the relation of emotional problems
to external "reality" (Herman, 1991; Spence, 1982), and they imply different approaches to treatment (Saari, 1994). Despite this, aspects of all three
models seemed relevant to Sally and Bob's situation. The challenge was to
find a way of using the elements from each that provided insights into Sally

and Bob's situation and that could provide therapeutic leverage, but in a way that would join the elements smoothly.

I was helped in this task by the following metaphor. I would picture Sally and Bob walking down a road together with a companion. The road passes through three sections: a woods of safety, a swamp of remembrance and mourning, and a hilly field of reconnection. As Sally and Bob travel along this road, they talk, telling each other stories. Initially, their companion (who is really their combined superego) shouts at them, haranguing and scolding them. At first, their stories are scary ones, tales of horror and terror. But gradually, as they progress down the first two sections of the road, their (superego) companion becomes softer and gentler, and eventually warm and embracing. As they enter the safer terrain, and with their companion no longer interfering with their story-telling, their stories become more benign. They are freed to use their imaginations to dream up a world of their design. The road they were walking along comes to the entrance of this new world and they are magically able to enter this world and live there as long as they want.

THE CLINICAL WORK

Sally and Bob, now in their fifties, married when they were both 19. They had their sons, who were two years apart, a couple of years later. Being parents was what they most wanted. They loved having children and doing things together as a foursome. Family life was organized around camping, biking, sports, skiing, mountain climbing, going to the beach, and running. The illustrations of a colorful children's book came to mind, where the family is depicted bursting with energy, and activity is just about falling off the page. Like the Brady Bunch, this sounded like a family anyone would want to join. Everyone was loved and they all spent time doing things together.

Amid the whirlwind of activities, the talker and listener in the family was Jim, Bob's father, who had just died of cancer. Bob said that his father was "fiercely intelligent and it was intellectually invigorating to be in his presence. I could turn to my father for advice in setbacks. He had such a clarity that I don't have in myself." Sally joked that she married Bob in part because she was in love with his father. Everybody else in the family, they reported, was "busy, busy, busy, doing, doing, doing." Peter, the younger of the two boys, had been especially close to Jim.

Sally and Bob, seeming so emotionally close that their body language — whether expressing grief, guilt, or consternation — seemed choreographed and the exchange of eye contact seemed so constant, were actually opposites in many ways. Sally would come to therapy in her muddy rubber gardening boots, cut-offs, and straw hats. She looked and sounded like a very feminine, easily apologetic little girl who had a lot of energy for fun. Bob, tall and athletic, with a gentle, sensitive face that revealed his pain, alternated between being cautious and confident. Sally spent her work hours with her hands in the soil planting the flowers for the gardens she designed. Bob's work hours were spent in the sky, working for an airline.

They were likable and charming, and seemed like very good and well-intentioned people, but they were very hard to sit with because of the profundity of their pain. Sitting with them as they sobbed, faces and bodies contorted with the deepest grief I had ever seen, was exhausting. In the early sessions, I felt my heart was breaking with them. Although I knew they would need to find another narrative in which they did not take all the responsibility for their son's death, I was unable to imagine what narrative these good people could come up with that would help them make peace with this tragedy. Although I felt hopeful that they would heal or at least get their lives back on track, the specifics of the hope were not there. Thoughts of my own child and insecurity about my own well-intentioned parenting were triggered, as were questions about what unhappy mysteries are locked inside those we love.

Sally and Bob had thought the family had been happy together and they had assumed there would be years and years ahead of them filled with camping and rafting and the addition of grandchildren and daughters-in-law. The deaths of Peter and his grandfather were the first deaths — indeed, the first tragedies — they remembered experiencing. Now life seemed completely different and all that mattered were less happy memories that had once been all but forgotten, since they believed examining these unhappy times would help solve the mystery of their son's suicide.

In answer to my questions about Peter's childhood, they acknowledged some troubled times. Bob recalled that "Peter did have a dark view of his childhood. It was like he was different from the rest of the family. When he was teased and pestered by his brother he would shut down, sulk, withdraw. . . . In high school he was using drugs. I wish we had talked more. I wish we had been observant. But we were afraid of more conflict and storminess. We looked for positive things to reinforce." Sally reported that "I missed the depression in Peter's life. Tom was verbal and would tease; Peter wasn't verbal and he said as an adult that he wished we had done more to stop Tom when he taunted him. We loved the outdoors. I would take them to the beach, but I would forget water or sunscreen. . . . Peter had no anger in him. He was so sweet. He was good as a little boy, but he broke all the rules as a teenager. Except for Bob's father there wasn't a talker in the family. Maybe Peter wanted to talk but we were too busy running out to throw a frisbee. I'm like my mother. I just always thought, 'Everything will work out.' But Peter clung to a dark side."

Before Peter's death, the happy times as a family were in the foreground; the dark times, buried. Now, those dark times, times that hadn't "fit" and were discarded, were all that mattered, as Sally and Bob "searched" for a son they hadn't known, a son who chose to end his life. Peter's "dark side" was the part of their son they had least understood, the part that made him different from the rest of the family. The only person who had been able to listen and talk to Peter's dark side, Peter's grandfather, was no longer here to share his "clarity." Who Peter was, what the nature of his dark side was, how he experienced his relationship with his parents, and why he chose to end his life seemed shrouded in mystery.

With great shame and pain they told me that a year ago, after reading *Generation X*, Peter had bought a gun. Bob flew out immediately when he found out. At this time Peter started treatment: antidepressants, individual and group therapy. It appeared that the crisis passed. Peter had a job, he was competing in sports, and he was spending a lot of time working with his brother healing the injuries of his childhood.

Then, after a ten-year fight with cancer, his grandfather, to whom he was very close, decided to end his life. One week later Peter also decided to end his life.

When Sally and Bob later found out that Peter's grandfather had said that "Peter will not make old bones," that Peter would die young, they denied feeling angry that the grandfather had not shared this with them. Rather, they reacted with guilt that they had not realized this themselves and tried to prevent their son's suicide.

Although the family had suffered two recent deaths, Bob and Sally stated that they had been prepared for Bob's father's death and that cancer brought with it a sense of closure that suicide did not. If we were to have worked together for longer than six months, perhaps feelings related to the grandfather's death, his knowledge of their son, the effect his decision to commit suicide had on his grandson's decision to suicide, may have surfaced. However, Sally and Bob were not interested in going down those paths; instead, they wanted help dealing with the trauma of their son's suicide.

The sessions were filled with long periods of sobbing that later turned to crying together, clinging to each other that later turned to holding each other, bitter recriminations that later turned to regrets, disbelief that Peter was no longer alive to sensing his "presence," and many wishes that they had been less busy, better listeners, better talkers. The wish to be better talkers and listeners was enacted in the session as they struggled to talk with me and listen to painful experience that they could no longer push aside.

Work with Sally and Bob did roughly fall into Herman's three stages of establishing safety, remembering and mourning, and moving toward integration. In the early stages, Sally and Bob needed to tell the story of their son's life and death to someone other than each other – to someone whose ego would not be flooded. I don't know if anyone could be prepared for living with a trauma victim at the same time that one is struggling to stabilize oneself from trauma. Much as they desired to be a holding environment to each other, they could not hold without expanding the pain and internal disorganization of the other.

Before their son's death they had been sources of support for each other. But now, when they would go to each other for help with guilt or with grief about their son, they would reinforce or escalate the guilt and grief. In Bob's words "we just pull the scab off each other." They were not able to be a container for each other in the early months after Peter's death; they would only escalate guilt, grief, and anxiety about future losses in a world that now seemed less reliable. Talking to a therapist, by contrast, was safe and stabilizing. The therapist could perform the job of containing the affect and providing a safe place to talk, remember, and mourn. Having a therapist present as a stable selfobject for their sharing of the traumatic memories they needed to replay, and for the guilt-saturated storying of their son's death, enabled them to begin to stabilize.

They were able to use the therapeutic relationship to stabilize, which allowed the remembering and mourning of Peter to occur without endangering their relationship, jobs, and social life. Increasingly, in session many tears were shed about the joys of life that their son would never know, much guilt was expressed about parenting decisions they had made with the best of intentions at the time, and great affection was felt as they shared happy memories of their son. They also put into words the shame they felt about their son's suicide, the loss of self-worth they experienced, and their isolation from others, who could never really understand what it was like to have a son who chose to end his life. Attempts were made to understand their son's decision. Time and talking, I believed, would lead to less guilty and self-attacking narratives.

At times in session, feelings of low self-worth, angry disappointment in the self, and harsh self-criticism would surface. At these times, to speak metaphorically, I imagined the superego yelling at them, and I would direct my interventions to this "screaming superego" part of them, attempting to deconstruct the judgmental assumptions of the superego companion. For example, Sally and Bob had many "what ifs." When Sally would say something like "If only I had asked him more questions when he was a child," I would first ask her what feelings she had about not asking these questions and then, after exploring that, I would then ask if she were sure beyond a shadow of a doubt that Peter would have responded to her asking more questions. I would then ask if she thought it could be an opinion and not a fact that being more probing would have made a difference. Recognizing that her opinions were not facts was freeing for Sally.

Bob's "superego companion" would often say to him, as if it were a fact, that, even though Peter had been living two thousand miles away for the past six years, Bob should have had control over his son's life. After exploring the feelings of helplessness that one has because one cannot control the people one loves and feels responsible for, the harshly critical and judgmental assumptions of his superego were deconstructed in conversations designed to permit more freedom of thought and narrative construction. Bob was asked questions such as: "You are assuming that you should have had more control and responsibility when it came to Peter's life. Is that something that Peter wanted?" "When Peter was alive, did you feel you should have more control over his life?" "Do Tom and Sally want you to have more control over their lives?" "Do they have responsibility for you?" These questions helped Bob to realize that, because others want to have responsibility for their own lives and mistakes—as he does for his—existential helplessness was something he was feeling powerfully. Laying aside the guilty feelings to explore these core feelings of helplessness led to productive work.

After four months of working with Sally and Bob, I felt we had come as far as we could with couples work. The metaphoric road they were walking down would fork. The superego companion was talking more forgivingly and more gently, especially to Sally. Sally and Bob were both preparing to reconnect with the world and construct new narratives; however, Sally was being drawn to a spirituality she had discovered inside herself, and she was allowing herself to think that perhaps her son was in a happier place than when he was alive. She would comfort herself by picturing Peter traveling to a new land where he was happy. When imagining this image, she could feel close to Peter, as if he were in her presence. Bob could not share this, and it was inhibiting her full exploration of her spirituality.

Since Bob did not share Sally's spirituality, Sally needed permission in session to pursue her own differentiated storying of Peter without feeling that she was abandoning her husband. After thirty years of a marriage they both described as happy and satisfying, Sally and Bob were used to thinking alike. They would combine their individual narratives of life to express an "averaged narrative." They storied their lives together in a way that reduced conflict, and this co-constructing had worked well for them. While this accommodation may have served them well in dealing with certain challenges their marriage encountered, it was inhibiting the full use of their own unique coping mechanisms, and hence, their recovery from the trauma of their son's suicide.

We decided to schedule several individual sessions to explore the develop-

ment of differentiated narratives. In these sessions Sally discussed her interest in Native American spirituality — an interest that she thought Bob saw as
silly. She needed permission from Bob and from her superego to use Native
American spirituality to story her experience of Peter when he was alive as
well as when he was dead. In Sally's individual work, a pivotal deconstruct-
ing question — that she answered in the affirmative — was "Is it okay to think
that Peter could be happy somewhere?" She seemed ready to construct a
new narrative, one where guilt played a quieter role. Sally imagined her son
crossing a boundary from one world to another — from a world where he
could not find happiness to a new world where he was finally happy.

Bob was not quite as ready. "To let go of my grief is to let go of Peter.
To touch my sorrow is to touch Peter." Bob agreed that the story he was
authoring was one designed to maximize the pain he would feel. Assuming
that a man who fathered a son who chose to die had no right to future
happiness, he was startled by my statement that it was actually a decision to
look at it this way and that he could decide to look at it differently.

A turning point for Bob was his recognition that his other son, Tom, had
become "stagnant" as a result of grief and guilt regarding his brother's
suicide. For the sake of his living son, Bob was now motivated to begin to
change his own stagnating narrative. Drawing on Bob's need for a co-
constructor of a new narrative and his strong sense of responsibility to his
remaining child to help begin this process, I gave Bob the following quote
to discuss with his son: "Individuals are never entirely at the mercy of events
so long as they retain the power to reconceive them" (Morson & Emerson,
1990, p. 230, discussing Bakhtin).

TERMINATION

The sands had run through the managed care hourglass and it was time to
end our work. A part of Sally and Bob would probably always be frozen in
grief, so they would never completely recover from their son's suicide.
But they were reconnecting to life with altered identities and with a new
appreciation of each other and of their son Tom and of what was important
to them. Their story about their son was not as guilt-saturated; their grief
was not as palpable; their lives, they could finally accept, were going to
move forward.

In the last session I asked them whether they thought they were allowed
to be happy again.

Bob said that he and Sally had just been talking about that and that Sally
had put it best when she said it was "okay."

It was okay to be happy again one day. Their superego companion, albeit begrudgingly and without enthusiasm, was beginning to release them from the dark elegy.

EMOTION RECOLLECTED IN TRANQUILITY

Poetry is the spontaneous overflow of powerful feelings: it takes its origin from emotion recollected in tranquility.

— Wordsworth, *Lyrical Ballads*

My knowledge of Sally and Bob was to end where it had begun: with an article in the newspaper. About two years after I had last seen Sally and Bob in session, there was an announcement in the paper that they were leaving their home of many years to be near their remaining son, who lived thousands of miles away. In the announcement they said good-bye and thank you to all of the people they had known.

I felt a mild implosion inside. I would miss knowing that they were in the area and that I might never see them again. Periodically I would run into Sally. The reconnections were always brief but touching and intense as our minds traveled back in time to the work we had shared. We had traveled to hell and back, and now Sally and Bob would be traveling away to build a new life — authoring and co-authoring new chapters in a new land. I felt like they were taking a part of me with them. What part I didn't know, but it seemed important to me that I send a card to wish them well. The contrast between the sunniness of a farewell card by Hallmark and the emotionally thick interpersonal field that had existed between us was striking.

Enough time had passed that I could now let myself remember what it had felt like to work with this couple. At the time I could think about the work only for short periods before I would get too anxious. Not wanting to lose my confidence in my work with them, I would not think about it too long or too deeply. Like the caterpillar who best not stop and think about where she's going or she'll lose her coordination, I needed to move forward and suppress some of my reactions.

Wordsworth (1979) defined poetry as "emotion recollected in tranquility." That is a good description of my reminiscing about my work with this couple. Call it poetry or countertransference, the intense marriage of words and feelings expressed in session were still vivid. At the time my feelings and mental confusion had been like a collection of little storms or tornadoes, each with its own issue. How can I bear looking at their pain? whirred one internal tornado. Why *did* Peter kill himself? stormed another. With a hurricane of feelings and puzzlements I wondered: How could they ever survive this trauma? Could they ever be happy again? Will they ever stop crying and screaming? Will their heavy, heavy grief ever lighten? Will they just be robots for the rest of their lives? What went wrong? What could help a pain so out of control? How could they—or anyone else—see this any other way than as a horrible, avoidable tragedy?

Working with this couple produced countertransference reactions of varying intensity. There were the usual countertransference reactions that help the therapist make sense of the couple's life together. Then there was the other kind of countertransference—the kind I felt most strongly in the early sessions with Sally and Bob. This I will call the "locomotive" kind of countertransference. This locomotive countertransference hits one like a train. There is no danger that the therapist will—emotionally or mentally—leave the room because one is feeling the force of another's feelings in a powerfully visceral, physical way.

When Sally and Bob walked into my office that first day, settled into their seats, then looked at each other and ignited in grief, I felt that the pain they were showing me was registering in my body. It was as if I were getting heavier and heavier in my chair. How hard it was to look at and see their pain, especially the pain of a man who, as an airline pilot, was used to being unflappable. When grief is all-consuming, there is no shame to hide the pain from another's view. Shameless grief is fetal, it rocks, it doubles one over in pain, it contorts one's face and body into an unrecognizable state. Sally and Bob expressed their pain so uninhibitedly, they seemed to beg the universe to "say it isn't so." I had seen this intense emotion only in war photographs and documentaries about concentration camps. I was horrified at first.

As they sobbed, my arms and legs felt heavier and heavier and eventually, by the end of the session after hearing about their loss, my body was exhausted. But this physical absorption of their pain intuitively felt like exactly the right thing to do—to just sit with them in an almost boundary-less way, listening and emotionally absorbing. Establishing a place of safety for them was calming for me as well. Existentially, it was reassuring to see that pain so big could be contained by human connectedness.

The next session was a bit less emotional and more narrative. My heart felt like it was not just open to them but breaking for them. I felt very, very sad for them and so at a loss for how to help them come to terms with their tragedy. It was easier for me to hold their pain than to imagine a healing narrative for them.

From their story and from who they seemed to be as people they had been good enough parents. Their son who had committed suicide had been so loved. How could it be that love and well-intentioned parenting had not been more protective? Why was love not able to protect a child? I felt a tear in the fabric of my own parenting. The thought of my child killing himself was inconceivable.

I then started to worry about other family members and to feel an increased responsibility for making sure they were happy. I thought of my brother. He never looks very happy. I called to reassure myself that he was still there. Next I thought of my stepson, who wears black all the time and is always reading Dostoyevsky. What if he isn't afraid to die and has days when he thinks life isn't worth the bother? Whom do I know and love who secretly contemplates suicide? I wondered. I felt insecure.

I panicked at the idea of having responsibility for helping this couple make their peace with the unthinkable. How could they see this event any other way than the way they were seeing it? A parent would feel like he or she had made terrible mistakes and must be to blame. How could one look at it any other way?

I panicked also that my child could be loved but need something more to sustain his desire to live. What could this be and what steps did I need to take immediately to start controlling this? I longed to hold my little boy and feel reassured that he was still here. What steps did I need to take immediately to prevent him from ever considering choosing death over life? Maybe, I wondered, I was not doing enough to make him happy. I'll do more, I promised myself. Then this could never happen to me. My own superego alarm system was triggered, and a new set of parental "shoulds" was being generated.

I felt paralyzed by the inadequacy I felt at helping Sally and Bob construct a healing narrative. "How," I would ask my psychologist-husband, to whom I go for occasional peer supervision, "could they ever forgive themselves?" Sally and Bob believed that as parents they had shaped their children's lives and that the suicide was the worst thing that had ever happened to them. I knew if it had happened to us we would look at it the same way and our happiness would end forever — just what Sally and Bob feared would happen to them. "I don't know," replied my usually helpful husband. "I don't like to think about it. Actually, I *can't* think about it. My mind moves on to other things." Constructing with the couple a narrative that could help them make some peace with their son's suicide and enable them to reconnect with ordinary life seemed as impossible as resurrecting the dead.

Then I saw the ridiculousness of planning to take so much responsibility for others' emotional lives and for wanting to micro-control my son's moods and become "neurotransmitter mother," who, ideally, could do everything to keep her child happy, even regulate his serotonin levels if necessary. This reaction paralleled Sally and Bob's unrealistic assumption that they had been responsible for their son's death. The ridiculousness of my countertransference was helping me make a diagnosis and treatment plan.

The bizarre fantasy of the neurotransmitter mother helped me conceptualize my work in terms of helping them get rid of a guilt that was cruel and unfair to them. Their parenting, I believed, had been more than adequate. The real story was that our children *can* choose at any moment to end their lives and we cannot control this. They can choose at any moment to leave our lives. Forever. Anyone can. We can't control this. Even love is powerless to prevent a permanent separation. How can I keep forgetting this? This powerlessness is the issue, not parenting mistakes. At last I found a clue to how to help them story their tragedy in a way that they would feel they did not need eternal punishment.

Another kind of countertransference experience was the terrifying rediscovery that, despite how well we think we know people, they are — in part — strangers filled with mysteries and terrible secrets. "We seldom know each other and can only guess at the lives that want to be lived in every human being," wrote novelist James Lee Burke (1995). Sally and Bob's son had a side to him that they had not known and that, because of their difference from him, they may not have been capable of knowing. He was in part invisible to the people who had given him life and watched him grow. I shared their incomprehension about why Peter killed himself. I still wonder. Perhaps clues lay in his relationship with his grandfather. This was never explored with the couple due to time constraints of brief treatment; in any case, Sally and Bob were not motivated or ready to explore it. Since they thought they must have been to blame, exploring other issues was resisted. My curiosity had to be put aside.

The last powerful countertransference issue triggered for me was my own impasse at coming to terms with death. The poet Rainer Maria Rilke (1968) wrote that "Death is the side of life that is turned away from us." Death was not turned away from Sally, Bob, and myself. Staring right at us, Death challenged us to find a narrative that would take us beyond frustration, impotence, fear, and the inadequacy of spiritual impasse.

References

Burke, J. L. (1995). *Burning angel*. New York: Hyperion.
Combs, G., & Freedman, J. (1994). Narrative intentions. In M. Hoyt (Ed.), *Constructive therapies* (pp. 189–216). New York: Guilford.
Freud, S. (1917/1957). Mourning and melancholia. In J. Strachey (Ed. and Trans.), *The standard edition of the complete psychological works of Sigmund Freud* (Vol. 14, pp. 237–258). New York: Norton.
Herman, J. L. (1992). *Trauma and recovery*. New York: Basic.
Jacobson, E. (1964). *The self and the object world*. New York: International Universities Press.

Morson G., & Emerson, C. (1990). *Mikhail Bakhtin: Creation of a prosaics*. Palo Alto, CA: Stanford University Press. Cited in M. Hoyt (Ed.), *Constructive therapies* (pp. 189–216). New York: Guilford.

Rilke, R. M. (1968). Letter to W. Von Hulewicz. In John Bartlett, *Familiar Quotations, 14th ed.* (p. 938). Boston: Little, Brown.

Roth, S., & Chasin, R. (1994). Entering one another's worlds of meaning and imagination: Dramatic enactment and narrative couple therapy. In M. Hoyt (Ed.), *Constructive therapies* (pp. 189–216). New York: Guilford.

Saari, C. (1994). An exploration of meaning and causation in clinical social work. *Clinical Social Work Journal, 22*, 251–261.

Schafer, R. (1960). The loving and beloved superego in Freud's structural theory. *Psychoanalytic Study of the Child, 15*, 163–188.

Spence, D. P. (1982). *Narrative truth and historical truth: Meaning and interpretation in psychoanalysis*. New York: Norton.

Unger, M., & Levene, J. (1994). Selfobject functions of the family: Implications for family therapy. *Clinical Social Work Journal, 22*, 303–316.

White, M., & Epston, D. (1990). *Narrative means to therapeutic ends*. New York: Norton.

Wordsworth, W. (1979). *Preface to the lyrical ballads*. Westport, CT: Greenwood.

15

Countertransference with Abusive Couples

CAROL A. FRANCIS

MEAN-SPIRITED, abusive behaviors often bring couples to therapy. When mental cruelty, emotional abuse, or physical violence is revealed, the couples therapist must instantaneously manage intense countertransferential reactions, including judgmentalness, anger, or disdain. Such knee-jerk reactions are natural responses to cruel, inhumane behaviors, responses typically derived from conventional social values. Couples therapists must rise above these reactions, however, and attend to the complex complementary and concordant countertransference reactions pertaining to both the abuser and the abused.

Here I apply Racker's (1948/1953, 1972) concepts of complementary and concordant countertransference to the effective treatment of abusive couples. In my years of providing treatment to abusive couples and supervision to therapists stymied by patients' abusiveness, I have discovered behaviors or characteristics that typically provoke these two types of countertransferences. Tara and Thomas are introduced to illustrate how I grappled with different provocative behaviors. As I discuss their process, I will present eight specific characteristics that commonly ensnare therapists in social or countertransferential traps.

TARA AND THOMAS, A COUPLE ENTANGLED IN ABUSE

I had provided individual therapy to Tara for two years. When we started working together, Tara had recovered from the outward effects of her third marriage—a relationship, like the two before, characterized by a cycle of violence. At first her relationships were intensely romantic and appeared enviously ideal. After several years, verbal and physical abusiveness would insidiously begin. Her husbands each had become frustrated by Tara's intriguing personality and sexual allure, which would frequently be accompanied by unpredictable, wild verbal accusations and hitting. Each husband was at first succoring during these explosive episodes. As the years passed, however, each husband would become enraged by the false accusations and then became physically expressive of a wish to shake Tara free from her delusions. Their physical expressions of frustration became assaultive (hitting, yelling, throwing items, breaking objects, locking Tara up, etc.). Eventually, each relationship ended with Tara terrified of her husband, needing to flee for her life to battered women's shelters or live out of cars.

During her second marriage, memories began to occur first as flashes then as intact scenarios. She began flirting with therapeutic help, but never fully recovered her history or understood how she repeated its pattern until after the similar demise of her third marriage.

Individual work with me and her three previous therapists revealed a life of horrible victimization. By six, Tara was the unwilling "whore" of her father. During nightly lengthy visits pervaded by her father's declarations of "You want me, I know; you can't get enough of me; I'm the best lover you'll ever have," Tara fled mentally and wept silently. She was confused by the wish to be special and the horror of being raped repeatedly by her father.

By day Tara's father would watch and lust and adore. Her mother, who saw and knew, would seethe and calculate Tara's punishment for seducing her father. Then, when father was gone, Tara was beaten with brooms, harassed with commands to tend to the house and the seven younger children, as well as battered verbally with charges of being a "bitch" or "whore." Her jealous and cruel mother considered Tara the only woman in her husband's large harem whom she could torture with revenge.

During one of those dark and terrifying years, Tara grew fat and sickly. One evening, she was rushed to the hospital with gut-wrenching pains. She was immediately admitted. She was convinced that she was about to die as she was anesthetized to sleep. Fifteen years later, she would discover that this was the night she gave birth to her father's twins. Her first children oho would call "sisters" until she discovered the well-hidden truth at age twenty-five.

While I was working with Tara individually, she met many men and began and ended flirtatious relationships with few abusive incidents. She was gun-shy and eager to note any signals of abusive tendencies she could detect. If she could have fun or be sexual without emotional involvement or if she could flirt and feel attractive without any actual ongoing commitment, she would feel safe and alive. However, she was eager to have the one lasting and trusting relationship of her life. Eventually she met Thomas.

Tara was determined to form a lasting relationship, one in which she would not be abused or abusive. We agreed that inviting Thomas into the therapeutic arena would enable her to address the nature of her interpersonal transferences, projections, and impaired relationship skills.

Thomas was a former professional athlete. He seemed huge as he ducked into my office door, squeezing his shoulders through the opening one at a time. His quiet, passive presence provided Tara with a sense of safety, much as a teddy bear might a young child.

Tara had attracted Thomas in much the same way she lured other men, with her charismatic vivacity and voluptuous body. Shortly thereafter, he fell in love with her and had made a tentative commitment to be the means through which she would triumph over her past. He had no history of violence. Even as an athlete he had been deemed too gentle and placid to become a long-term valued contender. Although divorced from a wife who had used street drugs for too long, he maintained an apparent civil relationship with her and lovingly co-parented their four adolescent children.

Before I met Thomas, Tara described him as a gorgeously attractive, strong man who conversed easily and straightforwardly. He was attentive, passionate, humorous, kind, and generous. I felt tremendously happy and hopeful for Tara, feeling that at last she had discovered a man who was without a violent history and had traits of a knight. She had found an ideal prince — but was this idealization or fact?

When I met this large, unkempt, out-of-shape man, he did not match Tara's portrayal. Although kind and calm, good-natured and well-meaning, he was slow to understand Tara's explanations, Tara's plight, the therapeutic process, or his positive and negative roles in Tara's current drama. He was not quick to anger, but he expected simple answers and simple solutions to be enough and would become frustrated and confused easily. Tara had found yet another individual who would be quite prone to falling into the same pattern of eventual unwitting spousal abuse. Her ideal knight proved susceptible to becoming physically and verbally abusive as soon as Tara displayed her provocative complications.

Verbal abuse began to transpire between Thomas and Tara even before couples therapy began. Tara would initially and frequently state, "If only Thomas will now learn to not talk to me that way!" "Now things will be different, since he knows that I won't take any type of abuse from him." By such statements, Tara clearly expressed her desire to avoid dealing with the weightiness of the situation and the complexity of her issues. She understandably wished to resume the pleasant aspects of the relationship with the help of quick remedies and superficial insights.

Hopefulness and Conditional Threats of the Abused

Hopefulness ("Now everything will be different. This won't happen again.") and *conditional threats* ("If he does this again, I'm leaving!")—as expressed by Tara after their first fight—are common reactions of abused individuals within a couple. These hopeful or conditional statements reflect the wishful urge to be able to apply superficial remedies and magical controls on the partner. Tables 15.1 and 15.2 outline the abused patient's needs and the therapist's basic social and countertransferential responses to these two types of behaviors.

My first impulse was to share Tara's hopefulness; I too hoped that this first fight would be a one-time event that would be instructive and curative in one simple stroke. I also wanted their reconciliation to be sufficient to

TABLE 15.1
Hopefulness of the Abused

Characteristics of the Abused	Abused's Fundamental Needs	Therapist's Socialized Reactions	Complementary Countertransference	Concordant Countertransference
Hopefulness: "If only s/he'd do___, everything would be okay." "S/he'll be different now; I know it will be okay."	Denial and minimization created by such hopefulness is often associated with the abused's inability to endure the impact of the truths he or she is failing to face.	Urge to confront the patient on the realities of the abusiveness or the urge to be hopeful are common social responses. These reactions, however, fail to address the fundamental needs of the abused, such as developing an ability to face and deal with reality.	Like the abuser, the therapist may fleetingly feel inclined to promote reconciliation without requiring any recognition of the wrongs done, the abuser's responsibilities, and the abused's blindness.	Like the abused, the therapist may feel the urge to gird up to "try again" and attempt superficial interventions instead of facing the abused's structural needs, such as groundedness in reality, capacity to affect one's life's circumstances etc.

TABLE 15.2

Conditional Threats of the Abused

Characteristics of the Abused	Abused's Fundamental Needs	Therapist's Socialized Reactions	Complementary Countertransference	Concordant Countertransference
Conditional threats: "I'll stay only if s/he changes _____." "S/he better never do that again; next time I'm leaving or reporting him/her to the police."	The abused individual resorts to these threats because there is a wish to magically control the abuser with simple words. There is often a fear that the abused could not live without the abuser and so the abused resorts to attempting to artificially gain control when the actual need is to become capable of effectively dealing with life. There is also a wish that the abuser will do all the changing.	Cheerleading the abused while he/she makes these ultimatums is sometimes a socialized response adopted from the wish to "empower" the abused. However, since threats rarely work and usually aggravate power struggles and rebelliousness, the abused is not empowered but rather deluded that threats actually can effect the necessary deep-level changes needed in both the abuser's and abused's lives.	Similar to the abuser's role, the therapist may feel inclined to belittle threats and thereby devalue or disgrace the abused even further. This type of intervention may actually have an abusive effect.	Similar to the abused's position, the therapist might emphasize the "list" of conditions being suggested by the abused and tailor therapeutic goals and interventions that attempt to control the abuser's behaviors. This type of response will breed a misalliance with the abuser and produce only artificial and temporary changes.

heal the now marred relationship without needing to address Tara's patterns and recapitulations or Thomas' now confused and guilt-ridden responses.

I even attempted to gear Tara up for returning to the relationship, informing her that all relationships have their difficulties and almost all relationships have some verbally abusive fights. She was confused as to what normal fighting was in a relationship and I addressed her confusion heuristically out of my blinding countertransference to her hopefulness.

In contrast to these countertransferentially driven interventions, I needed to trace the intricate and complicated patterns that Tara was reenacting, demonstrating to her with painful and indisputable accuracy how she was contributing to the creation of this burgeoning abusive situation.

Tara resorted to *conditional threats* ("I'll stay only if he changes _____.") as well. She hoped to intimidate Thomas into "never fighting again" by threatening abandonment or calling the police. Thomas at first acquiesced to Tara's demands in part to avoid losing her and in part to assuage his guilt about hitting her. Two weeks later, however, Thomas rebelled against the controlling effects of her commands; he protested "you can't order me around any more" and refused to return calls or pages for the next two weeks. When they reunited, he offered his own conditional threats, "If you ever try to control me again, I'll just stop talking to you."

Conditional threats usually digress into petty power-struggles and breed angry and rebellious responses that typically result in more abusive interactions. Therapists might sometimes feel inclined to capitalize upon the ultimatums and then list the changes the abuser is to make. Therapists might also believe that the temporary changes made after such threats are fundamental changes. These are typical concordant countertransferential responses, that is, responses that harmonize with those of the abused. Subtly confronting or deriding the abused for attempting to control the abuser with these threats is a complementary countertransferential response and can cause a minimization of the abused's efforts to find some means with which to effect changes.

Innocence and Guilt of the Abused

In my experience, most abused individuals feel both profoundly wronged by the abuser (*innocence*—"I did nothing to deserve this abuse.") and painfully responsible for the abuse (*guilt*—"I know what buttons to push and I don't stop harassing till she/he hits me. It's therefore all my fault."). Internal tension and confusion are created by the coexistence of these emotional reactions and moral positions in the abused. As a consequence, dealing with any abused individual's feelings of innocence and guilt is a delicate procedure that must be governed by extreme respect, empathy, profound appreciation of the complicated dynamics between two individuals in provocative circumstances, and a detailed understanding of an abused individual's history. Moreover, no therapist can trudge into an abused individual's interior world without the earned trust from and merited alliance with the patient.

After two years of individual work, I knew Tara's history, had developed respect for her strengths and cognizance of her weaknesses, and had earned her cautious trust. It was now time to approach her *innocence* and *guilt* as each manifested in the abusive activities taking place with Thomas.

During the course of a week, Tara would swing from feeling guilty about the abuse that was occurring to feeling innocent. Sometimes she would declare that she was the "innocent victim" of Thomas' abuse. If in reality she had done nothing to aggravate the abusiveness, she nondefensively could acknowledge her innocence and also could more easily recognize her innocence as an abused child.

If she was declaring her innocence even when she had shared information that indicated that she was definitely being provocative, she would actually become more abusive toward Thomas, using *blame* as a means of cruelly ridiculing him. At these times she would feel *entitled* to treat Thomas abusively as a means of vindication and self-protection. (See discussion below about *entitlement* and *blame* of the abuser.) If she could admit her guilt, that is, her participation in the abusive incident, and also appreciate that no one, including herself, had the right to be abusive, she would become clear-headed and able to approach Thomas thereafter without being provocative and without disregarding her need to be self-protective and self-respecting. Table 15.3 outlines various aspects of *innocence* associated with an abused's needs and potential reactions from a therapist in these circumstances.

Various forms of guilt plagued Tara and often stymied her ability to insightfully understand the nature of her abusiveness and abused innocence. However, through the therapeutic work on her experience of guilt, we managed to release her from being both the victim and victimizer. One day, out of her guilt, Tara weepingly explained yet another fight:

"I know I started it. I was so scared and certain he would hurt me, so I wanted to hurt him first. That's why I said what I said. Now I know it really hurt him and made him very angry. But I wouldn't stop; I just kept accusing him even though I had begun to realize that he hadn't done it (*have an affair*). I sounded like my mother. I kept hounding him and hounding him. When he started to leave, I grabbed him by the arm and accused him of abandoning ship. I threw some magazines and books at him. I began to hit him on his arm over and over. He tried to leave. I wouldn't let him. That's when he grabbed me. I thought he was going to hit me, but I think he was trying to stop me from hitting him. He began to yell at me. He called me a 'crazy witch' and said that he hated me. He let go of me by flinging me away. I fell to the couch. My arms are bruised by his grip. See? He left, banging the door behind him and swearing loudly."

Conventional social wisdom of this era guides therapists to sympathize sincerely with the abused individual's experience and to state clearly that under no circumstances does a man, or woman, have the right to be physically abusive. Also, it would be common and socially wise to advise that

TABLE 15.3
Innocence of the Abused

Characteristics of the Abused	Abused's Fundamental Needs	Therapist's Socialized Responses	Complementary Countertransference	Concordant Countertransference
Innocence: "I'm completely innocent." "I don't deserve his/her abuse because I did nothing wrong." "I never do anything provocative."	While the abusive behavior is never justifiable or acceptable, the abused individual needs to see what participation s/he has in the situation, including staying, escalating fights, badgering, needing to be self-punitive, or attacking verbally to elicit another physical attack that proves the other's badness.	Therapist's socialized responses, an accurate truism, is to declare "Of course you don't deserve the abuse" or to provide sympathy. These responses are meaningful and morally and legally correct. Yet the therapist must realize that these responses may prematurely stop the abused from recognizing his/her participation and therefore his/her power in the situation.	In identification with the abuser's frustrations or feelings of being provoked, the therapist may feel compelled to confront or deride the abused into accepting blame and may push the abused into wrongfully experiencing guilt.	When a therapist is identified with the abused's innocence, a failure to understand the abused's power, contributions, and potential need for the abuse and abusive relationship will result.

contact with an abuser be immediately stopped. These responses aim at promoting self-protection; Tara, like most abused individuals, needed to learn the art of realistic and effective self-protection.

The value of these types of socialized interventions cannot be minimized. However, these responses fail to recognize that an abused individual has the capacity to be abusive and coercive. Many therapists are ostracized for making such a statement. Various supervisees of mine have been ashamed to entertain these thoughts, as if they were betraying the abused individual and placing all blame on him/her. Working with the abused individual's guilt does not justify the abuser's actions and does not mitigate the abuser's guilt, but it does free the abused individual from buried and helpless feelings and the need to be abused in order to pay for one's guilt.

Complementary countertransference toward an abused individual who is expressing guilt typically stimulates a therapist to become subtly accusatory, much like to the identified abuser. For example, I might have suggested to Tara that she truly hurt Thomas and that his responses were self-defensive. This might have been helpful but not as insightful as Tara needed. Tara might have responded to this intervention by immediately expressing remorse and agreement with this idea. However, she might also have misconstrued my statement, thinking that I was suggesting that Thomas was justified in his actions. Moreover, she would have felt accused and misunderstood, because such a focus would have failed to identify the complex messages in her guilty feelings, as I will delineate below.

Concordant countertransference toward an abused individual means consoling the individual and assuaging the guilt parallel to the wish of the abused. For example, I might have empathically described how frightened she was of once again being betrayed by yet another man and explain how she defensively attempted to protect herself by attacking him first. While my intentions in this type of response might be (1) to empower her, (2) to help her find rationale for her behavior, and (3) to empathically assuage the severity of her guilt, I needed to guard against interfering with her developing ability to genuinely care for her victims (unlike her father) and deeply feel the urge to remedy her own inclination to be abusive (a hard inclination for anyone to face).

When an abused individual is feeling guilt, a complex process is transpiring, which needs to be delineated for the patient. First, the guilt should not be silenced or calmed; its presence is essential for helping a patient struggle with the issues described below. Second, the guilt should not be reinforced. An abused individual's guilt is multifaceted and should be unraveled with tremendous compassion. Therapeutic work with abused individual's guilt can lead to:

1. *Recognition of the capacity to be abusive.* This essentially helps an individual gain both a sense of personal power (I can hurt others, too!) and a realistic recognition of the many aspects of intense anger and the capacity for destructiveness that exist inside. An abused individual needs to recognize (a) the power he/she has to destroy, (b) his/her wish for destructive retaliation, and (c) his/her urge to identify with the abuser as a means of feeling powerful and in control.

2. *Recognition of his/her ability to admit personal guilt, unlike the abuser.* The capacity to admit mistakes, feel guilt and remorse, and pursue genuine reparation is a powerful and healthy response. This

response often differentiates the abused individual from his/her abuser, who could not admit any wrongdoing or could not sustain personal changes.

3. *Confusion associated with childhood beliefs that she/he is being deservedly abused because she/he is bad.* Children are very inclined to wish to perceive their abuser as wise and therefore often confuse the abusive behaviors with appropriate discipline. The child feels guilty for apparent bad behaviors that have "caused" the abuse. Of course, this type of guilt is not based upon an accurate appraisal of the situation. Many abused children carry feelings of this type of guilt into their adult perceptions. Some patients will feel more comfortable viewing themselves as bad. Their guilt becomes the means by which they mistakenly convert their bad abuser into the "wronged" individual. (This attitude is reflected in the adage "It is better to be a bad person in a good world than a good person in a bad world.")

4. *Recognition of how one can use guilt to remain trapped in the abusive relationship.* When abused individuals use their guilt to force themselves to remain within the familiar confines of an abusive relationship, the reasons for this need to be carefully examined in therapy. ("I don't deserve better treatment," is a common, convoluted form of guilt.)

5. *The wish to gain a sense of artificial powerfulness* by feeling responsible for creating a frightening and violent circumstance appears in therapy as another convoluted form of guilt.

6. *The wish to avoid being abused more, yet still remain in the relationship* sometimes motivates an abused person to accept blame. By quickly feeling guilty, one avoids issues, genuine responsibilities, or damages caused. If one apologizes or swiftly shows remorse, one might avoid the other's anger, retaliation, or rejection.

7. *Genuine and deeply moving emotions about hurting another individual and the wish to truly remedy the situation.* Removing guilt of this nature prematurely by way of explanations, justifications, blame, or sympathy will rob the patient of being deeply moved and empowered to alter his/her urge to hurt or punish the innocent individuals in his/her present life. Melanie Klein's article "Love, Guilt and Reparation" (1937/1977) details the value and development of this function of guilt.

With Tara, each of these aspects of her guilt had to be identified, exemplified, and defined with careful and clear explanations. For example, one aspect of her guilt was associated with her wish to inspire Thomas to quickly overlook and forgive her accusations and to justify her hitting.

She displayed painful and remorseful tears and agonizing apologies. She superficially vowed to Thomas to alter her behaviors and gave him detailed lists of lessons learned that she would never need to repeat. Notably, at these times she shifted roles and used "guilt" phrases typical of abusers. At these times, she needed to be therapeutically addressed as one would deal with an abuser who was expressing artificial contrition.[1]

After the middle phase of the couples therapy, Tara displayed guilt that truly enabled her to understand the serious harm her violent self-protective responses could do to a person who was innocent of the crimes once committed against her (even though he might be responsible for recent offenses). Her guilt could help her feel love and concern for her current victim, Thomas. Her genuine guilt would help her grasp at what point Thomas was as innocent as she had been as a daughter. Her guilt, associated with a wish to be fair and fairly treated, helped her recognize her unfairness toward Thomas and enabled her to differentiate her internal responses toward her father and mother from her blinding rage acted out upon Thomas.

Another advantage of Tara's recognizing her capacity to be abusive and feel remorse became evident. She began to be able to differentiate when Thomas was actually guilty of abuse and when she was misinterpreting or aggravating the situation. She could tune into internal signals that told her when she was guilty and when someone else was the offender. Table 15.4 contains information about the generic principles underlying the understanding of the abused's guilt and various reactions therapists experience.

Each time Tara expressed guilt, I would explain: "Let's try to understand what your remorse and painful guilt mean today." This type of phrase released Tara to explore her guilt without being judged or released prematurely. After we explored the nature of her current guilt, I would review the list that we had understood thus far. For example, "Two weeks ago, after the big fight, you felt guilty in a way that made you hate yourself for being so much like your mother. Last week, we discovered that some of your guilt was a way to try to win Thomas back without having to work at truly understanding how he was hurting. Today, your guilt seems moved from a place inside that understands how deeply he and you can be hurt when someone yells, hits, and falsely accuses."

---

[1]Role reversals (such as oscillating from the position of the abuser to abused back to abuser or vice versa) occur quite commonly in couples therapy when violence is present. This is difficult to detect and to appreciate since we are typically ostracized from ever viewing the predominantly abused individual as also capable of being abusive. However, to free a couple from the chains of violent cycles, this and other complex dyadic exchanges must be observed, appreciated, and addressed with respect and clarity, never accusation. In this situation, Tara was using the abusive characteristic *superficial contrition* (artificial guilt) to avoid the actual issues. Superficial contrition is a characteristic of abusive individuals, as I have discussed elsewhere (Francis, 1996).

TABLE 15.4
Guilt of the Abused

Characteristics of the Abused	Abused's Fundamental Needs	Therapist's Socialized Reactions	Complementary Countertransference	Concordant Countertransference
Guilt: "S/he's right; I start the fight. I know what will trigger him/her."	The abused individual needs to understand and resolve issues associated with (1) needing to feel guilty, (2) needing to be the initiator, and (3) needing to feel bad. The abused needs to find authentic ways to be powerful, self-protective, and remorseful.	Sympathy and dissuasion are socialized responses that typically derail the therapy from exploring the complexity of guilt in an abused patient.	When a therapist is identified with the abuser's position, the therapist will wrongfully seize the opportunity to find the abuser innocent when the guilt-ridden abused is temporarily willing to take the blame. The abused is weakened when s/he owns another's guilt. When the abused faces authentic guilt, s/he is usually strengthened.	Concordantly, the therapist may feel an urge to dissuade the abused of his/her guilt, since the abused individual may desperately wish to be released from the burden of the guilt. On the other hand, the therapist may concordantly become caught up in the perception that the abused is self-destructive. The cycle is created.

Obliviousness of Abusers

Even though Thomas did not recall either being in an abusive relationship previously (although one would wonder what it was like to be married to a cocaine addict for five years) or hitting, yelling at, or hurting a woman before, he began to display reactions that are typical of abusers. These included forms of mild verbal abuse, such as swearing, vulgar name-calling, and screaming during arguments. He also began to resort to physically pushing Tara away, both defensively and offensively. He began to miss their planned dates inconsistently but frequently, always with weak and seemingly dishonest reasons. He would accuse her falsely with rage and threats, as well as spy on her activities at home.

None of these actions came close to the abusive treatment Tara had experienced in other relationships. Nonetheless, the deterioration of Thomas's behavior became evident and increasingly more hurtful. In fact,

Thomas began to develop a tolerance for his own impulsive and destructive behaviors. What might have once startled him or made him guilty now barely fazed his conscience.

I have found that *obliviousness* in abusers stems from a lack of self-reflection, lack of empathic capacity, an erosion of the capacity to feel remorseful or appalled, and/or use of substances that lead to memory loss. Abusive backgrounds, coupled with progressively hostile conduct in a relationship, also mute a person's ability to recognize the pain, fear, and destruction resulting from battering episodes for both the victim and perpetrator.

Often therapists are eager to confront the abuser with the realities of the abuse and solicit guilt or remorse by applying interventions that promote shame or compliance. Therapists must determine why the abuser is unaware of his/her impact on another person and also help the abuser develop the capacity to feel the suffering that he or she caused and the remorse associated with creating such pain. Table 15.5 delineates more details pertaining to dealing with obliviousness in abusers.

Jealousy of the Abuser

Jealous possessiveness ("I love her/him so much, I'm afraid she'll/he'll leave me if I don't control her/him.") commonly expresses the abuser's severe insecurities about being lovable and fears of being abandoned. Therapy often needs to address the abuser's inability to receive, give, and experience love. Complementary countertransference (identification with the object of jealousy or mistrust) often causes therapists to resort to excessive reassurances and a false belief that loving gestures will eventually reduce the jealousy. Concordant countertransference (when the therapist feels as the jealous abuser feels) causes the therapist to place the abused in a position of trying to constantly succor the abuser and avoid even the slightest behavior that might be misconstrued as betrayal (see Table 15.6).

Thomas's jealousy strongly motivated his subtle gestures of abusiveness toward Tara. As couples therapy progressed, Thomas eventually shared the misery he suffered when he discovered his ex-wife's affairs. To Thomas, Tara was the most enticing woman he had met and he lived in terror of other men finding her irresistible. He often berated Tara, as her mother had, so that she would not feel confident enough to flirt with other men. Thomas's jealousy snared Tara into a "no-win" attempt to avoid any appearance of associating with men (although her career required active, charismatic interfacing with men and women). She also secretively began to regain her self-confidence by collecting compliments from other men since Thomas had stopped displaying attraction.

TABLE 15.5

Obliviousness of Abusers

Characteristics of the Abuser	Abuser's Fundamental Needs	Therapist's Socialized Responses	Complementary Countertransference	Concordant Countertransference
Obliviousness: "I never did any of that. That's an exaggeration. I don't remember any of this." "S/he's misunderstanding; it was only a disagreement."	The ego functions of self-reflection, empathy, and taking responsibility are often missing in abusers who are oblivious to the impact their behavior has on another. In addition, sometimes substance abuse leads to blank memories about the abusive events.	Therapists, out of disbelief or irritation, often wish to confront or give up on the abuser when obliviousness is a profound defense or mental state.	In accord with the abused individual, therapists might be inclined to minimize the abusive incident out of pity for the abuser. On the other hand, like the abused individual, they may be an inclined to be abusive, often in subtle ways, to try to make the abuser feel how painful abuse is.	Like the abuser, the therapist may feel subjective fogginess or the inclination to minimize the abusive episode. A wish to smooth over, forget, start over again with a magically cleaned slate, or other such attempts to ignore the incident may also be experienced.

At first, I felt the typical social responses of pity or irritation toward his jealousy and had urges to deflect it as unfounded. I also experienced the complementary countertransference of wishing to build him up so that he would not feel such insecurity. Fortunately, I resisted urges to place Tara in the role of providing succor for the insecurities leading to his jealousy.

Thomas's issues of insecurity had to be examined on deeper levels. His history of being teased for his size, teased for his passive nature when bullied by smaller boys, and teased for his slower mental abilities exacerbated the corrosive effects of his first marriage to an erratic, faithless wife who hounded him for failing as a sports hero and earning wages as a welder.

Thomas had hoped that Tara's intense idealization of him would continue forever as a magical way of healing his bruised self-respect. He was terrified that she would inevitably despise him as he did himself and as his previous wife had done. At times, he attempted to focus the relationship on Tara's insecurities, childhood abuse, and her severe problems, so that he

TABLE 15.6

Jealousy in the Abuser

Characteristics of the Abuser	Abuser's Fundamental Needs	Therapist's Socialized Responses	Complementary Countertransference	Concordant Countertransference
Jealousy and possessiveness: "I love him/her so much, I'm afraid s/he'll leave me if I don't control her/him." "I've been betrayed once; I won't be fooled again."	When jealousy is the source of abusiveness, the abuser often needs to (1) address severe issues of insecurity, abandonment, and envy; (2) address severe inability to feel lovable and confidence in another's love; and (3) learn how to endure the vulnerability and risk associated with loving someone, yet not controlling him or her.	(I have not yet discovered common socialized responses to an abuser's jealousy.)	Therapists identified with the abused may feel a surge of pity and eagerness to console the wounded abuser who abuses out of insecurity. On the other hand, the therapist may note an unusual comfort in the abuser's jealousy, which parallels the abused's feelings of being desirable or loved. Another possibility is that the therapist may be recognize that the abused is actually subtly abusing the identified abuser by aggravating jealousy.	Therapists identified with the abuser who is suffering from jealousy will feel inclined to have the abused try to reassure or love the "patient" out of the insecurities associated with the jealousy. This will entangle the couple in an abusive dyadic process by encouraging the abuser to see the abused as responsible for fixing the reasons for the jealousy.

could continue to appear to be better adjusted and a better "catch." More commonly, his insecurities made him jealous of men attracted to Tara and envious of Tara's charisma. His jealousy and envy drove him to demean and belittle Tara in an abusive fashion.

Once Tara understood these aspects of Thomas's dynamics, she sometimes abused him by pretending to be with other men or berating him for his character flaws. At these moments, Thomas would behave as an abused individual. Once again, the roles would reverse. I needed to be able to flexibly switch perceptions of who was abusing and who was being abused.

"Entitlement" of the Abuser

Entitlement ("I can do whatever I want!") expressed by an abuser often incites the therapist's outrage. Confrontational interventions, however, typically prove ineffective. In addition, the therapist must wrestle with complementary countertransference (feeling like the abused individual) by noting responses of defensiveness, fear, retreat, or acquiescence. Complementary countertransference to a spirit of entitlement may also include a strong urge to develop the abuser's guilt or conscience by way of instruction or blame. Concordant countertransference (feeling like the abusive individual) is manifested by a resonance with the patient's urge to be empowered and refusal to be manipulated or controlled by the partner.

Therapists working with a patient's abusive expressions of entitlement must recognize developmental needs associated with narcissistic and antisocial qualities, such as (1) long-term history of failed empathy, (2) long-term abusiveness, (3) developed belief in the right to retaliate against all aggravations, (4) failure to develop object constancy, (5) failure to develop compassion and healthy guilt, or (6) familial attitudes of machismo dominance.

Tara took on the role of the abuser when she manifested the attitude that she was entitled to physically hit and verbally attack Thomas in order to defend herself against a perceived or potential threat. At these times, therapy addressed her need to be self-protective without resorting to counterattacks. Tara gradually recognized that the "right" to retaliate against her father's cruelty did not include harming Thomas — or any other suitor for that matter.

Thomas, too, felt entitled to verbally attack Tara. "After all," he would argue, "she started it." The urge to retaliate is often used as moral justification for becoming abusive toward another. Therapists infected by a concordant countertransference to the entitled abuser may (1) privately or overtly cheer the abuser on because the abused "deserved it"; (2) forget to differentiate self-defense and proactive self-protection from retaliatory abusiveness; or (3) resonate with the abuser's wish to avoid being manipulated or controlled by a partner.

Entitlement to be abusive also triggers antagonistic responses or complementary countertransference. For instance, when Thomas felt that Tara deserved being abandoned, yelled at, or pushed around, I felt incensed at Thomas's self-justifications (a moralizing, socialized response). I grappled with the nontherapeutic urge to stimulate his conscience with confrontational, guilt-producing techniques. Instead, empathy, exploration, description, and interpretation enabled Thomas to move toward his own genuine regrets and desire to take responsibility for his cruelty, regardless of provocations from Tara. Table 15.7 delineates these aspects of an abuser's sense of entitlement.

Blame of the Abuser

Blame ("She/he made me do it! If she/he hadn't . . . I wouldn't have hurt her/him! It's her/his fault!") can trigger the therapist's urge to confront the abuser with the "facts." However, first the therapist must sort through potential complementary reactions, such as a wish to counterblame the abuser or defend the honor, weakness, or rights of the abused. Complementary countertransference to blaming statements may also make the therapist feel accused and vulnerably unarmed. These reactions are common among abused individuals subjected to strong pounding and eroding blame and accusations by the abuser. Concordant countertransference (feeling the same as the abuser) results in the therapist's identifying with a sense of having been manipulated and goaded by the abused. At these times the therapist feels inclined to side with the abuser and confront the abused as an inciter (see Table 15.8).

Thomas once blamed Tara when he physically lifted her out of his car on a freeway on-ramp during an argument because she was inflaming him by her wrongful accusations. He intensely defended his actions in the subsequent session: "She started the whole thing. I wasn't hurting her; I was just making a clear statement that she can't keep throwing these accusations at me. I am not the mean person here; she is!"

Clearly Tara was exceedingly irksome. Nonetheless, Thomas was failing to appreciate how he had resorted to physical solutions instead of safe interventions. The central need of the abuser who resorts to blame is to develop the capacity to experience a sense of responsibility even when provoked. Constructive guilt and remorse, coupled with empathy for another's welfare, enable one to refrain from abusiveness even when inflamed. Past relationships frequently demonstrate a deprivation of empathy and an excessive use of projections. This held true for Thomas, who had severely suffered the effects of a drug-addicted ex-wife who blamed Thomas for all her unhappiness.

Other Characteristics

Several other characteristics of the abused and the abuser that provoke countertransferential reactions and socialized responses have been devel-

TABLE 15.7
Entitlement of the Abuser

Characteristics of the Abused	Abused's Fundamental Needs	Therapist's Socialized Reactions	Complementary Countertransference	Concordant Countertransference
Entitlement to abuse: "I can do what I want because I am who I am." "She deserves this." "I have a right to defend myself."	In some families, the aggressive or abusive individual wins respect. The abuser wishing to change needs to alter the effects of this background. In like manner, issues typical of narcissistic and antisocial personality disorders are often prevalent. Retaliation and self-protection can also generate an attitude of entitlement.	Therapists often become outraged when an abuser acts entitled to be cruel to another human. The urge to confront or demean may interfere with therapeutic processes.	As with the abused individual, sometimes therapists become frozen or stymied by the "entitled" abuser because the abuser has the capacity to make others (therapist included) feel deserving of demeaning words and devaluing responses. In these cases, the therapist feels abused or devalued, yet confused by irrational feelings of guilt. Therapists can also become intense moralizers in hopes of changing the wrongful and self-centered perspective of the "entitled" abuser.	Therapists who are identified with the entitled abuser may confusingly applaud the empowerment expressed by the individual, especially if the abuser was once abused. The abuser can also charismatically convince the therapist that good intentions were behind the abusive actions. Therapists can also become so frustrated with the "martyred" image of the abused individual that they sympathize with the abuser's inclination to attack.

TABLE 15.8
Blame of the Abuser

Characteristics of the Abuser	Abuser's Fundamental Needs	Therapist's Socialized Responses	Complementary Countertransference	Concordant Countertransference
Blame: "S/he made me do it." "If s/he hadn't done_____, I never would have hurt him/her." "It's her/his fault!"	Developmental issues associated with the capacity to feel guilt, remorse, responsibility, and compassion need to be addressed when blame is evident. In addition, abusers who pass off the responsibility by blaming the victim often report a family history wherein projection and blame were pervasive.	Irritation, dismissiveness, and the urge to confront the abuser's blame are common spontaneous responses.	Therapists identified with the abused who is being blamed often will come to his/her defense, creating a misalliance in the couples therapy. If the abused is hyper-responsible (via guilt or shame), the therapist may blindly act like the abuser and confront the abused with the "blame material" the abuser is presenting.	Therapists identified with the abuser will herald the rights of the abuser and confront the abused with guilt and shame in subtle ways. Justification for the abuser's actions often comes in the form of "I could certainly appreciate where he/she was coming from; the abused was so provocative."

oped elsewhere (Francis, 1996) with appropriate case examples. They are briefly listed in Table 15.9.

CONCLUSION

The abusive couple is among the most provocative dyads with which to work. The couple's dynamics are highly entangled, twisted, enticing, convoluted, and gripping. Moreover, rarely is there space for the therapist, who is humane and concerned, to feel comfortably neutral. The discipline and constraint with which an effective couples therapist must approach abusive couples require insightful, clinically informed reflections. Each intervention must be done with deliberation and double-checking. It is my hope that readers will increase their self-reflection on socialized responses as well as

TABLE 15.9
Characteristics of Abused and Abusers which
Trigger Nontherapeutic Reactions

Abuser's sadism (pleasure from causing another person harm)	"I like to see him/her squirm. S/he likes it, too."
Abuser's lies	"I never did any of this; s/he's making this all up to make me look bad!"
Abuser's need or desire for control or mastery	"It's for her/his own good. S/he's more loving afterward."
Abuser's superficial contrition	"I feel awful about doing this. I'll never do this again. S/he can trust me. I've learned my lesson. We don't need to keep coming to therapy. S/he can move back in."
Abused's helplessness	"I know what I should do, but I just can't. I don't know how I could survive without him/her."
Abused's masochism	"I enjoy the energy and connection that occurs afterward. We're so close now." "I know that s/he needs to pick on someone because s/he's so wounded inside." "I understand the way s/he is. It's okay; I can take it."
Abused's addiction	"I know I should leave, but I love him/her so much. I guess I'm co-dependent."

on complementary and concordant countertransference and then be able to face the abuser and the abused with helpful interventions. Work with abusive couples is not for all therapists but for those who dare to forge into battles that embroil even the most objective.

REFERENCES

Francis, C. (1996). *Countertransference and the abusive couple, Part II.* Unpublished manuscript.

Klein, M. (1937/1977). *Love, guilt and reparation.* New York: Dell.

Racker, H. (1948/1953). Contribution to the problem of countertransference. *International Journal of Psychoanalysis, 34,* 313–324.

Racker, H. (1972). The meanings and uses of countertransference. *Psychoanalytic Quarterly, 41,* 487–506.

16

Rage and Aggression in Couples Therapy: An Intersubjective Approach

RONALD ALEXANDER
NANCY P. VAN DER HEIDE

FEW THERAPEUTIC SITUATIONS evoke such challenging countertransference reactions as rage and aggression. When these affects arise in couples therapy, their sheer intensity can stimulate especially powerful reactions on the part of the therapist. This can permit the therapist a deeper understanding of the couple's relational dynamics. The way we conceptualize these affects — their origins and role — will greatly impact on our stance as therapists in contending with them.

The premise that anger, rage, and aggression are rooted in early relational patterns and become reactivated in the context of later relationships provides an invaluable therapeutic approach, particularly in helping couples cope with seemingly destructive elements of their relationships. Comprehending the source of narcissistic rage in couples therapy and the functions it serves allows us to decenter from our personal feelings of anxiety or disgust in the face of frequently obnoxious defensive posturing.

ALICE AND JIM

Alice and Jim were successful business people working in the same field. This couple began conjoint therapy with another therapist who felt that she

The authors wish to thank Dr. Jeffrey Trop for his invaluable input, review, and contributions to the relational and intersubjective positions in the organization and preparation of this article.

could not contain their violent acting-out behavior. She was afraid to sit with them in her office, where they would attack each other with slaps, hits, and kicks. Tempers would erupt in restaurants, where they threw wine at each other and dumped tables over. Alice tried to push Jim into the street in front of a moving car; he attempted to throw her out of a moving car.

Frequently, Alice and Jim capped these explosive exchanges with intense sexual encounters. They had sex in elevators, in parking lots, on rooftops, and in parked cars, generally after having beaten each other up. The sex was often vicious and painful.

A fight was already raging in the waiting room before the session began. As I (R.A.) entered the room, they continued to taunt each other with obscenities and pushed and slapped at each other until they were inside the office. They almost had to be separated like boxers in the ring and continued to snarl threats at each other until they were seated, both directly facing the therapist.

Alice began with some restraint, "I hate him. I want to kill him." Her voice then rose to a feverish pitch, and shortly the two were fully engaged in a screaming and yelling match. Somewhat remarkably, I was able to stay focused in the midst of this intensity. Perhaps because my mother never engaged in violent battles with my father, I had no preformed, unconscious connotations of danger organized around the scene enacted in my office.

THERAPIST: Alice, you sound so hurt and so mad. Do you know why you are so angry with Jim that you feel like killing him? Do you feel something inside of you hurting so badly?
JIM: She's a bitch, an angry bitch who's a cheat and a whore.

I felt it was important not to get distracted by his affect and decentered from my own reaction to this outburst, staying, rather, with Alice.

THERAPIST: Alice, can you answer my question?
ALICE: Inside of me is a volcano of rage and anger and poison. I want to spit it all over him because he hurts me so much.
JIM: You're a piece of garbage. I'm sick to death of your bullshit. I ought to dump you somewhere.
THERAPIST: Jim, you sound so furious with Alice. I wonder what you feel she's been withholding from you that has you so incensed.
JIM: She's a bitch. All I get is her venom. I never get sex unless we go through these episodes.
THERAPIST: I see. So some of your rage at Alice is really seeking a response from her that drives up the heat, an attempt to find some passion for you to get into bed together.

JIM: Yeah. It's a real sicko type thing between us. She tries to kill me, I start whacking her, and she's whacking me, and the next thing you know we're doing it.

THERAPIST: I imagine you think about whether there are other ways to get the heat going in this relationship.

ALLICE: He's an impotent, fat pig, is what he is. He wouldn't know how to love me if I showed him myself.

THERAPIST: Have you tried to show him?

ALLICE: No. Why try? Nothing ever works with him. He's an asshole. Worthless nothing.

THERAPIST: You're trying to get the heat going with what you're saying to him, aren't you?

Suddenly, Alice was on her feet, screaming obscenities in his face, trying to humiliate and provoke him. Fearing that blows were about to go down, I stood between them, restrained her from hitting him and got them both seated again. Since my need to establish limits took precedence, I let them know in no uncertain terms that I would stop the session and refuse to work with them if they did this again.

JIM: Yeah. See what I mean, how whacko she is with all that stuff?

THERAPIST: Alice and Jim, I think you both feel deeply powerless and very confused about how to connect and have passion without the enactment of ritualized rage and humiliation, which seems to light up your fires and culminates in your making love, which provides you with the space to feel at one, warm and together.

ALICE (*quieting down*): How can we get close without all the craziness? I really do love you, Jim.

THERAPIST: Yes. Are there ways for bonding, pulling passion up without visiting the rage/hate dimension?

JIM: I want your love, but I hate you as much as I love you.

THERAPIST: Jim, perhaps when you feel hate, it is really your way of protecting yourself from being hurt and feeling something terrible inside. How dangerous it is for you to feel vulnerable and exposed. When in your early life did you feel exposed, shamed, or embarrassed?

Jim revealed an early humiliating event from junior high school when he opened up to a girl who then read his love letter to the guys on the football team.

THERAPIST: I can certainly understand why opening up would feel very dangerous.

ALICE: I want to open up, too, and feel I can be myself without your controlling me.

THERAPIST: Yes, our task is to discover how to make that possible for both of you. We need to take a look at how both of you need and want what the other has to give, but how it feels that the only way to maintain the bond between you is through intense and terrifying fights. I believe that at the heart of the matter each of you feels desperately out of control, panicked, and enraged when either one of you seems to be breaking the bond. Terrified of the emptiness and deadness you feel when the connection threatens to disintegrate.

Understanding the emotional atmospheres in which Jim and Alice grew up was critical to establishing and maintaining a therapeutic relationship with them. Until a context emerged for the incredible levels of venom and physical violence that threatened to erupt at any time, it was nearly impossible to feel warmth or even the desire for an empathic connection to this couple. Their respective histories shed some light on the developmental deficits generating the organizing principles by which these two people were functioning.

As an only child, Jim grew up with a mother who expressed two emotional settings: she was either cold, icy, and withdrawn or raging at her husband and son. Jim's father was passive and uninvolved with Jim. Lacking sensitively attuned caregivers in his world, Jim's experience was woefully bereft of sufficient opportunities to have critical mirroring and idealizing needs met. His chances of developing a positive sense of self-esteem through seeing his worth reflected in the gleam of his mother's eye were nonexistent. In fact, the only gleam in his mother's eyes was one of fiery anger. (As an intriguing aside, Jim's first wife tried to burn him up in bed.) It is easy to hypothesize that as an adult Jim is operating from the premise that there is no hope, ever, of a warm, emotional connection with another person, except through rage. The rage he activates thus serves two functions: (1) to establish a way of relating to Alice, and (2) to defend against the feelings engendered by his desperate sense of nonexistence.

Alice, too, sustained narcissistic injury in her early developmental milieu. Alice appears to have provided affect-regulating functions for her mother during her father's frequent absences from the home. Additionally, her father's perfectionistic expectations of Alice hindered the development of her own self attributes. The use of the child by the parents in these ways is instrumental to the derailing of optimal self-development and encouraging narcissistic defenses of rage and grandiosity.

UNDERSTANDING AGGRESSION

Kohut (1984) reversed decades of traditional thinking on aggression by considering it to be a disintegration product related to faulty environmental attunement. Rather than perceiving aggression to be an inevitable discharge of instinctual viciousness, Kohut saw it as a reaction to disappointment and narcissistic injury, thereby opening the line of psychoanalytic inquiry into the nature of that injurious process.

Kohut also noted that the most dangerous form of aggression is that which is attached to activities involving the grandiose self and the omnipotent object. The rage arising from narcissistic injury is fueled by an urge to reverse the injury, regardless of cost. For some, the regulation of self-esteem is tied so thoroughly to having control over the archaic selfobject environment that the unavailability of the idealizable selfobject for merger or approval and mirroring triggers intense narcissistic rage.

Narcissistic rage always occurs in the context of a relational configuration. The nature of the specific trigger to this affect, be it selfobject unavailability or such injuries to self-esteem as derision, denigration, or observable defeat, points to its reactive nature. The same qualities of rage that render it so destructive to a relationship contain vital information regarding both its etiology and alternative pathways of relating. In the therapy setting rage serves a critical function by providing a portal to the underlying pain and its amelioration.

Rage and aggression in conjoint therapy can best be understood and treated as reactivated affect states emerging from situations co-created by the participants in the relationship. The assimilation of even a seemingly minor, if thoughtless, transgression by one partner into the preformed relational theme carried unconsciously by the other evokes rage of an intensity that seems out of proportion to the actual event. The concept of organizing principles (Atwood & Stolorow, 1984) illuminates this unconscious shaping of one's subjective world into familiar patterns and themes of experience.

Of importance, too, is the intensity of the affect arising in conjoint therapy. Trop (1996, personal communication) states that, "patients retreat to earlier affective experiences of childhood as a way of organizing experience in the here and now. The intense affect state is therefore a replay." In a particular situation, the sense of self is organized around a predominant affect, for example, rage. This configuration is the self state most familiar to the individual.

Researchers of infant behavior have increasingly demonstrated the relationship between affectivity and the child-caregiver system of mutual regulation (Demos, 1988; Sander, 1985). Affects and their relationship to the organization of self experience can no longer be considered outside of the context of intersubjective transactions (Basch, 1984). Elaborating on Kohut's formulations concerning the role of the caregiver's ability to provide appropriate selfobject functioning to the developing infant, Soccarides and Stolorow (1984) direct our attention to specific ways in which affect integration is impacted, as well as the consequences on the organization and consolidation of self experience.

One important process facilitated by appropriate selfobject functioning is that of affect synthesis. The child's ability to comprehend various intense, contradictory affects as emanating from a unitary internal source is dependent on the optimal responsiveness (Bacal, 1985) of caregivers to those affect states. When parents are capable of tolerating and understanding only particular affects to the exclusion of others that may engender anxiety in themselves, the child's affect synthesizing capacity is compromised. Rather than becoming integrated into a complete sense of self experience, the unacceptable affects, together with the experiences associated with them, are segregated from other affective experience.

A related issue is the development of the capacity to employ the signal function of affect. A caregiver's ability to tolerate and contain intense, shifting affect states enables the child to track and respond to these shifts in a coherent, congruent manner. Inappropriate responsiveness to intense affect results in terrifying experiences of psychic disorganization and fragmentation. When traumatic states are sequestered, they are unavailable for use as signals of a changing self state. Instead, these affects portend fragmentation.

Repetitive experiences of selfobject failure, therefore, preclude the development of a cohesive self experience by preventing affect identification, tolerance, and integration. The net result is an individual whose self experience is exceedingly vulnerable to disorganization and fragmentation. Corresponding to the infant's dependence on the parental selfobject function for self cohesion, the adult, too, develops selfobject ties in the hope of acquiring necessary self-enhancing experiences. Rupture in a needed selfobject tie evokes anxiety, which heralds a potentially terrifying disorganization in the self state. In the need to order and organize current experience, an encapsulated affect state or self experience organized around intense, disavowed affect may be reactivated (Atwood & Stolorow, 1984). When this happens, disintegration anxiety prompted by the breakdown in selfobject relatedness (or the collision of organizing principles) may be ameliorated. Ultimately, through this process self cohesion is maintained. Activation of an intense affect state like rage can also function to protect the self against anticipated retraumatization by either preventing the emergence of unbearably painful feelings of worthlessness, despair, and hopelessness, or by reorganizing the sense of self around an archaic experience of omnipotence.

Couples enter therapy replete with interacting subjectivities, some of which typically precipitate narcissistic injury and rage in one or both partners. Many couples act out aggressive affects in violent physical and sexual behaviors. A major therapeutic task lies in containing the intensity of the acting-out behavior so that the couple might develop new ways of relating. It is our capacity as therapists for vicarious introspection that permits us to comprehend the meaning of the archaic selfobject needs that lie, frustrated, beneath the rage. In the tradition of the intersubjective context, we, too, bring our own organizing principles into the arena, which influence and are influenced by those of the couple. The inevitability of misattunements experienced by the couple, as well as the superimposition of our subjective realities on those of the partners, requires a reflective self-awareness on our part. This enables us to decenter from our organizing principles and understand the subjective meaning of these experiences to the couple.

BILL AND MARY

Bill and Mary were referred for conjoint therapy when their original therapist realized the extent of her reaction to the rage engendered in the therapy sessions. She was particularly shaken by Bill's violent acting-out and had images of Nazi torturers, stemming from events in her own past. She took seriously his threat that, if a separation resulted from the therapy, he would kill her dogs.

An entrepreneur in his mid-forties, Bill was rich, successful in his father's business, and struggling in his second marriage. His father was a cruel, harsh alcoholic, prone to violent outbursts, frequently beating Bill and actually killing one of Bill's dogs in a fit of rage. Although Bill was Dad's "Golden Boy," he received the brunt of his father's abuse. Bill's mother was passive, quiet, and uninvolved. She kept largely to her room, where she, too, drank heavily; she blamed Bill for provoking his father.

In his personal life, Bill was always drawn to sweet, passive women who eventually frustrated and disappointed him. Mary described her home life as quiet, calm, and peaceful. Both of her parents were warm, loving people who were happy with the simple life they shared, though her father felt he had never achieved the success or recognition for which he yearned. Mary shared cozy memories of a "Father Knows Best" family life, with Mom and the two girls deferring to Dad's wishes.

Mary's adolescence, however, paints a picture of low self-esteem. Mary's sexual behavior with boyfriends was motivated by a strong desire to placate and please. "I felt like my mother. It was my role, my purpose, to take care of them, to sacrifice myself, my needs, to make them feel better." Like her mother, Mary put her own agenda last and disavowed her separate center of initiative. As an adult, Mary found herself attracted to powerful, narcissistic, successful men who were demanding, critical, and emotionally or physically abusive.

Sessions with Bill and Mary were as horrifying as the first therapist had indicated. From the first meeting, Bill was loud, angry, and full of rage. His initial contributions to the session were threats to punch Mary's face, smash things in the office, kick the therapist, and blow up the office building. Not surprisingly, my (R.A.) countertransference was readily engaged.

My immediate feelings were of being frightened and intimidated. I was reminded through flashes of imagery of my own tyrannical father. I felt like the Dickens character Tiny Tim, overpowered by a force of enormous magnitude. I became aware of being in the presence of someone desperate to maintain his equilibrium by whatever means available.

My first instinct was an urge to stand up to him, defeat him—the child me magically facing down my father and saving my mother. This was followed by a feeling of nausea and a sick feeling inside my body that I recognized as the terror of a child faced by a suddenly monstrous parent.

What should I do with all of this information? Contain it? Or put it back in the room? These were the questions I was asking as I permitted myself to experience the kaleidoscope of sensations swirling inside. Some of the feelings, clearly, were reactivations of my own early experiences with parental violence. Surely Bill, too, had experienced some loss of self cohesion in similar encounters with his father. Was this, perhaps, a self state he was warding off by way of intimidating posturing?

I also wanted to attend to my own emotional responses. In this way I could begin to identify disowned affect and bring it to awareness in the interpersonal field.

I began to share a small portion of my subjective inner experience with Bill and Mary. "Sitting here, I'm finding myself aware of the presence of fear, anger, and frustration in the room. I wonder if you are also aware of the feelings of helplessness I can sense?" As both replied affirmatively, I continued, "I find myself deeply drawn to helping each of you heal the conflict that creates the gap in intimacy, the gap that I believe is fueling some of the tension and turmoil. I sense that each of you is feeling very alone and misunderstood. At the same time I find myself thinking of how it feels to be a small and helpless child at a hostile family dinner table. Do either of you experience something like that?"

Bill nodded yes. I was aware of feeling both helpless and fearful of responding to him, as his explosive behavior was so reminiscent of my father's behavior. In addition to restimulating powerful countertransference feelings, I hypothesized that the feelings contained information about Bill's internal experience. I asked him, "I'm wondering if you felt powerless and afraid to respond when your father was attacking you or your broth-ers? And, at the same time, very angry, with a strong urge to show him how terrible his behavior was?" Simultaneously with bringing these presumably disavowed affects into the field, I was also communicating to Bill that it was safe to have so much intense affect, that it was being contained.

As Bill's rage subsided somewhat and he regained some connection with his feelings of helplessness and fear, other sensations became clearer to me. "I am also imagining what Mary must experience when you feel so rageful and yet so helpless to really tell her about the hurts and fears inside of you. Mary, I imagine you want to recede, to hide and escape from Bill when he acts like this."

MARY: Yes, I can't stand it. I'm so afraid, and frustrated and angry.
THERAPIST: And under that anger?
MARY: (*sobbing*) I hurt so much and I'm so scared.
BILL: I'm glad you said all of that. Usually you just disappear and I feel so isolated and alone with all this badness inside of me.
THERAPIST: You mean when people are silent or leave you, you feel even worse about yourself and more hopeless, which leads to more rage about not being seen or heard?
BILL: That's why I want to scream and lash out at her.

At this point it becomes clear that beneath Bill's rage the primary affects are anxiety and despair about separation. One of Bill's organizing principles is emerging, specifically that when people close to him withdraw from the intensity of his emotion or are silent Bill assimilates it into his subjective experience of being ignored or abandoned by critically needed others. This collides with Mary's organizing principle, which discerns rage and intimida-tion as dangerous, something to avoid, rather than a plea for engagement. In fact, Bill's intense affect state is protecting a fragile sense of self from disintegration in the face of the frozen wasteland of his childhood.

THERAPIST: Bill, it sounds like what you really need from Mary when you're rageful is for her to somehow see how alone you are feeling.
BILL: Yes. I'm lost in it.

Aware of the terror that I experienced in response to Bill's rage, I knew that I wanted to help him, but felt frozen myself, much as Mary might feel.

THERAPIST: I'm wondering, Mary, if you find yourself frozen and unable to move toward Bill at times?
MARY: I'm terrified that he might hurt me.

THERAPIST: Bill, do you imagine there might be any way to help Mary come closer to understanding how hurt and alone you're feeling?

BILL: What do I do?

THERAPIST: That's really something to be curious about. I wonder what your unconscious will discover that will help you to respond directly with your feelings of helplessness and fear, rather than the intensity of the rage. When you were small and in the presence of your father's rage, there probably was not a safe place for you to be with your feelings. Is that right?

Bill suddenly began to rage at both of us, screaming at Mary that she was a lifeless, sexless, inept bitch whore, and raining more obscenities down on me.

My first impulse was to yell back at him, as he embodied my own raging father. Taking a breath, I reflected that Bill was expressing his own internalized father-son relationship, showing us what it is like to be consumed by that much rage. It was overwhelming.

THERAPIST: Your father's rage, it consumed you and now it's consuming us, overwhelming all of us. There really was no refuge from it, was there?

BILL: My mother let him kick the shit out of me and humiliate me and she didn't do anything! Nothing! Just left, and went to her room, drunken bitch!

THERAPIST: I wonder if that's what it feels like when Mary shuts down, leaving you to deal with all that terrifying rage by yourself?

I had the experience of Bill being somewhat distanced from me and from Mary.

THERAPIST: Bill, can you *see* Mary at this moment?

(*Mary is crying and appearing to grow smaller, shrinking into herself.*)

BILL: Yes.

THERAPIST: What does her body look like she is experiencing?

BILL: She looks scared and frightened.

THERAPIST: What does she look like she is doing?

BILL: Withdrawing. That's what gets me so angry. She starts to cry and leaves me.

THERAPIST: Then you get so mad because you feel so small and alone. Mary, when Bill gets rageful, could you consider telling him that you are scared, frightened, and feel the need to withdraw to protect yourself?

That you don't want to leave him but you have to protect yourself against his upset feelings that are frightening you?

MARY: Yes, but I don't know what to do when he gets so loud.

THERAPIST: Okay. Bill, I imagine that when you get loud you're actually feeling very little, alone, and scared of yourself inside. And what you feel most frightened of is that Mary will abandon you. Is that correct — that you are afraid of that terrible feeling of how helpless you feel that she will leave you?

BILL: Yes. She just doesn't see how little I feel inside.

THERAPIST: Like a scared little boy.

BILL: Yes. (*starts to sob*)

THERAPIST: Yes. And what I felt in my body when you first started yelling and screaming and threatening us was the fear, terror, and helplessness of a child who can't do anything to protect himself against someone big.

MARY: (*also crying*) That's what I feel all the time. Afraid to stay and afraid to leave him. I'm scared that he will hurt himself or hurt me.

THERAPIST: Bill, have you ever hurt yourself or anyone else in this state of rage?

BILL: When I was younger, I beat up my friends and once in a while, when they provoked me, I slapped a few girlfriends in the face to get them to stop making me feel so bad.

THERAPIST: Have you ever hit Mary?

BILL: No. Only a few times, I felt the urge to push her against the wall to get her attention.

THERAPIST: Bill, do you think you can control yourself, when you're enraged, to keep from hitting her?

BILL: I think so, but I don't really know. The rage gets so intense and powerful. I once beat our dog so badly it almost died. I broke one of the dog's legs.

THERAPIST: I can see, Bill, that what you are needing from Mary is some reassurance that she knows you're in there, hurting, and that she's not going to leave you. And you, Mary, need to feel that you aren't in any physical danger. Bill, if you were to receive some reassurance from Mary she is still there for you, do you think you could find another way to release all that energy and cool down enough to reconnect on the level of your pain rather than the rage?

BILL: Well, I do have a set of punching bags in the garage that I used to work out with. I guess I could go in there if I knew she would still be there.

THERAPIST: Mary, when Bill has calmed down, I want you to do some mirroring work with him. Look at him and tell him you are here and that you won't abandon him if he takes responsibility for controlling his rage.

Tell him you can see how scared he is of being left alone and that you can feel his pain and sadness. And tell him how much hurt there is inside of you and how you need comforting, too.

MARY: I feel better knowing that he needs to take care of his rage and that it's not my job.

THERAPIST: That's right. Bill's a big fellow and he's the kind of guy that can learn to handle a big job like cooling out all that rage so he can eventually start to show you his pain. You can show him that you are as afraid as he is of being abandoned. It's a big job for Bill to start to learn to feel — contain and understand his emotions and feelings — because nobody ever helped him with that when he was little. So it's a real challenge. And then he can end up with what he wants, which is to feel closer to you. Isn't that what you are really wishing for, Bill?

BILL: Yes. I always feel so badly after I get mad and we are so far apart. I only want to be closer to you.

THERAPIST: Mary, how do you feel hearing that Bill has a new job and it's one you can let him handle on his own?

MARY: Great. I've felt my whole life that I have to take care of men and what they feel.

THERAPIST: Just like your mother felt.

MARY: Yes. What a relief to let him handle it, and then, I'm available to help comfort and support you, Bill.

THERAPIST: You, Mary, also have to know that if you ever feel unsafe you can leave the room, go outside, wait at a friend's house. Call Bill and tell him that you're still around, you haven't abandoned him, but are making yourself feel safe and getting some comfort while he cools down.

As we continued working together in this style, the couple was able to develop the means for moving into a more fluid state of communication and to express their painful experience. In the process, their trust of each other deepened and they evolved the capacity to connect with each other empathically, thereby enhancing their intimacy.

After six months of intensive conjoint therapy the couple stabilized and transformed their destructive patterns of behavior into more functional, healthy, and loving interactions with each other. Bill continued to see me for individual therapy at that point and subsequently quit working in his father's firm to pursue his own interests in the finance business. That and other lifestyle changes enabled the couple to develop a more intimate, connected life together, and they have since had three children. For some time, I would see Bill occasionally when he would experience some recurrence of the rage. Rather than acting it out with his wife and children, he recognized his need for support and availed himself of help. Bill and Mary continue to be able to discuss their differences with each other on a regular basis and are enjoying their life together.

DISCUSSION

Both cases illustrate a shift in stance that makes it possible for us to search our own selves for affective analogs to our clients' experience and begin to co-create an atmosphere of safety and understanding. A focus on rage as a byproduct of misattunement to healthy developmental longings allows the therapist to attune to the disavowed, unarticulated affective longing unfolding within the dyad.

For both couples, the rage served a variety of functions in the service of maintaining a very fragile sense of self. Bill's rage protected him from the underlying terror resulting from the perceived threat of separation. Alice and Jim both experienced extreme panic when the bond between them seemed endangered, and both reacted with the kind of violence that demanded a response from the other, thereby maintaining this precarious connection. It is also clear that feeling vulnerable was experienced as extremely dangerous by both Bill and Jim, and that the rage served to protect each man from intolerable feelings.

Viewing rage as serving a self-sustaining function allows the therapist to decenter from organizing principles relating to rage and become curious about the meaning of the individual's underlying, frustrated selfobject needs. The compassion thus generated makes it much more likely that the therapist's responses will be experienced as therapeutic by the client.

REFERENCES

Atwood, G. E., & Stolorow, R. D. (1984). *Structures of subjectivity: Explorations in psychoanalytic phenomenology.* Hillsdale, NJ: Analytic Press.

Bacal, H. A. (1985). Optimal responsiveness and the therapeutic process. In A. Goldberg (Ed.), *Progress in self psychology* (Vol. 1). Hillsdale, NJ: Analytic Press.

Basch, M. (1984). Selfobjects and selfobject transference. In P. Stepansky & A. Goldberg (Eds.), *Kohut's legacy.* Hillsdale, NJ: Analytic Press.

Demos, E. V. (1988). Affect and the development of the self. In A. Goldberg (Ed.), *Frontiers in self psychology: Progress in self psychology* (Vol. 4). Hillsdale, NJ: Analytic Press.

Kohut, H. (1984). *How does analysis cure?* Chicago: University of Chicago Press.

Sander, L. (1985). Toward a logic of organization in psychobiological development. In H. Klar & L. Siever (Eds.), *Biologic response styles.* Washington, DC: American Psychiatric Association.

Soccarides, D. D., & Stolorow, R. D. (1984). Affects and selfobjects. *The Annual of Psychoanalysis, 12/13*, 105–119. New York: International Universities Press.

Trop, J. (1994). Self psychology and intersubjectivity theory. In R. D. Stolorow (Ed.), *The intersubjective perspective.* Hillsdale, NJ: Jason Aronson.

17

Therapeutic Depletion and Burnout

MARION F. SOLOMON

ALL HELPING PROFESSIONALS, no matter what their level of proficiency and experience, eventually confront the gnarly issue of therapeutic depletion. How we handle this difficult situation either strengthens us as therapists or moves us perilously close to professional burnout. My own confrontation with burnout remains vivid in my mind. I had been working with Louis and Jean, a volatile, turbulent borderline couple who were eliciting powerful feelings of anger, fear, dread, and confusion in me, to an extent I had never experienced with prior clients. I felt like a terrified passenger on a sinking ship: powerless, exhausted, and very alone. It was not until much later that I realized, upon reflection, how seriously my emotional state had been altered by my dealings with Louis and Jean; although I had been manifesting many of the symptoms of exhaustion and depletion, at the time I did not connect them to burnout. As I came to better understand the surreptitious nature of burnout, I sought ways to ensure that such a dilemma would not occur again.

Louis was a successful TV producer who was heavily addicted to cocaine and amphetamines. His wife, Jean, was a popular TV actress who had become disillusioned with Louis after he immersed himself in the drug world and became increasingly paranoid and distant as a result of the substances' pernicious effects. The couple approached me for help when they realized their marriage was on the verge of collapse. Louis was battling a number of hypochondriacal illnesses that plunged him further into drug-saturated despair, and he began using cocaine to ward off the pain of his various ailments; meanwhile, Jean was expressing violent rage toward Louis because she felt abandoned and deceived by him.

At first I welcomed the challenge of working with this intensely passionate, fascinating, beleaguered couple. In my office, Louis and Jean connected quickly to our work together and expressed appreciation for the help. But soon they became even more hostile toward one another, despite my efforts to help them. Louis expressed paranoid fears that Jean was sedating him so that she could gain control of his financial holdings. Jean believed that Louis didn't want her to succeed on her own and was therefore "gas-lighting" her — intentionally making her crazy so that she could not secure further work away from him. When I attempted to engage Louis and Jean in rational discussion around the problem of Louis's drug addiction, chaos ensued. The two would launch into shouting matches, blaming each other, professing how much they loved and had done for the other, then threatening legal action or divorce and predicting devastating property settlements.

Because I was concerned about the fragility of both personalities and the tenuousness of their marriage, I made myself available whenever one or the other called for emergency telephone consults. Almost immediately, Louis and Jean each began calling me at least once daily; soon their constant calls were nearly unmanageable. Louis would launch into diatribes about Jean, alternately crying about his bottomless love for her and cursing her existence; Jean would chatter endlessly about the disappointments in her adult life. When I would attempt to end the telephone conversations with Jean, she would tersely say, "Okay, we're done," and slam down the phone. As she had experienced so often in her life, she expressed feeling cut off and abandoned when I terminated our sessions. Louis had to speak to me *immediately* whenever he called. If I was not available when he called, he would not be available when I returned the calls.

I felt frustrated and mildly angry at my inability to help this tortured couple. My feelings increased when both Louis and Jean began expressing discontent because I had "not seemed to make any headway" in resolving their problems. Soon, Louis and Jean were screaming in unison — at me. Their threats, once pointedly directed at one another, were subtly being lobbed at me. Without realizing it, I had placed myself in the vortex of an unresolvable situation. I had permitted a borderline couple to place out-of-control emotional issues in my care and then had tacitly accepted their redirected feelings, believing that it was *up to me* to solve their woes.

As I struggled to determine a better way to handle Louis and Jean — and my own stressed-out feelings — I watched their marriage slide toward inevitable disaster. Louis locked Jean out of their home and shared office;

Jean retained legal counsel to initiate a series of actions against Louis, his business associates, his doctors, and a variety of professionals who had attempted to help them with their financial, medical, and psychological problems. Their split was messy and very public. Although Louis precipitated it, Jean talked to everyone — friends, colleagues, gossip columnists — and there were threats and restraining orders that made reconciliation unlikely. Louis and Jean were destroying each other, yet couldn't seem to leave each other alone. Throughout the fighting, each partner would call, fax, or e-mail the other in an attempt to reopen the relationship.

When Louis called me to ask whether I would continue as their couples therapist in order to help them save their marriage, I realized I was in a very tenuous position. I could not simply abandon this couple. Besides, Jean was now threatening lawsuits against virtually anyone who crossed their paths, and I could not walk away without inviting similar attacks. Yet, I could not continue with them as I had in the past, because my approach had not been helping them and was causing me to feel depleted and inadequate. At this delicate juncture, I carefully weighed my options. For several months, my tensions had continued to increase. Whenever my phone rang, I would wince and my heart would beat rapidly: Was it one of them calling me yet again? What did they want now? And if it was Louis or Jean, would I be able to handle the call professionally, despite my growing resentment toward both of them, and despite the vehement emotions that would be directed at me?

After much rumination, I referred Louis and Jean to individual therapists, but agreed to remain available to them as a couples counselor. I did not abandon them, despite my inclination to do so. But I was certain that, even if they decided to attend conjoint sessions again, the therapy would likely end without my having helped the relationship. I continued to receive calls from both Louis and Jean for the next six months. They were always asking me to explain some "bizarre" act of the other. Each wanted me to agree with his or her side. I envisioned being subpoenaed in a divorce action and wondered what I would do. When the calls abruptly terminated, I was relieved, but many questions remained. Why did I take on a couple in which one partner was actively addicted without insisting on a drug treatment plan to precede conjoint therapy? Why did I allow the conjoint therapy to turn into "on-demand feeding" whenever one or the other called? Was I influenced by their fame to allow the therapeutic frame to disintegrate? Could I have done anything to help this couple, or was it futile from the beginning? Did the treatment make the situation *worse*? What would I say if subpoenaed to court? Did *I* need a lawyer?

To exact closure for this difficult learning experience, and to better understand my own reactions, I decided to research the subjects of countertransference, burnout, and therapeutic failure more fully and then write about my findings. Reviewing the subject, I realized that burnout is much more common than what is reflected in the literature. Acknowledging and admitting burnout seems to arouse shame in many therapists.

DEFINITIONS OF BURNOUT, PAST AND PRESENT

Burnout originally referred to the chronic depletion, apathy, and hopelessness experienced by drug abusers. Freudenberger first reapplied the term to describe the occupation-related exhaustion felt by many helping professionals (Freudenberger & Robbins, 1979). He studied volunteer workers in community social service agencies and noted that workers who displayed enthusiasm and commitment at the beginning of their careers were now exhibiting symptoms of exhaustion, ennui, and psychosomatic ailments. In fact, those who had seemed to be the most deeply committed and idealistic at the inception of their work appeared to be most consumed by disillusionment and disappointment when their professional efforts did not pay off.

Working with "hard-to-treat" individuals and couples can be incredibly challenging and rewarding. Those helping professionals who do so must constantly monitor themselves to be sure they are not losing their effectiveness, becoming cynical and pessimistic, losing their empathic attunement, growing angry with and resentful of their clients, or attempting to deny any mounting difficulties in their work. Therapists who regularly deal with borderline and narcissistic couples are particularly prone to burnout symptoms of hopelessness, anger, and exhaustion. Such feelings, in their acute forms, arise in response to stressful encounters with difficult patients. But these emotions may turn chronic and disabling if therapists attempt to repress them or refuse to seek help once their work begins to feel overwhelming.

Joseph (1978) warns of the pitfalls of grandiose expectations. When the anticipated results of hard work fail to bring about the promised success and reward, he observes that, " . . . with this disillusionment can come a debasement of the whole process with attempts to find shortcuts and modifications that will promise the ultimate rewards sought. Finally there may come a complete abandonment of the entire field" (p. 382). Giovacchini (1972) describes the existential annihilation of the therapist that comes about as the result of the narcissistic needs and demands of the patient, in which case the person of the therapist is neither perceived nor responded to. This same quasi-annihilation comes about by the very nature of the role we play in the treatment process, whatever the patient's pathology. When there is a substantial narcissistic core, this experience may become even more acute.

Burnout, which is in large part a depressive reaction, comes about as a consequence of a wide range of losses: the loss of ideals, purpose, self-definition, self-esteem, and highly valued self-other interactions in which one feels alive or validated. In addition, burnout may surface as a consequence of the chronic narcissistic wounding and annihilation of the self that are part and parcel of being a therapist.

Several reasons for susceptibility to burnout among those who select psychotherapy as a career have been suggested in the research (Freudenberger, 1990; Grosch & Olsen, 1994). Psychologists spend hours each day engaged in intense, emotionally charged dialogue, often with difficult and demanding clientele. Therapists may not have control over the course of therapy, in that patients can and do decide to terminate seemingly productive therapeutic relationships. Finally, therapists must sustain a difficult form of intimacy in that they interact closely with individuals who, because of the nature of the therapeutic relationship, are supposed to disconnect from the therapists once treatment has ended. Due to issues of confidentiality, unless there is internal gratification, therapists may receive little affirmation or appreciation for their work (Grotstein, Solomon, & Lang, 1985).

The prolonged, intense nature of some types of therapy is capable of emotionally and spiritually depleting even the most experienced of therapists. In particular, the continual psychic draining by people with intense needs and the wear-and-tear of the daily practice wherein much anger and hate are verbalized toward the therapist contribute to burnout (Freudenberger & Robbins, 1979).

The therapeutic milieu additionally influences susceptibility to burnout. Particularly predisposed to depletion are those therapists who:

- handle large caseloads of chronic, resistant, and seemingly untreatable patients who act out and direct anger at the therapist;
- dwell on patients' problems after sessions, bringing home residual feelings of frustration, anger, and bewilderment;
- have not been able to adjust to the nonreciprocal nature of their work;
- are individuals whose self-esteem and professional identity require that patients succeed in treatment;
- fail to acknowledge powerful countertransference feelings that are affecting treatment with one or more clients; and
- have not been trained to deal properly with their countertransference feelings;
- battle stressful, unresolvable personal issues (such as marital conflict, financial woes, or lack of time for hobbies and recreation).

SYMPTOMS OF BURNOUT

In 1990, Farber identified a number of burnout symptoms that typically befall overstressed helping professionals: exhaustion, emotional and physical depletion, inattention to patients, irritability, disillusionment, loss of belief in one's effectiveness, and displacement of feelings onto one's family and friends. These are phenomena that most of us have experienced at least occasionally, but burnout sufferers experience these symptoms as chronic assaults. Other researchers, after conducting a range of studies, added further symptoms to the burnout syndrome: loss of energy, idealism, motivation, purpose, and positive regard for patients; a lessening of concern about work; decreased job morale; increased absenteeism; and a decline in overall effectiveness (Freudenberger & Robbins, 1979; Maslach, 1976, 1982). These researchers further noted that burnout sufferers were particularly susceptible to fatigue, insomnia, frustration, depression, colds, headaches, gastrointestinal problems, ulcers, hypertension, and abuse of alcohol and drugs.

Table 17.1 presents a synthesis of the symptoms identified by Freudenberger, Grosch and Olsen, and Maslach.

TABLE 17.1
Symptoms of Burnout

Physical	Emotional/ Psychological	Cognitive	Behavioral
Insomnia	Irritability	Boredom and apathy	Withdrawal from family and co-workers
Headaches	Loss of enthusiasm	Indecision	
Indigestion			Boundary violations
Feelings of depletion	Depression	Making the same interpretations and suggestions with many different clients	
Feelings of exhaustion	Feelings of hopelessness		Abandonment of personal hobbies and interests
Gastrointestinal disturbances	Resentment and envy of other people	Lack of concentration and easy distractibility	Accidents or injuries
Increased sick leave	Frustration with life in general	Negative attitude toward work	Unexplained reduction in clientele
	Feelings of inadequacy	Increased thoughts about leaving the profession	Preoccupation/ obsession with particularly difficult clients
	Feelings of omnipotence and grandiosity		
	Mood swings		

All of us may experience one or several of these symptoms on occasion. But when the symptoms persist and accumulate, causing disconnection from patients and loss of faith in the psychotherapeutic process, help from peers and mentors should be sought. Admitting burnout may feel shameful at first. And this, unfortunately, may prevent troubled therapists from seeking the very aid they need. Depletion and burnout should be discussed as common risk factors for all therapists. In specific cases, burnout should be understood as a therapeutic reaction to *patients'* feelings of helplessness and despair. When therapists focus on understanding the countertransference burnout and discussing and utilizing it without fear of judgment, it provides replenishment and helps them get through periods of what are otherwise seen as resistance and therapeutic impasses.

Burnout is particularly insidious to helping professionals because it robs previously effective individuals of their ability to relate empathically to others. This not only jeopardizes therapists' practices and client relationships but endangers their personal lives as well. Therapists suffering from depletion and burnout may disengage from family and friends, become hypersensitive to criticism, and harbor beliefs that they are incapable of helping anyone, including themselves. Some may become rageful at those around them or demonstrate self-destructive behaviors; others may simply become listless and apathetic.

THE CONNECTION BETWEEN FAMILY ETIOLOGY, THERAPIST MOTIVATION, AND BURNOUT

A person's vocational choice typically reflects his or her developmental dynamics; it is driven by myriad unconscious forces that continue to influence adult life. Certain individuals, whom Alice Miller (1979) describes as "parentified," "not only become confidants, comforters, advisors, supporters to their own parents, but also take over the responsibility for their siblings. Eventually they develop a special sensitivity to the unconscious signals put out by others to advertise their needs. Such people may be in danger of growing up to become therapists. As children, they could not get their needs met and were required to adopt parental roles in order to receive attention and care from others" (Boszormenyi-Nagy & Krasner, 1986). The behaviors that such children develop, trading a caretaking role for the reciprocity of affection, serve them well as adults in this profession.

Psychotherapy is a relatively "safe" way to relate intimately with others, for the therapist's role is free of the typically requisite vulnerability and self-disclosure that is expected in other intimate settings. The role of therapist can serve a twofold benefit to "parentified individuals": it allows them to continue manifesting their caretaker persona and receive acknowledgment for these skills, and it enables them to form highly structured intimate relationships from a position of apparent power and control.

The parentified individual may enjoy great fulfillment as a helping professional. However, if the motivation to help others is tainted by unresolved unconscious conflicts, the therapist may become particularly susceptible to burnout when: values, beliefs, and personal needs clash with the reality of patients' decisions and actions; clients' needs and dilemmas become overwhelming and unresolvable; or external forces make utilization of therapeutic skills increasingly difficult and stressful. This is particularly true in our age of managed care, reduced budgets for agencies, patients' limited financial resources, and a decline in referrals to therapists in private practice. Studies have shown that the single most common cause of burnout is lack of therapeutic success (Farber & Heifett, 1982).

Recently I was asked to consult with a therapist whose disillusionment with the profession increased as her patients continued to disappoint her. Like many other helping professionals, Dr. F was an older child in a family where the parents tacitly required that their offspring demonstrate caretaking skills and emotional attunement in exchange for "love." Thus, at a young age, Dr. F was forced to trade empathy for acceptance. She became a "child-parent," in effect. When she took care of her parents and younger siblings, she was rewarded and praised, but when she demonstrated other natural affective states – such as anger or competitiveness – she was scolded and rejected. Dr. F's mother and younger brother were frequently ill, which further compounded Dr. F's sense of guilt and obligation. Seldom was she able to express her own needs or protest when family members placed exceptional demands upon her. Dr. F maintained deeply conflicted feelings about her younger brother, who had been crippled since birth and who was the focus of the family's attention. Rationalizing that her resentment toward her brother was "inappropriate," she fought to repress it. Eventually Dr. F developed a persona that deftly banished all negative feelings from consciousness and appeared all-nurturing and ever-giving. By remaining in this persona, Dr. F was able to receive the love and positive regard she desperately craved.

Despite her apparent success in her profession, Dr. F remained personally unfulfilled. Her "shadow parts," disowned aspects of her personality, continued to manifest – at first in unobtrusive, clandestine ways, but later in ways that thwarted her therapeutic efficacy. Although some patients continued to praise and idealize her, their accord was no longer satisfying: "It never felt like enough. I kept waiting for someone, or something else, to make me feel more fulfilled."

As Dr. F told me more about her practice, she described the patients with whom she most enjoyed working. Such information often provides important details about countertransference factors. Dr. F told me that she most enjoyed working with those patients she defined as "narcissistically vulnerable"—and she least liked working with those she saw as "borderline." The narcissists superficially satisfied Dr. F's needs for admiration and positive connection; they provided her with temporary, albeit ineffective, substitute family members. She avoided treating borderline patients— many of whom she described as angry, volatile individuals who "split" people into good and bad objects, including Dr. F, leaving her feeling "dumped upon."

These patients apparently resurrected all the ugly childhood issues that Dr. F thought she had neatly resolved. As her practice had grown, she was able, at least initially, to weed out difficult patients and focus on clients who fulfilled her sycophantic, vulnerable "need to be needed." She was happy to field her patients' calls at all hours and schedule emergency sessions at their slightest behest. But even this quasi-perfect scenario did not quash the burning emptiness Dr. F felt deep inside. Slowly, she was forced to admit she was lonely, disappointed, and disillusioned. "I began to realize how ungrateful they all were," Dr. F confessed. "I put so much effort into each of them—endless on-demand feeding—but they never really recognized my efforts. Day by day I became more drained, more bitter, more chewed up and used up. Some of my clients left therapy without even a thank-you. Then, of course, new people would appear in their place, with their set of insatiable demands. Today, when my phone rings, I can barely answer it. I want to run away. I want to quit the profession. But I can't because I have to pay the bills and keep my kids in school."

Initially rejecting supervision, peer consultation, and other options that would have allowed for professional dialogue, Dr. F single-mindedly pursued two unattainable goals: satisfying her bottomless need to be needed, and solving the woes of deeply disturbed, narcissistic individuals and couples through her "good mother" persona. Compulsively seeking to fulfill these futile fantasies only led Dr. F down a road of frustration, depletion, despair, and bitterness. Because the need to be an all-powerful rescuer conceals an underlying, cavernous need to be loved and admired, a sense of anxiety, impotence, and despair descends when rescue fantasies are thwarted. As Dr. F learned, the discrepancy between effort and reward, between constant giving and lack of quantifiable progress, frequently cannot be reconciled in exceedingly challenging cases. Learning to tolerate this cognitive dissonance is the challenge of our profession.

Unrealistic Expectations and Common Disappointments

The therapeutic relationship is an inequitable one, particularly at its inception. Patients typically experience the therapist as an unrealistically powerful and even perfect person, who possesses magical healing powers. The therapist/patient relationship often begins as an idealized parent-infant relationship and progresses in maturity until, near completion of treatment, the patient evolves into a whole, nonregressed adult, capable of perceiving the therapist more realistically. Unfortunately, however, the inequitable nature of the therapeutic relationship tends to foster feelings of aloneness, uncertainty, inner conflicts, countertransference, and, in some cases, impotence in particularly sensitive therapists. If not dealt with, these feelings can evolve into their compensating counterparts: arrogance, an imposed superhuman image, and extraordinary self-expectations (Freudenberger, 1990; Hedges, 1992). Abend (1986) describes how the demands of therapy place a strain on our ability to consistently uphold the standards set by our profession: " . . . our hard-earned ability to perform . . . is subject to pressure during every hour we spend with patients. On the face of it, it is inconceivable that any one of us can sustain an optimum level of functioning with anything remotely like an absolutely unvarying state. Why, then . . . do we appear so prepared to expect it of ourselves and believe it of our problems?" (p. 565) Here, Abend addresses one of the factors that contributes to burnout: the persistence of unrealistic and unrealizable ideals that continues to influence theory and aspirations. "The shame associated with a failure to live up to the implied ideal leads to a resistance to discuss these issues in private with colleagues or more publicly in books and journals," adds Horner (1993, p. 138).

More often than not, the depletion brought on by burnout tends to only intensify. Affected therapists then begin to lose confidence in their skills and training models. Horner (1993) notes that the occupational hazard of burnout is based on the climate of isolation and an identification with the idealized icons in the field. Some of these leaders in our field use charismatic behaviors with couples and families in demonstrations of their teaching excellence. Ordinary therapists cannot achieve the results they see the "master teachers" in the field achieving. They may begin to question the healing potential of the therapeutic relationship and, as a result, become less effective in treating patients.

Poised at the edge of the burnout precipice, these therapists are faced with a critical choice: they can acknowledge their dilemma and seek help, as Dr. F did, or they can burrow deeper, hoping "all will resolve itself." I was forced to face this choice when I was working with Louis and Jean. I was seeing too many other patients. I had little time for reflection. Their unending crises demanded more of my evening hours than I wanted to give. It was time to share my feelings with a peer consultation group to which I belonged. Sharing burnout feelings with peers is difficult because of an underlying sense of failure and the acknowledgment of inappropriate or less than stellar practice. It is helpful to remember that countertransference issues are universal and can propel any of us to do things that our better judgment would oppose. Discussion with peers and feedback help the mind to regroup and emotions to replenish.

Sadly, perhaps because of pride or diffidence, too many therapists avoid the resources that are most likely to help. They stop attending meetings of their professional organizations, no longer seek continuing education to learn new treatment possibilities, and do not discuss their work with anyone who can provide important feedback. Ultimately the work begins to feel empty and boring. They fall into unfocused and apathetic states during sessions, their thoughts wandering to family matters, income problems, errands and chores, poignant memories, future plans, and even ways to leave the profession—all as patients confide critical information—and the clock ticks far too slowly.

This is how Dr. A felt. A therapist with many years of experience, she described feeling as if she were "covered with a dark cloud." She no longer looked forward to meeting with clients: "While I'm in the middle of a session, I'll suddenly start fantasizing about weekend getaways and I'll miss some of what my clients say. And even after vacations, I've come back home wanting to pack up again and go somewhere else. I hate to admit it, but I've been seriously considering becoming a travel agent or purchasing a bakery shop in Aspen!"

When therapists have unmetabolized, unrecognized feelings and needs that come up repeatedly in their sessions, they may be unable to summon the energy and empathy needed to support their clients. An older therapist, Dr. B, exemplifies this dilemma. "Lately, I've been wanting to post a sign that says 'The doctor is out' and just walk away," he said. "No matter how much I give, they want more." Dr. B had been trained as an analyst, but had become interested in couples therapy because many of his referrals were people wanting to deal with marital crises. He sought advice about a difficult couple with whom he was working. When questioned about his difficulties, Dr. B blurted out, "They live in a beautiful home, have a Mercedes, a Range Rover, and beautiful four-year-old twins. They argue over whether the wife should return to her highly intense and involving career. The husband wants her to stay home for two more years; she wants to go back to work. And I want to yell at them, 'You think you have problems? Let me tell you about real problems—what it's like to be in *my* shoes.'" He then confided that he had a learning-disabled son needing special schooling, aging parents who need his help, power struggles at home, and financial woes. Dr. B went on to describe his wish to terminate with this couple but said that he didn't terminate because he could not afford to lose their fees.

Occupied by his countertransference feelings, Dr. B had been unable to uncover the couple's underlying destructive issues, revealed in their arguments, which had been jeopardizing their marriage—lack of mutual validation, excessive dependency, issues of power imbalance and envy—all quite evident in a session audiotape that Dr. B played for me. Because Dr. B was struggling with pressing personal issues that mirrored yet exceeded those of his troublesome couple, and because his burnout symptoms were diminishing his efficacy, he turned a blind eye and deaf ear to the couple's true dilemmas, which would have been instantly apparent to this capable therapist in less stressful times.

DISEMPOWERING RESPONSES TO THE THREAT OF BURNOUT

Freudenberger (1993) identified three coping strategies typically marshaled in response to early signs of therapeutic depletion, which, because of their ineffectiveness, tend to intensify depletion and lead therapists toward chronic burnout: (1) the urge, when frustrated, to intensify one's work at all costs in order to produce results one feels one *must* achieve; (2) the tendency, when frustrated, to simply renounce one's goals and succumb to exhaustion; and (3) the tendency, when frustrated, to "tune out"—to perform one's work perfunctorily, and to turn against therapy as a career choice.

The most likely employer of the first coping strategy of frenetic overinvolvement is the young, highly idealistic therapist who has recently completed a training program and has become overly invested in resolving certain types of cases. Such a therapist would thrive in the role of idealized savior for borderline patients (who are usually referred to the least experienced therapists) or as a nurturing parent figure for dependent adults who were neglected in childhood. The therapist's "payoff" would be "cures," which would bring acclaim from colleagues as well as heaps of loving appreciation from newly transformed patients. But the idealistic therapist's fantasies are highly unrealistic. Patients who function at borderline, narcissistic, or other levels of primitive mental functioning are exceedingly difficult to treat; many are completely resistant to the therapeutic process. Even in promising cases, such patients can be argumentative, rejecting, and ungrateful—responses that the self-idealized therapist is reluctant to address. Nonetheless, newer clinicians may force themselves to carry on as though all were well. This is because idealistic therapists frequently harbor the delusion that, if they just work harder, or learn a new technique, or set up the definitive consultation, or peruse the latest scholarly journal for information about their clients' ailments, they will be able to "cure" even the most intractable client. But these unrealistic goals merely heighten their susceptibility to burnout. Feelings of frustration, exhaustion, and bitterness eventually eclipse their earlier boundless enthusiasm and optimism.

The second ineffective therapeutic coping style tends to be employed by overworked, typically underpaid psychotherapy professionals who hold staff positions in rigidly structured, hierarchical organizations, such as agencies and institutions. Such environments tend to have complicated regulations and daunting restrictions that inhibit their therapists' effectiveness. Stark, demanding work settings, by their nature, tend to diminish the satisfaction that staff therapists might feel when treating difficult, predominantly impoverished patients. Such therapists, bound by rules, prohibitions, and political protocol, quickly experience an institutional form of burnout. Eventually, they stop trying to make a difference. They may become professional clock-watchers and paper-pushers. Therapist and patient suffer continually in such scenarios.

The final coping style described by Freudenberger seems to affect therapists who continue to work with agency clients or in private practice, but who have lost faith in themselves and their treatment modalities, becoming apathetic and cynical because their work no longer challenges them, but they do not know what else to do. These therapists create a treadmill-like existence for themselves, in which they can continue function with minimal effort in their chronic burnout state. They view the psychotherapy profession merely as an unpleasant means of earning money. They have chosen status and control over fulfillment and challenge.

CHRONIC AND ACUTE BURNOUT

Employing one of these three ineffective coping strategies for a protracted period typically leads to chronic, end-term burnout syndrome, which can only be ameliorated through extended intervention and lifestyle restructuring. But many helping professionals — far more than those who suffer from chronic burnout syndrome — suffer from what I classify as beginning state, "acute burnout." The stresses of one or more intense, unrectifiable cases suddenly propel these men and women to the brink of despair and exhaustion.

Some health-care professionals, when stricken with burnout, see a reduction in caseload as the answer and begin to refer their clients to other therapists. They are like panicked captains of sinking ships — jettisoning cargo overboard in the hopes that they can sufficiently lighten their disabled vessels to make it safely to shore. But banishing clients from the office will not assuage burnout for two reasons: (1) although the immediate *trigger* for the therapist's feelings of burnout has been eliminated, the underlying *cause* of the burnout remains, and (2) the therapist may face serious moral and ethical dilemmas (additional burnout provokers) for having terminated treatment without proper cause. Acute burnout sufferers' first task is to acknowledge that they need help; if they do not, their burnout symptoms are likely to become chronic.

Dr. C, a prominent and successful therapist, admitted in a peer consultation group that he was struggling with acute burnout. He described a particularly pugnacious couple, Geoffrey and Hilda, who used his office as a combat zone. Their screaming, arguing, cursing, and bitter rancor caused Dr. C to feel burned out and overwrought. Dr. C told me he desperately wanted to refer them to a colleague: "I cannot get a word in edgewise with them. Each time they leave, I feel worn out and enraged. I wonder why they keep coming, but they say it helps. I don't know what it is they think is helping, but they keep coming back."

Dr. C was not dependent upon revenue from this couple, since he had patients waiting for an available hour, and he felt he would benefit emotionally by exiling them from his office. But as a professional, he realized that doing so might prove ethically unsound: the couple felt his therapy was helping them and they truly wanted to continue in his care. Did Dr. C have an obligation to provide further treatment, even if working with them provoked anxious, out-of-control feelings in him? The more we explored this issue, the more obvious it became that Dr. C had become a container for the couple's discord. Mired in his own personal difficulties, Dr. C had not been aware of this; he had simply accepted their psychic baggage as his own because it so closely matched his personal woes. Each week, the couple left the intolerable parts of themselves and their marriage with him; each week, he felt increasingly irritated, fatigued, and drained. Dr. C decided to tape the sessions and review the tapes in weekly supervision to see where he was getting caught in the couple's unconscious acting-out. He learned to read his own countertransference feelings as signals of the pain, rage, and fear provoked within the couple. Doing this helped him maintain his role as observer, as well as recognize the transference and projections occurring. This option seemed to maximally serve all concerned.

PROGRESSION OF ACUTE BURNOUT

Too frequently, I have observed therapists try to hide their "burned-out" condition by prematurely terminating therapeutic relationships or immersing themselves in academic and professional havens where they can give speeches, write papers, offer consultations, and otherwise dodge the emotional ghosts that haunt their offices. But burnout, untreated and ignored, simply does not go away.

The following case history chronicles a progression of acute burnout symptoms, which led to more intractable, chronic difficulties.

Dr. D, an older therapist returning to her practice after raising three children, had high hopes for her reentry into the psychotherapy profession. One of her first new patients was Jason, 16, a teenager who was acting out aggressively and abusing drugs in order to gain the attention of his somewhat distant parents.

Dr. D threw herself into Jason's rehabilitation: "I wanted to be there for him, unlike his mother and father," she explained. She allowed Jason to summon her via beeper when he needed to talk late at night and agreed to see him for "emergency sessions" on weekends, when he felt tempted to act out or take drugs.

As Dr. D immersed herself deeper into Jason's case, her husband and children began to grow concerned. They questioned Dr. D about her involvement with Jason: "Don't you think you're going beyond your limits?" her husband repeatedly asked her. "Don't you think you should pull back from the boy so he won't get too dependent?" But Dr. D dismissed her husband's questions as the anxious probings of a layperson and, despite her husband's and children's pleas to spend more time with them, continued to focus her attention upon Jason, who was now calling Dr. D at all hours.

Some weeks into the therapy, Jason's parents requested family counseling with Dr. D; Jason agreed to attend. At first, Dr. D was thrilled at this request. She fantasized about reuniting the family, restoring peace, and resolving their deep-seated hostilities toward each other. But the family sessions proved anything but healing: Jason screamed and cursed at his parents; Jason's father threatened Jason and revoked his privileges; Jason's mother wept through most of the sessions and blamed all the family's problems on Jason's difficult birth.

Each week, Dr. D would study case histories, read up on current professional literature, and speak with colleagues about Jason's case. And each week, after the family session, Dr. D would return home even more disappointed and frustrated. Though she was reluctant to admit it, Dr. D realized unconsciously that, rather than helping this embattled family, her sessions appeared to be further alienating family members from one another. Jason was now barely speaking to his parents; he was abusing more drugs and routinely violating his parents' orders. Jason's father had stopped attending the sessions altogether, leaving word on Dr. D's answering machine that he felt the sessions were "not of any real value." Jason's mother was coming late to sessions, sitting silently across from Jason and despairing in weepy tones that all was growing worse and she was terrified that her husband intended to leave her. Worst of all, according to Dr. D, Jason had stopped calling her between sessions and sharing his secrets.

As the case slid further out of control, Dr. D began losing sleep, picking arguments with her husband and children, withdrawing from social activities, and enduring crying spells. She sometimes fantasized about leaving the profession again; maybe, she rationalized, returning to it had not been the right thing to do.

Finally, after a particularly grueling session in which Jason threatened to hit his mother, Dr. D called a colleague and asked him to take over Jason's case. She told her husband she was giving up therapy, that this episode proved she didn't "have what it takes." But Dr. D was wrong—she was suffering from burnout exacerbated by limited training and insufficient supervision for a reentering therapist. She took on more than she could cope with as a result. She had caved in from overwork, intense stress, and idealization of her client (and his potential for rehabilitation). In the end, when all her efforts were failing, she had become overwrought with despair. Dr. D's case is of particular interest because her symptoms were so intensely acute, given her very short time reengaged as a helping professional.

Idealistic therapists such as Dr. D operate from the unconscious belief that, if they could only become perfect caretakers, they could effect the healthy recovery of all of their patients. Dr. D became depressed and bitter when her struggle to rehabilitate her adolescent client—who, she later realized, felt somehow like a "shadow" of herself—failed despite her best efforts to exploit the role of long-suffering, all-tolerant "good mother." It was only after joining a peer consultation group that Dr. D. recognized her well-meaning intentions and idealistic expectations would not automatically translate into successful outcomes. Intellectually she always knew this, but emotionally she experienced it as a reflection of her inadequacy. Her sense of failure and depletion only made her work harder, persisting in a downward cycle that left no room for replenishment or vitality.

DISEMPOWERING REACTIONS TO THE REALITY OF BURNOUT

When therapists are burned out, they often develop secondary reactions to their disability that are destructive. They may abuse alcohol and drugs, overmedicating themselves to quell a host of vague physical symptoms.

Some burned-out therapists may attempt to "cut corners"—shirk or shrink certain professional obligations—in order to combat the fatigue, boredom, and restlessness they are experiencing. For example, one burned-out therapist cut back his sessions from 50 minutes to 45 minutes and felt great relief from the reduced workload; the extra time, he said, gave him the minutes needed to refresh himself. But several months later, he again felt depleted, so he further cut back his sessions to 40 minutes: "They get more of me in the 40 minutes," he boasted, "but sometimes they get angry and cancel therapy."

Still other therapists, who have given up on their modalities and training, begin practicing—intentionally or not—a sort of "grass-roots, do-your-own-thing" type of therapy in which they offer homespun advice, discuss dilemmas in their own lives, or, as Grosch and Olsen (1994) describe, cross professional boundaries in sundry other ways. Healthier patients often leave treatment when they intuit that these therapists' agendas clash with their own or are counterproductive. But needier, more deeply wounded patients may be so dependent upon the connection with their therapists that they accept the therapists' seemingly capricious behaviors and advice . . . usually to ill effect.

All therapists have seen patients who describe previous catastrophic therapeutic experiences that went on for months or even years. Knowing it happens with even highly esteemed therapists does not keep us from feeling we are immune to doing harm to our own patients. We protect our idealized professional image by labeling problems as patients' projections or resistance to treatment. We explain our failures in terms of patients' psychopathology. We have many defenses against facing our own resistances, projections, feelings of exhaustion, and envy that a patient has the resources to get the help he or she needs (Searles, 1979).

The burned-out, overstressed therapist may seek to heal his/her own psychic wounds through exploitative encounters with very needy, confused patients. In severe cases, therapists may completely repress their discomforting emotions, ignore their flagging effectiveness, and, with affectless stares and monotone voices, try to explain away flagrant signs of danger, such as dwindling clientele, mental lapses during sessions, crying jags, rage attacks, etc. Some may overstep professional boundaries, ignoring the potentially deleterious effects of overinvolvement with clients. In the particular case of the couples therapist, he/she may form bonds with one partner that could erode precarious couples' marital relations.

A percentage of burned-out therapists may enter into illicit relationships with their clients. In such cases, these therapists commit dangerous professional self-sabotage rather than asking for help or even acknowledging that they have a serious problem. I have worked with therapists who acted out destructive fantasies, with the unconscious wish that their desperate actions would attract the attention of someone who could help them. Unfortunately, the price paid by transgressing ethical boundaries is too dear; such therapists frequently face censure, litigation, loss of practice, and public disgrace.

ANTIDOTES TO BURNOUT

There are many ways to actively prevent burnout. Most importantly, helping professionals should conduct periodic assessments of their own skills, clientele contentment level, treatment efficacy, and professional and personal satisfaction. Therapists can further empower themselves by forming strong professional networks with trusted colleagues, keeping up-to-date with ideological and practical changes in the profession, and by regularly conducting caseload evaluations, during which they honestly answer the following questions:

- Which couples do I most enjoy working with? Why?
- Which couples do I least enjoy working with? Why?
- Which couples are most difficult to work with? Why?
- Which couples are easiest to work with? Why?
- Of the clients with whom I am working, which ones show the most positive growth? What might I be doing to facilitate this?
- Which clients are experiencing impasses? Am I doing something (or failing to do something) that may be hindering their progress?
- Am I secure in my model of couples treatment? If I have insecurities about my model, with whom might I consult, or what relevant periodicals can I study?
- Do I feel a sense of control over my work environment, client caseload, intake procedures, professional income, etc.? If not, what might I do to regain my sense of control in these areas?

After careful self-evaluation, should a therapist find that difficulties with particular patients or issues require assistance, there are ways to create a detailed plan for corrective action—for example, seeking ongoing consultation with a more established professional, attending relevant conferences, joining peer group discussions, and/or taking continuing education courses. Such strategies can augment professional knowledge, offer new treatment choices, and perhaps ameliorate feelings of isolation and frustration.

Workplace supervision is another potential remedy for burnout. It is ordinarily convenient and free in agency settings, though such a setting requires the supervised therapist to share countertransference vulnerabilities with a superior who is in a position to determine salary, promotional potential, and career future. If agency-based therapists want supervision but are unwilling to risk critical or adverse evaluations by their superiors, they may choose to hire a private supervisor who will keep their issues confidential while offering qualified advice and support. Such privately arranged supervision may be found in a number of ways: via referral, at professional workshops, at university classes, through contact with local authors of relevant scholarly articles, etc. The inquiring therapist would be wise to interview several supervisorial candidates privately before hiring one. The therapist should ask potential supervisors detailed questions about training, professional background, experience in the therapist's area of expertise, opinions about therapy, favored modalities of treatment, etc.

Group supervision is another helpful option for those therapists whose financial resources are limited and/or who seek the support of fellow therapists experiencing similar challenges. Usually, such groups meet for regular weekly sessions, where participants have an opportunity to exchange information, receive peer support, gain new insights, and receive guidance from a senior clinician who presides over the sessions. Though new information is undeniably invaluable, even more importantly, these sessions enable group members to overcome the isolation and aloneness that is strongly associated with burnout.

Should no such professional groups be offered locally, or should one or more therapists wish to organize a discussion group around a specific theme, a supervision group can be inaugurated by inviting like-minded peers and hiring a consultant who is willing to commit to weekly sessions for a set hourly fee for group supervision. Shared costs are then relatively low for the group's participants. For example, should eight therapists agree to split the consultant's hourly fee for an eight-week series of two-hour meetings, each might agree to pay the cost of one week's session. Most senior clinicians are willing to take on such a time-limited group; indeed, if the sessions prove satisfying to the consultant and helpful to the members, all parties involved may wish to renegotiate for continuing supervision. With enhanced communication, group supervision by telephone with someone across the country or across the globe is quite possible.

PERSONAL EMPOWERMENT AS AN ANTIDOTE TO BURNOUT

Burnout is most likely to be exacerbated when therapists neglect their personal and familial relationships while in the throes of difficult professional crises. Those helping professionals who have built rich lives outside of their practices are most strongly defended against the stresses and assaults of burnout. Should therapists feel isolated, overwhelmed by personal issues, or unable to cope with the combined pressures of work and home life, they should consider the following options:

- seek the guidance of one or more established therapy professionals,
- seek the support of family and friends,
- join a professional support group,
- set up strong boundaries regarding work hours, caseload volume, availability for client consultations, etc.,
- treat any addictions and unresolved psychological issues that may be impeding personal and professional well-being,

- take a relaxing vacation, if feasible,
- develop interests and hobbies outside of the therapy field,
- take classes, go to concerts, attend conferences to meet new people with interests in common.

CONCLUSION

Burnout can affect any therapist whose combined work and personal stresses exceed his or her coping ability. I have experienced it and know that it is a signal to stop, reexamine priorities, change personal and professional habits, and find avenues of self-replenishment. When symptoms of emotional and physical depletion, exhaustion, disillusionment, depression, and alienation lead to a loss of belief in one's professional abilities and a decline in overall effectiveness, it is time for change.

Burnout tends to be exacerbated, as it was for me, when the therapist is faced with particularly difficult, abusive clientele who demand long hours, limitless empathy, and miraculous overnight cures. But it may be the drop-by-drop decline in our reservoir of empathic energy and a growing feeling of depletion that lead to a therapeutic dry well.

Therapists who struggle with "savior complexes" or who feel an intense yearning to be needed are at particular risk for burnout. They tend to idealize their profession, become overinvolved with their clients, and over-estimate their ability to resolve exceedingly difficult cases. Any perceived failures, because they bear a personal and historical significance in these clinicians' lives, end up causing depression, despair, and hopelessness — symptoms of chronic burnout syndrome. If untreated, these symptoms may get worse, leading some therapists to contemplate ending their careers.

Seeking help from established professionals, joining support groups, and sharing one's feelings with family, close friends, and trusted co-workers are strong antidotes to burnout. Acknowledging burnout symptoms and reaching out for appropriate treatment improve one's prognosis for complete recovery and provide the replenishment needed for a more challenging and satisfying career.

REFERENCES

Abend, S. (1986). Countertransference, empathy, and the analytic ideal. *Psychoanalytic Quarterly, 55*, 563–575.

Boszormenyi-Nagy, I., & Krasner, B. R. (1986). *Between give and take.* New York: Brunner/Mazel.

Farber, B. (1990). Burnout in psychotherapists: Incidence, types, and trends. *Psychotherapy in Private Practice, 8*(1), 35–44.

Farber, B. & Heifett, L. (1982). The process and dimensions of burnout in psychotherapists. *Professional Psychology, 13*, 293–301.

Freudenberger, H. J. (1990). The hazards of psychotherapeutic practice. *Psychotherapy in Private Practice, 8*(1).

Freudenberger, H. J., & Robbins, A. (1979). The hazards of being a psychoanalyst. *The Psychoanalytic Review, 66*(2), 276–296.

Giovacchini, P. L. (1972). Technical difficulties in treating some characterological disorders: Countertransference problems. *International Journal of Psychoanalytic Psychotherapy, 1*, 112–128.

Greenberger, D., & Padesky, C. (1995). *Mind over mood.* New York: Guilford.

Grosch, W. N., & Olsen, D. C. (1994). *When helping starts to hurt: A new look at burnout among therapists.* New York: Norton.

Grotstein, J., Solomon, M., & Lang, J. (1985). *The borderline patient: Emerging concepts in diagnosis, etiology, psychodynamics, and treatment.* Hillsdale, NJ: Analytic Press.

Hedges, L. (1992). *Interpreting the countertransference.* Northvale, NJ: Jason Aronson.

Horner, A. (1993). Occupational hazards and characterological vulnerability: The problem of burnout. *The American Journal of Psychoanalysis, 53*(2), 137–142.

Joseph, E. (1978). The ego ideal of the psychoanalyst. *International Journal of Psychoanalysis, 59*, 377–385.

Maslach, C. (1976). Burned-out. *Human Behavior, 5*(9), 16–22.

Maslach, C. (1982). *Burnout: The cost of caring.* Englewood Cliffs, NJ: Prentice-Hall.

Searles, H. (1979). *Countertransference and related subjects — Selected papers.* New York: International Universities Press.

18

Countertransference as the Focus of Consultation

JUDITH P. SIEGEL

COUNTERTRANSFERENCE can be viewed as a therapist's foe or best ally. When not addressed, it can lead the therapist to harbor intense feelings that complicate and impede therapy; however, when properly attended to, it can enable the therapist to rapidly comprehend the inner worlds of the couples who stimulate it.

The therapist is often provoked to accept feelings and roles that pertain directly to the clients' internalized object relations as spouses engage in projective identifications with each other and also enact critical themes with the therapist. The therapist will inevitably respond to these dynamics in ways that include confusion, anxiety, and atypical clinical reactions to the couple. Because the therapist's defenses can obscure his or her awareness, the connection between countertransference reactions and subsequent clinical activity may not be easily deciphered. Often the themes presented in countertransference are either so tenuous or so provocative that the clinician passes over potentially rich material. For these reasons, case consultation in either an individual or group format is an indispensable way of developing and expanding awareness. By questioning and directing attention to subtle and more obvious countertransference reactions, the consultant is able to generate a deeper level of understanding.

Not all therapists are open to or interested in utilizing the information available in their countertransference reactions. The topic was neglected for years after it was first introduced, possibly because of the shame and anxiety involved in revealing vulnerable aspects of self to another (Racker, 1953). To admit feelings that seem unprofessional or countertherapeutic, such as anger toward or sexual attraction to a client, may create considerable distress or cause a therapist to doubt his/her suitability for the profession (Tauber, 1953). To admit these feelings to another requires considerable bravery, especially when the supervisor's or consultant's reaction cannot be predicted.

Therapists must come to terms with their own narcissistic vulnerability in admitting to therapeutic responses or activities that are less than ideal. Racker (1957) suggested that the analytic posture encourages a sense of superiority in the analyst that makes awareness of countertransference difficult. Expanding upon this, Brightman (1984) has pointed out how the therapist's wish to be helpful, powerful, and healing can complicate his/her ability to accept and take responsibility for feelings and actions that contradict this image. This is especially so for the novice therapist, whose limited experience and fragile sense of professional competency can create performance anxiety. The resulting defenses, such as avoidance and denial, make countertransference material especially difficult to access.

Another challenge to the utilization of countertransference is the therapist's capacity for self-awareness and growth. Reactions stimulated by clients stem from a variety of sources, including the therapist's beliefs and unresolved internalized self and object conflicts. Effective work with countertransference reactions necessitates the examination of all facets of meaning. The therapist who is fearful of encountering unknown aspects of self may erect strong barriers against this kind of exploration.

In order to work successfully with countertransference it is useful to consider countertransference universal and beneficial to therapy. The works of Kernberg (1965) and Giovacchini (1985) are particularly helpful in explaining the value of using countertransference as information about the client. Approaching countertransference as projective identification enables clinicians to accept their most repugnant reactions as information to help expand understanding and empathy. Usually the relief they feel from accepting the universality of their reactions stimulates further interest in learning how to make sense of countertransference-related thoughts, feelings, and activities. Therapists who are working with clients who have schizoid, borderline, or narcissistic personalities especially need support in working through what are usually complex and intense reactions. Knowing that the intensity of the countertransference is diagnostically revealing (Kernberg, 1995) ameliorates some of the anxiety that accompanies the process of exploration. Briggs (1979) has outlined specific kinds of countertransference reactions that occur frequently in therapy with borderline clients. Knowing that other therapists have experienced similar reactions to like clients helps the therapist face his/her own experiences in a more re-laxed and tolerant manner.

Countertransference acts as a tool to facilitate comprehension within the consultation room as well as within the therapy environment (Kahn, 1979). Searles (1955) noted that, just as the patient may enact what is repressed or forgotten, so, too, will the supervisee bring this material to be acted out with the consultant. The consultant will be stimulated to experience a reaction that mirrors or allows a repetition of the patient's internalized object relations (Siegel, 1995). The consultant, by paying attention to his/her own shifting internal experiences, can help the supervisee focus, digest, and process important material.

CASE PRESENTATION

The following session of a case consultation demonstrates how the process of unraveling the therapist's countertransference facilitates both awareness and empathy.

AP (THE THERAPIST): This is a case that seems to be going well, but for some reason I'm not totally confident. I've seen them for seven sessions over a three-month period. They were initially in a state of emotional divorce, barely talking to each other except about household issues and their children. They have a married son whose wife is pregnant and a twenty-eight-year-old daughter who is moderately retarded and living in a community residence.

Harvey is unemployed now and is having a hard time finding a new job. He held one of those middle-management banking positions that was eliminated in the company's downsizing. He's bright and tries to stay optimistic, but has gone through a series of unsuccessful interviews and a recent stretch of closed doors. In general he has a hard time expressing emotions. He tries to stay in control, but he explodes over trivial things and releases his tension that way. Lucy has a stable job, but is very much overworked and often comes home exhausted. It seems like she can't cope with his angry outbursts and his need to control things, so she just withdraws. If he doesn't approach her to try to reconcile, they can stay disconnected for months.

Let me give you a little family background. They've been married 33 years and have had marital problems most of that time. I think that they stayed in it mainly for their daughter. She lived at home until she was fifteen, and she required the care of both parents. Beyond that, they are pretty conservative. I don't think that divorce was an option because of the social stigma attached to it. I gather that Lucy started talking about it seriously a few months ago, and that was the reason they called me. Both of them have denied having affairs. They were in couples therapy once before a long time ago, but stayed only a few sessions. Neither thought the therapist understood them or was very helpful.

Harvey is 58 years old, and feels too young to retire. He is an only child and has very few memories about his childhood. He thinks everything was "normal" but says that his father worked long hours—I think he held two jobs—and that his mother overprotected him. His father died suddenly when Harvey was seventeen, and Harvey said his mother tried to lean on him a lot after that. Harvey got married at a relatively young age and I think part of that was to reinforce the boundaries. His mother died five years ago.

Lucy is the elder of two sisters from a more financially affluent family. She went to a well-respected private college, which is quite an accomplishment for a woman of her generation. Her family dynamics are pretty complicated. Apparently her father dominated the family and severely demeaned her mother. He had a vicious temper and would shout more than he would talk. Lucy was his favorite, the only one who could reason with him. There were times her mother got quite anxious and severely depressed. Lucy held the family together.

JS: What was the first session like?

AP: They were initially very intellectual and guarded. He was a little sarcastic both about Lucy and about the benefits of therapy, and was off-putting in a narcissistic kind of way. Lucy also seemed ambivalent, and I sensed an underlying depression. I wasn't sure if they were going to make a second appointment. There were some real complicating factors, especially her work schedule, but I felt there was a strong reluctance about getting involved in the therapy. I decided to see them separately, which I do not always do, but I thought necessary because of the ambivalence.

JS: Tell me more about the individual sessions.

AP: They were both more open to me. Lucy came first. She was able to speak quite clearly about her ambivalent feelings toward Harvey, but hadn't thought of herself as being depressed. She doesn't like to admit to weaknesses in herself, but was able to see how her negative outlook, her exhaustion, and her wish to be alone were all symptoms of depression. She was emphatic that even if she is depressed she is not willing to go on medication. Basically she thinks that she and Harvey are two very different people who don't always bring out the best in each other. She doesn't think that she has the right to make demands or request changes in him, but can't cope with the way he takes control and the way he explodes. Her experience is that all attempts to talk lead to conflict, and she can't stand being around his anger, so she withdraws.

JS: It sounds like chronic marital conflict, like they've been doing this for years.

AP: I really felt that she was almost at the point of pursuing a divorce — she said that she had given it a lot of thought lately and that marriage therapy was the last resort. I had the feeling that she wanted it to fail, or that she wanted to not be able to work with me so that she could justify the divorce, and that my getting connected to her or saying that the marriage could be improved was not at all what she wanted.

JS: I'm sensing a lot of pessimism. What was your session like with the husband?

AP: My session with Harvey went pretty well. He started out sarcastic again, but just needed to vent some of his frustrations. He has few people other than his son whom he can talk to, and he was feeling a lot of pressure. I think Harvey is more committed to wanting the marriage to work, but feels frustrated by Lucy's pattern of withdrawal, which he says has been going on since the marriage started. He really feels controlled by her and resents her, but doesn't want to lose the marriage. He is very limited in his ability to talk about feelings, but he was able to use the therapy in a positive way — to get advice on how to change. He gets very focused and intense, and I did see how he can be somewhat controlling.

JS: Toward you?

AP: When he wanted a list of things he could do differently, I felt cornered by him.

JS: How have the remaining couples session gone?

AP: Well, recently they went away for a long weekend and were able to reconcile a little. In one of our earlier sessions I focused on their anger and how they each handle it so differently. Lucy gets passive, but does things that make Harvey furious. Harvey's explosions remind Lucy of her father, and she gets totally paralyzed and disgusted. Harvey really seemed to listen to that, and he's made a significant effort to change. He's tried not to lose his temper or fight with her, and she's noticed his self-restraint. I think they are both being a little more civil toward each other, and that helps them get along better, but a lot of the underlying things haven't changed. For example, I don't think that Harvey has any insight into his own behavior, and why he handled anger the way he did before.

JS: Maybe that's why you aren't sure about their progress. If they don't understand why things worked the way they did, it's hard to believe they can just turn it around. I'm struck by a number of things you have said so far. Can we look at some of your reactions in more depth and see if we can learn more about this couple? I was particularly interested in your initial reaction to her. You seemed to have an awareness about her wish to end the marriage and her hope that the marital therapy would fail. Was this a feeling or something that was openly discussed?

AP: A feeling.

JS: If you were to exaggerate it so we could understand it better, what would it be like?

AP: I guess like forcing her back into a marriage where she was unhappy. Like I was taking away her only chance at freedom.

JS: It feels to me like a very intense experience. That must have put a lot of responsibility on you. Kind of like taking a bird and putting it back into a small, dark cage.

AP: Yes. I remember feeling like I was hurting her and taking away her last chance for happiness.

JS: That must have been a difficult feeling to tolerate.

AP: It was. I really think she wanted out of the marriage and was building up the courage to ask for a divorce. These people have been married a long time, and I don't know how much change is really possible. I didn't want to do anything hurtful to her or contribute to her staying in an unhealthy marriage.

JS: The feeling of Lucy as captive and the theme of responsibility strike me as being very important here. Maybe we can learn more about her by exploring them. How might that make sense in light of her past?

AP: Well, I think that she was excessively responsible throughout her childhood. Her mother was treated badly by her father and Lucy was held up as being much more reliable and competent. I think her mother's depressions were fairly substantial; Lucy said that her mother was hospitalized once for a "nervous breakdown."

JS: That probably explains why she is so uncomfortable with your assessment of depression and her position of refusing medication. Children of demeaned parents have a choice—to identify with the competent, controlling parent or be like the incompetent parent. Sounds like both options are difficult for her.

AP: Lucy still cannot respect her mother. She bristled when Harvey compared them. I can see Lucy as being a very competent, parentified child.

JS: Who never got her needs met. . . . I think your feeling of responsibility and dread is really a reflection of that. I'm also thinking about their handicapped daughter. These are parents who took care of a very needy child for a long time. Can you tell me more about that?

AP: It's a very sad story. She was born with brain damage and was delayed in all of her milestones. She has a seizure disorder and is hearing-impaired as well. They were told there was probably an undiscovered infection during the pregnancy. I think Lucy has been fighting depression for years. She breaks into tears so easily. Harvey is very different. He has handled it by trying to take charge getting information, taking her to the best doctors, and doing whatever can be done. But he hasn't been able to grieve about losing a normal daughter, and he got tense and agitated in the session when I started to explore that. Lucy was able to cry in the session, but stops in response to his tension. There's been a recent setback in Marsha's health, and I think that might be an important issue, but there's no way to talk about it together — at least the emotional piece of it.

JS: So they are on their own. She carries the emotions, but has to be alone with them, and he feels burdened and overwhelmed. I'm thinking that this, too, is related to the initial sense of her need to be free. This is a woman who has carried excessive responsibility and has never really been supported or responded to. Your sense of responsibility here is another clue to her internal state.

AP: That's helpful to think about.

JS: Harvey's inability to talk about feelings is an important dynamic in all of this.

AP: Yes. I think his energy and taking charge of things is an attempt to cope in the only way he knows.

JS: Any thoughts on why he's so closed down emotionally?

AP: I think that I know less about him than I do about any other client I have.

JS: You mean about his past or his present?

AP: Well, definitely his past, but even when we are talking about his present I get facts, never the feelings behind them, and it's all very one-dimensional.

JS: You used the word narcissistic when you first described him to me. Can we look at that together for a minute? When I think about narcissism I think about the need to preserve grandiosity and the splitting that underlies it.

AP: I was very aware of his need to be respected, and some of the discomfort he had about being a client instead of being in charge. He can be very domineering. But he's so out of touch with his real self and I think of his narcissism as having a lot to do with that.

JS: Okay. So that helps you understand and accept where he is coming from. You started out feeling cornered by him, but it looks like you handled things really well.

AP: Yes. I gave him a feeling of acceptance and safety, and things turned around. He started to like me — I guess I would call it a very positive alliance.

JS: Well, you seem accepting of his limitations in a very tolerant kind of way.

AP: You know, now that I think about it, I wonder if I'm colluding with his defenses. I really feel like I'm walking a fine line here. He is very limited in his capacity to tolerate feelings, and I don't want to overwhelm him. But I am suddenly thinking of how his mother used to overprotect him, and I'm wondering if that's the role I've unconsciously been playing with him.

JS: That seems like an important observation. It's worth thinking about. I was also thinking about the splitting piece as well.

AP: I'm not following.

JS: You seem a little sleepy. Am I going too far with this?

AP: No. I want to go on. I just don't understand what you mean.

JS: Well, you seem to have established a positive relationship with Harvey, which is exactly what you need to do. But you also know about Harvey's anger and sarcasm and domineering side. It's possible that staying away from the emotional world helps preserve the good relationship he has with you, or at least allows you to avoid having to deal with the bad. I'll bet that dynamic is alive in their relationship as well.

AP: That she goes out of her way not to provoke him?

JS: Well, not directly anyway. It might be helpful to imagine the way in which avoidance of anger can influence things. There's another piece of it that's worth looking at. You know, we have to remember that his silence serves a function for her, too.

AP: Okay. She is definitely intimidated by his anger and his style of dominating. Her response is to withdraw, but that doesn't help.

JS: Right—it would create an immediate identification with a mother who could not stand up for herself and who was controlled and demeaned as a result. I think the feeling of being like her mother creates additional depression for her.

AP: His anger is definitely a reminder of her father and that sets up a lot for her.

JS: It's interesting—she has chosen to be with a man who can't talk about feelings or be responsive to her except by taking over for her. She has trouble bringing up grievances or problems because of his reaction. So, as a result, she is shut off from her true self as well. My guess is that she is a woman who cannot tolerate weakness in herself—so Harvey creates a scenario where she is forced into a silent competency, much like her childhood.

AP: What you said before about her not tolerating depression fits into that. I'm thinking that she must be struggling with an unresolved depression about her daughter and a depression from feeling like her mother because of Harvey's anger and sarcasm.

JS: Does that seem to fit?

AP: It does. But I'm left not sure how much or even how to get them talking about these kinds of things. He really is intolerant of feelings.

JS: You said before that he can easily get sarcastic and tense. You also described their first session as a kind of intellectual exercise, and that they were bantering in an ineffective way. Do you remember your reaction to that?

AP: Not really. If anything, it makes me annoyed because it's so futile and distracting.

JS: Well, it is distracting. My guess is that he often provokes her out of her depression, so she can be with him—even if it is an uncomfortable exchange. They end up staying away from any genuine emotions, which probably serves a purpose for both of them.

AP: There are so many things that we need to open up and really talk about. But I honestly don't know how much he can tolerate.

JS: It would feel very different to be in a session with them where they could share real feelings and issues with each other. To me it has something to do with being dependent. If they have to resolve all of their problems on their own, then they never have to face needing another person. In different ways they both have made you feel like you were being pushed away—Lucy with her reluctance, and Harvey with his sarcasm and control.

AP: I think the theme of dependency is really an important one with this couple.

JS: We can speculate that Lucy's childhood family dynamics made it unsafe for her to trust or depend on any one. Do you have any thoughts about Harvey?

AP: I only know that he lost his father very suddenly when he was quite young. I guess that is partly connected to it.

JS: I think so, too. And you also talked about his difficulty regulating the boundaries with his mother, who could be controlling in her own way and later, needy.

AP: This is all worth thinking about. His narcissism adds another piece, too.

JS: Can you say more about that?

AP: He easily interprets her comments as a criticism or an attempt to censor or control him. He reacts very defensively and usually in a way that she experiences as conflictual. That's when they get into the intellectual bantering that leaves them both frustrated.

JS: Frustrated and alone. They reaffirm their shared belief that it is not safe to trust others, that they will always be diminished or disappointed. They prove their own self-sufficiency and preserve their own safety, but end up feeling lonely and unloved.

AP: Maybe if we start to look at this dependency issue it will make it possible for them to understand or at least tolerate looking at some of their other patterns.

JS: It's worth trying. I think that until some of these issues are brought out into the open it will be hard to feel confident about the real changes that need to happen or to feel confident about their progress.

DISCUSSION

Many therapists are attracted to the concept of countertransference, but are not entirely sure how to use it in their work. In this example, the therapist was able to look at reactions to which she had not given serious thought, but which had greatly influenced her clinical activity. By reflecting on the meaning of specific reactions, she was able to see how she had in fact experienced the couple's dynamics in several important ways.

Not reflected in this interview are my own countertransference reactions to AP, which I often share as parallel process (Gediman & Wolkenfeld, 1980; Grey & Fiscalini, 1987). Supervisors are often stimulated through empathy and identification to take on aspects of the transference and countertransference that exist between client and therapist. This case was initially presented as a tentative success, and I had an urge to support this perspective and compliment AP on her good work. When we started to look into the splitting and the dynamics underlying the withholding of real feelings, I felt AP get sleepy and withdraw. My response was to feel protective and to slow down, as if my comments, however well-received, were overwhelming. In retrospect, my own holding back of this information paralleled AP's avoidance of emotions and other confrontations that might upset this couple's rather fragile recovery. I also felt that my capacity to provide a holding environment, where difficult feelings could be validated and thoughtfully examined, would ultimately provide AP with the potential to do the same in her couples sessions. In this way the parallel process allowed the original projective identification to be returned, in a more palatable way, to the couple.

TEACHING THERAPISTS TO WORK WITH COUNTERTRANSFERENCE

Therapists who wish to develop their abilities to use countertransference in couples therapy need to refine their intellectual understanding of the concept; more importantly, they must develop an accepting posture in which the totality of their reactions can be processed. Just as the client needs a safe environment to examine and make sense of relationship dynamics, the therapist requires a context of acceptance and tolerance from self as well as others.

In my own consultation and teaching, students and supervisees are urged to use their "self" like a barometer. When they know their internal states independent of their clients', they are in an excellent position to detect subtle shifts and changes. As students begin to value the information available from analysis of countertransference, they become more comfortable shifting the focus of attention from the couple to their own subjective states. The reaction must be welcomed and the space protected for further development (Bollas, 1983). My students are also urged to stay with the process until the dynamic makes sense, in the same spirit as "negative capability" (Scharff & Scharff, 1987, p. 210). Analysis of countertransference seems most productive when therapists allow themselves to be imaginative and creative in trying to experience and make sense of their reactions. Fantasies and metaphors often open the door to a richer and more complete sharing of meaning.

Equally important is understanding the process of returning to a psychological state that is not impacted by the countertransference reaction. If therapists are able to define and comprehend their experiences, it becomes possible to give back to their clients material that has been externalized and to tuck away the reactions that need to be more thoughtfully processed through self-analysis or ongoing therapy. The therapist is less likely to act out or take home facets of therapy that too easily become excessive burdens. Once understood, the countertransference reaction becomes less potent as an irrational, compelling force and more easily contained as knowledge that can inform but not command.

REFERENCES

Bollas, C. (1983). Expressive uses of countertransference. *Contemporary Psychoanalysis, 19*, 1–34.
Briggs, D. (1979). The trainee and the borderline client: Countertransference pitfall. *Clinical Social Work Journal, 7,* 133–146.
Brightman, B. K. (1984). Narcissistic issues in the training experience of the psychotherapist. *International Journal of Psychoanalytic Psychotherapy, 10*, 293–317.
Gedimen, H. K., & Wolkenfeld, F. (1980). The parallelism phenomenon in psychoanalysis and supervision: Its reconsideration as a triadic system. *Psychoanalytic Quarterly, 49*, 234–255.
Giovacchini, P. L. (1985). Countertransference and the severely disturbed adolescent. *Adolescent Psychiatry, 12*, 449–467.
Grey, A., & Fiscalini, J. (1987). Parallel process as transference countertransference interaction. *Psychoanalytic Psychology, 4*, 131–144.
Kahn, E. M. (1979). The parallel process in social work treatment and supervision. *Social Casework, 60*, 520–528.
Kernberg, O. (1965). Notes on countertransference. *Journal of the American Psychoanalytic Association, 13*, 38–56.
Racker, H. (1953). A contribution to the problem of counter-transference. *International Journal Psychoanalysis, 34*, 313–324.
Searles, H. F. (1965). The informational value of the supervisor's emotional experiences. *Collected papers on schizophrenia and related subjects*. New York: International Universities Press.

Scharff, D., & Scharff, J. (1987). *Object relations family therapy.* Northvale, NJ: Jason Aronson.

Siegel, J. (1995). Countertransference as projective identification. *Journal of Couples Therapy, 5,* 61–69.

Tauber, E. S. (1953). Exploring the therapeutic use of countertransference data. *Psychiatry, 17,* 331–337.

Index